PROPERTY RIGHTS

**Understanding Government Takings
and Environmental Regulation**

On the Cover:

Montpelier—Home of President James Madison, author of the Bill of Rights

American Portrait Gallery, Engraving, 1858

This engraving appeared as a frontispiece in the then-popular *American Portrait Gallery* publication on famous Americans. It shows the house and grounds of this site as they appeared in the mid-19th century. The architecture is classical revival, a style meant to link the new republic to the Roman and Greek origins of democratic institutions and practices. The site faces west, symbolizing the conviction of Madison, Jefferson and others among the more farsighted and egalitarian of the founders that the future of the new nation and its people was in the west, beyond the Blue Ridge.

This engraving appears courtesy of Stan Jorgenson and American Heritage Engraving of Alexandria, Virginia.

PROPERTY RIGHTS

Understanding Government Takings and Environmental Regulation

Nancie G. Marzulla
Roger J. Marzulla

Foreword by Senator Orrin G. Hatch
Introduction by Chief Judge Loren A. Smith

Government Institutes
Rockville, Maryland

Government Institutes, Inc., 4 Research Place, Rockville, Maryland 20850
Phone: (301) 921-2355
Fax: (301) 921-0373
Email: giinfo@govinst.com
Internet Address: http://www.govinst.com

Copyright © 1997 by Government Institutes. All rights reserved.

01   00   99   98   97   5   4   3   2

No part of this work may be reproduced or transmitted in any form or by any means, electronic or mechanical, including photocopying, recording, or any information storage and retrieval system, without permission in writing from the publisher. All requests for permission to reproduce material from this work should be directed to Government Institutes, Inc., 4 Research Place, Suite 200, Rockville, Maryland 20850.

The reader should not rely on this publication to address specific questions that apply to a particular set of facts. The authors and publisher make no representation of warranty, express or implied, as to the completeness, correctness or utility of the information in this publication. In addition, the authors and publisher assume no liability of any kind whatsoever resulting from the use of or reliance upon the contents of this book.

Library of Congress Cataloging-in-Publication Data

Marzulla, Nancie G.
   Property rights : understanding government takings and environmental regulation / by Nancie G. Marzulla, Roger J. Marzulla.
      p.   cm.
   Includes bibliographical references and index.
   ISBN 0-86587-554-5
   1. Eminent domain--United States. 2. Right of property--United States.
I. Marzulla, Roger J. II. Title.
KF5599.M3   1996
343.73'0252--dc21   96-47384
                                                                CIP

Printed in the United States of America

Table of Contents

Foreword: The Honorable Orrin G. Hatch ix
Introduction: The Honorable Loren A. Smith xiii
About the Authors xvii
Acknowledgments xxi

**Chapter 1. The Origins of Constitutionally
          Protected Property Rights** 1

Eminent Domain   3
Physical Invasions or Occupations   6
Regulatory Takings   7

Chapter 2. What is Property? 11

Land   13
Trade Secrets and Intellectual Property   13
Contracts   14
Money   14
Pension Plans   15
Causes of Action   16
Business Interests   17
"Heavily Regulated" Industries   17
Water Rights   18
Billboards   18
New Forms of Property   19

Chapter 3. What is a "Taking"? 23

When Does a Regulation Go "Too Far"?   23

Per Se Takings   24
   Nexus—No Substantial Advancement of a
      Legitimate State Interest   25
   Deprivation of All Beneficial and Productive
      Use of Property   27
   Destruction of the Power to Exclude Others   27
Fact-Based Inquiries   28
   Economic Impact   28
   Interference with Investment-Backed Expectations   30
   Character of the Government's Action   32
   Other Equitable Factors Under *Penn Central's*
      "*Ad Hoc*" Test   33
The Nuisance Exception   34
Temporary Takings   37
Conclusion   38

Chapter 4. Wetlands 43

The Wetlands Regulatory Scheme   44
   Isolated Wetlands   46
   Definition of "Wetland"   47
   Wetland Manuals   49
   Case Study: Wetland Definition and
      Agency Contradiction   50
Wetlands Enforcement Provisions   53
Wetlands and Property Rights   54
   The Property Rights Defense   56
   Takings and Wetlands   58
      Florida Rock Industries, Inc. v. United States   58
      Loveladies Harbor, Inc. v. United States   60
   Wetlands Criminal Prosecutions   61
      United States v. Paul Tudor Jones, II and
         William B. Ellen   61
      United States v. Ocie Mills and Carey C. Mills   63
      United States v. James J. Wilson   65

Chapter 5. The Endangered Species Act **71**

The Endangered Species Regulatory Scheme 72
    The "Take" Prohibition 72
    Prohibitions on Federal Agencies 73
    Recovery Plans 74
    Incidental Take Permits and Habitat
        Conservation Plans 75
    Jeopardy Opinions 76
Civil and Criminal Enforcement Provisions 76
Endangered Species Habitat and Property Rights 78
    The *Sweet Home* Decision 79
    Case Studies on Habitat Modification 81
        Florida Scrub Jay 81
        Golden-Cheeked Warbler (Central Texas) 83
        Tipton Kangaroo Rat (Bakersfield, California) 84
    Ranching and Farming and Endangered Species 84
    Water Rights 85
        Edwards Aquifer (Texas) 86
        Kern County (California) 87
    Timber 88
State Land Use Regulation and Development 88

Chapter 6. Superfund, Mining, and Other
        Environmental Statutes **93**

Superfund and Property Rights 94
    The Superfund Regulatory Scheme 94
    Superfund and Property Rights 95
        Hendler v. United States: Superfund is a Taking 96
        Triumph, Idaho: The Taking of a Town 98
Mining 99
    The SMCRA Regulatory Scheme 99
    The *Whitney Benefits* Decision 102
Other Major Federal Environmental Statutes 102
Common State Environmental Statutes 106

Chapter 7. Land Use and Zoning 111

Generally Legitimate as Exercise of Police Power   111
When Does Zoning Go Too Far?   112
    Downzoning   112
    Open Space Zoning   113
Exactions   115
    Nollan v. California Coastal Commission   115
    Dolan v. City of Tigard   116
    Ehrlich v. City of Culver City et al.   116
Historic Preservation   117
Flood Plain Zoning   118
    The Flood Plain Regulatory Scheme   118
    Flood Plain Zoning Held Violative of
        Property Rights   119
Condemnation Blight   120
Transferable Development Rights   122

Chapter 8. Due Process, Equal Protection and Governmental Seizure of Property 125

Due Process   125
    The Administrative Procedure Act:
        Statutory Due Process   126
Due Process as Applied to Property Rights   128
Due Process and Unreasonable Delay   130
Substantive Due Process and Property Rights   132
Equal Protection and Property Rights   133
Freedom From Unreasonable Search and Seizure   135
    Unreasonable Searches   136
    Unreasonable Seizures   136
    Searches, Seizures, and Environmental Regulation   137
Asset Forfeiture and Property Rights   137
    Civil Forfeiture   138
    Criminal Asset Forfeiture   138

Chapter 9. The Practical Difficulties of Litigating a Takings Case 143

Choosing the Right Court: State versus Federal   145
Choosing the Right Federal Court: District Court versus
    Court of Federal Claims   148
Choosing a Claim: Facial versus Applied Challenges   149
Ripening the Claim   150
Exhausting Administrative Remedies   151
Statute of Limitations   151

Chapter 10. Developing Issues Regarding What is a Taking 157

Unreasonable Delay as a Taking   157
Partial Takings   158
    Diminution in Value   158
    Relevant Parcel   159
Res Judicata   160

Chapter 11. Legislative Solutions to the Property Rights Problem 163

Is Property Rights Legislation Needed?   163
Federal Executive and Legislative Attempts to Protect
    Property Rights   166
    Federal Executive Order—12630   166
    Origins of the Executive Order   167
    Framework of the Executive Order   168
    Congressional Legislation   170
State Property Rights Legislation   171
    Planning or "Look Before You Leap" Bills   171
    Compensation Bills   172
Pros and Cons of Property Rights Legislation   174
    Planning Bills   174
    Compensation Bills   175

Appendix A: The Bill of Rights and the 14th Amendment to the U.S. Constitution **179**

Appendix B: Executive Order 12630 (President Reagan's Executive Order on Takings) **187**

Appendix C: The U.S. Attorney General's Guidelines for Implementing Executive Order 12630 . . . . **193**

Guidelines   195
Index to Guidelines   222
Appendix to Guidelines   229

Appendix D: The Dolan Decision **247**

Appendix E: The Lucas Decision **271**

Index **315**

Foreword

The right to own and use private property free from arbitrary government interference is fundamental to American life, and it is a right every American should strive to protect whether he or she owns property or not.

This right is increasingly under attack from the regulatory state. Indeed, despite the constitutional requirement for the protection of property rights, the America of the late twentieth century has witnessed an explosion of federal regulation of society that has jeopardized the private ownership of property with the consequent loss of individual liberty. Under current federal regulations, thousands of Americans have been denied the right to the quiet use and enjoyment of their private property.

Despite the outrage that has followed arbitrary restraints of property use, few understand the genesis, complexities, and depth of the problem. Yet a full understanding is what is needed if efficacious protection of private property and reform of the overreaching regulatory state are to be accomplished.

I am pleased that the book *Property Rights: Understanding Government Takings and Environmental Regulation* not only illustrates the intricacies of regulations limiting use of private property and how conflicts arise from those regulations, but also calls for reform legislation that ensures the constitutional guarantee for just compensation whenever government takes private property for public use. The book's analysis cuts through the confusion about the fundamental right to private property and sets the terms for debate over environmental regulatory programs that impact private property owners.

Because contemporary discussion of environmental regulation so often focuses exclusively on the very real need for prudent ecological practices, the general public rarely realizes the associated costs in terms of resources and forfeited fundamental property rights. The Marzullas clearly outline the myriad of procedural and financial hurdles property owners face when dealing with government regulation of private property and alert the reader to the true costs of land-use restrictions. The key point is that many of these ineffective, costly hurdles could be eliminated without risking environmental safety through legislation that clarified the law and defined effective remedies.

Individuals are struggling to preserve their constitutional rights to private property, and courts are wrestling with the difficult tensions between these rights and the government's power to regulate. It is in response to this confusion that many legislators, like myself, have introduced legislation that would fortify the right to private property ownership and simplify the procedural process of obtaining just compensation. Unfortunately, at this writing, bills such as the Omnibus Property Rights Acts, S. 605 and S. 1954, have not yet been enacted despite the mounting need and public outcry for clarity.

The purpose of the just compensation clause of the Fifth Amendment to the Constitution, as interpreted by the Supreme Court in *Armstrong v. United States*, 364 U.S. 40, 49 (1960), is "to bar Government from forcing some people alone to bear public burdens, which in all fairness and justice, should be borne by the public as a whole." The current government practice of singling out private property owners to bear the costs of regulation blatantly violates this principle. This book provides numerous examples of citizens facing unjust and burdensome litigation in their fight to protect their property. Each example further leads the reader to the conclusion that a fair balance between environmental protection and the protection of the private property of individuals must be reached. Proposed legislation defines what constitutes "property" and "just compensation" and specifies precautionary procedures regulatory agencies would be required to follow preceding any action that might affect private property.

This book outlines the concerns about the senseless procedural hoops through which property owners must jump to bring their claims against the government in court. Currently, aggrieved parties seeking both monetary and injunctive relief face an unclear division of proper jurisdiction and are shuffled between U.S. District Court and U.S. Court of Federal Claims in what is commonly known as the "Tucker Act Shuffle." Bills, such as the Omnibus Property Rights Acts, were designed to eliminate this technical legal maneuver used by the government to evade justice. The "shuffle" is only one of many difficulties a claimant might experience. Unlike the government agencies whose resources are as deep as the collective pocket, most individual property owners do not have the resources to maintain a legal battle which very well may last over a decade.

It is our mission as legislators to restore a proper balance between efficient and sound land use and the fundamental rights to private property embedded in our Constitution. But policy makers can be significantly aided by the mission of this book, which is to help inform the public about the assault on private property rights and to point the way to insightful, rational solutions. I congratulate the authors on a job well done.

THE HONORABLE ORRIN G. HATCH
UNITED STATES SENATOR, UTAH

Introduction

I suspect most people generally do not read the introduction to a book. Why bother with an "appetizer" when the "meat and potatoes" are already on the table? For those of you, however, who wish to savor every literary bite, I write.

Like an appetizer, this introduction is not intended to supplant the full meal, but rather to make its consumption a bit more satisfying. I merely hope to sensitize your intellectual palate, if only a little.

I write this introduction from the very same perspective that you have: not having read this book as I write this, brimming with the positive anticipation of reading, based upon the authors and the subject. I am deeply honored to write this introduction because it is for the Marzullas.

Roger and Nancie Marzulla bring to this task a broad range of skills, experiences, and perspectives. As the head of Defenders of Property Rights, Nancie is a strong advocate of private property right holders and their claims—both moral and legal. Roger, as the former Assistant Attorney General for the Environment and Natural Resources Division of the Justice Department, was responsible for defending the myriad of actions taken by the federal government that were challenged in the courts as violations of property and due process rights. On top of that, however, he also carried out the government's duty to defend property rights, as all government officials must.

The Marzullas thus have the natural and learned resources to carry out their task comprehensively. More importantly, both have a deep love of liberty and what liberty means in human terms. When Roger and Nancie speak or write, it is never a dry abstract study of law or philosophy. Rather, they approach the fundamental human right to property in the same spirit as did James Madison and the other framers of our Constitution—as part of the fundamental integrity and dignity of the human being. In order to be a good lawyer, one must be a good person. Roger and Nancie are very good people, and this makes their writings very good writings, based on a solid legal and philosophical foundation.

The other reason I agreed to write this introduction is the importance of the subject, both to the development of our law as well as to the broader and more important concern for the preservation of a free society—a society based upon a written constitution with the protection of fundamental God-given rights. While this is the main topic of this book, I wish to add enough here as an appetizer without satiating any intellectual hunger.

We are at the end of an unparalleled era of human history. Totalitarian ideologies arose throughout this century, imposing radical alternatives to the classical liberal 19th century system of individualism based on the fundamental rights of life, liberty, and property.

These totalitarian ideologies (which include National Socialism, Communism, Socialism, Fascism, and several other variants) spilled the blood of well over 100 million human beings in the names of race, class, or mindless utopian concepts. These ideologies sought to create heaven on earth, but almost built hell instead. All had the overriding objective of destroying the fundamental human rights of life, liberty, and property. Their reasoning was that only by destroying these fundamental rights in individuals could their utopias arise—giving all power to the mystical volk, proletariat, people, or masses.

We have learned much from this century. The most important is that the fundamental rights of life, liberty, and property are the bulwark of all political and societal freedom. These rights are what stands between us and the mad dreams of a perpetual totalitarian night.

Property is the least understood of the fundamental rights, perhaps because it is the practical foundation of the other two. Property rights restrain tyranny while allowing private individuals to organize their lives and affairs. In order to understand the foundations of free societies, we must understand the importance of property rights, the threats to them, their protection, and their explication.

At the very beginning of our nation's existence, property rights were considered sacred. John Adams, in his *Defense of the Constitutions of Government*, said, "the moment the idea is admitted into society that property is not as sacred as the laws of God, and there is not force of law and public justice to protect it, anarchy and tyranny commence." The horrors of the 20th century, however, have dulled us to the vital importance of property rights. I believe this book will help restore a true understanding of this importance.

Since even the finest book is only a beginning, I also hope it will stimulate a veritable flood of writing and scholarship on what is the mainspring (in today's jargon, the CPU) of the free society: property rights.

THE HONORABLE LOREN A. SMITH
CHIEF JUDGE
UNITED STATES COURT OF FEDERAL CLAIMS

About the Authors

Nancie G. Marzulla

Nancie G. Marzulla is the nationally recognized leader of the property rights movement. She is President and a founder of Defenders of Property Rights, the nation's only public-interest legal foundation dedicated exclusively to protecting property rights. Defenders has been dubbed both the "brain trust of the property rights movement" by the Center for Responsive Politics and the "litigation arm of the property rights movement" by Greenpeace. Defenders' clients include small property owners who have been unfairly singled out to bear the cost of achieving public good. Ms. Marzulla is also a sought-after commentator for radio and television and has published scores of articles.

Ms. Marzulla has played a key role in dozens of successful state and federal lawsuits, including the recent Supreme Court cases of *Lucas v. South Carolina Coastal Council* and *Dolan v. City of Tigard*. She has also testified before the U.S. Congress, U.S. Senate and numerous state legislatures on property rights legislation. She assisted with the drafting of virtually every property rights bill in both the House and the Senate in the 104th Congress.

Ms. Marzulla is the founder and presiding chair of the Property Rights Roundtable—the national action-network for more than 150 property rights groups and leaders across the country. She is on the faculty of the Lincoln Land Institute and was the first co-chair of the U.S. Federal Circuit Court of Appeals Natural Resources Committee.

She holds a master's degree in public administration and a law degree from the University of Colorado. While in law school, she was a member of the law review and co-founded the Colorado chapter of the Federalist Society. Ms. Marzulla was an appointee in the Reagan Administration Justice Department and was a litigator in private practice, prior to founding Defenders of Property Rights in 1991.

Ms. Marzulla is a contributing author to the following books: *Regulatory Takings: Restoring Private Property Rights*, (National Legal Center for the Public Interest 1994); *Environmental Gore,* (Pacific Research Institute for Public Policy 1994); and *Land Rights—The 1990s Property Rights Rebellion*, (Rowman & Littlefield Publishers, Inc. 1995).

Roger J. Marzulla

Roger J. Marzulla is one of the nation's leading authorities on Environmental Law and Constitutionally Protected Property Rights. He is a partner in the Washington, D.C. law office of Akin, Gump, Strauss, Hauer and Feld, where he heads the Environmental Law Practice. His clients include real estate developers as well as companies involved in diverse industries such as aerospace, chemicals, manufacturing, mining, timber, oil and gas. Mr. Marzulla regularly litigates cases under the Clean Air Act, the Clean Water Act, Wetlands Regulations, Superfund, Endangered Species Act and other environmental and natural resource statutes.

A prolific author and lecturer on environmental and constitutional issues, Mr. Marzulla is often called upon to testify as an expert witness in environmental cases. Congress, too, has often sought his testimony as an expert on property rights, environmental crimes, wetlands and the Tenth Amendment. His views on environmental issues are often sought by national newspapers and news magazines, network television news and network radio.

Mr. Marzulla previously served as Assistant Attorney General in charge of the U.S. Justice Department's Land and Natural Resources Division, where he was responsible for all environmental, land management and natural resources litigation on behalf of the federal government. During his tenure at the Justice Department, he spearheaded the federal government's participation in regulatory takings litigation, including cases such as *Nollan v. California Coastal Commission* and *First English Evangelical Lutheran Church v. County of*

Los Angeles. He was also responsible for the presidential executive order "Avoiding Governmental Interference with Constitutionally Protected Property Rights" signed by President Reagan in March 1988.

Mr. Marzulla began his career as a real estate trial lawyer in California, bringing his first constitutional challenge to a local land use regulation in 1972. Since that time, he has participated in dozens of constitutional and regulatory cases in state and federal courts.

Mr. Marzulla received his juris doctorate degree, *magna cum laude*, from the University of Santa Clara School of Law, graduating first in his class. He also holds a bachelor of arts degree in political science from the University of Santa Clara. He is Chairman of the Board of Directors of Defenders of Property Rights.

This is the first book he has published with his wife, Nancie, although they have collaborated on numerous articles and legal briefs. Mr. Marzulla has been a contributing author to numerous books on environmental issues, including: *American Values—An Environmental Vision*, (The Environmental Policy Analysis Network 1996); *Environmental Criminal Liability: Avoiding and Defending Enforcement Actions*, (BNA 1995); *Farmers, Ranchers and Environmental Law*, (National Legal Center for the Public Interest 1995); *The Clean Air Act Amendments: BNA's Comprehensive Analysis of the New Law*, (BNA 1991); and *Environmental Due Diligence: The Complete Resource Guide for Real Estate Lenders, Buyers, Sellers and Attorneys*, (BNA 1989).

The authors live in Washington, D.C. with their two children, Allegra and Marco.

Acknowledgments

We wish gratefully to acknowledge the extraordinary contributions of those without whose talents and hard work this book simply could not exist.

- Michael Bloomquist, whose thorough research, insightful analysis and dogged determination transformed an incomplete manuscript into the finished book you now hold in your hands.

- Pat Smoot, Andrew Langer and David Almasi, whose word processing, editing, cite-checking and endless revising polished out most of the flaws in our manuscript.

- Mary Diandrea, whose brilliant graphic design skills brought the cover of this book to life. What better choice than a picture of Montpelier, the home of James Madison—author of the Bill of Rights.

- Wanda Gerald and Patricia Gainey, who cheerfully slogged through the massive job of inputting all the changes, paginating and reprinting, and, ultimately, physically assembling the manuscript.

Nancie G. Marzulla
Roger J. Marzulla

PROPERTY RIGHTS

**Understanding Government Takings
and Environmental Regulation**

Chapter 1

THE ORIGINS OF CONSTITUTIONALLY PROTECTED PROPERTY RIGHTS

The protection of rights in property lies at the heart of our constitutional system. The founding fathers, in drafting the Constitution, drew upon classical notions of legal rights and individual liberty dating back to the Justinian Code, Magna Carta, and the Two Treatises of John Locke—all of which recognize the importance of property ownership in a governmental system in which individual liberty is paramount. Concurrently, the constitutional framers also drew upon their own experience as colonists of an oppressive monarch, whose unlimited powers invested him with the ability to deprive his subjects of their God-given rights of "life, liberty, and property" (subsequently revised by Thomas Jefferson to substitute "the pursuit of happiness" for "property").

To the framers of the Constitution, the protection of individual liberty was essential. Accordingly, they devised a system of government which fractured governmental power among the three branches of federal government, and between federal and state governments. By enumerating specific powers granted to various government officials, many felt they had created a government of sufficient checks and balances to ensure that individual liberties would be protected. Others, however, felt it necessary to make explicit the most important of those liberties which the Constitution sought to protect; thus, the Bill of Rights—to protect those fundamental liberties—was drafted by James Madison and ratified contemporaneously with the original Constitution.

These fundamental liberties guaranteed by the Bill of Rights include freedom of speech and religion; freedom of press and assembly; the right to bear arms; the right to trial by jury and cross examination of accusing witnesses; and freedom from cruel or unusual punishment. Recognizing that a government could easily abuse these civil rights if a citizen's property and livelihood were not guaranteed, the United States Constitution also imposes a duty on government to protect private property rights. Thus, within the Bill of Rights, numerous provisions directly or indirectly protect private property rights. The Fourth Amendment guarantees that people are to be "secure in their persons, houses, papers, and effects. . . ." The Fifth Amendment states that no person shall "be deprived of life, liberty, or property, without due process of law; nor shall private property be taken for public use without just compensation." In addition to the Bill of Rights provisions, the Fourteenth Amendment echoes the Due Process Clause of the Fifth Amendment, stating that no "State shall deprive any person of life, liberty, or property without due process of law. . . ." Indirectly, the Contracts Clause of the Constitution also protects property by forbidding any state from passing any "law impairing the Obligation of Contracts."

The Constitution places such strong emphasis on protecting private property rights because the right to own and use property was historically understood to be critical to the maintenance of a free society. To understand why this is true, one must appreciate that property is more than just land. Property is buildings, machines, retirement funds, savings accounts, and even ideas. In short, property is the fruit of one's labor. The ability to use, enjoy, and exclusively possess the fruits of one's own labor is the basis for a society in which individuals are free from oppression. Indeed, some have argued that there can be no true freedom for anyone if people are dependent upon the state for food, shelter, and other basic needs. Understandably, where the fruits of citizens' labors are owned by the state and not individuals, nothing is safe from being taken by a majority or a tyrant. Ultimately, as government dependents, these individuals are powerless to oppose any infringement on their rights (much less the degradation of the environment) due to the absolute government control over the fruits of their labor.

One of the most eloquent early commentators on the relationship between freedom and property rights was Noah Webster. The noted American educator and linguist said, "Let the people have property and they will have power—a power that will forever be exerted to prevent the restriction of the press, the abolition of trial by jury, or the abridgment of many other privileges." Not surprisingly, the world's greatest oppressors have also understood the intrinsic link between property rights and freedom. Karl Marx developed this insight in his *Communist Manifesto*: "You reproach us with planning to do away with your property. Precisely, that is just what we propose . . . The theory of the Communists may be summed up in a single sentence: Abolition of private property."[1]

In its most practical sense, however, the United States Supreme Court has repeatedly explained that the primary purpose for protecting property rights is to bar government "from forcing some people alone to bear public burdens which, in all fairness and justice, should be borne by the public as a whole."[2]

EMINENT DOMAIN

Within a framework where private property rights are paramount, government must be able to acquire land in order to carry out its ordinary and legitimate functions, not the least of which include the construction of buildings, highways, and military installations, as well as the preservation of parks, wildlife refuges, and other natural areas. The government's power to acquire property through condemnation, even over the objections of the owner, is called "eminent domain," and is possessed by federal and state governments alike. Situations arise, however, where the government takes property without instituting formal eminent domain proceedings to condemn land. In these cases, a private landowner may go to court and bring an action for inverse condemnation to force the government to remit compensation. The power of eminent domain is an inherent attribute of governmental sovereignty; accordingly, it need not be (and is not) specifically listed as an enumerated power of the federal government in the Constitution.

The Just Compensation Clause of the Fifth Amendment— "nor shall private property be taken for public use, without just compensation"—provides two conditions that limit a government's power to obtain land and other property through eminent domain.[3] First, the acquisition or taking of the private property must be for "public use." That is, the taking must not be for the private benefit of some government official (*e.g.*, constructing a road to his property) but must be for public benefit and in furtherance of actual powers possessed by the government (*e.g.*, national defense, commerce, etc.). The "public use" limitation on the government's ability to condemn private property has been construed broadly. For example, the United States Supreme Court has held that a reallocation of land or other property through an urban renewal project or similar process meets the "public use" requirement even though title is held by private individuals as a result of the process.[4] The key issue in determining "public use" is whether the activity furthers governmental (rather than private) purposes.[5]

The second condition placed by the Constitution upon the exercise of the eminent domain power is that the owner be paid "just compensation" for the property taken. "Just compensation" is the monetary value of the property taken.[6] Failure of the government to provide just compensation invalidates the attempted exercise of eminent domain power or, at a minimum, gives rise to a claim for the value of the property taken. Later chapters will discuss this issue in greater detail. But it should be noted here that the Just Compensation Clause does not, in and of itself, forbid the exercise of otherwise legitimate governmental power. Indeed, it is only designed to "secure compensation in the event of otherwise proper interference amounting to a taking."[7]

A substantial body of law has developed around the process by which government exercises its eminent domain power and provides just compensation. Federal law permits the government to obtain immediate possession (the so-called "quick take") if it deposits the estimated just compensation in escrow and files an action. Alternatively, the government may sue first to acquire title, placing a *lis pendens* on the property to give notice of its claim. Either way, in the federal court system, the just compensation issue is normally determined in a trial before a board of commissioners appointed by the court to make a report to the judge.

Different states have different procedures for determining just compensation and acquiring title. Some require deposit of estimated just compensation into court, while others do not. Some allow for trial before a jury, while others use the commissioner system of knowledgeable persons appointed to advise the court. The litmus test for any of these proceedings is whether it ultimately affords just compensation for the property taken.

The value of the property is generally decided on the basis of testimony given by the owner, appraisers, or both. The fundamental issue is: what price would a willing buyer pay to a willing seller for this property? This amount is its "fair market value," and is the universally accepted measure of damages in an action for just compensation.

Although various appraisal methodologies may be employed, the most common is the "comparable sales" approach in which the appraiser first determines the "highest and best" use of the property, then compares the property to others in similarly situated locations. "Highest and best use" is the most profitable use which could reasonably be expected to be made of the property in light of all of the circumstances. Naturally, these circumstances include economic conditions prevailing at the time of the taking, together with the physical suitability of the land. A strong demand for particular types of land (*e.g.*, residential, commercial, office) will drive up the price, and a soft market will drive down the price.

The existing two hundred years of eminent domain law serves as foundation for analysis of the "newer" development of inverse condemnation—*i.e.*, physical and regulatory takings. But the touchstone of the constitutional analysis in each instance is the Fifth Amendment's Just Compensation Clause; accordingly, all takings cases—including eminent domain—are constructed of the same logical and constitutional components.

PHYSICAL INVASIONS OR OCCUPATIONS

Sometimes the government may physically occupy or invade property for a sufficient time and to such an extent that this activity alone will constitute a taking. Thus, even in the absence of the exercise of eminent domain, property may be "taken" and the constitutional requirements of "public use" and "just compensation" triggered. Such physical invasion or occupancy amounts to a taking even though no legal process has been instituted and even though the government may not have wished to take the property.

In *Dow v. United States*, for example, the federal government laid down a pipeline on the plaintiff's property, then later instituted a condemnation action to acquire title to the land beneath the pipeline.[8] The government contended, unsuccessfully, that it only owed the landowner the value of the property at the time the condemnation action was filed and not the value of its use of the land prior to condemnation. Rejecting the government's argument, the United States Supreme Court held that the temporary occupancy of the plaintiff's land was in the nature of a lease, giving rise to an obligation to pay just compensation for the time during which the government physically occupied the right-of-way.

Had the government abandoned the property in *Dow*, rather than condemned it, the activity would have been what is generally referred to as a "temporary taking." Such temporary occupancy or invasion of land by the government constitutes a non-permanent taking of the property. In such cases, the measure of just compensation is the value of the use of the property—just as though the government had condemned a leasehold for the time it occupied. Thus, while it is true that an individual cannot force the government to "condemn" private property, an individual can force the government to pay for what it has taken.

This is also true when the government takes a part—even a small part—of an individual's property. In *Loretto v. TelePrompter Manhattan CATV Corp.*,[9] Justice Thurgood Marshall, writing for the United States Supreme Court, held that the placement of a three-foot-by-two-foot television cable box on the exterior of an apartment building in New York City gave rise to a claim for the value (however slight):

> 'when the character of the governmental action,'. . . is a permanent physical occupation of property, our cases uniformly have found a taking to the extent of the occupation, without regard to whether the action achieves an important public benefit or has only minimal economic impact on the owner.[10]

The government may also be liable where the physical invasion occurs as a result of governmental action, even though the government receives no real benefit from the taking. Thus, the government is liable where its actions cause flooding, create aircraft noise so as to interfere with the use of property, or cut off access to highways from the property. These physical infringements on property rights amount to an invasion of the property, even though no building is erected, and no government agent ever sets foot on the property itself.

Distinct from these instances of physical invasion amounting to a taking, however, are cases in which government agents act unlawfully. Thus, while the unlawful invasion of a house may be a tort or the unauthorized flooding of property may be a trespass, these actions do not give rise to a taking claim precisely because they were wrongful. If "the taking is unauthorized the acts of defendant's officers may be enjoinable, but they do not constitute a taking effective to vest some kind of title in the government and entitlement to just compensation in the owner or former owner."[11]

REGULATORY TAKINGS

Finally, a "regulatory" taking occurs if a regulation "goes too far" in restricting the use of property.[12] The United States Supreme Court has fashioned a two-part, disjunctive test to complement Justice Oliver Wendell Holmes' flexible "too far" definition of a taking. A regulation "effects a taking if the ordinance does not substantially advance legitimate state interests . . . *or* denies an owner economically viable use of his [property]" (emphasis added).[13] This test requires that challenged government action must pass *both* portions of the test.

Outside this general framework, however, the Supreme Court has not been able to formulate specific and consistent standards by which to evaluate takings claims. The takings inquiry is essentially an equitable, fact-based, case-by-case, *ad hoc* inquiry.[14] If the government action does not substantially advance state goals and no compensation is provided by the government, an enjoinable taking has occurred. If legitimate action causes significant economic hardship to the property owner, a compensable taking has occurred.

Whether the requested relief is declaratory or monetary in nature, and whether the claim alleges failure to substantially advance a legitimate government interest or denial of economic use, a plaintiff must, as a threshold matter, prove the existence of a protected property right.

ENDNOTES

[1] Karl Marx and Friedrich Engels, *The Communist Manifesto* (Samuel Moore trans., 1992).
[2] *Armstrong v. United States*, 364 U.S. 40,49 (1960).
[3] U.S. CONST. amend. V.
[4] *Berman v. Parker*, 348 U.S. 26 (1954).
[5] *Hawaii Housing Authority v. Midkiff*, 467 U.S. 229, 240-41 (1984).
[6] *Almota Farmers Elevator and Warehouse Co. v. United States*, 409 U.S. 470, 473 (1973).
[7] *First English Evangelical Lutheran Church of Glendale v. County of Los Angeles, California*, 482 U.S. 304, 315 (1987).
[8] 357 U.S. 17 (1958).
[9] 458 U.S. 419 (1982).

[10] *Loretto*, 458 U.S. at 435-36 (quoting *Penn Central Transportation v. City of New York*, 438 U.S. 104, 124 (1978)).
[11] *Tabb Lakes v. United States*, 10 F.3d 796, 802-34 (Fed. Cir. 1993) (quoting *Armijo v. United States*, 663 F.2d 90, 95 (Cl. Ct. 1981)).
[12] *Pennsylvania Coal Co. v. Mahon*, 260 U.S. 393, 415 (1922).
[13] *Agins v. City of Tiburon*, 447 U.S. 255, 260 (1980).
[14] *Penn Central Transportation v. City of New York*, 438 U.S. at 124.

Chapter 2

WHAT IS PROPERTY?

The right to own property is as ancient as mankind itself, and has been a part of every legal system since the dawn of history. In the United States, rights in property are defined by positive law, including state statutes, state common law, and traditional Anglo-American principles going back hundreds of years.[1] In *Ruckelshaus v. Monsanto Co.*,[2] the Court noted that "we are mindful of the basic axiom that '[p]roperty interests . . . are not created by the Constitution. Rather, they are created and their dimensions are defined by existing rules or understandings that stem from an independent source such as state law.'"

Within that context, no single definition of the term "property" encompasses all of the aspects of this concept which is so central to our legal system. Rather, the term refers to an aggregate of individual rights which are guaranteed and protected against the government by the Constitution, and against trespass and infringement by others under traditional Anglo-American law. James Madison defined property as:

> that dominion which one man claims and exercises over the external things of the world, in exclusion of every other individual. In its larger and just meaning, it embraces every thing to which a man may attach a value and have a right; and *which leaves to every one else the like advantage* [emphasis in original].[3]

Modern definitions echo this original definition of property as a combination of rights, powers, and duties. For example, former President

Richard Nixon alleged that the taking of his presidential papers was compensable under the Fifth Amendment.[4] The United States Court of Appeals for the D.C. Circuit agreed and, in so holding, also fashioned an extremely broad definition of property that is applicable to business interests: "The essential character of property is that it is made up of mutually reinforcing understandings that are sufficiently well grounded to support a claim of entitlement."[5] Thus, an essential component in takings analysis is whether the plaintiff had a reasonable expectation to "possess, use, enjoy, dispose, or exclude others" from the putative property interest.[6]

Property has also been described as a "bundle of sticks" or "group of rights" associated with ownership of the property. This notion of property is inherently broad:

> It is conceivable that [the term "property" in the Just Compensation Clause] was used in its vulgar and untechnical sense of the physical thing with respect to which the citizen exercises rights recognized by law. On the other hand, it may have been employed in a more accurate sense to denote the group of rights inhering in the citizen's relation to the physical thing, *as the right to possess, use and dispose of it.* In point of fact, the construction given the phrase has been the latter [emphasis added].[7] Indeed, it is much more than possession that defines the term property; the use of land, and the ability to alienate "physical things" are rights just as fundamental to the concept of property. It is "[t]he right to *exclusive ownership* as a property right that is fundamental to our theory of social organization."[8]

In short, the Constitution protects against government infringement of the rights to use, own, exclude others, possess or dispose of virtually everything of value—tangible or intangible.[9,10,11,12]

LAND

While property is far more than just land or a building, *real property* is what most people commonly associate with the term "property." Indeed, there is some suggestion from the United States Supreme Court that land is entitled to special protection under the Just Compensation Clause:

> In the case of land, however, we think that the notion pressed by the council that title is somehow held subject to the 'implied limitation' that the State may subsequently eliminate all economically valuable use is inconsistent with the historical compact recorded in the Just Compensation Clause that has become part of our constitutional culture.[13]

Some commentators have taken this language to suggest that there is a distinction between real and personal property in terms of the constitutional protection which should be afforded those forms of property. This view, however, conflicts with a well-established line of cases which holds that it is the characteristics of the property, not whether it is personal or real, that determine whether the owner is entitled to constitutional protection. More importantly, as noted constitutional scholar Richard Lazarus has pointed out, "the Court's distinction [in *Lucas v. South Carolina Coastal Council*] between the expectations of real and personal property holders does not derive from the text of the Just Compensation Clause, which appears to apply to 'real' and 'personal' property alike."[14]

TRADE SECRETS AND INTELLECTUAL PROPERTY

The United States Supreme Court has explicitly recognized that intangible property rights are deserving of Fifth Amendment protection. In *Ruckelshaus v. Monsanto Co.*, the Court adopted language that recognizes property interests in a wide range of business situations:

"[T]he perception of trade secrets as property is consonant with a notion of 'property' that extends beyond land and tangible goods and includes the products of an individual's labor and invention."[15] Other Fifth Amendment cases have adopted this rule for determining the existence of a property right.[16]

CONTRACTS

Similarly, valid contracts are protected by the Just Compensation Clause.[17,18,19] One court has even held that the *diminution* in value of a contract implicates a Fifth Amendment property right. In *General Offshore Corp. v. Farrelly*, a plaintiff alleged that the Virgin Islands Wrongful Discharge Act worked an unconstitutional taking of his business because it restricted his right to terminate employees pursuant to provisions of signed employment contracts.[20] The court wrote:

> It seems evident that the right to fire an employee has value to an employer, so, if the contract is a source of a property interest, then the partial deprivation of the right to fire an employee diminishes the value of the contract. The threshold issue must thus be resolved in favor of the Plaintiff.[21]

MONEY

In the leading case of *Webb's Fabulous Pharmacies, Inc. v. Beckwith*, the United States Supreme Court was called upon to determine whether interest accruing on an interpleader fund deposited in the registry of a county court was a property interest protected against uncompensated takings under the Fifth Amendment.[22] The Court held that it was, and, in so doing, set forth a definition of property that reflects the original conception of the reach of the Just Compensation Clause.

Justice Harry Blackmun, writing for the Court, warned that protected property is more than "a mere unilateral expectation or an abstract need."[23] The Court concluded that "Webb's creditors, however, had more than a unilateral expectation."[24] Therefore, the property taken was protected by the Fifth Amendment:

> The deposited fund was the amount received as the purchase price for Webb's assets. *It was property held only for the ultimate benefit of Webb's creditors, not for the benefit of the court and not for the benefit of the county.* . . . Eventually, and inevitably, that fund, less proper charges authorized by the court, would be distributed among the creditors as their claims were recognized by the court. The creditors thus had a state-created property right to their respective portions of the fund [emphasis added].[25]

PENSION PLANS

Concerned about the financial liabilities of employer pension plans, Congress enacted the Multiemployer Pension Plan Amendments Act of 1980 (MPPAA) that sought to discourage employers from withdrawing from multi-party pension plans. MPPAA made employers who voluntarily withdraw from pension plans liable, upon their withdrawal, for a fixed share of the pension plan's unfunded vested benefits. They applied the withdraw liability provisions retroactively to employers withdrawing from plans beginning in 1979.

Three cases presented challenges to the 1980 provision by arguing that appellants had valid and existing private pension contracts which obligated them to pay fixed amounts to the pension plans. Under the terms of the 1980 withdrawal liability provision, each appellant was forced to pay more than the private contracts required. In *Connolly v. PBGC Corp.*, the appellant challenged the 1980 withdraw provisions as violative of the takings clause.[26] In *Concrete Pipe of Calif. v. Laborers Pension Trust,* the appellant challenged the law on takings and due process grounds.[27] In *Pension Benefit Guaranty Corp. v. R. A. Gray*, the challenge was based on the due process clause only.[28] In all three cases, the property owner lost. Thus, based upon these leading decisions, it appears that pension benefits are not entitled to the same degree of protection as real property because the pension industry is "heavily regulated."

CAUSES OF ACTION

Government destruction of a legal claim or cause of action can also trigger the Just Compensation guarantee. In *Dames & Moore v. Regan,* the United States Supreme Court upheld federal abrogation of the right to maintain a cause of action based upon contract where a non-appealable award by an international tribunal was substituted.[29] The Court rejected the plaintiff's assertion that a Presidential Executive Order, which abrogated the plaintiff's state law contracts claim, attachment, and final judgment, itself constituted a taking of property.

Courts have also deferred to congressional expressions that its substitution of a federal fund for a cause of action constitutes "just compensation," thus precluding the court from even considering a takings claim. *Juda v. United States* upheld the federal government's substitution of a $150 million federal fund for all existing claims against the United States by residents of the Marshall Islands arising from government testing of nuclear weapons on and around the islands from 1946-1958.[30] Because the fund provided compensation to residents, the court rejected certain residents' claims that this fund's abrogation of their ongoing actions in federal court constituted a taking of property. "Congress did not intend to take the plaintiffs' right to just compensation for the takings or their right to obtain damages for breach of contract, as distinguished from removal of their remedy. The settlement procedure . . . provides a 'reasonable' and 'certain' means for obtaining compensation."[31]

However, Congress has on numerous occasions used the device of statutorily substituting the United States (with its sovereign immunity) as a party defendant in place of private parties who might well be liable (thus effectively depriving the plaintiff of his ability to recover) without incurring takings liability. Indeed, Congress has, on occasion, simply eliminated a state law cause of action without providing any substitute at all.

BUSINESS INTERESTS

A number of courts have held that the regulatory destruction of business interests triggers the duty of government to compensate the owner for a taking. In *Yancey v. United States*, the federal law required the quarantine of the plaintiff's turkey flock.[32] The quarantine resulted in the destruction of the Yancey's turkey breeder stock business. The U.S. Court of Appeals for the Federal Circuit upheld the lower court's determination that the plaintiffs held a protected property interest in their healthy, but quarantined, turkey flock. The court stated that "for Fifth Amendment purposes, the Yancey's ownership of their turkey flock deserves just as much protection as if ownership of their farm had been appropriated."[33]

"HEAVILY REGULATED" INDUSTRIES

Courts have occasionally refused to recognize some business interests as protected property interests if it can be said that the industry in which the business operates is "heavily regulated." The explanation given is that the property owner in such instances could have reasonably expected that government might, some day, change the rules and thereby destroy the business. For example, in *Allied-General Nuclear Services v. United States*, the United States Court of Appeals for the Federal Circuit denied a claim for just compensation for the denial of an operating license for a nuclear power reprocessing plant.[34] The owners had invested $200 million in building the plant pursuant to government assurances that the license would be granted. However, the Carter administration initiated a "nuclear freeze" which vitiated any hope for that license.

Upon review, the Federal Circuit concluded that compensation was not warranted:

> Appellants do not deny they accepted the regulatory scheme so far as it might have resulted in denial of construction or operating licenses on the ground the plant, as appellants would operate it, was unsafe. They deny that nuclear proliferation grounds were within the contemplation of the parties . . . The attendant circumstances: the novelty of nuclear fission, the fearsome effect of its use in war, the public fears, all forbid us to suppose that the government had committed itself to use of its licensing power not to respond to some new ground of hesitation just because it was not originally foreseen.[35]

WATER RIGHTS

The right to use or to receive water, especially in the arid western states, is often an incident of property ownership more valuable than the land to which it attaches. Elaborate systems of water allocation and regulation of use have developed under state law to apportion this limited resource. While the water itself remains the property of the state, the right to use that water (called a usufructuary right) is a property right recognized by all of the states where scarce water must be allocated. In a case of first impression, the Court of Federal Claims recently stated that "water rights, like other property rights, are entitled to the full protection of the Constitution."[36] Therefore, if such rights to use water are condemned, physically appropriated, or destroyed through regulation, the owner of the water right is protected by the Constitution just as any other property owner.

BILLBOARDS

Some courts have held that outdoor advertising signs or billboards, while property, are not entitled to constitutional protection against uncompensated takings if the government provides an "amortization" period prior to the taking. Unique thus far to the billboard industry, courts have held that the destruction of a billboard business is not compensable on the fiction that the amortization period—usually five years—confers a benefit on the owner. That is, the owner is allowed to continue making a profit from the billboards for a specified period of time before he has to tear them down. But while a fair number of courts have held that "amortization" is an acceptable form of compensation, the United States Supreme Court has yet to rule on this issue.

NEW FORMS OF PROPERTY

In a sense, new forms of property are continually being created. Security interests and mortgages, lottery tickets, derivatives, technological discoveries, software and applications, and professional practices all are examples of property that did not exist at the time the Constitution was ratified (or even twenty years ago). Since "property" encompasses all rights in virtually anything of value, these forms of property, too, receive the constitutional guarantees described in subsequent chapters. Because the Constitution does not purport to limit its protection of property rights to any particular kind of property, the constitutional guarantees described in this text apply equally to all forms of property.

ENDNOTES

[1] *Lucas v. South Carolina Coastal Council*, 112 S. Ct. 2886, 2889 (1992).
[2] 467 U.S. 986, 1001 (1984) (quoting *Webb's Fabulous Pharmacies, Inc. v. Beckwith*, 449 U.S. 155, 161 (1980), quoting *Board of Regents v. Roth*, 408 U.S. 564, 577 (1972)).

20 / *Property Rights*

³ *Property,* Nat. Gazette, Mar. 27, 1792, in 14 J. Madison, *The Papers of James Madison* 266 (R. Riland ed. 1977).

⁴ *Nixon v. United States,* 978 F.2d 1269 (D.C. Cir. 1992).

⁵ *Id.* at 1275 (citing *Kaiser Aetna v. United States,* 444 U.S. 164, 179 (1979) (property consists of recognized expectancies)). Some courts (in cases cited with approval in *Nixon*) have gone so far as to suggest that rights created by custom may be so "robust" as to "trump" positive law or common law. *Id.* at 1276. *See, e.g., Ghen v. Rich,* 8 F.159, 162 (D. Mass. 1881) (usage in finback whaling industry overcomes the common law rule).

⁶ *Delaware v. Cavazos,* 723 F. Supp. 234, 240 (D. Del. 1989), *aff'd,* 919 F.2d 137 (3d Cir. 1990) (denying state's claim to a property right because state had no reasonable expectation to use Guaranteed Student Loan funds for purposes other than the GSL program).

⁷ *Monsanto,* 467 U.S. at 1003 (quoting *United States v. General Motors Corp.,* 323 U.S. 373, 377-78 (1945)).

⁸ *Hendler v. United States,* 952 F.2d 1364 (Fed. Cir. 1991).

⁹ *See, e.g., Kaiser Aetna v. United States* (right to exclude public access to a privately owned pond), 444 U.S. 164 (1979).

¹⁰ *See, e.g., Hodel v. Irving* (right to devise private property), 481 U.S. 704 (1987).

¹¹ *See, e.g., Penn Central Transp. Co. v. City of New York* (right to use air space above a privately owned building), 438 U.S. 104 (1978).

¹² *See, e.g., Pennsylvania Coal Co. v. Mahon* (right to mine subsurface coal), 260 U.S. 393 (1922).

¹³ *Lucas v. South Carolina Coastal Council,* 112 S. Ct. 2886 (1992).

¹⁴ Richard J. Lazarus, *Putting the Correct Spin on Lucas,* 45 STAN. L. REV. 1411,1424 (1992).

¹⁵ *Monsanto,* 467 U.S. at 1003 (quoting 2 W. BLACKSTONE, COMMENTARIES at 405).

¹⁶ *See, e.g., Lariscey v. United States,* 20 Cl. Ct. 385 (1990), *rev'd,* 949 F.2d 1137 (Fed. Cir. 1991), *opinion vacated and withdrawn on grant of reh'g,* 962 F.2d 1047 (Fed. Cir. 1992) (unpatented invention held to be a protectable secret).

¹⁷ *See, e.g., Lynch v. United States* (insurance policies protected against uncompensated takings), 292 U.S. 571 (1934).

¹⁸ *See, e.g., Armstrong v. United States* (materialmen's liens), 364 U.S. 40 (1960).

[19] *See, e.g., Louisville Joint Stock Land Bank v. Radford* (real estate liens), 295 U.S. 555 (1935).
[20] 743 F. Supp. 1177 (D.V.I.), *aff'd*, 919 F.2d 137 (3d Cir. 1990).
[21] 743 F. Supp at 1202.
[22] 449 U.S. 155 (1980).
[23] *Id.* at 161.
[24] *Id.*
[25] *Id.*
[26] 475 U.S. 211 (1986).
[27] 113 S. Ct. 2264 (1993).
[28] 467 U.S. 717 (1984).
[29] 453 U.S. 654 (1981).
[30] 6 Cl. Ct. 441 (1984).
[31] 6 Cl. Ct. 441 (1984).
[32] 915 F.2d 1534 (Fed. Cir. 1990).
[33] *Id.* at 1541.
[34] 839 F.2d 1572 (D.C. Cir. 1988).
[35] *Allied-General Nuclear Services*, 839 F.2d 1572 (D.C. Cir. 1988).
[36] *Hage v. United States*, No. 91-1470L, 1996 WL 102801, at *28 (Cl. Ct. Mar., 8 1996).

Chapter 3

WHAT IS A "TAKING"?

After a property right is found to exist, the next question is whether the government action has, in fact, "taken" the property. While the Constitution does not define the term "taking," common sense and history use the term to refer to any acts that diminish, deprive, or disturb any of the legally protected rights to use, possess, or dispose of one's acquisitions or property. Clearly then, not every interference with one's use of property is a "taking." Attenuated or indirect government acts most likely do not "take" property rights. While the analysis is often straightforward if the government physically invades or occupies the property, the analysis for an alleged taking due to government regulation can be anything but simple. Indeed, Justice William Brennan in his now-famous dissent in *San Diego Gas & Electric Co. v. San Diego* stated: "The touchstone of the takings analysis in the regulatory context was stated in 1922 by Justice Holmes to be a determination of whether the regulation has gone 'too far?'"[1] That remains essentially the test employed by the courts today.

WHEN DOES A REGULATION GO "TOO FAR"?

In 1922, Justice Oliver Wendell Holmes declared that "the general rule at least is, that while property may be regulated to a certain extent, if regulation goes too far it will be recognized as a taking" [*Pennsylvania Coal Co. v. Mahon*].[2] Since that time, courts have struggled with the question of when a regulation does, in fact, go "too far." There has been no clear articulation of when the exercise of regulatory authority will violate the Just Compensation Clause. In 1978, after surveying fifty years of takings jurisprudence, Justice Brennan threw up his hands in dismay and declared that "This Court, quite simply, has been unable to develop any 'set formula' for determining when 'justice and fairness' require that economic injuries caused by public action be compensated by the government, rather than remain disproportionately concentrated on a few persons" [*Penn Central Transp. Co. v. New York City*].[3] Justice Brennan then identified three factors to guide courts in determining whether the Fifth Amendment has been violated: (1) the character of the government's action; (2) the reasonableness of the owner's investment-backed expectations; and (3) the economic impact of the regulation.

Since 1978, however, the Court also has identified at least three areas which constitute *per se* violations of the Fifth Amendment. In *Nollan v. California Coastal Commission*, the Court determined that a property regulation which does not substantially advance its avowed governmental purpose constitutes a taking.[4] Most recently, in *Lucas v. South Carolina Coastal Council*, the Court held that the destruction of all productive and beneficial uses of private property violates the Fifth Amendment.[5] Additionally, in *Hodel v. Irving*, the Court held that destruction of the right to devise private property violates the Fifth Amendment.[6] Despite these efforts to flesh out Fifth Amendment guarantees, there are still many open questions in takings jurisprudence. Indeed, the most troublesome question is determining when a regulation goes too far.

PER SE TAKINGS

In 1980, the United States Supreme Court announced a two-part, disjunctive test to analyze potential Fifth Amendment violations. Namely, the application of a government regulation to a particular property effects a taking if "the ordinance does not substantially advance legitimate state interests"; or if it "denies an owner economically viable use of his land" [*Agins v. City of Tiburon*].[7]

Nexus—No Substantial Advancement of a State Interest

The United States Supreme Court examined the first prong of the *Agins* test in *Nollan v. California Coastal Commission,* where it held that a regulatory scheme that affects property rights must "substantially advance" the purported purpose of the scheme.[8] Without such a "nexus," the regulatory scheme will be considered a taking of property, entitling the owner to injunctive relief. The Nollans wanted to tear down their bungalow on a California beach and build a new three-bedroom house. The California Coastal Commission granted the permit to do so, but included the condition that the Nollans provide public access to their beachfront. The state contended that this condition was designed to minimize the "psychological barrier" to public access that arises from continuous privately owned structures along the beachfront. The Nollans objected to the condition, and the permit was denied. The California Superior Court struck down the condition and, while the case was on appeal, the Nollans built their new home. The California Court of Appeals reversed the ruling, finding that the condition attached to the permit was a legitimate exercise of the state's regulatory powers for which no compensation was necessary.[9] An appeal to the United States Supreme Court followed.

Because the beach access condition did not substantially advance the California Coastal Commission's stated goal of removing the "psychological barrier" facing viewers from the road, the United States Supreme Court found that there was no "nexus" between the goal and effect of the regulation. The Court then struck down the condition.[10]

The most significant feature in the *Nollan* opinion is the level of scrutiny the Court applied in reviewing the government's action. The Court held that in order to decide whether a taking had occurred, it must first determine whether the condition attached to the permit *substantially advanced* a legitimate government interest. The Court found that this inquiry is one that required a heightened degree of scrutiny. Writing for the Court, Justice Antonin Scalia specifically rejected Justice Brennan's dissenting argument that the rational basis test should be used to review government action in takings cases. As a result, courts may no longer "rubber-stamp" governmental action by using the rational basis test.

Other "nexus" cases under the Fifth Amendment have followed the rule set forth in *Nollan*. In *Seawall Associates v. City of New York*, the courts analyzed New York City Local Law No. 9.[11] The law required single room occupancy (SRO) owners to rent rooms at controlled rents, refrain from demolishing SRO apartment buildings, repair these buildings, and maintain high occupancy levels. The stated statutory purpose was to alleviate homelessness. Despite the fact that most rent control ordinances have been found not to constitute a taking,[12] the New York Supreme Court found that the law was invalid as a taking of private property without just compensation.[13]

After the Appellate Division reversed,[14] the New York Court of Appeals found that both a physical and regulatory taking had occurred.[15] Analyzing the economic effect upon the property owners, the court noted that there was no indication that the law substantially advanced its stated goal, *i.e.*, to reduce homelessness. The court noted that its inquiry was guided by the "heightened judicial scrutiny" test articulated in *Nollan*. Finally, the court found it compelling that one of the city's own studies indicated that "a ban on converting, destroying, and warehousing SRO units would do little to resolve the homeless crisis." Thus, the law failed the nexus test and was held unconstitutional.

Similarly, the district court in *Richardson v. City and County of Honolulu* invalidated an ordinance that limited rent increases in certain residential condominiums.[16] While the goal of the law was to ensure that there was an adequate supply of "reasonably" priced rental housing, the court found that the law did not allow landowners a reasonable rate of return, nor did it prevent lessees from subletting at higher rents. Citing *Nollan*, the court found that the statute was intended to further a legitimate governmental purpose but that the means did not substantially further that goal. Because just compensation had not been paid, the law was held unconstitutional.

Deprivation of All Beneficial and Productive Use of Property

The second part of the *Agins* disjunctive test—which requires a court to determine whether government action has denied a property owner the economically viable use of his property—was applied by the Supreme Court in *Lucas v. South Carolina Coastal Council*.[17] In *Lucas,* the Coastal Council denied permission to build homes on two desirable, and otherwise suitable, lots along the South Carolina coastline. The central holding of *Lucas* is that "regulations that deny the property owner of all 'economically viable use of his land' constitute one of the discrete categories of regulatory deprivations that require compensation without the usual case-specific inquiry into the public interest advanced in support of the restraint."[18] The Court emphasized that this is a *per se* rule of law. This means that to prove an unconstitutional taking under *Lucas*, a property owner need only show that the government took all economic or productive use of his property. The court need not engage in the *ad hoc* factual inquiry where the government is free to introduce countervailing evidence to defeat the taking claim.

The whole tenor of the *Lucas* decision is also worthy of note. The Court relied heavily on the roots of traditional Anglo-American property law and the values and the premise of the Just Compensation Clause itself in reaching its decision: "This accords, we think, with our 'takings' jurisprudence, which has traditionally been guided by the understanding of our citizens regarding the content of, and the State's power over, the 'bundle of rights' that they acquire when they obtain title to property."[19]

Destruction of the Power to Exclude Others

The "power to exclude" others, in the view of the United States Supreme Court, is one of the most valuable aspects of owning property. Where property exists, and the owner has not voluntarily compromised the attendant right to exclude, permanent physical occupancy directed by government authority presents an "unusually serious" impact on the property right.[20] In the face of such an impact, the Court has found a taking without regard to the public interest involved or the minimal economic impact imposed. The Court in *Nollan* stated that it had "repeatedly held that, as to property reserved by its owner for private use, 'the right to exclude [others is] one of the most essential sticks in the bundle of rights that are commonly characterized as property.'"[21]

FACT-BASED INQUIRIES

As mentioned above, in *Penn Central*, Justice William Brennan set forth a three-part test to assist courts in this *ad hoc* inquiry applicable in all cases not governed by the *per se* rules. Courts are to assess: (1) the economic impact of the restriction on the plaintiff's property; (2) the restriction's interference with investment-backed expectations; and (3) the character of the government's action. While (in many ways) the factors relate to the economic effect of the government action and are thus appropriate for assessing a damages action in the Claims Court, courts have relied on these factors in cases requesting declaratory and injunctive relief.[22]

Economic Impact

In 1922, the United States Supreme Court in *Pennsylvania Coal* decided the first great "economic impact" case. After Justice Holmes penned the now famous "too far" standard for evaluating takings claims, he found that a law limiting the mining of coal near support structures had the effect of "appropriating and destroying [the coal's value]."[23] This degree of destruction ran afoul of the Fifth Amendment.

Over fifty years later, Justice Brennan quoted Justice Holmes' *Pennsylvania Coal* admonishment that "courts were 'in danger of forgetting that a strong public desire to improve the public condition is not enough to warrant achieving the desire by a shorter cut than the constitutional way of paying for the change.'"[24] In *Penn Central Transp. Co. v. New York City*,[25] the Court analyzed the takings implications of the denial of a building permit by the New York City Landmarks Preservation Commission. Plaintiffs requested a permit to construct an office tower over Grand Central Station, property that had been designated an historic landmark. The Commission denied the permit, stating that the historic integrity of the landmark would be irreparably harmed. Justice Brennan, writing for the Court, neither questioned the legitimate goal of protecting historic sites, nor the means the Commission used to achieve that goal. Instead, the Court focused on the economic impact of the permit denial.

The Court found that the restriction was part of an overall plan designed to preserve historic buildings for the benefit of society as a whole, and did not single out Penn Central to bear the burden alone. The Court also found that the permit denial did not interfere with present uses of the Station and that the Station could be operated so as to realize a reasonable rate of return. Finally, the Court noted that New York's transferable development rights program allowed the plaintiffs to develop other properties in the area, thereby minimizing the economic impact of the government action. The Court rejected the plaintiffs' claims that a taking had occurred.

Though *Penn Central* adversely affected the property holder, Justice Brennan's fact-based, *ad hoc* inquiry has been applied to other property holders with different results. In *Loveladies Harbor, Inc. v. United States*, for example, the Claims Court judged the impact of the Army Corps of Engineers' denial of a wetlands permit.[26] Comparing the fair market value of the property before and after the denial of the permit, the court found that the denial caused a ninety-nine percent diminution in the value of the property. After a searching inquiry, the court found that there was no economically viable alternative use for the property absent a permit to fill in the wetlands and a taking had occurred.

Similarly, in *Whitney Benefits Inc. v. United States*, the Federal Circuit upheld the Claims Court's finding that operation of the Surface Mining Control and Reclamation Act (SMCRA) took property.[27] The

Act prevented the owners from mining coal from the "Whitney" mine in Wyoming. Because they owned only a small portion of the surface rights, but all of the mineral rights to the coal, the economic effect of SMCRA on the Whitney property was devastating. When the government argued that it had not physically taken the property, the court rejected the argument and noted that "[a] taking occurs when economic development is effectively prevented."[28] Distinct from *Penn Central*, where no taking was found because the station held economically viable alternatives, the property owners in *Pennsylvania Coal* and *Whitney Benefits* had no economically viable alternatives. Thus, *Whitney Benefits* joined a long list of cases that used the economic impact test first stated in *Pennsylvania Coal*, and then refined in *Penn Central*, to find a taking.[29]

Interference with Investment-Backed Expectations

Although Justice Brennan in *Penn Central* did not discuss the concept of interference with investment-backed expectations at length, this inquiry has been outcome-determinative in several significant takings cases. In *Ruckelshaus v. Monsanto Co.*, the plaintiff sued the Environmental Protection Agency (EPA), alleging that the agency's disclosure of confidential material to the public revealed valuable trade secrets.[30] To register a pesticide under the Federal Insecticide, Fungicide, and Rodenticide Act (FIFRA), Monsanto submitted confidential information to EPA. To assess whether Monsanto had an expectation that this information would be kept secret, the Court wrote that "[a] 'reasonable investment-backed expectation' must be more than a 'unilateral expectation or an abstract need.'"[31] Under this definition, the Court found that between the years 1972 and 1978, FIFRA expressly provided for the protection of trade secrets:

> Thus, with respect to trade secrets . . . the Federal Government had explicitly guaranteed to Monsanto and other registration applicants an extensive measure of confidentiality and exclusive use. This explicit government

guarantee formed the basis of a reasonable investment-backed expectation. . . . [Disclosure] would frustrate Monsanto's reasonable investment-backed expectation with respect to its control over the use and dissemination of the data it has submitted.[32]

On these grounds, the *Monsanto* Court found a taking.

Government interference with investment-backed expectations in *United Nuclear Corp. v. United States* also resulted in the conclusion that a taking occurred.[33] United, which had signed a lease to mine uranium on the Navajo Indian reservation, spent more than $5 million in exploration costs. After determining that a sizable amount of uranium existed on the property, United applied for all the necessary permits. Although United [Nuclear] met all the technical requirements, the United States withheld the permits to mine on the grounds that the Navajo tribe had not approved the mining plan. The permit delay caused the lease to lapse, and the tribe kept all lease bonuses, rents, and royalties. The Claims Court held that United had no reasonable expectation that its application to mine would be approved or that the regulations would not change, and denied the company's takings claim.[34]

On appeal, the Federal Circuit reversed the ruling, finding that the government's new policy of allowing the tribe to veto ratified leases "seriously interfered with United's investment-backed expectations by destroying them."[35] The court recognized that expectations may be frustrated by future regulations but that:

> The fact that United agreed that the leases would be subject to future regulations does not indicate that United fairly can be said to have anticipated that the Secretary would apply a new policy requiring tribal approval of mining plans to leases entered into almost six years earlier in reliance on which United had expended some $5 million.[36, 37]

32 / Property Rights

Thus, courts are not reluctant to grant monetary relief when the government "pulls the rug" out from beneath property owners.[38]

Character of the Government's Action

The final inquiry in the three-part *Penn Central* test is to judge the "character of the government's action." The more intrusive the character, the more likely there is a taking. Justice Brennan's third inquiry provides a court with flexibility to judge whether the character of the government action imposes an unfair or unnecessary burden on the property owner. The leading authority is the Supreme Court decision of *Hodel v. Irving*.[39] In order to avoid excessive fractionalization of Indian lands, Congress passed a law stating that Indians on the Ogalala Sioux reservation could not pass their interest in land at death to heirs. The purpose of the law was to prevent ownership scenarios such as the one regarding tract 1305:

> Tract 1305 is 40 acres and produces $1,080 in income annually. It is valued at $8,000. It has 438 owners, one-third of whom receive less than $.05 in annual rent and two-thirds of whom receive less than $1. . . . The smallest heir receives $.01 every 177 years.[40]

The relevant provisions of the Indian Land Consolidation Act require that upon death, the land escheats to the reservation. The plaintiffs, descendants of landowners, alleged an unconstitutional taking.

Assessment of the first two *Penn Central* factors in *Hodel v. Irving* led the Court to determine that the economic impact was *de minimis*, and that there were not investment-backed expectations. The Court found, however, that "the character of the government regulation here is extraordinary, since it amounts to virtually the abrogation of the right to pass on property to one's heirs, which right has been part of the Anglo-American legal system since feudal times."[41] Therefore, the Court held that the statute violated the Just Compensation Clause of the Fifth Amendment.

The Federal Circuit in *United Nuclear* similarly found the character of the government's action to be indefensible. As described above, the government refused to issue a uranium mining permit because the Navajo tribe failed to approve of the mining plan. The government's justification was assailed by the court:

> In its brief before us, the government asserts that the Secretary's requirement of tribal approval of the mining plan was intended to promote the Indians' right to and development of self-determination. It is difficult to understand, however, how encouraging the Indians not to live up to their contractual obligations, which they entered into freely and with the Secretary's approval, could be said to encourage self-determination.[42]

Other Equitable Factors Under *Penn Central's* "Ad Hoc" Test

Justice Brennan's three-part test in *Penn Central* does not undermine the fact that, at its core, the takings inquiry is a fact-based, *ad hoc* inquiry that examines the "totality of the circumstances." Thus, although not usually articulated as a factor, the equities clearly are weighed in determining whether or not a taking has occurred. The fact that a plaintiff might not "score" well on all three factors does not necessarily mean that he will not prevail on his takings claim. For example, in *Hodel v. Irving* the Court specifically noted that the economic impact of the government's restriction on alienation of Indian property was *de minimis*. Similarly, no investment-backed expectations were affected. Still, the Court found that the character of the government's action was so intrusive that declaratory relief was appropriate.

In *Yancey v. United States*, the plaintiffs did not score high on any of the three *Penn Central* factors, yet the inequity of having the government "take" healthy turkeys was too much for the court to allow. Thus, a taking was found in that case as well.

> Bluntly stated, the consequences of the Government's action cannot be ignored. Why should the Yanceys be forced to bear their own losses when their turkeys were not diseased? The Yanceys' losses came about because of the Government's action. If the intent of the poultry quarantine was to benefit the public, the public should be responsible for the Yanceys' losses.[43]

In *Monsanto*, the Court found the interference with investment-backed expectations to be controlling: "It is to the last of these three factors that we now direct our attention, for we find that the force of this factor is so overwhelming . . . that it disposes of the taking question regarding those data."[44] Indeed, the three factors do not have to be weighted equally, as any one alone could win the day.

In sum, the overarching rule in *Armstrong v. United States* goes hand in hand with the *Penn Central* test: the "Fifth Amendment guarantee . . . [is] designed to bar Government from forcing some people alone to bear the burdens which, in all fairness and justice, should be borne by the public as a whole."[45]

THE NUISANCE EXCEPTION

The right to use and enjoy property is not, however, unlimited. Thus, the jurisprudence of property rights forbids those uses of one's property which unreasonably interfere with the rights and liberties of others. An owner may not build a ditch to divert flood waters onto his neighbor's property; generate noxious smoke and fumes; conduct ultrahazardous activities which threaten his neighbor's safety; or otherwise impinge on the liberties of others as he uses and enjoys his own property. Like any other liberties, the right to own property has its limits. The outer boundaries of one's property rights are coextensive with the boundaries of the rights of others, just as the right of free speech does not protect defamatory statements and the right to free assembly does not encompass riots and malicious mischief.

The outer boundary of the right to use property proscribes those uses and labels them "nuisances." The common law has long recognized the authority of neighbors to obtain relief from uses of adjacent property which constitute nuisances. More recently, government has been held to possess the legal authority to assert a claim on behalf of the public as a whole for "public nuisances." Indeed, early environmental law was essentially the assertion of nuisance claims regarding noise, pollution, and other noxious uses of property. The "nuisance exception" to the right to use and enjoy one's property, since then, has become embedded in our legal system. Therefore, even if the plaintiff prevails in demonstrating that his "property" has been taken in violation of the Fifth Amendment, compensation need not be paid if the government can meet its burden of showing that the taking was necessary to abate a "public nuisance." It is well established that one may not use his property so as to damage others. Conceptualizing this a little differently, the use of one's property so as to harm others is not a legitimate property right, and hence has no value which can be taken.[46]

More recently, however, some environmental advocates have attempted to use the "nuisance exception" to swallow virtually the entire body of constitutionally protected property rights. Under this theory, any use of property of which they disapprove—the felling of a tree, the building of a fence, the leveling of a field—is said to constitute a "nuisance" which the law may enjoin. Not surprisingly, the most stringent wetlands regulations are routinely defended on the grounds that any disturbance of a wetland constitutes a "nuisance."

Importantly, the validity of a nuisance defense cannot be determined by legislative pronouncements.[47] The mere passage of a statute outlawing certain activity does not determine whether a nuisance exists at the particular property.[48] First, government cannot be allowed to define property rights out of existence simply by calling otherwise legitimate uses of property a nuisance.

> It does not rest with the public, taking the property, through Congress or the legislature, its representatives,

> to say what compensation shall be paid, or even what shall be the rule of compensation. The Constitution has declared that just compensation shall be paid, and the ascertainment of that is a judicial inquiry.[49,50]

Should this be the case, the existence of particular property rights would be dependent upon legislative grace rather than being constitutionally protected against public seizure without just compensation.[51]

Additionally, the legislative branch is institutionally incapable of performing the judicial function of weighing the evidence necessary to determine whether the proposed use of the particular parcel of property will constitute a nuisance.

> Indeed, we have frequently observed that whether a particular restriction will be rendered invalid by the government's failure to pay for any losses proximately caused by it depends largely "upon the particular circumstances [in that] case."[52]

Moreover, if the legislature could take private property without notice and hearing, then serious due process concerns are implicated. As indicated by the court in *Florida Rock Industries, Inc. v. United States*:

> [S]imple invocation of the term pollution cannot foreclose a plaintiff's right to compensation under the Fifth Amendment. "[M]ere labels" of this sort afford "no talismanic immunity from Constitutional limitations." (citations omitted) Government may not circumvent the takings clause by defining activity as noxious by fiat. . . . To avoid the payment of compensation on this theory, the government must show that the prohibited activity in fact causes harm.[53]

Thus, the court, and not the legislature, is the appropriate forum in which to determine whether a nuisance exists.

Finally, it should be noted that the government bears the burden of proving such a nuisance defense.[54] In *Lucas*, for example, the South Carolina Coastal Council failed to sustain this burden, choosing instead to rely on the legislative findings supporting the statute. Since those legislative findings, standing alone, did not constitute sufficient evidence to sustain the burden of proving the existence of a nuisance on the facts *of that particular case,* the United States Supreme Court held that the government must remit compensation for taking Lucas' property.

Distinct from the nuisance defense, in *Mugler v. Kansas*, the Court established the "noxious use" doctrine.[55] The doctrine was a narrow exception to the Just Compensation Clause. It was applied in those instances where the proposed use of property involves quite profound and immediate adverse physical effects upon the health, safety, or welfare of others.

TEMPORARY TAKINGS

Shortly after the Supreme Court concluded in *Pennsylvania Coal* that a regulation could effect a taking of private property, the Court also concluded that a taking could be limited in duration, or temporary, as opposed to permanent.[56] It was not until the late eighties, in *First English Evangelical Lutheran Church of Glendale v. County of Los Angeles, California*, however, that the United States Supreme Court fleshed out this notion.[57] Chief Justice William Rehnquist stated that "'temporary' takings which, as here deny a landowner all use of his property, are not different in kind from, permanent takings, for which the Constitution clearly requires compensation."[58]

Lower courts have subsequently applied this concept. In *Yuba Natural Resources, Inc. v. United States,* the federal government prevented a company from exercising its mineral rights.[59] After losing a quiet title action that spanned six years, the United States withdrew its objection that prohibited mining. Yuba sued the government for temporarily taking the property. Because the government's mining prohibition altered Yuba's mineral property right for six years, the court held that the government temporarily took Yuba's property.

CONCLUSION

The potential taking of a parcel is determined through judicial interpretation of the government's action to assess whether the government has gone "too far." In order to give full value to the protection offered by the Fifth Amendment, courts examine potential takings from a variety of perspectives. The different facts and contexts involved in each of these cases provide landowners with a number of different judicial models to determine whether the government's conduct unconstitutionally interfered with their property.

ENDNOTES

[1] 450 U.S. 621 (1981).
[2] 260 U.S. 393 (1922).
[3] 438 U.S. 124 (1978).
[4] 483 U.S. 825 (1987).
[5] 112 S. Ct. 2866 (1992).
[6] 481 U.S. 704 (1987).
[7] 447 U.S. 255 (1980).
[8] 483 U.S. 825, 836-39 (1987).
[9] *Nollan v. California Coastal Commission*, 177 Cal. App. 3d 719 (1986).
[10] 483 U.S. at 841-42.
[11] 544 N.Y.S.2d 542 (N.Y. 1989).
[12] *See, e.g., Bowles v. Willingham*, 321 U.S. 503 (1944) (federal regulations placing ceiling on war-time rents did not exact a taking).
[13] *Seawall Associates v. City of New York*, 523 N.Y.S.2d 353 (N.Y. Sup. Ct. 1987).
[14] 534 N.Y.S.2d 958 (N.Y. App. Div. 1988).
[15] 544 N.Y.S.2d at 548.

[16] 759 F. Supp. 1477 (D. Haw. 1991).

[17] 112 S. Ct. 2886 (1992).

[18] *Id.*

[19] *Id.*

[20] *Loretto v. TelePrompter Manhattan CATV Corp.*

[21] 483 U.S. at 825 (quoting *Loretto v. TelePrompter Manhattan CATV Corp.*, 458 U.S. 419, 433 (1982), quoting *Kaiser Aetna v. United States*, 444 U.S. 164, 176 (1979)).

[22] In federal district court, a claim for declaratory and injunctive relief must be carefully drafted to avoid requesting relief for specific economic harm. A claim for damages may result in a motion to transfer jurisdiction to the United States Claims Court, which has exclusive jurisdiction over just compensation cases for damages under the Tucker Act. 28 U.S.C. § 1491 (Supp. 1990). "Equitable relief is not available to enjoin an alleged taking of private property for public use, duly authorized by law, when a suit for compensation can be brought against the sovereign subsequent to the taking." *Ruckelshaus v. Monsanto Co.*, 467 U.S. 986, 1016 (1984).

[23] 260 U.S. at 414.

[24] *Penn Central Transp. Co. v. New York City*, 438 U.S. 104, 152 (1978), quoting *Pennsylvania Coal v. Mahon*, 260 U.S. at 416.

[25] 438 U.S. 124 (1978).

[26] 21 Cl. Ct. 153 (1990).

[27] 926 F.2d 1169 (Fed. Cir.), *cert. denied,* 502 U.S. 952, (1991).

[28] 926 F.2d at 1172.

[29] *See, e.g., Richardson,* 759 F. Supp. at 1489; *Yancey,* 915 F.2d at 1539-40.

[30] 467 U.S. 986 (1984).

[31] *Id.*

[32] 467 U.S. at 1011.

[33] 912 F.2d 1432 (Fed. Cir. 1990).

[34] *United Nuclear Corp. v. United States*, 17 Cl. Ct. 768 (1989).

[35] 912 F.2d at 1437.

[36] *Id.* at 1436.

[37] *United Nuclear,* 912 F.2d 1432 (Fed. Cir. 1990).

[38] *See also Yancey,* 915 F.2d at 1539-40 (government-mandated quarantine of turkeys interfered with plaintiff's investment-backed expectations to sell the flock out of state).

[39] 481 U.S. 704 (1987).
[40] *Hodel v. Irving*, at 713.
[41] *Id.* at 716.
[42] 912 F.2d at 1437.
[43] *Yancey*, 915 F.2d 1534, 1542 (Fed. Cir. 1990).
[44] 467 U.S. at 1005.
[45] 364 U.S. at 49.
[46] *Keystone Bituminous Coal Association v. DeBenedictis*, 480 U.S. 470 n.20 (1987).
[47] *Loveladies Harbor, Inc. v. United States,* 15 C. Ct. 375, 388 (1988). The court stated that "the mere fact that the governmental regulation was intended to promote a public benefit is not sufficient to [determine whether the regulation substantially advances a public purpose.] This determination must also involve the Court's weighing of the intended public benefit against the harm inflicted upon the landowner involved." *Id.* (quoting *Agins v. City of Tiburon,* 447 U.S. at 261).
[48] This is not to say that the legislature cannot decree that certain activities injurious to public health and safety (*e.g.,* maintaining a facility for producing illegal drugs) constitute a *per se* nuisance. However, the Court must ascertain whether the activity actually falls within the common law notion of "nuisance," and may not simply accept the proposition that a formerly lawful activity is a "nuisance" merely because the legislature says it is.
[49] *Monongahela Navigation Co. v. United States*, 148 U.S. 312 (1893).
[50] *Id.* at 327.
[51] *See, e.g., Whitney Benefits, Inc. v. United States,* 18 Cl. Ct. 394 (1989), *modified,* 20 Cl. Ct. 324 (1990), *aff'd* 926 F.2d 1169 (Fed. Cir.), *cert. denied,* 502 U.S. 952 (1991) (Enactment of SMCRA which deprived owner of all value of property is a taking); *Bell v. Town of Wells,* 557 A.2d 168 (Me. 1989) ("[L]egislature cannot simply alter these long-established property rights to accommodate new recreational needs.").
[52] *Penn Central Transp. Co. v. New York City,* 438 U.S. 104, 124 (1977) (citing *United States v. Central Eureka Mining Co.,* 357 U.S. 155, 168 (1958)).
[53] 8 Cl. Ct. at 171.
[54] *Loveladies Harbor, Inc. v. United States*, 21 Cl. Ct. at 154-58.
[55] 123 U.S. 623 (1887); *see also Keystone Bituminous Ass'n. v. DeBenedictis,* 480 U.S. 470 (1987) (subsidence threatening buildings and ground water); *Miller v. Schoene,* 276 U.S. 272 (1928) (state action to destroy

certain trees carrying infectious disease hazardous to principal agricultural crop in Virginia).
[56] *Jacobs v. United States*, 290 U.S. 13, 16 (1933).
[57] 482 U.S. 304 (1987).
[58] *Id.* at 318.
[59] 821 F.2d 638, 642 (Fed. Cir. 1987).

Chapter 4

WETLANDS

The legal prohibition against the wanton destruction of wetlands rests upon the importance of marshes, bogs, and tidal areas to ecological balance.[1] Wetlands can perform important functions by protecting against erosion and controlling floods. Moreover, because of the role wetlands play in filtering out pollutants which would otherwise flow into our nation's waterways, there is reason for including them as part of the overall system of water pollution control.

Water pollution is governed by the permitting system of the 1972 Federal Water Pollution Control Act, commonly known as the "Clean Water Act." The law is simple: if one wishes to discharge pollutants into navigable waters, one must obtain a permit from the government.[2] That permit describes the nature and amount of the pollutants one may discharge. The release into navigable waters of unpermitted pollutants is a violation of the Clean Water Act, punishable by monetary penalties, injunctions, or even imprisonment.[3] The system is straightforward, and has resulted in immense improvements in water quality across the nation.

Wetlands protection, nevertheless, is more like land use regulation than pollution control. Moreover, Congress has failed to pass a comprehensive and coherent wetland protection statute. Instead, inventive (and often well-intentioned) bureaucrats and political leaders try to force the square peg of wetlands protection into the round hole of pollution control, specifically, the point source discharge permitting scheme of the Clean Water Act. The result is a haphazard, conflicting wetlands regulatory scheme that mismanages our nation's natural as well as financial resources. A federal district judge in Florida recently declared that:

> in a reversal of terms that is worthy of *Alice in Wonderland*, the regulatory hydra which emerged from the Clean Water Act mandates in this case that a land owner who places clean fill dirt on a plot of subdivided dry land may be imprisoned for the statutory felony offense of "discharging pollutants into the navigable waters of the United States."[4]

THE WETLANDS REGULATORY SCHEME

The Clean Water Act was adopted by Congress for the express "purpose of restoring and maintaining the chemical, physical and biological integrity of the Nation's waters."[5] Section 404 of the statute forbids "the discharge of any pollutant by any person" except in accordance with a statutory scheme which requires a permit for most "point source" pollutant discharges into "navigable waters."[6] The "knowing" violation of this requirement is punishable as a felony, and even a negligent violation of the Clean Water Act can draw a prison sentence of up to one year.[7] The statute is primarily concerned with regulating industrial and sanitary waste water streams at the point they discharge into navigable waterways.

Parallel to this statutory scheme for controlling waste water discharges is a program under which the Secretary of the Army (traditionally charged with maintaining navigability of rivers and harbors) may issue permits "for the discharge of dredged or fill material into the navigable waters at specified disposal sites."[8] Reacting to the political clout of environmental groups and the activism of some federal judges, the bureaucracy within the United States Army Corps of Engineers has "interpreted" a program regulating "discharges" of "fill materials" at "disposal sites" into the "navigable waters" to apply to any disturbance of a broad class of ecological systems which they dubbed "wetlands."[9] Since the term "wetland" has neither a legal definition nor a scientific meaning, the effect of this regulatory expansionism was to criminalize a class of land-disturbing activities, while failing to define that class in an intelligible and consistent manner.

Under the current United States Army Corps of Engineers' regulations,[10] moreover, the scope of "navigable waters" is theoretically stretched to—and perhaps beyond—its furthest *constitutional* reach.[11] Only if the regulated waters are navigable or otherwise part of the interstate commerce does Congress have the constitutional authority to regulate them. The United States Army Corps of Engineers' regulations extend the definition to cover not only traditionally navigable waters, but also an unprecedented range of "areas" that they label "waters." These include:

- all interstate waters, including interstate wetlands;

- all other waters, such as intrastate lakes, rivers, streams (including intermittent streams), mudflats, sandflats, wetlands, sloughs, prairie potholes, wet meadows, playa lakes, or natural ponds, the use, degradation or destruction of which *could* affect interstate or foreign commerce [emphasis added];

- all impoundments of water that fit these definitions;

- tributaries of any defined waters;

- the territorial seas; and

- wetlands adjacent to waters, other than those adjacent to other wetlands.[12]

Isolated Wetlands

The phrase "all other waters, . . . the use, degradation or destruction of which could affect interstate . . . commerce"[13] is the means by which the government today claims it can assert jurisdiction over "isolated wetlands" that are not even adjacent to another body of water. The Seventh Circuit has noted, however, that "[i]solated wetlands, unlike adjacent wetlands, have no hydrological connection to any body of water. By their very definition, isolated wetlands have no relationship or interdependence with any other body of water" [*Hoffman Homes, Inc. v. EPA*].[14] Ignoring this essential element, the United States Army Corps of Engineers continues to determine whether isolated wetlands are subjugated to the Section 404 Clean Water Act permitting regulations by making an *ad hoc* factual inquiry to see whether the use of those waters could hypothetically affect interstate commerce. Under this practically boundless regulation, the United States Army Corps of Engineers continues to exert its authority over isolated wetlands which are both within private property boundaries and have no discernible impact on interstate commerce. Quite simply, if the United States Army Corps of Engineers can come up with some plausible relationship between the isolated or nonadjacent wetland and interstate commerce, the water body will fall under the Clean Water Act's jurisdiction.

The United States Army Corps of Engineers regulation lists several nonexhaustive examples of the type of link that can draw private property into the heavily regulated wetlands arena. For example, it regulates waters "which are, or *could be,* used by interstate travellers, from which fish or shellfish are or could be taken and which are used or could be used for industrial purposes" (emphasis added).[15] The broadest application of this definition has been the attempt of the United States Army Corps of Engineers to establish an interstate commerce connection by the potential, not even the actual, use of the isolated wetland by migratory birds or other wildlife. Several cases have examined this far-reaching application, but there is no consensus on the constitutionality of this rule to date.[16] Although the decision was recently vacated, the Seventh Circuit in *Hoffman Homes* expressed the incredibility of allowing this hypothetical scenario to satisfy the interstate commerce link.

> Since creation (of the states), migratory birds have flown interstate. But this annual traverse by itself does not affect commerce. The birds obviously do not engage in commerce. Until they are watched, photographed, shot at or otherwise impacted by people who do (or, we suppose, have the potential to) engage in interstate commerce, migratory birds do not ignite the Commerce Clause. The idea that the *potential* presence of migrating birds itself affects commerce is even more far-fetched [emphasis added].[17]

Definition of "Wetland"

Under the current regulatory program, the United States Army Corps of Engineers has primary responsibility for processing wetlands permits, although individual permits are also reviewed (and may be vetoed) by the EPA. Additional "consulting agencies" include the United States Fish and Wildlife Service, the National Marine Fisheries Service, and the Soil Conservation Service. Lacking any congressional direction, the wetlands permitting program allows each agency to make permitting decisions or recommendations with reference solely to its own particular interests. Hence, "wetlands" has come to mean different things to different regulators. Further, because it is a program created by regulators, there is no designated body with jurisdiction or authority to settle their squabbles. As one commentator describes it:

> To the frustration of permit applicants, for years each agency used different definitions of wetlands and different methods to determine their boundaries. What was acceptable to one agency might not be to another, often resulting in one agency approving a permit request that another had denied or raised objections to.[18]

Unsurprisingly, each agency sees and defines wetlands from its own programmatic perspective. For Fish and Wildlife, wetlands are primarily a habitat for birds, fish, reptiles and other creatures who live in the transitional zone between water and land. For the Soil Conservation Service, wetlands are an integral part of controlling erosion and flooding, and thus maintaining our nation's agricultural base. The EPA sees wetlands as a filter for pollutants which would otherwise run off the land and into bodies of water. And the United States Army Corps of Engineers sees them as topographic and geographic features integral to navigation and earth works. As the same commentator put it, there has been "a lot of trench warfare between the agencies over what constituted a wetland."[19]

The agencies' inconsistent wetland policies under the Clean Water Act have been especially troubling for farmers and ranchers, since their wetlands are also highly regulated under other statutes. Moreover, the different statutes seek varying ends and are not integrated to create a harmonious and cohesive wetlands policy. What is legal or illegal, nonwetland or wetland, under one statute may not necessarily be so under another. For instance:

> Under the FSA [Food Security Act], lands that meet the physical definition of wetlands are exempted from the definition of wetlands, based on their agricultural usage. This structure differs from the [Clean Water Act], which provides far-reaching physical jurisdiction and a blanket prohibition on filling without a permit; exceptions to the [Clean Water Act] are exceptions to the requirement to obtain a permit, not exceptions to the definition of wetlands. These contrasting legislative structures have led to confusion by regulated persons, *who wonder why the same parcel is legally a wetland under one federal law, but not under another* [emphasis added].[20]

Wetland Manuals

After years of negotiation during the mid 1980s, an interagency working group adopted a document which spent roughly two hundred pages defining wetlands. This 1987 wetlands manual was immediately attacked on all sides as inadequate, resulting in two more years of wrangling that produced a 1989 manual. That manual, also prepared without benefit of public comment or congressional debate, would have nearly doubled the acreage subject to wetlands regulation. The 1989 manual was almost immediately repudiated by everyone, including its authors, and work began on the 1991 manual. Late in 1992, unable to reach accord, government agencies declared a truce by agreeing to use the 1987 wetlands manual on an interim basis pending resolution of the matter by the new administration. Ultimately, Congress mandated that a report on designating wetlands must be prepared by the National Academy of Sciences before any further revisions of the wetlands manual could be conducted.[21]

Despite dozens of hearings and a number of bills introduced over the past several years, Congress has also made little progress in declaring what it wants to regulate as a wetland and how. Senator Max Baucus (D-Montana) aptly described the wetlands permitting program:

> It is confusing. It is difficult for the public to understand the program's requirements and, therefore, how to comply with them. It is particularly difficult for farmers and ranchers to sort through and reconcile the various requirements of Section 404 and the swampbuster provisions of the Food Security Act.
>
> It is often financially or technically difficult for small landowners to take the steps, such as identification and delineation of wetlands, necessary to even apply for a Section 404 permit to fill portions of a wetland.
>
> The Section 404 permit process can still drag on for too long without a decision one way or another. And permit

50 / Property Rights

applicants have no avenue other than the courts to appeal a decision on their application.[22]

Despite the inexact science of defining a wetland and the many conflicting formulas created by the agencies, the current Section 404 wetlands permit program makes the property owner bear the initial burden of discovering whether or not his property falls within the Clean Water Act's wetland jurisdiction.[23] Thus, the lack of an agreement among the agencies on what constitutes a wetland often comes at the expense of the baffled property owner.[24]

Case Study: Wetland Definition and Agency Contradiction

A Pennsylvania dairy farmer's fight with the bureaucracy produced results which one is hard-pressed to believe Congress intended or even imagined when promulgating the Clean Water Act.[25] This farmer had a "wetspot," measuring several hundred square feet and typical to the region's terrain, located in the middle of his hay field. During dry years, he harvested hay on it. He mowed around it during wet years. This lone spot did not serve as floodwater control, nor did it have any water quality benefits. Furthermore, because it was situated on glaciated hardpan soils, it did not contribute to groundwater recharge. Finally, as the area was seasonally mowed for hay, it did not serve as prime habitat for endangered plants or animal species. The wetspot did, however, serve the critical function of a watering pond for a farm that on several occasions had almost had its well dry out.

Because of the need for additional water supplies, the farmer decided in the spring of 1988 to expand this wetspot into a two-acre pond. As a conscientious farmer, he first went to the local Conservation District office which is theoretically required to keep abreast of the current environmental regulations and interpretations affecting the county. The Conservation District referred the farmer to the United States Fish and Wildlife Service because of the potential wetlands classification this project involved. Six months later, the Fish and Wildlife Service visited the land and declared that regulated wetlands existed and a Clean Water Act Section 404 permit would be required—but most likely granted, due to the diminutive size of the land.

The next step in the bureaucratic maze was to fill out a permit. With the assistance of the Conservation District, a joint United States Army Corps of Engineers and Pennsylvania Department of Environmental Resources permit application was prepared and submitted. Months later, this entire package was returned with a letter explaining that no permit was required for this activity. The farmer sought clarification from the Conservation District, which reiterated the Department of Environmental Resources' words that "construction of a dam in a wetland area that has less than one-hundred acres drainage, is less than fifteen feet high, and impounds less than fifty acre-feet, is not regulated by the Department of Environmental Resources."[26] But the farmer was further informed that although the land is not under the Department of Environmental Resources' jurisdiction, it is still subject to the United States Army Corps of Engineers' permitting program, and an application must be filed accordingly. Apparently, the "joint application" did not serve its purpose. Accordingly, in the spring of 1989, the farmer again sent his application to the United States Army Corps of Engineers.

While this application was pending, the Conservation District discovered that certain wetland-disturbing activities could be authorized under a "nationwide permit" under the United States Army Corps of Engineers' regulations. Under these permits, specific activities in areas of less than one square mile are allowed, provided that one first obtains a state "water quality certification." The Conservation District was told that the regional Department of Environmental Resources Bureau of Water Quality is in charge of issuing these certifications, and that one is required before the nationwide permit is available. The frustrated farmer decided to wait for a response from the United States Army Corps of Engineers in regards to his initial permit application before he ventured down a different agency path. In the meantime, he was forced by dry weather to drill another well in order to keep his stock watered. After waiting for over a year for a response from the United States

Army Corps of Engineers, he decided to apply for the nationwide permit. When the Conservation District contacted the Regional Department of Environmental Resources office for guidance on how to obtain a water quality certification, this time the Department of Environmental Resources replied that until the nationwide permit is issued, certification cannot be obtained (instead of vice versa).

Having received these conflicting instructions, the Conservation District tried unsuccessfully to contact the United States Army Corps of Engineers office for further clarification. Apparently, no one was answering the telephone in the Pennsylvania office. The Conservation District therefore contacted the Fish and Wildlife Service, who unambiguously stated that they are prohibited from giving out information regarding national permits, since that information must come from the United States Army Corps of Engineers. The Conservation District then called the central United States Army Corps of Engineers headquarters in Baltimore, only to be told that they must contact the Pennsylvania office. After explaining their difficulty in contacting that office, they were assured by the Baltimore office that it would instruct the Pennsylvania office to telephone the Conservation District. The Pennsylvania United States Army Corps of Engineers office still failed to reach the Conservation District. Ultimately, at the Conservation District's suggestion, this farmer sent letters simultaneously to the Department of Environmental Resources for a water quality certification *and* to the United States Army Corps of Engineers for a nationwide permit, in a vain attempt to expedite this ridiculously lengthy process.

Whatever the ultimate outcome, this diligent farmer has been prevented from constructing a much-needed stock watering pond which would not affect any navigable waters, and which would be entirely contained on his own private property. An American Farm Bureau Federation representative summarized the process:

> Ignorance of the law is seldom a valid excuse when dealing with rules and regulations that affect our day to day operations. Yet, there appear to be instances where

the regulations, and process to become "enlightened" or "less ignorant" about those regulations, is so vague and confusing, that it appears the majority of us are doomed to remain as ignorant as when we began. This can also be extended (through no fault of their own) to the people required to enforce those regulations. . . . While [this one dairy farmer] perseveres to do the work the "right way," we can't help but wonder if the "right way" works at all.[27]

WETLANDS ENFORCEMENT PROVISIONS

Unlike most environmental law statutes, the Clean Water Act vests independent enforcement authority with two agencies, the EPA and the United States Army Corps of Engineers. Either one may pursue an enforcement action against any person that exhibits control over the illegal wetland activity. There are three methods by which the wetlands provisions are enforced: administrative enforcement; civil enforcement; and criminal enforcement.

Section 309 of the Clean Water Act addresses enforcement penalties. Under this Section, administrative enforcement takes the form of EPA administrative orders, or "cease and desist" orders by the United States Army Corps of Engineers. Generally, under the Clean Water Act, EPA is the lead enforcement agency for cases involving unpermitted discharges into a wetland, and the United States Army Corps of Engineers is the lead agency for Corps-issued permit violations. Although these orders are not independently enforceable (enforcement is through judicial action), the compliance orders are not judicially reviewable and pre-enforcement review is unavailable.

Civil and criminal enforcement proceedings risk the assessment of severe penalties. Under Section 309(b) of the Clean Water Act, any person who discharges dredged or fill material without a permit or who disobeys an administrative order "shall be subject to a civil penalty up to $25,000 per day for each violation." The statute requires courts to consider certain factors, including the seriousness of the violation and the economic benefit to the violator, before assessing the penalty. Criminal enforcement under Section 309(c) provides sanctions for negligent and knowing violations of the statute. A negligent violator may be fined no more than $25,000, or less than $2,500 per day of violation, or be imprisoned up to one year, or both. Knowing violators may not be fined more than $50,000, or less than $5,000 per day of violation, or be imprisoned more than three years, or both. More stringent punishments apply to knowing violators that, through their violation, place another person in imminent danger of death or serious bodily injury.

Section 505 of the Clean Water Act empowers citizens to bring lawsuits against violators of the Clean Water Act. To maintain an action under the citizen suit provision, the citizen must follow detailed procedures that offer EPA the chance to intervene. Additionally, the suit must involve a continuous and ongoing violation that satisfies the "actual violation" standard set forth in the landmark United States Supreme Court decision of *Gwaltney of Smithfield Ltd. v. Chesapeake Bay Foundation, Inc.*[28]

WETLANDS AND PROPERTY RIGHTS

A true "discharge of fill material into navigable waters of the United States" would not be constitutionally protected, since the individual does not own those waters. The public has an interest in ensuring that its rivers, lakes, and streams remain navigable, and that helter-skelter dredging, filling, and building of obstacles in these watery highways does not occur. Indeed, the United States Army Corps of Engineers has possessed permitting authority over construction of such obstacles to navigation for nearly a century under the Rivers and Harbors Act of 1899.[29] Similarly, one may not wantonly discharge pollutants into those same public waters, fouling the drinking water supply and destroying fisheries and vegetation. Again, the impact of this activity is upon the publicly owned resources offsite, and its effects are substantial and detrimental. The people who drink the water and fish the lake have a right to preclude such environmental degradation, and that right forms the outer boundary of the individual's right to use his property. Requiring permits for the discharge of pollutants or fill material into truly navigable waters is, in most instances, an appropriate and effective regulatory scheme for protecting the chemical, physical, and biological integrity of our nation's waterways.

As we have seen, however, the wetlands permitting program reaches far beyond those waterways owned by the public. Instead, it purports to regulate virtually all land-disturbing activities occurring on as much as one hundred million acres of privately owned property. Where the activity and its impacts are confined to the boundary lines of the property itself, with no discharge of pollutants or fill material leaving that property, the "nuisance" rationale evaporates. The rights of no individual suffer from the owner's use of his private lands. Indeed courts have, in a number of instances, invalidated purported exercises of the Corps' wetlands jurisdiction on precisely this ground, that the regulation of the wetland does not substantially advance a legitimate governmental interest in protecting its citizens against pollution or obstruction of navigable waters.[30]

In addition, some courts have held that if the government wishes to preserve these wetlands, it must purchase them from the property owners and pay "just compensation" as required by the Just Compensation Clause of the Fifth Amendment.[31] Other courts have labeled governmental regulatory actions as arbitrary and capricious when the impact of the wetlands disturbances is limited to the boundaries of the private property, because no individual right to be free from pollution or obstruction is implicated.[32] Finally, other federal statutes addressing wetlands actually recognize that their regulations "take" valuable property rights, and therefore include provisions that compensate for those losses. For example, the Conservation Reserve Program pays farmers annual rent if they agree to stop cultivating highly erodible land; similarly, under the Wetlands Reserve Program, the government will purchase wetlands easements from the landowner.

Ironically, the Clean Water Act itself regulates discharges of pollutants only outside the boundaries of the property. Thus, polluted water may be circulated through a "closed loop" system in a plant without a permit. It may also be discharged into a settling pond, a waste water collection system, or a waste water treatment facility without a permit, so long as it is retained on site. In short, the Clean Water Act itself appears to recognize that the government lacks any legitimate interest in regulating the pollution of water so long as any impact of that pollution is confined to the boundaries of the private property.

Yet the Section 404 program, predicating its enforceability on precisely the same provision of the Clean Water Act which forbids "discharge of pollutants" into "navigable waters of the United States," purports to regulate all wetlands disturbances whether or not their impact is confined to the private property itself. Pressed to identify the rights of others that are infringed by the owner's exercise of his right to use and enjoy private property, defenders of the system will assert that wetlands perform important functions such as flood control, filtration of pollutants, and providing habitat for migratory birds.

This argument proves too much, however. It fails to distinguish wetlands from other natural ecosystems—mountains, meadows, beaches, and prairies—all of which perform unique functions in maintaining the intricate web of our nation's environment. Indeed, it is difficult to imagine any private property in its natural state which does not perform some ecological function. Every rivulet, earthworm, rock, and blade of grass has its place in this ecological system and, if it may not be disturbed without the permission of the government, then private property rights no longer exist. The class of "wetlands" whose disturbance shows no discernible impact beyond the boundaries of the private property simply cannot be distinguished from the stand of trees, the glen, the dale, or the brook, all of which likewise have their place in nature.

The Property Rights Defense

The legality of prosecution for wetlands violations depends upon the legality of the underlying exercise of wetlands' regulatory power. If the United States Army Corps of Engineers did not have the legal power to require a permit, then the disturbance of the wetlands without a permit is simply not punishable. Courts have often held that the exercise of a constitutional right in violation of a regulatory scheme does not constitute a crime. In the case of the First Amendment's guarantees of freedom of expression and assembly, a criminal complaint for failure to obtain a permit prior to a parade or demonstration will be dismissed if the permitting requirement infringes upon constitutionally guaranteed liberties.[33] The Fourth Amendment forbids prosecution for many acts performed within the sanctuary of one's home even though the performance of those same acts elsewhere might be a criminal offense.[34] The Fourteenth Amendment forbids the prosecution of those who violate state laws by refusing to attend segregated schools.[35]

The property rights provisions of the Constitution stand "as a shield against the arbitrary use of government power."[36] Where the wetlands disturbance lies within the realm of constitutionally protected property rights, the owner may not be prosecuted for failing to obtain a permit. Adding to the arbitrariness of wetlands enforcement is the fact that there is no blanket authority to prosecute every wetlands disturbance. In testing purported exercises of wetlands jurisdiction against the measure of constitutionally protected property rights, the courts have consistently required an "*ad hoc* factual inquiry" as to which no settled formula is used.[37] Under a recent United States Supreme Court holding where all the beneficial and productive use of land was taken, and the government was unable to meet its burden of proving that the "nuisance exception" does not apply, a *per se* taking of property was found.[38] Alternatively, where the wetlands regulations fail to "substantially advance" their stated purpose, the government simply lacks the constitutionally delegated authority to regulate those acts because the regulation as applied to the property owner is invalid.[39]

Takings and Wetlands

A number of successful cases have been brought against the federal government to recover just compensation for the taking of property due to the denial of a wetlands permit.

Florida Rock Industries, Inc. v. United States

Florida Rock Industries, Inc. v. United States[40] involved proposed limestone mining on wetlands. In 1972, Florida Rock Industries, a large-scale miner of limestone for cement production, bought a tract of 1,560 acres for $2,964,000 in Dade County, Florida, for the sole purpose of limestone mining.[41] The property was located above a large limestone formation which was approximately fifty feet deep, and tests showed that it would yield approximately 100,000 tons of usable rock per acre.[42] When Florida Rock bought the property, it obtained all the necessary state and local permits or waivers to operate a limestone quarry. At that time, there were no applicable state or federal wetlands regulations.[43] Because of a slump in southern Florida construction, however, Florida Rock did not attempt to mine the limestone until 1978. When it did, it was told that, by reason of a change in the law, it would have to obtain a Section 404 "dredge and fill" permit pursuant to the Clean Water Act.[44] On October 2, 1980, the United States Army Corps of Engineers denied Florida Rock's permit application, finding the permit would not be in the public interest.[45]

In its initial determination of whether Florida Rock's expectation to mine its land was reasonable, the United States Court of Claim for the Federal Circuit was influenced by the fact that the company had bought the property before the regulations were promulgated:

> [T]he government has drawn a line in time, and has dictated that covered activity begun after a certain point is restricted. As defendant has conceded, if plaintiff had attempted to mine its property earlier, it probably would have been grandfathered in under the then-existing

statutory scheme. Moreover, . . . limestone mining operations that had begun prior to the amendments to the Clean Water Act were ongoing at the time of trial.[46]

However, the overriding issue at stake in the *Florida Rock* case was whether the mining was an alleged nuisance and an unreasonable threat to the surrounding environment. The government argued that destruction of the wetland would inflict a noxious injury upon the community, and therefore, prohibition of that use is not a taking because it prevents a public nuisance.[47] The Claims Court rejected this nuisance exception argument, in part because of the dearth of evidence introduced to support the defendant's contention that the claimant's proposed mining would endanger or destroy wetlands and risk contamination of the Biscayne Aquifer. The judge visited the property and observed:

> [I]t is clear from the court's aerial visit of the site that the proposed use of plaintiff's property would not have created any significant increase in the risk of contamination posed to the Biscayne Aquifer. The extensive quarries in the area of plaintiff's property belie any claim that a nuisance is involved here.
>
> ....
>
> Rock mining of the type planned for plaintiff's property never has been considered a nuisance. In fact, it is in this area, as the court observed, the precursor of stylish, if not elegant, residential development.[48]

In short, the court found there was no nexus between the prohibition of mining and the protection of the aquifer, and found that the value of the limestone was unconstitutionally taken.

Loveladies Harbor, Inc. v. United States

Loveladies Harbor, Inc. v. United States,[49] a wetlands case, is similar to *Florida Rock*. *Loveladies Harbor* was decided the same day as *Florida Rock* and by the same judge. The case involved the plaintiff's acquisition of 250 acres of undeveloped land in Long Beach Township, New Jersey, for $300,000 in 1956. By 1982, the construction of new homes and the improvement by landfill consumed 199 of those acres, making the fair market value of the developed property increase over $200,000 per acre. The enactment of state and federal statutes which required permits before the filling of any wetlands prevented the development of the remaining fifty-one acres.[50] The state eventually agreed to allow the plaintiffs to fill eleven and a half acres, provided that they create a corresponding amount of new wetlands. The United States Army Corps of Engineers, however, denied the plaintiffs' application to fill in any acreage. At issue before the Claims Court were the eleven and a half acres and a previously filled single acre.

The court's decision to award compensation for the loss of the fair market value of the limestone rested largely on the inequity of the denial of the fill permits. Loveladies Harbor investors bought the property for one purpose only—development. By denying the required development permits, the government effectively stripped away all of the property's anticipated economic return. Unlike *Florida Rock*, however, the court did not question the nexus between the government's objective and its action. Rather, it asserted that: "[T]he central reason behind the denial [of the plaintiffs' fill permits] was the government's desire to preserve the wetlands along with its attendant wildlife and vegetation."[51] The court indicated that even though the government had an important objective at stake, the regulation in this instance had gone too far in that it destroyed the entire value of plaintiffs' property:

> The Fifth Amendment guarantees that private property shall not be "taken for public use, without just compensation." This constitutional guarantee is more than just a limitation against the physical seizure or invasion of

property by the government in the name of the public good. The Fifth Amendment also provides just compensation against governmental regulations which effectively accomplish the same destructive end.[52]

Further, what is interesting about this analysis is the court's rejection of the government's proposed alternative uses for the property, and instead its focus on the expectation of the property owner: "[D]efendant argues that among the potential uses plaintiffs' appraiser overlooks are birdwatching, hunting, and harvesting salt hay. Defendant offers little or no proof of any of these uses, relying instead on its perception that plaintiffs bear the entire burden of proof and persuasion."[53] In looking at the intended development of the property, the court found that the plaintiffs suffered an almost total diminution of value due to the government action, and concluded that compensation of more than $2,658,000 was warranted.[54]

Wetlands Criminal Prosecutions

Defendants in federal wetlands criminal prosecutions have not fared as well as those prosecuted civilly. In none of these cases was the property rights defense fully tested. In both of the following cases, the federal government was neither required to show any injury to the environment, nor that the activities in question had any adverse impact even within the boundaries of the private property itself. Nevertheless, William Ellen was required to spend six months in federal prison, while Ocie and Carey Mills served twenty-one months in federal prison.

United States v. Paul Tudor Jones, II and William B. Ellen

In 1987, Paul Tudor Jones, II, retained William B. Ellen to assist in developing a showplace wildlife sanctuary and hunting retreat.[55] As conceived by Jones and Ellen, the goal of the project was:

(1) to create a state-of-the-art sanctuary that would enhance wildlife habitat and provide other public benefits; and (2) consistent with that objective, to develop an estate for private recreation.

They selected land in Dorchester County, Maryland, for the project. The land was mostly wooded, but it also contained some marshes and farm fields. The land had been used by previous owners for farming, hunting, trapping, and logging.

Ellen served as project manager for the sanctuary. He assisted Jones in locating land for the project, and designed the conceptual plan. He also had the responsibility to obtain permits for the project. He shared supervisory responsibility with Jones, the project architects, several construction contractors, and the farm manager.

By March, the project, known as Tudor Farms, consisted of over 2,800 acres. Construction of ten ponds and associated emergent wetlands—meant to serve as habitat for migratory waterfowl and other wildlife—was nearing completion. Also under construction was a dirt road, a lodge, and a group of sheds, kennels and other buildings known as the Management Complex. Migratory waterfowl were protected. Activities and research to promote marsh productivity and enhancement were undertaken at Ellen's direction.

In March 1989, construction was halted when the United States Army Corps of Engineers issued a cease-and-desist order for filling wetlands without a permit. Subsequent analysis indicated that 14.7809 acres of non-tidal wetlands had been filled at Tudor Farms while 56 acres of wetlands had been created. Most of the area filled was woodland with minimal ecological value. The wetlands that were created, on the other hand, provided valuable wildlife habitat and served other important environmental functions.

Ellen, a licensed marine engineer who specialized in design and construction of projects in and around rivers, estuaries and marshes, had obtained hundreds of wetlands permits. In the case of Tudor Farms, he set about to avoid all wetlands disturbance by delineating the acreage which he thought was wetland, referring to maps prepared by the State of Maryland, topographic maps prepared by the United States Corps of Engineers (which used two feet above sea level as an appropriate wetland boundary on the property), and aerial photography. He obtained nearly forty different state and federal permits for the project, and was visited regularly by officials of half a dozen or more government agencies. His standing order to all contractors was: no construction in wetlands. Jones, the owner, approved of this approach.

In May of 1990, a Baltimore grand jury indicted Ellen on six counts of felony violations of the Clean Water Act (discharging pollutants into navigable waters). At trial, the government produced evidence that Ellen, a professional marine engineer, knew that wetlands permits were required for most construction in wetlands. The government did not prove (and was not required to) that any pollutant had been discharged into public waters, nor that Ellen directed or intentionally permitted construction to occur in wetlands. Ellen was convicted by a jury on five counts of felony Clean Water Act violations, and sentenced to six months in the Petersburg Federal Prison, together with one year of supervised release conditioned upon four months of home detention and sixty hours of community service.

Paul Tudor Jones, after extensive negotiations with the government, plea-bargained to a misdemeanor count of negligently violating the Clean Water Act. He paid a criminal fine totaling $2 million, and agreed to "restore" the wetlands at a cost exceeding $1 million. A large portion of the "restoration" involved blasting a four-hundred-foot channel through wetlands at the United States Corps of Engineers' direction.

United States v. Ocie Mills and Carey C. Mills[56]

Ocie and Carey Mills, father and son, purchased two waterfront lots on Escambia Bay, Florida in 1986. One of the lots was later conceded by the government to be upland, while the second lot was mostly wooded. The second lot contained trees such as magnolia, oak, gum, bay, and large pine, as well as some smaller trees and shrubs. Although some of these trees do well in saturated soils, others require upland soils to prosper. The lot also contained a narrow strip of marsh grass along the bay beachline, but the marsh grass was never disturbed.

In its natural condition, the lot in question also contained a dish-shaped drainage area which apparently conveyed rainwater runoff from inland to the bay. This lot, however, had no standing water on it, nor did it appear to be a marsh, swamp, or bog. It contained no features readily identifiable by the layman as characteristic of "wetland."

Soon after purchase, the Millses began grading, clearing, and other site preparation activities for construction of two homes on the lots. They were subsequently visited by the United States Army Corps of Engineers, who demanded that they cease and desist their actions and begin restoring the lot to its original condition. After refusing to do so, the Millses were charged, in late 1988, with five felony counts of discharging pollutants into navigable waters of the United States. Each charge represented the five separate dates on which the site preparation activities occurred.

In 1989, the Millses, who defended themselves in a jury trial, were convicted on all five felony counts, as well as a misdemeanor count of unlawfully excavating a drainage ditch. Each was sentenced to twenty-one months incarceration in federal prison, followed by one year of supervised release. Each was also fined $5,000, plus a special monetary assessment of $250, and ordered to restore the property to its original condition. The convictions and sentences were summarily upheld on appeal.

In a subsequent proceeding regarding their supervised release and their obligations under the site restoration plan, the court determined that, at the time in question, the subject lot was probably not a wetland at all. The court determined that the drainage area did not carry rainwater runoff inasmuch as it had been blocked and partially filled as early as 1978, well before the Millses bought the property. Indeed, the drainage ditch (for the construction of which the Millses had been convicted) had apparently been dug at the same time in 1978. These findings came too late to change either the conviction of the Millses or to avoid their serving twenty-one months in federal prison.

United States v. James J. Wilson

In 1977, the Interstate General Company (IGC) and its President and CEO, James Wilson, began construction of a 9,000-acre planned community. Because the development was to be built in conjunction with the Department of Housing and Urban Development (HUD), an environmental impact statement was performed. In the course of the environmental impact statement, the United States Army Corps of Engineers and the EPA concluded that only seventy-five acres of the project were wetland.

Construction proceeded unabated until 1990, when the United States Army Corps of Engineers issued a cease and desist order involving a five-acre area known as "parcel L." After attempting to resolve the dispute, the IGC filed a just compensation claim in 1991, alleging that its property had been taken in violation of the Fifth Amendment. After successfully moving to dismiss IGC's taking claim as too uncertain to be ripe, the government astonishingly found the facts to be sufficiently concrete to begin a criminal investigation against IGC and James Wilson.

In the spring of 1996, Mr. Wilson and his company, IGC, were convicted of unlawfully filling a "wetland" without a permit. In May 1996, Mr. Wilson was sentenced to twenty-one months in prison and fined $1 million. His companies, IGC and St. Charles Associates, were fined $3 million—which may bankrupt them.

ENDNOTES

[1] This is a relatively new understanding of the function of swamps and marshes. *See, e.g., Leovy v. United States*, 177 U.S. 621 (1900).
[2] 33 U.S.C. § 1311(a) (1986). "Except as in compliance with this section and sections 1312, 1316, 1317, 1328, 1342 and 1344 of this title, the discharge of any pollutant by any person shall be unlawful."
[3] 33 U.S.C. § 1319(c) (Supp. 1994).

66 / Property Rights

[4] *United States v. Ocie Mills*, 904 F.2d 713 (11th Cir. 1990).
[5] 33 U.S.C. §§ 1251 et seq. (1986 and Supp. 1994).
[6] 33 U.S.C. § 1311(a) (1986).
[7] 33 U.S.C. § 1319(c) (Supp. 1994).
[8] 33 U.S.C. § 1344(a) (1986).
[9] The Corps defines the physical characteristic of a wetland as:

> [A]reas that are inundated or saturated by surface or ground water at a frequency and duration sufficient to support, and that under normal circumstances do support, a prevalence of vegetation typically adapted for life in saturated soil conditions. Wetlands generally include swamps, marshes, bogs, and similar areas.

33 C.F.R. § 328.3(b) (1993).
[10] The Army Corps regulations are found at 33 C.F.R. §328.3(a) (1993).
[11] *Cf.* United States v. Riverside Bayview Homes, Inc., 474 U.S. 121, 131 (1985) (concluding that the Corps' definition of "waters of the United States," which included wetlands "adjacent to but not regularly flooded by rivers, streams, and other hydrographic features more conventionally identifiable as 'waters,'" was not unreasonable because it was consistent with the legislative history requiring that the Clean Water Act be interpreted broadly so as to protect the entire aquatic ecosystem); *see also Natural Resources Defense Council, Inc. v. Callaway*, 392 F. Supp. 685, 686 (D.D.C. 1975) (holding that Congress, by defining the term navigable waters as "'the waters of the United States, including territorial seas,' asserted federal jurisdiction over the nation's waters to the maximum extent permissible under the Commerce Clause of the Constitution").
[12] Margaret N. Strand, *Federal Wetlands Law: Part I*, 23 ENVTL. L. REP. 10,193 (1993).
[13] *Id.*
[14] 961 F.2d 1310, 1314, *vacated, reh'g granted*, 975 F.2d 1554 (7th Cir. 1992), *supplemental op.*, 999 F.2d 256 (7th Cir. 1993).
[15] *Hoffman Homes*, 999 F.2d at 260 (citing 33 C.F.R. §328.3(a)(3) (1993).
[16] See *Tabb Lakes, Ltd. v. United States*, 715 F. Supp. 726 (E.D. Va. 1988) (skeptical of whether the possible use of isolated waters by migratory birds was an adequate nexus to interstate commerce) *aff'd without op.* 885 F.2d 866 (4th Cir. 1989); *Leslie Salt Co. v. Froehlke*, 896

F.2d 354 (9th Cir. 1990), *cert. denied*, 498 U.S. 1126 (1991) (avoiding the direct issue of whether bird usage creates a nexus between interstate commerce and isolated wetlands, the court remanded the case for further evidence of migratory bird habitat).

[17] *Hoffman Homes, Inc. v. EPA.*, 961 F.2d 1310, 1320.

[18] Jeffery Cohn, *How Wet Must A Wetland Be?*, NAT'L J. GOV'T EXECUTIVE, 16 (Mar. 1992).

[19] *Id.*

[20] Margaret N. Strand, *Federal Wetlands Law: Part III*, 23 ENVTL. L. REP. 10,357 (1993).

[21] Departments of Veterans Affairs and Housing and Urban Development and Independent Agencies Appropriations Act, Pub. L. No. 102-389, 106 Stat. 1571 (1992).

[22] 139 CONG. REC. S9,721 (daily ed. July 28, 1993) (statement of Sen. Baucus).

[23] Strand, *supra* note 18.

[24] For example, Ray Britton came to an agreement with the Army Corps to create new wetlands as mitigation for his "filling" another wetland in order to build some townhomes. After constructing the townhomes, the EPA disregarded his agreement with the Army Corps and found that Mr. Britton illegally filled a wetland. Mr. Britton faces up to $125,000 in fines.

[25] This incident was taken from an American Farm Bureau Federation's "Wetlands Problems Documentation Form," provided by the District of Columbia office of the American Farm Bureau Federation (June 15, 1990).

[26] *Id.*

[27] American Farm Bureau Federation, "Wetlands Problems Documentation Form" (June 15, 1990).

[28] 484 U.S. 49 (1987).

[29] 33 U.S.C. § 401 et seq. (1990).

[30] *See, e.g.*, *1902 Atlantic, Ltd. v. Hudson*, 574 F. Supp. 1381 (E.D. Va. 1983).

[31] *Loveladies Harbor, Inc. v. United States*, 15 Cl. Ct. 381, 385 (Cl. Ct. 1988).

[32] *See, e.g.*, *Hoffman Homes*, 961 F.2d 1310.

[33] *Cox v. Louisiana*, 379 U.S. 536 (1965) (practice of allowing local officials to use unfettered discretion when regulating the use of streets for peaceful parades and meetings violated appellant's freedom of speech and

68 / *Property Rights*

assembly in violation of the First and Fourteenth Amendments). *See also Cohen v. California*, 403 U.S. 15 (1971) (the state violated the First and Fourteenth Amendments by making the simple public display of a single four-letter expletive a criminal offense).

[34] *Stanley v. Georgia*, 394 U.S. 557 (1969).

[35] *Heart of Atlanta Motel, Inc. v. United States*, 379 U.S. 241 (1964) (stating that the Fourteenth Amendment forbids prosecution of blacks who demand service at segregated lunch counters, schools, and public accommodations); *see also Boynton v. Virginia*, 364 U.S. 454 (1960) (stating that the interest in interstate commerce protects against racial discrimination by owners and managers of terminal restaurants); *Henderson v. United States*, 339 U.S. 816 (1949) (language under Commerce Clause is broad and bars discrimination of all kinds; it forbids railroad dining cars to discriminate in service to passengers on account of their color).

[36] *1902 Atlantic, Ltd. v. Hudson*, 574 F. Supp. at 1381.

[37] *See, e.g., Florida Rock Inds., Inc. v. United States*, 791 F.2d 893 (Fed. Cir. 1986), *cert. denied*, 479 U.S. 1053 (1987), *on remand*, 21 Cl. Ct. 161 (Cl. Ct. 1990), *vacated*, and *remanded*, 18 F.3d 1560 (Fed. Cir. 1994).

[38] *Lucas v. South Carolina Coastal Council*, 112 S. Ct. 2886 (1991).

[39] *Nollan v. California Coastal Commission*, 107 S. Ct. 3141 (1987).

[40] 791 F.2d 893 (Fed. Cir. 1986), *cert. denied*, 479 U.S. 1053 (1987), *on remand*, 21 Cl. Ct. 161 (1990).

[41] *Florida Rock*, 791 F.2d at 895.

[42] *Florida Rock Indus., Inc. v. United States*, 8 Cl. Ct. 160, 162 (1985).

[43] *Id.* at 163.

[44] *Florida Rock*, 791 F.2d at 895.

[45] *Id.* at 896.

[46] *Florida Rock*, 21 Cl. Ct. 161, 169 (1990).

[47] *Id.* at 166.

[48] *Id.* at 166-67.

[49] 21 Cl. Ct. 153 (1990). For a thorough discussion of *Loveladies Harbor*, see Note, *Loveladies Harbor, Inc. v. United States*: The Claims Court Takes a Wrong Turn—Toward a Higher Standard of Review, 41 CATH. U. L. REV. 701 (1991).

[50] *Loveladies Harbor*, 21 Cl. Ct. at 154.

[51] *Loveladies Harbor, Inc. v. United States*, 15 Cl. Ct. 381, 384 (1988).

[52] *Id.* at 385.

⁵³ *Loveladies Harbor*, 21 Cl. Ct. at 158.

⁵⁴ The Claims Court summarily rejected the nuisance exception argument:

> Defendant also argues that plaintiffs' appraisal must be disregarded because the highest and best use proffered depends on an "impermissible activity," namely, placing fill in wetlands. This argument is reminiscent of defendant/appellant's argument in *Florida Rock*, to which the Federal Circuit responded, "We suppose appellant added this contention to provide a little humor for an otherwise serious and scholarly brief, and say no more about it." Neither shall this Court.

Loveladies Harbor, 21 Cl. Ct. at 157, n.5 (quoting *Florida Rock*, 791 F.2d at 905); *see also Ciampetti v. United States*, 18 Cl. Ct. 548 (1989) (involving a wetlands development issue wherein the Claims Court did not reach the nuisance issue the defendant raised, but it did reject defendant's motion for summary judgment on that issue).

⁵⁵ *United States v. Ellen*, 961 F.2d 462 (4th Cir. 1992).

⁵⁶ *United States v. Ocie Mills*, 904 F.2d 713 (11th Cir. 1990).

Chapter 5

THE ENDANGERED SPECIES ACT

Congress enacted the Endangered Species Act in 1973 in response to increasing concern about the extent to which "various species of fish, wildlife, and plants" had been rendered extinct "as a consequence of economic growth and development untempered by adequate concern and conservation." The purposes of the Endangered Species Act include providing "a means whereby the ecosystems upon which endangered species and threatened species depend may be conserved."

Under the Endangered Species Act, the Secretary of the Interior determines the wildlife species that are "endangered" or "threatened" within the meaning of the Act and maintains a list of such species.[1] In deciding whether to list a species, the Secretary must consider, among other concerns, "the present or threatened destruction, modification, or curtailment of its habitat or range."

When a fish or wildlife species is listed as endangered, it is protected by Section 9(a)(1) of the Endangered Species Act.[2] Section 9(a)(1)(B) makes it unlawful for "any person" (which includes governmental entities) to "take" an endangered species. The prohibition may be enforced through suits for injunctive relief, as well as civil and criminal penalties. By regulation, the Section 9 "take" prohibition also applies generally to species that are listed as threatened.[3]

THE ENDANGERED SPECIES REGULATORY SCHEME

The "Take" Prohibition

The Endangered Species Act defines the term "take" to mean "to harass, harm, pursue, hunt, shoot, wound, kill, trap, capture, or collect, or to attempt to engage in any such conduct." As part of its initial set of programmatic regulations implementing the Endangered Species Act, the United States Fish and Wildlife Service promulgated a regulation in 1975 interpreting the term "harm" for purposes of the Endangered Species Act. As the United States Supreme Court noted in *TVA v. Hill*, the 1975 regulation defined "harm" to mean an act that "actually injures or kills wildlife, including acts which annoy it to such an extent as to significantly disrupt essential behavioral patterns, which include, but are not limited to, breeding, feeding or sheltering," and which include "significant environmental modification or degradation which has such effects."[4] The preamble to the 1975 regulation explained that the regulation represented a "reasonable response to the habitat needs of listed species," which Congress had specifically acknowledged in the Purposes section of the Endangered Species Act. The preamble further noted that the environmental degradation encompassed within the regulatory definition of "harm" was:

> expressly limited to those actions causing actual death or injury to a protected species of fish or wildlife. The actual consequences of such an action upon a listed species is paramount.

In 1982, the Secretary modified the regulation to make it consistent with the original intent that a Section 9 "take" violation does not arise out of "habitat modification alone without any attendant death or injury of the protected wildlife." At the same time, however, the Secretary reaffirmed that "harm" is not limited "to direct physical injury to an individual member of the wildlife species," and that in redefining the term, he "did not intend to imply that significant habitat destruction which could be shown to injure protected wildlife through the impairment of its essential behavioral patterns was not subject to the Act." The "harm" regulation as revised in 1981 provides:

> *Harm* in the definition of "take" in the Act means an act which actually kills or injures wildlife. Such an act may include significant habitat modification or degradation where it actually kills or injures wildlife by significantly impairing essential behavioral patterns, including breeding, feeding or sheltering.

Prohibitions on Federal Agencies

In addition to the Section 9 "take" prohibition, the Endangered Species Act includes other methods of protecting listed species. Section 7(a)(2) provides that each federal agency shall, with the consultation and the assistance of the Secretary:

> insure that any action authorized, funded, or carried out by such agency . . . is not likely to jeopardize the continued existence of any endangered species or threatened species or result in the destruction or adverse modification of habitat of such species which is determined by the Secretary . . . to be critical,[5] unless such agency has been granted an exemption for such action . . . pursuant to subsection (h).[6]

This obligation to ensure against "jeopardizing" a species' continued existence or destroying or adversely modifying its "critical" habitat applies to action undertaken by the agency itself, as well as private parties that are issued a federal license or permit. If an endangered species is present or may be present, the acting agency, or federally permitted private party, must perform a biological assessment to determine the impact of the proposed action on the species. If the action will impact the species, or the Fish and Wildlife Service does not agree with a finding of "no impact," the Fish and Wildlife Service must prepare a biological opinion. Within this formal document, the Fish and Wildlife Service will make its determination of whether the proposed action will jeopardize the species and, if so, what reasonable and prudent conservation alternatives might permit the project to go forward.

Recovery Plans

Sections 4, 5, and 7 of the Endangered Species Act are aimed not merely at preventing extinction of listed species, but also at their conservation. For purposes of the Endangered Species Act, "conservation" means "the use of all methods and procedures which are necessary to bring any endangered species or threatened species to the point at which the measures provided pursuant to this chapter are no longer necessary." Available conservation measures include, but are not limited to, "all activities associated with scientific resources management such as research, census, law enforcement, habitat acquisition and maintenance, propagation, live trapping, and transplantation, and, in the extraordinary case where population pressures within a given ecosystem cannot be otherwise relieved, may include regulated taking."

The conservation provisions of the Endangered Species Act are intended to achieve the eventual removal of the species from the endangered and threatened lists. To that end, Section 4(f) authorizes the Secretary to develop and implement recovery plans to promote the conservation of species. Section 5 empowers the Secretary to utilize land acquisition and his authority under other wildlife protection statutes to acquire land to implement a program that will conserve endangered and threatened species. Section 7(a)(1) requires that federal agencies shall, with the consultation and the assistance of the Secretary, "utilize their authorities in furtherance of the purposes of [the Act] by carrying out programs for the conservation of endangered species and threatened species."

Incidental Take Permits and Habitat Conservation Plans

The "take" prohibition in Section 9 of the Endangered Species Act and the "jeopardy" and "critical" habitat restrictions in Section 7 are not absolute—the Secretary may permit "incidental takings" if the instance meets the detailed criteria set forth by Congress in 1982. Specifically, through amendments to Sections 7 and 10, Congress authorized the Secretary to permit takings that would otherwise be prohibited under Section 9(a)(1)(B), "if such taking is incidental to, and not the purpose of, the carrying out of an otherwise lawful activity."

Section 10(a)(2)(A) provides for the issuance of an incidental take permit to nonfederal and private party applicants only barred by the "take" prohibition of Section 9 and not applicants also barred by Section 7. Congress also conditioned issuance of a Section 10 incidental take permit on the applicant assuming certain duties. The Endangered Species Act states that "[n]o permit may be issued by the Secretary" authorizing an incidental taking unless the applicant submits to the Secretary a conservation plan that specifies:

> (i) the impact which will likely result from such taking;
>
> (ii) what steps the applicant will take to minimize and mitigate such impacts, and the funding that will be available to implement such steps;
>
> (iii) what alternative actions to such taking the applicant considered and the reasons why such alternatives are not being utilized; and
>
> (iv) such other measures that the Secretary may require as being necessary or appropriate for purposes of the plan.

The Secretary will issue the permit if he finds, *inter alia*, that the taking will be incidental; that the applicant will "to the maximum extent practicable, minimize and mitigate the impacts of such taking;" that "the applicant will ensure that adequate funding for the plan will be provided;" that "the taking will not appreciably reduce the likelihood of the survival and recovery of the species in the wild;" and that the applicant will meet "such other measures that the Secretary may require as being necessary or appropriate for purposes of the plan."

Jeopardy Opinions

Congress provided a somewhat different mechanism for authorizing "incidental takes" resulting from a project involving the federal government subject to Section 7(a)(2) of the Endangered Species Act jeopardy prohibition and critical habitat restrictions. The biological opinion that Fish and Wildlife Service prepares during the formal Section 7 consultation process must include what is known as an "incidental take statement." That statement must identify the impact of any anticipated take that is incidental to the proposed federal action and supply "reasonable and prudent measures" that the Secretary considers "necessary or appropriate to minimize such impact;" it also sets forth the "terms and conditions . . . that must be complied with by the Federal agency or [permit or license] applicant (if any) or both to implement the measures specified." Any taking that is in compliance with the terms and conditions set forth in the biological opinion is not considered a taking in violation of Section 9.

CIVIL AND CRIMINAL ENFORCEMENT PROVISIONS

The Endangered Species Act provides for both civil and criminal penalties for its violation, as well as injunctive relief. Any person who knowingly violates the major provisions of the Endangered Species Act may be assessed a civil penalty of up to $25,000 for each violation. He is entitled to an administrative hearing before the Secretary of the Interior, and, if a penalty is assessed by the Secretary, the Attorney General of the United States may institute suit to collect that penalty. Lesser penalties for paperwork and reporting violations may be assessed at up to $500 for each such violation.

Section 11 of the Endangered Species Act provides that "any person who knowingly violates . . . any regulation shall, upon conviction, be fined not more than $50,000 or be imprisoned for not more than one year, or both." This provision does not require that the defendant know that he is violating the regulation; rather, it is a "general intent" criminal provision which merely requires that the defendant knowingly commit the act which constitutes the violation. For example, in *United States v. St. Onge*, the court rejected defendant's motion to permit him to introduce evidence that he thought he was shooting a non-endangered elk rather than an endangered grizzly bear.[7] Citing the holding in *United States v. Billie*,[8] the court refused the proffered instruction, finding instead that Section 11 is more properly understood to impose a "general intent" requirement:

> The critical issue is whether the act was done knowingly, not whether the defendant recognized what he was shooting. The scienter element applies to the act of taking; thus, defendant could only claim accident or mistake if he did not intend to discharge his firearm, or the weapon malfunctions, or similar circumstances occurred. Given the regulatory nature of the Act, and its broad purposes to protect listed species, the government cannot be required to prove that he had the specific intent to take a grizzly bear.

Finally, the Attorney General may also seek an injunction against any person who is alleged to be in violation of any provision of the Endangered Species Act, or any regulation issued under it. Such injunctions could forbid "habitat modification," *i.e.*, the use of one's property, as discussed below.

ENDANGERED SPECIES HABITAT AND PROPERTY RIGHTS

According to a report by the Government Accounting Office, the U.S. Fish and Wildlife Service prosecuted 126 alleged violations of the Endangered Species Act on private lands between 1988 and 1993. Of the 126 cases, 86 were brought criminally, and 40 were brought as civil prosecutions. Of the seventy-one criminal prosecutions for which results were available:

- fines ranging from $25 to $50,000 were levied in fifty-nine instances; in twenty-one instances, fines were $1,000 or more;

- fines were suspended in two instances;

- jail sentences ranging from 10 days to 1,170 days were given in eighteen instances;

- jail sentences were suspended in two instances; and

- probation ranging from 182 days to 1,825 days was given in thirty-three instances.

According to Fish and Wildlife Services officials, during this same period (1988-1993), 321 investigations of alleged "takes" of endangered species on private lands were opened, resulting in 100 actual prosecutions. Of these, a substantial number arose from habitat modification without any injury to actual plants or animals.

A predominant number of the species protected under the Endangered Species Act have the major share of their habitat on private lands. Specifically, of the 781 listed species for which the Fish and Wildlife Service was responsible as of May 1993, 712—over ninety percent—have habitat on private lands. Of these, according to the

Service, 517 have over sixty percent of their total habitat on private lands.

Thus, it is unsurprising that constitutionally protected property rights collide with endangered species protection programs from the ancient growth forests of the Northwest (spotted owl habitat) to the Everglades of Florida (Florida panther habitat); from the deserts of Southern Nevada (desert tortoise habitat) to the beaches of Malibu (Stevens kangaroo rat habitat). Indeed, the increasing emphasis of the federal government on the protection of *habitat* as a means of species protection guarantees that such collisions will continue—and likely increase—in the future.

Under a Memorandum of Agreement signed September 28, 1994 by the Departments of Agriculture, Defense (Department of the Army, U.S. Army, Corps of Engineers), Commerce (National Marine Fisheries Service), Interior, Transportation, and the Environmental Protection Agency, these diverse arms of government pledged to use their powers and programs "to achieve the common goal of conserving species listed as threatened or endangered under the Endangered Species Act by protecting and managing their populations and the ecosystems upon which those populations depend." To implement this agreement, these agencies formed a National Working Group to coordinate the efforts of their various departments, as well as Regional Working Groups to concentrate on specific species, habitat, and ecosystems. The intended result is better conservation of species (endangered, threatened or candidate) through, among other things, protection of their habitat on, in most instances, private lands.

The *Sweet Home* Decision

On June 29, 1995, the U.S. Supreme Court handed down its landmark decision in *Babbitt v. Sweet Home Chapter of Communities for a Great Oregon*, upholding the Interior Department's regulation defining a "take" of an endangered species to include "significant habitat modification or degradation where it actually kills or injures wildlife by significantly impairing essential behavioral patterns, including breeding, feeding, or sheltering."[9] The challengers argued that a "take" of an endangered species required actual harm to an identified individual animal (*e.g.*, killing, wounding, injuring, harassing or capturing), while the Interior Department argued that its regulation should be upheld because habitat modification could generally affect a species without actually causing harm to an identified creature. The Court sided with the Interior Department, ruling that habitat modification which might affect the ability of animals to breed, feed, or shelter constitutes a "take" of an endangered species, punishable civilly or criminally.

In *Sweet Home*, the Court built upon its famous "snail darter" case of 1978 [*TVA v. Hill*].[10] In that case, it halted construction of the Tellico Dam, built to provide power for the Tennessee Valley Authority, on the grounds that "the plain intent of Congress in enacting this statute was to halt and reverse the trend towards species extinction, whatever the cost." Over strenuous dissent, the Court extended the "snail darter" rule to private land, as well as land owned by a federal agency.

The Supreme Court began its analysis by underscoring its interpretation of the Endangered Species Act's importance:

> In *TVA v. Hill*, we described the Act as "the most comprehensive legislation for the preservation of endangered species ever enacted by any nation." Whereas predecessor statutes enacted in 1966 and 1969 had not contained any sweeping prohibition against the taking of endangered species except on federal lands, the 1973 Act applied to all land in the United States and to the Nation's territorial seas. As stated in Section 2 of the Act, among its central purposes is "to provide a means whereby the ecosystems upon which endangered species and threatened species depend may be conserved. . . ."

Federal agencies reacted immediately and forcefully, touting the Endangered Species Act as, in effect, an ecosystem protection act that grants broad authority to the federal government to control the use of private land for the benefit of endangered species. In furtherance of its ecosystem protection program, the Fish and Wildlife Service identified hundreds of thousands of acres as *possible* habitat for various endangered species, and imposed upon property owners extensive duties to avoid habitat modification which might injure the "population" of the species. Importantly, this includes a prohibition against modifying habitat (*i.e.*, using or developing land or water) in any way which might detract from the recovery of the species. Just how far this federal power may reach—and how it inevitably conflicts with constitutionally guaranteed property rights—may be best understood through a few examples.

Case Studies on Habitat Modification

Florida Scrub Jay

In June 1991, the Fish and Wildlife Service sent letters to 550 ranchers, farmers, and homeowners identified through a review of county property records as "owning property which may contain 'scrub' habitat, essential to [the Florida scrub jay]." The Fish and Wildlife Service defined scrub habitat "as a sandy area which supports a dense, but often patchy, layer of woody shrubs, with little or no ground cover." This sandy area with woody shrubs is the "type of habitat that may be occupied by Florida scrub jays."

The Fish and Wildlife Service then informed the residents of the prohibition of taking endangered or threatened species, provided the regulatory definition of "harass" and "harm," and made the following pronouncement:

> Harm is further defined as an act which actually kills or injures wildlife. It is the Service's position that destruction of scrub habitat will significantly affect this species .... As a landowner, you are responsible to ensure that actions carried out on your property are not harmful to the scrub habitat or listed species it supports.

The letter, sent to all landowners regardless of whether the scrub jay currently inhabited their property, assured landowners that "[a]lthough this may appear to be a burden, there is a procedure to resolve this conflict." The procedures for resolution required the landowner to apply for and receive "take" permits under either Section 7 or Section 10(a) of the Endangered Species Act. Thus, by verbal sleight of hand, the Secretary transformed "injury to the species" into "destruction of the scrub habitat," rendering such habitat modification an illegal "take" under the statute.

Another Florida rancher received a letter from the Fish and Wildlife Service demanding the cessation of certain activities that had the "potential to impact Florida scrub jays." There was no confirmation that scrub jays actually occupied—or had ever occupied—the property, but the rancher was prohibited from clearing land to plant some blueberry bushes for his personal, non-commercial use. The Fish and Wildlife Service stated:

> This letter is regarding ongoing land-clearing activity taking place at River Ridge Ranches, Inc. . . . This and any planned clearing activities have the potential to impact Florida scrub jays. These birds are federally listed as threatened, and any land-clearing activity may result in an incidental take of the species. Any activities at this site must be stopped immediately.

The letter informed the rancher of the procedure to seek a permit under Sections 7 and 10(a) of the Endangered Species Act, and concluded with a warning: "'Taking' a listed animal, such as the Florida scrub jay, without fulfilling the requirements of one of these two methods, would violate the Act."

Accordingly, the Fish and Wildlife Service's broad interpretation of "take" required the landowner to obtain a "take" permit from the federal government for any land-clearing activities that had the potential to impact Florida scrub jays, without reference or regard to whether any such scrub jays actually existed on the property. In this way, the Fish and Wildlife Service prohibited habitat modification that in no way "*actually* killed or injured wildlife" (emphasis added) which might or might not be on the property.

Golden-Cheeked Warbler (Central Texas)

In Texas, the potential impact to the golden-cheeked warbler prohibits habitat modification on private property without regard to whether any golden-cheeked warblers inhabit or use the specific property. The Fish and Wildlife Service sent a letter to a landowner in a residential area near Austin, Texas to inform her that her property "would be suitable habitat for the federally listed [as] endangered golden-cheeked warbler." Based on the belief that her land "would be suitable habitat" for endangered species, and without any indication that an endangered species actually used or existed on the land, the Fish and Wildlife Service informed the landowner that "[w]e believe that clearing or land development-related activities of this acreage would constitute a 'take' as defined by the Endangered Species Act."

The Fish and Wildlife Service has even used the broad language of habitat preservation regulation to prevent the development of land which would contribute to "encroaching urbanization." This development, while not directly affecting any specific animal, would reduce the habitat adjacent to places where the golden-cheeked warbler was sighted. A landowner seeking to develop his property was denied that right by the following interpretation of the harm regulation:

> Current biological information indicates that encroaching urbanization adversely affects the golden-cheeked warbler through habitat reduction, fragmentation, increase in certain predators, and other factors. Development of lots on Foxtree Cove, which are adjacent to one of the largest blocks of contiguous, occupied golden-cheeked warbler habitat remaining in Travis County, would contribute to the negative impacts mentioned above.

The Fish and Wildlife Service failed to show that development of the above property would actually kill or injure wildlife, except under an elastic definition of those terms that equates "encroaching urbanization" with the killing or injuring of an endangered species.

Tipton Kangaroo Rat (Bakersfield, California)

Tuang Ming-Lin, a Chinese immigrant, bought land in Kern County, California, to grow bamboo and other Chinese vegetables. Unfortunately, this land turned out to be suspected habitat for the Tipton kangaroo rat, an endangered species. Mr. Tuang was charged criminally with violation of the Endangered Species Act. The prosecution alleged that, in the course of plowing his field, he had destroyed some of the holes in which the rat makes its home, and possibly killed several of the rats in the process. The U.S. Attorney even seized Mr. Tuang's tractor as the "instrumentality of the crime" under the Asset Forfeiture Statute.

Subsequent evidence strongly indicated that, if any rats had been killed, they were most likely common kangaroo rats—a pest routinely exterminated. Indeed, DNA evidence was required to distinguish between a Tipton kangaroo rat and a common kangaroo rat, and experts differed as to whether a separate species of kangaroo rat even existed. In the face of overwhelming odds, the federal government ultimately dropped its criminal prosecution—but not until after Mr. Tuang's funds were exhausted.

Ranching and Farming and Endangered Species

Ranching and farming are, quite simply, the use of land to produce food and fiber. Without land, these activities could not be undertaken. Ranching requires that the land be carefully tended to produce water, hay, grass, fodder, and other nutrients for livestock. Erosion or other damage to the land is avoided. In the course of their work, ranchers and farmers must clear the brush, fell trees, build fences, barns, stables and dwellings, and introduce other human activities to the land. The livestock produce food, fiber, and numerous by-products which are essential to our daily lives.

Ranching and farming require vast tracts of rural and relatively undeveloped land, much of which might be suitable habitat for one or more endangered species. Indeed, approximately sixteen percent of the land mass of the United States—371 million acres—is privately held ranch land. This amounts to an area the size of twenty-two states combined.

Not surprisingly then, ranchers and farmers such as Mr. Tuang find themselves the targets of many endangered species habitat protection efforts. In the Central Valley of California, endangered or threatened species such as the California kit fox, salt marsh harvest mouse, Tipton kangaroo rat, and fringe-toed lizard have brought farming and ranching activities to a screeching halt. The recent release of wolves (timber and gray) into wilderness areas in Idaho, Montana, and Wyoming caused a marked increase in predation upon cattle and sheep. Such actions have also increased among protected grizzly bears, whose critical habitat may encompass as much as 35 million acres. In Texas, various environmental groups sued the federal government to prohibit the continuation of farming programs which might impact water-dwelling salamanders and darters.

Under state law, ranching and farming activities which might disturb state-protected plants or animals are also prohibited. In Northern California, for example, Thule elk were imported into Mendicino County, where they prospered. Now, this state-protected elk herd ravishes surrounding farms and ranches with impunity because property owners are forbidden from harassing or injuring the animals. Similarly, farmers have been forbidden from plowing or allowing cattle to graze their land because populations of protected vegetation (*e.g.*, grasses, thistles, etc.) are found upon it. In fact, a federal statute, the Lacy Act,[11] makes it a federal crime to violate state laws protecting such wildlife—even if the animals are not protected as endangered or threatened species under the federal Endangered Species Act.

Water Rights

In much of the arid West, water rights are created and administered under state law. It is water that gives value to land, and makes development or agriculture possible. Where water is also the natural habitat for endangered or threatened species, property rights relating to the use of water collide with the Endangered Species Act. Two case studies help illustrate this conflict.

Edwards Aquifer (Texas)

The Edwards Aquifer is a 175-mile-long underground conduit which covers an expanse of about 3,600 square miles in central and southern Texas. Water enters the Edwards Aquifer—essentially an underground river—from surface streams which sink into the ground as they cross its recharge area. Thus, the water is delivered as a source of pure drinking water for approximately 1.5 million residents of the City of San Antonio and its suburbs, as well as for the irrigation of hundreds of thousands of acres of ranch and farm land. This water is extracted by sinking wells into the ground to tap the aquifer.

The aquifer also discharges naturally at springs—especially in Comal and San Marcos—which are the sole known habitat for the San Marcos fountain darter, Comal Springs salamander, San Marcos salamander, and Texas wild rice. In 1991, several environmental groups brought suit seeking an injunction to require San Antonio, the ninth largest city in the country, to obtain its drinking water elsewhere, and to compel the State of Texas to limit other withdrawals from the Edwards Aquifer. In 1993, a federal judge issued the injunction, essentially compelling the entire city and suburbs to abandon its dependence upon ground water. Instead, it was encouraged to build a reservoir system at costs estimated in the billions of dollars. Judge Lucius Bunton wrote:

> If the City of San Antonio would seriously and immediately develop additional supplies of water, implement conservation programs and mandates (like minimal lawn watering and credits for native landscaping), reuse water, and seek alternative sources of water, the City of San

Antonio is likely to obtain substantial additional water supplies within five to ten years.[12]

Although the injunction was subsequently modified, it seems clear that San Antonio—despite its undoubted right to extract water under state law—will be required to abandon, at least, a substantial portion of its water rights in order to comply with the Endangered Species Act.

Kern County (California)

Lying at the southern end of our nation's most productive agricultural area, the Central Valley of California, Kern County produces huge crops of vegetables, nuts, fruit, and cotton with water that is brought southward from the Sacramento-San Joaquin Delta through a series of natural and man-made structures known as the California Water Project. This multi-billion-dollar water project is financed by assessments upon all of those who use the water; in turn, state law allocates the right to receive and use specified quantities of water to farmers, ranchers, cities and industrial users. These water rights are recognized as a property right under California state law.

Beginning in 1992, the federal government started limiting the amounts of water which could be sent south to Kern County and other parts of California in order to maintain in-stream flows to protect the habitat of two endangered fish—the delta smelt and the winter run of Chinook salmon. As much as two million acre-feet of water—enough to cover two million acres to a depth of one foot—have been held back annually from municipal and agricultural use in order to maintain certain levels in streams and lakes which constitute the habitat of these fish. Farmers and ranchers have suffered many millions of dollars in lost crops and, in some instances, have lost their property as it has become unproductive. Their water rights have, in effect, been expropriated for the benefit of the endangered species, giving rise to a takings claim.

Timber

A sharp confrontation arose in the Pacific Northwest between the protection of an endangered species, the northern spotted owl, and the desire to ensure the continued health of the timber industry—which is extremely valuable to the communities of the region. The negotiations and litigation involving this contentious species are well chronicled elsewhere, but never before has the reach of the Endangered Species Act extended over so vast an area. The current ramifications of the Act's reach are only starting to be felt.

In an ongoing case, the Department of Interior sought to enjoin the timber harvesting of Anderson & Middleton Logging Co. At issue are seventy-two acres of old growth timber in the State of Washington that are owned by the logging company. In accordance with state law, the company received all the necessary state and federal permits to log old growth timber, and notified the federal government of its intent to proceed with harvesting. On December 9, 1993, the DOI filed suit to enjoin the logging of Anderson's acreage. It claimed that, in violation of Section 9 of the Endangered Species Act, the timber harvest would present a future threat that might harm or harass two spotted owls nested on federal land almost two miles distant. In the press release announcing the lawsuit, the government's biologist admitted that the Fish and Wildlife Service lacked proof that any spotted owl had ever flown through, let alone nested, roosted, or foraged on the property. If the court determines that the government's reach under Section 9 of the Endangered Species Act extends to future and distant threats, it would certainly give rise to a Fifth Amendment takings challenge.

STATE LAND USE REGULATION AND DEVELOPMENT

Finally, it is worth noting that the Endangered Species Act often hinders the implementation of state zoning and land development authority—possibly in violation of the Tenth Amendment to the Constitution. That amendment, recently re-invigorated by the U.S. Supreme Court, reserves to the states (or the people, respectively) all powers not specifically delegated to the federal government. The states of Arizona, Colorado, and Texas all filed briefs before the Supreme Court in the *Sweet Home* case making this point. As the Attorney General of Texas said:

> Under the federal system established by the Constitution, state and local governments enact, maintain, and enforce laws protecting private property. "Property interests, of course, are not created by the Constitution, but rather by existing rules or understandings that stem from an independent source such as state law."[13] Real property law, furthermore, has been recognized by the Court as a matter of special concern to the states.[14]
>
> Certain police powers are reserved to the states and protected by the Constitution. State and local governments are particularly responsible and entitled to enact, maintain, and enforce laws governing the use of land and water, such as laws regarding zoning, land use planning, and natural resource management.
>
> The "harm" regulation substantially intrudes into two areas in which Congress and the courts have consistently and pointedly deferred to state law: resource management (including the definition, protection, use, and control of private property), and the use, control, and allocation of water. Paradoxically, the result of FWS's overexpansive interpretation of "harm" is that the mere listing of species results in a resource management system controlled by a cadre of federal bureaucrats, scientists, and technicians—without any necessity to designate critical habitat as the ESA requires.

Sentiments such as these reflect the frustration of the state governments which are subjected to the strict and sometimes questionable regulations of agencies acting under the guise of the Endangered Species Act.

ENDNOTES

[1] "Endangered species" means any species (other than certain insect species) "which is in danger of extinction throughout all or a significant portion of its range." 16 U.S.C. § 1532(6). "Threatened species" means "any species which is likely to become an endangered species within the foreseeable future throughout all or a significant portion of its range." 16 U.S.C. § 1532(20). Endangered and threatened species are referred to collectively as "listed species."

[2] "Fish or wildlife" is defined in the ESA as "any member of the animal kingdom, including without limitation any mammal, fish, bird (including any migratory, nonmigratory, or endangered bird for which protection is also afforded by treaty or other international agreement), amphibian, reptile, mollusk, crustacean, arthropod or other invertebrate, and includes any part, product, egg, or offspring thereof, or the dead body or parts thereof." 16 U.S.C. § 1532(8). The term "plant" is separately defined; *see* 16 U.S.C. § 1532(14). The "take" prohibition in Section 9(a)(1)(B) does not apply to endangered species of plants, which are instead protected by Section 9(a)(2) of the Act, 16 U.S.C. § 1538(a)(2).

[3] Under Section 4(d) of the Act, 16 U.S.C. § 1533(d), the Secretary may, by regulation, prohibit with respect to threatened species any act prohibited under 16 U.S.C. § 1538(1)(1). The Secretary has extended the "take" prohibition in 16 U.S.C. § 1538(a)(1)(B) to threatened fish and wildlife species. *See* 50 C.F.R. 17.31(a), 17.21(c)(1). Thus, the "take" prohibition applies to all listed species of fish or wildlife except where special rules applicable to particular threatened species otherwise provide. *See* 50 C.F.R. 17.40-17.48. On February 17, 1995, the Secretary published regulations under Section 4(d) that address the application of the "take" prohibition to the northern spotted owl (a threatened species). 60 Fed. Reg. 9484.

[4] 437 U.S. 153 (1978).

[5] "Critical habitat" has a specific and limited meaning for purposes of the ESA . Section 4 empowers the Secretary to designate "critical" habitat for

listed species. 16 U.S.C. §§ 1533(a)(3), (b)(2) and (b)(6)(C). "Critical habitat" is defined by the Act to mean:

> (i) the specific areas within the geographical area occupied by the species, at the time it is listed in accordance with the provisions of section 4 of this Act, on which are found those physical or biological features (I) essential to the conservation of the species and (II) which may require special management considerations or protection; and

> (ii) specific areas outside the geographical area occupied by the species at the time it is listed in accordance with the provisions of section 4 of this Act, upon a determination by the Secretary that such areas are essential for the conservation of the species.

16 U.S.C. § 1532(5)(A). In appropriate cases, designating unoccupied potential habitat for listed species can play a role in the recovery of the species by providing for "natural range expansion into adjacent suitable habitat." 49 Fed. Reg. 38,904 (1984). However, "[e]xcept in those circumstances determined by the Secretary, critical habitat shall not include the entire geographical area which can be occupied" by listed species. 16 U.S.C. § 1532(5)(C). Thus, designation of critical habitat may add protections for a listed species against federal government actions that are likely to take place on some suitable, but unoccupied, habitat.

[6] 16 U.S.C. § 1536(a)(2).
[7] 676 F. Supp. 1044 (D. Mont. 1987).
[8] 667 F. Supp. 1485 (S.D. Fla. 1987).
[9] 115 S. Ct. 2407 (1995).
[10] 437 U.S. 153 (1978).
[11] 16 U.S.C. §§ 3371-3378 (1994).
[12] *Sierra Club v. Lujan*, No. MO-91-CA-069, 1993 WL 151353 *31 (W. D. Tex. Feb. 1, 1993).
[13] *Delaware v. New York*, 113 S. Ct. 1550, 1557 (1993) (citation and quotation marks omitted).
[14] *Fidelity Federal Savings & Loan Association v. de la Cuesta*, 458 U.S. 141, 153 (1982).

Chapter 6

SUPERFUND, MINING, AND OTHER ENVIRONMENTAL STATUTES

Environmental regulation touches virtually every American on a daily basis. It regulates the water we drink, the air we breathe, the clothes we wear, and the houses we live in. Nearly every sector of the economy is touched by environmental laws that are becoming increasingly global in scope.

Environmental regulation is both the newest and, at the same time, most extensive governmental regulatory program ever conceived. Economic, social, and personal activities that were considered acceptable—and even laudable—have, within the past decade or two, become undesirable. In many instances, they have even become unlawful. Moreover, much environmental regulation is predicated on incomplete and developing scientific knowledge that is without consensus. Much environmental policy is also predicated on philosophical and aesthetic tenets which are not necessarily universal and are, in many instances, conflicting and self-contradictory. Government has, in short, entered upon a novel and vastly expanded project regulating our daily lives. Not surprisingly, some have raised the question: How far can government go in the name of environmental protection?

Environmental regulation annually costs Americans between $150 billion and $300 billion. Pollution control and environmental technologies constitute a huge growth industry which already employs four million Americans. The federal government annually recovers more than one billion dollars in fines, cleanup costs, and injunctive relief in suits against American companies.

SUPERFUND AND PROPERTY RIGHTS

The Superfund Regulatory Scheme

The hazardous waste cleanup program has its roots in one of the most dramatic environmental and public health stories of recent decades—Love Canal in New York. As industrial wastes and toxic substances buried at Love Canal decades earlier began seeping into basements and bubbling to the surface, the country's awakening environmental consciousness mobilized to create the most far-reaching and expensive environmental program ever undertaken. Due to the perceived environmental emergency, Congress quickly drafted and passed the Comprehensive Environmental Response, Compensation and Liability Act of 1980 ("CERCLA" or "Superfund").[1] The Act devised a unique liability scheme, the breadth and reach of which are only now starting to be comprehended.

Novel problems beget novel legislation, and the CERCLA liability scheme is a collection of concepts drawn from tort, property, contract, and agency law principles engrafted upon a massive national program of hazardous waste cleanup. Under CERCLA, a potentially responsible party (PRP) is strictly liable regardless of the care exercised in disposing of the waste. Further, the PRP is severally liable for the entire cost of cleanup regardless of how many other PRPs there may be (when these costs are indivisible). Apart from proving that someone else was solely to blame for the release of the hazardous substance, the defendant in a CERCLA suit has only two remaining statutory defenses: (1) that the release was caused by an act of war, or (2) that it was caused by an act of God. A potentially responsible party may not seek court relief while the government is cleaning up the site with government money, but must wait until the government has completed all of the work. When a potentially responsible party finally does get to court, the defendant is not entitled to a jury trial. Furthermore, the potentially responsible party may present little, if any, evidence in the case, since review by the court is limited to the administrative record prepared by the government. This record is entitled to deference by the court unless it is found to be arbitrary and capricious.

Section 104 of CERCLA authorizes the federal government to respond to the release or threatened release of a hazardous substance into the environment by taking any action "necessary to protect the public health or welfare or the environment." In order to pay for these government response actions, CERCLA established the Hazardous Substances Response Trust Fund, popularly known as the Superfund. If the federal government taps the Superfund to pay for a response action, it may then sue the potentially responsible parties to recover its costs.

Section 107 of CERCLA sets forth the following four classes of persons who may be held liable for remedial response costs: (1) the current owner or operator of a hazardous waste disposal facility; (2) any person who owned or operated such a facility at the time of waste disposal; (3) hazardous waste generators who arranged for the disposal of such waste at the facility; and (4) transporters of hazardous waste who selected the facility for the disposal of hazardous waste.

As a result of congressional deadlock over the appropriate standard of liability, CERCLA originally failed to clearly specify the standard. Subsequent judicial interpretation, however, has confirmed that all classes of potentially responsible parties are strictly liable, and that they incur joint and several liability for all cleanup costs unless the contribution of each party to the need for cleanup is clearly severable. Thus, the proverbial "one barrel generator" at a Superfund site may be held liable for the entire cost of cleanup, as may the owner or operator of the site, unless the defendant proves one of the three available statutory defenses.

Superfund and Property Rights

The government's unwelcome entry upon property, together with the crushing cost of Superfund cleanups (often in the tens of millions of dollars), has proved an explosive mixture when ignited by claims of property right infringement. Property owners often assert that their land is not sufficiently contaminated to pose any threat to public health, safety, or the environment; that the government's proposed method of cleanup is excessively intrusive or expensive; or that excessive government zeal has actually resulted in the contamination of other portions of their land. Additionally, property owners have often sought to deny access to government officials, claiming them to be trespassers, and asserting that the government must purchase any uncontaminated portions of their land that became polluted in the cleanup process.

In 1986, Congress acted to cut off most of these claims by the simple expedient of denying property owners access to the federal courts. As a result of the Superfund amendments of 1986, Federal District Courts lack any jurisdiction to entertain a challenge to EPA's actions until after the cleanup has been completed. Since cleanups often last a decade or more, most of the issues have either become moot or so stale that they are not worth pursuing by the time EPA leaves the property.

The statute also permits EPA to file liens upon the owner's property—including uncontaminated portions—to satisfy liability claims. These liens, together with other EPA claims (such as bankruptcy priority), have generally been upheld against constitutional challenge. Indeed, the courts have generally reasoned that the cleanup of our nation's contaminated sites is so important that Superfund is paramount over most traditional statutes governing property—even court procedure.

Two case studies help illustrate how Superfund has generated unintended consequences, in derogation of constitutionally protected property rights.

Hendler v. United States[2]: Superfund is a Taking

Mr. Hendler owned property in Riverside County, California near the hazardous waste disposal site known as the Stringfellow Acid Pits. The EPA became aware that a plume of groundwater contaminated with toxic substances from the pits was threatening to enter a nearby source of drinking and agricultural water. The EPA requested, and was denied, access to the plaintiff's property to install wells for monitoring and extracting these migrating hazardous substances.

In September 1983, the EPA issued an administrative order granting itself and the State of California access to the property for, *inter alia*, "locating, constructing, operating, maintaining, and repairing monitor/extraction wells." Shortly after, the EPA went upon the plaintiff's property and began the installation of a series of wells: five were installed by contractors for the EPA, and (by the time of the first hearing) at least another thirteen were installed by the State of California.

In 1984, Mr. Hendler filed suit in the United States Court of Federal Claims. After many years of intense and acrimonious litigation, the case came before the Court of Appeals. The issue presented was whether the EPA's occupancy of the Hendler property—even for the purpose of allegedly safeguarding him against groundwater pollution—constituted a taking under the Fifth Amendment. First, the court found that Hendler's right to exclude others had been violated. This is perhaps the most important right in the "bundle of sticks" known as property rights:

> In the bundle of rights we call property, one of the most valued is the right to sole and exclusive possession—the right to exclude strangers, or for that matter friends, but especially Government. The notion of exclusive ownership as a property right is fundamental to our theory of social organization.[3]

Next, the court rejected the EPA's argument that the importance of Superfund might exempt its activities from the constitutional prohibition against taking without just compensation.

> The intruder who enters clothed in the robes of authority in broad daylight commits no less an invasion of these rights than if he sneaks in the night wearing a burglar's mask. In some ways, entry by the authorities is more to

be feared, since the citizen's right to defend against the intrusion may seem less clear. Courts should leave no doubt as to whose side the law stands upon.[4]

Triumph, Idaho: The Taking of a Town

Triumph, Idaho is a former mining town of fewer than 100 people located near the resort area of Sun Valley. During the last century, Triumph boomed with the extraction of silver and other metals from the surrounding hillsides, leaving great piles of exposed ore and rock in heaps a hundred feet tall ringing the town. Much of this exposed rock is high in lead, arsenic, and other metals.

In the 1980s, the EPA began an investigation of conditions in Triumph, concluding that the high levels of metals posed a threat to public safety. According to EPA projections, the residents (especially the children) were at risk for lead and arsenic poisoning. Although subsequent blood testing of all residents disproved the EPA's fears, the machinery of Superfund could not be stopped. Accordingly, EPA commenced the process of listing the entire town of Triumph as a Superfund site in 1992.

The effect of the Superfund listing on property values in Triumph was immediate and devastating. Residents could not sell or mortgage their homes since no one would willingly purchase a home which was part of a hazardous waste site. Banks were reluctant to issue loans secured by such unsalable properties. Moreover, under Superfund's liability scheme, anyone who purchased such a property would immediately become liable for the entire cost of cleaning up the site. Economic activity in the town ground to a virtual halt.

Residents banded together, seeking to have their story told. Ultimately, working through Congress, state agencies, and the media, they were able to hammer out a process under which the town would not be designated as a Superfund site, but would, instead, be cleaned up voluntarily by its residents. Economic activity has resumed, and property rights have, in large measure, been restored. Many residents, however, say that the federal government came perilously close to destroying their town in an effort to "save" it.

MINING

Government regulation over the extraction of minerals and fossil fuels has generated considerable property rights litigation. For example, the federal government's moratorium upon the extraction of oil and gas from off-shore leases, for which the major oil companies had paid the government, in aggregate, more than $500 million, led to a massive suit by twenty oil companies claiming more than a billion dollars in damages. A mining company whose mineral lease on Indian lands was destroyed by the action of the Secretary of Interior also recovered a multi-million-dollar judgment against the federal government. Environmental permitting and regulation requirements have twice brought coal companies before the United States Supreme Court in landmark property rights decisions.

The SMCRA Regulatory Scheme

The mining regulatory scheme that has produced the most litigation, however, is the Surface Mining Control and Reclamation Act of 1977 ("SMCRA").[5]

A comprehensive statute, SMCRA is designed to "establish a nationwide program to protect society and the environment from the adverse effects of surface coal mining operations." Title II of the Act established the Office of Surface Mining Reclamation and Enforcement ("OSM") within the Department of the Interior. The Secretary of the Interior ("Secretary"), acting through OSM, is charged with primary responsibility for administering and implementing the Act by promulgating regulations and enforcing its provisions.

The principal regulatory and enforcement provisions are contained in Title V of the Act. Section 501 establishes a two-stage program for the regulation of surface coal mining: an initial or interim

100 / Property Rights

regulatory phase, and a subsequent permanent phase. The interim program mandates immediate promulgation and federal enforcement of some of the Act's environmental protection performance standards, complemented by continuing state regulation. Under the permanent phase, a regulatory program is to be adopted for each state, mandating compliance with the full panoply of federal performance standards, with enforcement responsibility lying with either the state or federal government.

Section 501(a) directs the Secretary to promulgate regulations establishing an interim regulatory program during which mine operators will be required to comply with some of the Act's performance standards, as specified by Section 502(c). Included among those selected standards are requirements governing:

(a) restoration of land to its prior condition;

(b) restoration of land to its approximate original contour;

(c) segregation and preservation of topsoil;

(d) minimization of disturbance to the hydrologic balance;

(e) construction of coal mine waste piles used as dams and embankments;

(f) revegetation of mined areas; and

(g) soil disposal.[6]

The published interim regulations are currently in effect in most states.

The Secretary is responsible for enforcing the interim regulatory program. A federal enforcement and inspection program is to be established for each state, and is to remain in effect until a permanent regulatory program is implemented in the state. States may issue permits for surface mining operations during the interim phase, but operations authorized by such permits must comply with the federal interim performance standards. States may also pursue their own regulatory and inspection programs during the interim phase, and they may assist the Secretary in enforcing the interim standards. The states are not, however, required to enforce the interim regulatory standards and, until the permanent phase of the program, the Secretary may not cede the federal government's independent enforcement role to states that wish to conduct their own regulatory programs.

Section 501(b) directs the Secretary to promulgate regulations establishing a permanent regulatory program incorporating all of the Act's performance standards. The Secretary published the permanent regulations, but these regulations do not become effective in a particular state until either a permanent state program, submitted and approved in accordance with Section 503 of the Act, or a permanent federal program for the state, adopted in accordance with Section 504, is implemented.

Under Section 503, any state wishing to assume permanent regulatory authority over the surface coal mining operations on "non-federal lands" within its borders must submit a proposed permanent program to the Secretary for his approval. The proposed program must demonstrate that the state legislature has enacted laws implementing the environmental protection standards established by the Act and accompanying regulations, and that the state has the administrative and technical ability to enforce these standards. The Secretary must approve or disapprove each such proposed program in accordance with time schedules and procedures established by Sections 503(b) and (c). In addition, the Secretary must develop and implement a federal permanent program for each state that fails to submit or enforce a satisfactory state program. In such situations, the Secretary constitutes the regulatory authority administering the Act within that state and continues as such unless and until a "state program" is approved. No later than eight months after adoption of either a state-run or federally administered permanent regulatory program for a state, all surface coal mining and reclamation operations on "non-federal lands" within that state must obtain a new permit issued in accordance with the applicable regulatory program.

The *Whitney Benefits* Decision

In *Whitney Benefits v. United States*, the Court of Appeals for the Federal Circuit affirmed the Court of Federal Claims and held that the Surface Mining Control and Reclamation Act unconstitutionally took all economically beneficial use of the plaintiff's mineral estate.[7] The court held that the only use for the mineral estate was to mine coal and that the statute took all value of the property because it prohibited that use. The court rejected the government's argument that the trial court ignored the public use of SMCRA, and that uses such as farming the surface estate above the mineral estate still existed. In its decision, the court analogized the case to *Pennsylvania Coal v. Mahon* and distinguished it from *Keystone Bituminous Coal Association v. DeBenedictis*.[8] The court noted that "[Whitney] Benefits is in the position occupied by the citizens in *Mahon*, who were denied all economically viable use of their coal, and in a fundamentally different position from that of the citizens in *Keystone*, who were not."[9] In compensation for the unconstitutional taking, the government was ordered to remit more than sixty million dollars.

OTHER MAJOR FEDERAL ENVIRONMENTAL STATUTES

Existing federal environmental statutes comprehensively regulate vast segments of our nation's economy, touching upon land, natural resources, water, air, timber, wildlife, and a whole host of other components of the biosphere. Although federal environmental regulation can in some degree be traced back to the efforts of John Muir, Gifford Pinchot, and Theodore Roosevelt, the modern environmental regime was born on April 22, 1970—the first Earth Day. In rapid succession, Congress passed a string of environmental statutes which, when woven together, create a net of regulations which capture many aspects of modern life.

- The National Environmental Policy Act (NEPA) requires the preparation of an environmental impact statement for any major federal action significantly affecting the quality of the human environment. Since "major federal action" encompasses permits and authorizations of many kinds—road construction, mineral and timber sales, as well as the generic programs under which these activities occur (*e.g.*, oil leasing or gas exploration on federal lands)—NEPA also impacts a broad array of private resource development that is dependent upon or tangential to federal programs or activities. Opponents to such programs rely upon NEPA, often referred to as the "grandfather of all environmental statutes," as a means for stopping the project on the grounds that an environmental impact statement was either not prepared or was inadequate.

- The Clean Air Act, originally passed in 1970, significantly amended in 1977, and massively overhauled in 1990, regulates emissions of pollutants into the atmosphere. It requires permits for "major sources" of pollution, especially particulates, volatile organic compounds, sulphur dioxides, nitrogen oxides, air toxics and depleters of stratospheric ozone. The regulations which implement the Clean Air Act of 1990 are still being written, so basic questions about operating permits and air quality requirements remain unclear. Like the Clean

Water Act, the Clean Air Act is primarily implemented through state legislation which must be submitted for federal review in the form of a State Implementation Plan (SIP). The failure of a state to pass legislation satisfactory to the federal government may result in imposition of a Federal Implementation Plan, as well as sanctions including the cutoff of highway construction funds and punitive cutbacks in allowable emissions. The federal Clean Air Act is the most expensive environmental regulatory program to date.

- The Clean Water Act regulates the discharge of pollutants into waters of the United States. Passed in 1972, the Clean Water Act has not been significantly amended because the program is thought generally to work well. Like the Clean Air Act, the Clean Water Act is implemented through a state permitting program known as the National Pollution Discharge Elimination System (NPDES); unlike the Clean Air Act, however, the Clean Water Act has no State Implementation Plan (SIP). Instead, the federal government prescribes water quality standards which the state must achieve. The Clean Water Act is also a principal vehicle for funding municipal waste water treatment plants. Finally, Section 404 of the Clean Water Act serves as authority for federal regulation of approximately 100 million acres of wetlands.[10]

- The Resource Conservation and Recovery Act (RCRA) prescribes a "cradle-to-grave" program for managing hazardous waste. Drums of hazardous waste must be labeled, manifested, and tracked to their ultimate place of disposal. Such treatment, storage and disposal (TSD) facilities must obtain RCRA permits, and must comply with stringent regulations concerning construction, allowable wastes, ground water monitoring, closure plans and financial responsibility.

- CERCLA differs from the Clean Air Act, Clean Water Act, and RCRA in that it is a liability scheme rather than a permitting program. CERCLA imposes liability upon the owner, operator, transporter, or arranger for disposal of hazardous substances whenever those substances are released into the environment. Comprehensively overhauled in 1986 by the Superfund Amendment and Reauthorization Act (SARA), the statute imposes strict, joint and several liability for cleanup costs which may be recovered by the federal government or by an innocent third party.[11]

- The Oil Pollution Act of 1990, passed in the wake of the eleven-million-gallon Exxon *Valdez* oil spill in Prince William Sound, Alaska, imposes liability upon owners and operators of vessels or facilities from which oil is released, and requires the preparation of extensive oil spill contingency plans to guarantee readiness in the event of a serious oil spill.

- The Surface Mining Control and Reclamation Act of 1977 (SMCRA), administered by the Surface Mining Office of the Interior Department, requires reclamation of surface mine

106 / Property Rights

> lands to conditions approximating their original natural contours.[12]

- The Endangered Species Act of 1973 (ESA) forbids the "taking" of any species of animal or plant listed by the United States Fish and Wildlife Service as endangered, including disturbance of the habitat of that species. Severe civil and criminal penalties may be imposed for violation of the statute.[13]

- The Marine Protection Resources and Sanctuaries Act (MPRSA) governs the disposal of sewage, sludge, and other waste into the ocean.

- The Federal Insecticide, Fungicide and Rodenticide Act (FIFRA) requires testing, registration, and labeling of pesticides.

- The Toxic Substances Control Act (TSCA) requires registration and testing of new chemicals.

- The Coastal Zone Management Act of 1972 (CZMA) requires states to adopt plans for the protection of their coastlines and coastal waters.

- The Safe Drinking Water Act (SDWA) regulates small private water distribution systems.

COMMON STATE ENVIRONMENTAL STATUTES

Each of the fifty states has adopted an environmental protection scheme of greater or lesser complexity that is adapted to its own ecological, economic and social needs. Some of those programs are federally mandated, while others are purely home grown. The variety and peculiarities of state environmental regulation cannot be catalogued here; suffice it to say that in many instances, it is the state regulatory scheme rather than the federal one which most directly touches citizens everyday.

A number of federal environmental statutes set minimums or "floors" for state environmental protection, on the rationale that states should not be allowed to create "pollution havens" where industry may flee to avoid environmental regulation. These federal statutes, however, provide substantial flexibility to states in determining how they will achieve compliance with federal requirements, and allow states to adopt other and more stringent regulations than those which are federally mandated. Thus, under the Clean Air Act, for example, states are required to prepare State Implementation Plans (SIPs) which are submitted to the federal government for approval, but state air pollution control laws often reach far beyond the basic requirements of the federal Clean Air Act. States such as California, New York, and Colorado have adopted highly specialized air pollution regulations to address their unique and very different climatic conditions, geographies, and population distributions.

Similarly, programs for controlling water pollution, wetlands, non-municipal drinking water supplies, underground injection, and other treatment or disposal programs for hazardous waste must all be conducted in accordance with federal regulations. Other programs, such as mineland bonding and reclamation, application of agricultural chemicals, or protection of ground water, are effectively "state led" programs in which the federal government effectively defers to local authorities as more appropriate regulators of the activities in question. State "mini-superfunds," recycling laws, labeling requirements, and "community right-to-know" requirements are all examples of state analogies to federal statutes which either add embroidery to the federal regulatory program, or reach activities not otherwise regulated.

Although recent years have seen significant federal encroachment upon the states' formerly exclusive preserve, the field of public health and safety has traditionally been the domain of the states.

Similarly, zoning and land use restrictions on private property are essential functions of state and local governments, despite recent federal incursions typified by wetlands regulation. More recently, states have expanded their land use regulation to include historic preservation, battlefield protection, scenic designations, setbacks along waterways and streams, farmland protection, and establishment of greenways, designation of parks and preserves, and restrictions upon natural resource development, together with outright prohibitions upon disturbance based upon environmental, cultural, aesthetic, historical and other considerations.

Finally, licensing and permitting schemes, economic incentives, and taxation are also used by state and local governments as means of encouraging or discouraging certain economic activities which ultimately affect the environment. Taken together with the comprehensive battery of federal, state and local regulations directly applicable to activities affecting the environment and land use, these economic incentive/disincentive policies can effectively prohibit or eliminate many otherwise feasible and productive human activities.

ENDNOTES

[1] Pub. L. No. 96-510, 94 Stat. 2767 (1980)(codified as amended at 42 U.S.C.A. §§ 9601-9675 (West 1983 & Supp. 1989)).
[2] 952 F.2d 1364 (Fed. Cir. 1991).
[3] *Id.*
[4] *Id.*
[5] 30 U.S.C. §§ 1201-1328 (1988).
[6] 30 U.S.C. §1265(b) (1988).
[7] 926 F.2d 1169 (Fed. Cir. 1989) *cert. denied*, 112 S. Ct. 406 (1991).
[8] 480 U.S. 470 (1987).
[9] *Id.*
[10] *See supra*, Chapter 4.
[11] *See supra*, Chapter 6.

[12] *See supra*, Chapter 6.
[13] *See supra*, Chapter 5.

Chapter 7

LAND USE AND ZONING

GENERALLY LEGITIMATE AS EXERCISE OF POLICE POWER

The modern law of health and safety regulation finds its roots in the venerable doctrine that a landowner may not act to create a nuisance upon his land to the detriment of his neighbors in the community. Since there was no right to commit a nuisance upon one's land, the abatement of such a nuisance was not a "taking" of any property right. Thus, once the 1887 Supreme Court decided that production of alcoholic beverages was "a noxious use" calculated "to inflict injury upon the community," it followed that the State of Kansas could shut down the plaintiff's brewery without compensation [*Mugler v. Kansas*].[1] Early zoning regulations were upheld on the basis of the nuisance doctrine, for uses that in one district might be "entirely unobjectionable" could "very nearly be a public nuisance in another." Soon, however, the courts began to uphold land use regulation against takings challenges on the grounds that the conferring of public benefits under the police power was the equivalent, for Fifth Amendment purposes, of avoiding noxious uses. This approach reached its zenith in *Goldblatt v. Hempstead,* which, in saying that "the term 'police power' connotes the time-tested conceptual limit of public encroachment upon private interest," was widely interpreted to hold that private property rights began only where the state's regulatory authority terminated.[2]

Goldblatt represents the high water mark of deference to governmental regulatory authority under the Fifth Amendment, from which the Court thereafter began to recede. By the time of *Keystone Bituminous Coal Association v. DeBenedictis* in 1987, Justice John Paul Stevens could agree with Justice William Rehnquist's dissent in *Penn Central* that "the nuisance exception to the taking guarantee is not coterminous with the police power itself."[3] Three months later, Justice Antonin Scalia put the matter to rest: "*Goldblatt v. Hempstead* does appear to assume that the inquiries are the same, but that assumption is inconsistent with formulations of our later cases."[4] Although the recognition that police power and property rights were incomparable was crucial to the holding that property regulation could constitute a compensable taking in the Supreme Court's *First English* case, other cases such as *Keystone* only provide general guidance regarding which health and safety regulations may escape takings liability by virtue of the nuisance doctrine.

Importantly, while the *Mugler* Court's conclusion that the production of beer was a *per se* nuisance may now be questioned, the *Keystone* opinion assures us that *Mugler's* fundamental holding remains correct:

> The special status of this type of state action can also be understood on the simple theory that since no individual has a right to use his property so as to create a nuisance or otherwise harm others, the state has not "taken" anything when it asserts its power to enjoin the nuisance-like activity.[5]

WHEN DOES ZONING GO TOO FAR?

Downzoning

Downzoning involves an attempt by the government to rezone a parcel in order to reduce the number of ways a property owner may use the property. This type of arbitrary government action can drastically affect a property owner's plans for his property. The dramatic effect that downzoning may have on a property owner is best illustrated through an example.

In 1984, Long Beach Equities, Inc. ("LBE") purchased a 250-acre parcel of property that the County of Ventura had generally zoned for residential development, and that the City of Simi Valley had specifically zoned for 1,100 residential units. LBE proceeded to prepare plans for development and built the infrastructure necessary to service 1,100 residences. In 1985, after LBE had invested thousands of dollars in the property, the City and County imposed a partial moratorium on the approval of necessary permits. In 1986, the City announced a new policy that "temporarily" limited the number of building permits to be issued annually. Set to last until 1996, this temporary policy required a developer to first obtain City approval before a project could even become eligible for a waiting list that allowed the developer to apply for a building permit. Simultaneously, the County downzoned the property to only permit one residential unit per 160 acres. Thus, even if LBE ever got a City building permit, it would only be allowed to build one unit on its 250-acre parcel. Reducing the number of residential units that may be built from 1,100 to 1 effectively foreclosed LBE from all development of its property.

Open Space Zoning

In *Agins v. City of Tiburon*, the Court unanimously affirmed a judgment of the Supreme Court of California denying a landowner's facial taking challenge of a municipal zoning ordinance that restricted development to no more than five residences per acre.[6] After the appellants had purchased a tract of land, the City, acting under California law, prepared a land use plan and established ordinances for the development of the land. The Agins sued in state court, facially challenging the zoning ordinances as a taking in violation of the Fifth and Fourteenth Amendments. Appealed all the way to the United States Supreme Court, the zoning ordinance was held constitutional.

In *Agins*, the Court set forth a two-prong, disjunctive takings test: if the zoning ordinance does not "substantially advance legitimate state interests," or if it denies the owner "economically viable use" of his property, then an unconstitutional taking occurred. In upholding the City of Tiburon's zoning ordinance, the Court stated that the ordinance favored both the landowner and the public by "serving the city's interest in assuring careful and orderly development of residential property with provision for open-space areas."[7] Thus, the open space zoning ordinance substantially advanced legitimate state interest and was found to be constitutional.

In 1992, the Supreme Court decided *Lucas v. South Carolina Coastal Council*.[8] The Coastal Council had denied property owner David Lucas permission to build homes on two desirable, and otherwise suitable, lots along the South Carolina coastline. In doing so, the Commission was exercising the open space zoning authority granted to it under the South Carolina Beachfront Management Act. The Act, which prohibited new construction on portions of the coastline to prevent erosion, was passed in 1988. It, however, did not exist at the time Mr. Lucas bought his property in 1986.

In his lawsuit, Lucas asserted that the Act deprived him of all economically viable use of his property. Justice Scalia, writing for the Court in *Lucas*, stated that if a "logically antecedent inquiry into the nature of the owner's estate shows that the proscribed use interests were not part of his title to begin with,"[9] the owner's asserted right never existed and compensation was not due. In other words, for a takings claim to be compensable, a plaintiff's desired use of property must be lawful and not precluded by law at the time of the property's acquisition. Where the use is not precluded by these pre-existing bodies of law, the plaintiff's desired use is compensable property under the Fifth Amendment. Distinguishable from *Agins*, where pre-existing California law required the City to create a zoning plan, the South Carolina Beachfront Management Act did not exist when Mr. Lucas purchased the tracts. Therefore, it was found that the state's desire to preclude beachfront development unconstitutionally took Mr. Lucas' property, as on remand to the South Carolina Supreme Court, the state failed to prove that Mr. Lucas' property interest did not include the right to develop the parcels under pre-existing law.

EXACTIONS

Exactions are specific demands made by the government that bind a property owner to either take certain action or refrain from acting in a certain fashion as a *quid pro quo* for government approval of an owner's development. For example, a property owner wishing to develop residences along a road may be required to install a sidewalk as a condition for receiving a building permit. However, when the government exaction overly impinges on a property interest, Fifth Amendment takings implications are raised. In the last ten years, two U.S. Supreme Court cases and one California Supreme Court case directly addressed the issue of when exactions become an unconstitutional taking.

Nollan v. California Coastal Commission

In *Nollan v. California Coastal Commission*, the plaintiff wanted to build an addition to his house, an act that would raise the height of the beachfront dwelling.[10] The Coastal Commission granted a building permit on the condition that Nollan permit public access across his property and onto the beach. The state alleged that this would minimize the "psychological barrier" to the public that arises from continuous beachfront housing. The Commission responded to Mr. Nollan's objection to the exaction by denying his permit. In the subsequent lawsuit, the highest court in the State of California found the exaction to be a constitutional exercise of the state's regulatory powers.

The United States Supreme Court, however, reversed the decision, instead finding that an unconstitutional taking occurred. The Court ruled that there was an insufficient "nexus" between the stated goal of removing a "psychological barrier" and forcing a public easement on Mr. Nollan as a condition for the permit. The intermediate level of scrutiny test established by the Court was whether the condition attached to the permit "substantially advanced" a legitimate government interest.

Dolan v. City of Tigard

In 1994, the U.S. Supreme Court again examined whether an exaction by a municipality on a landowner went too far and resulted in a taking. In *Dolan v. City of Tigard*, Florence Dolan applied for a building permit to expand her plumbing and electrical supply store.[11] The City of Tigard, acting under state statute, had developed a comprehensive zoning plan that identified areas prone to flooding and proposed building a bike path to alleviate traffic. Although the City had no problems with Mrs. Dolan's permit, the City sought to exact two concessions. The first concession prohibited her from building on any land within the 100-year flood plain on her property, and the second was that she provide a swath of land adjacent to the flood plain for use as a bike path.

Denied in all of her previous appeals, Mrs. Dolan emerged victorious when the Court declared the desired exactions unconstitutional. The Court ruled that the City of Tigard's exactions failed the test of when "the government may require a person to give up a constitutional right . . . in exchange for a discretionary benefit conferred by the government."[12] The three-part test established by the *Dolan* Court applies the two elements set forth in *Nollan* (that the government seeks to promote a legitimate state interest, and that there is a sufficient "nexus" between the interest and the government's conditions) and a new, third part that requires the conditions to be "roughly proportional" to the "impact of the proposed development."

Ehrlich v. City of Culver City et al.[13]

In 1981, due to monetary losses, Mr. Richard Ehrlich applied for a change in the City's zoning code to build an office building. Denied by the City, Mr. Ehrlich continued to operate his health club until 1988, when he closed it due to the financial losses. Mr. Ehrlich again applied for a change in his land's designation, this time to build a condominium complex worth ten million dollars. Although the City felt that there was a lack of public sports/recreational facilities, the City chose not to purchase his property. After a threatened lawsuit, the City approved the necessary changes conditioned on two monetary exactions. Specifically, the City required $280,000 to compensate for the loss of recreational facilities, and an additional payment to its public arts program under an ordinance that covered new residential developments.

Mr. Ehrlich sued for a taking under the Fifth and Fourteenth Amendments to the Constitution. After an extensive litigation process, the California Supreme Court accepted the case for review. The court thoroughly examined the United States Supreme Court's reasoning in the *Nollan* and *Dolan* cases, applying the heightened standard of judicial scrutiny formulated to the monetary exaction sought by the City. Heightened scrutiny applied because the government imposed "special discretionary permit conditions on developments" by an individual property owner. The court held that although a city might constitutionally require a monetary exaction, the City did not meet its burden of proof in this case.

HISTORIC PRESERVATION

Equally important cases for property rights are those involving neither federal, nor state environmental takings—but local zoning or historic preservation statutes. The case of *United Artists Theater Circuit, Inc. v. City of Philadelphia* is a recent example.[14] The dispute arose when the City Historical Commission of Philadelphia, Pennsylvania designated the Boyd Theater as an historic site. As a result, the building's owners were required to maintain the facility to Commission standards at their own expense or risk criminal penalties. United Artists, the owners of the theater, petitioned the Pennsylvania Supreme Court for relief. In 1991, the court ruled that Philadelphia's historical preservation system was "unfair, unjust, and amount[s] to an unconstitutional taking without just compensation. . . ."[15] As a result of strenuous protests from the state attorney general, state representatives, the National Historic Trust, and others, the court agreed to rehear the case. But on November 9, 1993, the court again found for the plaintiff.[16] This case is significant because Philadelphia's historic preservation system is typical of those across the country.

FLOOD PLAIN ZONING

Among state and local ordinances, one of the most troublesome has been flood plain zoning. Predicated upon a federal program intended to provide flood insurance to homeowners who would otherwise be unable to obtain it, these ordinances, ironically, often preclude much or all development within land designated as a "100 year" or "500 year" flood plain, *i.e.*, where there is a one percent chance in any given year that the land will be inundated to a depth of one foot. Such an ordinance reached the United States Supreme Court in the landmark case of *First English Evangelical Lutheran Church v. County of Los Angeles*,[17] the first Court decision to hold that the Just Compensation Clause compels the payment of damages for the taking of property, even where the offending ordinance is subsequently invalidated or rescinded.[18]

The Flood Plain Regulatory Scheme

The National Flood Insurance Program (NFIP) was enacted by Congress in 1968 in order to provide national access to flood insurance that was commercially infeasible and unavailable.[19] NFIP makes flood insurance available in states or localities that map areas as flood plain and establish standards for construction that minimize damage to structures in those areas. Rather than forbidding construction on land zoned as flood plain, the program guarantees insurance to persons who have built appropriate structures within those flood plains.

Although there is much variety among city and county ordinances dealing with flood plains, they often include some or all of the following features:

- forbid the erection of permanent structures within the flood plain;

- exclude the flood plain from counting toward open space requirements;

- regulate the construction of above-ground utilities and roads;

- require maintenance of flood plain areas as wildlife habitat, public access greenways, or vegetative preserves.

Flood Plain Zoning Held Violative of Property Rights

In 1994, the United States Supreme Court invalidated a building permit condition requiring an owner to dedicate, as a public access greenway, a swath of land located within the flood plain alongside a creek which bounded the property in *Dolan v. City of Tigard*.[20] The Court rejected as inadequate the City's contention that the construction of a parking lot and store addition would increase the likelihood of rainwater run-off, thereby justifying the town's exaction of title to the flood plain as a condition for construction approval. Stating that there was an insufficient relationship between the City's interest in flood control and its demands on the owner, the Court held that the city's desire to impose a public easement on her land would not just diminish Mrs. Florence Dolan's "right to exclude [the public from her property] . . . it would be eviscerated."[21]

Numerous state courts have recognized that the zoning of lands as flood plain, which converts private property into water detention basins, "goes too far." For instance, the New Jersey Supreme Court invalidated a zoning ordinance that restricted use of property to purposes consistent with maintaining a wildlife preserve and flood control:

> While the issue of regulation as against taking is always a matter of degree, there can be no question but that the line has been crossed where the purpose and practical effect of the regulation is to appropriate private property for a flood water detention basin or open space. These are laudable public purposes and we do not doubt the high-mindedness of their motivation. But such factors cannot cure basic unconstitutionality. Nor is the situation saved because the owner of most of the land in the zone, justifiably desirous of preserving an appropriate area in its natural state as a wetland wildlife sanctuary, supports the regulations. Both public uses are necessarily so all-encompassing as practically to prevent the exercise by a private owner of any worthwhile rights or benefits in the land. So public acquisition rather than regulations is required.[22]

Similarly, the Connecticut Supreme Court recognized that the zoning of lands as flood plain extinguished all value from land:

> The plaintiffs have been deprived by the change of zone of any worthwhile rights or benefits in their land. Where most of the value of a person's property has to be sacrificed so that community welfare may be served, and where the owner does not directly benefit from the evil avoided (*see, e.g.*, the old smoke nuisance cases such as *State v. Hillman*[23]), the occasion is appropriate for the exercise of eminent domain. Our statutes empower the flood and erosion control board to purchase or condemn property if it is needed for flood control.[24]

CONDEMNATION BLIGHT

The United States Supreme Court has long held that threats of governmental action have legally cognizable consequences, particularly if constitutional rights are at stake. This has occurred most prominently in the First Amendment context. For example, in *New York Times Co.*

v. Sullivan, the Court held that prior restraints were so repugnant to constitutionally protected free speech rights, that even if the defamatory criticism of public officials had not been yet determined to be protected speech under the First Amendment, the state's plans to suppress it were unlawful.[25] The Court's primary concern was that the suppression would have a "chilling" effect on speech.

The Fifth Amendment parallel of a "chilling" effect on fundamental rights is seen in the context of "condemnation blight." This refers to those instances in which a government lets it be known that, sometime in the future, it may condemn a certain piece of property. With the government waiting in the wings to swoop in and pay less than top dollar for the property, the value of the property immediately drops. In the case of commercial land, the value of the land can plummet. Courts then face the issue of whether the mere threat of condemnation—which has real, tangible effects on the marketplace and the value of private property—can trigger the duty of the government to compensate the owner for that lost value.

The right to use one's property is a fundamental right, as is the right to enjoy its productive and beneficial use. In *Dolan v. City of Tigard*, the Court reaffirmed that property rights are indeed "fundamental rights" on equal footing with the other rights listed in the first ten Amendments.[26] Thus, similar to the guarantees provided by the First Amendment, the Fifth Amendment should also prevent government from clouding a title, and thereby destroying the use and enjoyment of property.

State courts have already recognized the need to vigorously defend property rights from threatened infringement by government. In *Washington Market Enterprises v. City of Trenton*, the Supreme Court of New Jersey held that threat of condemnation alone is sufficient to trigger the protections of the Just Compensation Clause.[27] "We hold that where the threat of condemnation has had such a substantial effect as to destroy the beneficial use that a landowner has made of his property, then there has been a taking of property within the meaning of the Constitution."[28]

Likewise, in *Knight v. City of Missoula*, the Supreme Court of Montana determined that excessive traffic, dust and runoff from state roads resulted in a taking of the plaintiff's property.[29] The court held "a property owner may recover in an inverse condemnation action where actual physical damage is approximately caused to his property by a public improvement as deliberately planned and built."[30]

TRANSFERABLE DEVELOPMENT RIGHTS

Transferable Development Rights (TDRs) have emerged as a popular "free market" alternative to compensation for a taking. TDRs occur when the government offers a property owner an alternative forum to pursue a desired action in place of the property owner acting on the current parcel.

In *Penn Central Transportation Co. v. New York City*, the City of New York declared Grand Central Station an historic landmark and precluded all construction above the station as it would damage the station's aesthetic and historical importance. The specific TDRs offered in *Penn Central* would allow the owner to build taller buildings on the surrounding parcels. In ruling that no taking occurred, Justice William Brennan commented favorably on the City of New York's grant of TDRs to the owner. He stated that it is important to remember that even if TDRs "may not have constituted 'just compensation' if a 'taking' had occurred, the rights nevertheless undoubtedly mitigate whatever financial burdens the law has imposed on appellants and for that reason are taken into account considering the impact of the regulation."[31]

As one option among many, TDRs may provide some landowners with a pleasant prospect. TDRs, however, should not be viewed as a panacea for the unconstitutionality of all takings. Unfortunately, in the time since Justice Brennan approved of TDRs in *Penn Central*, other cases, generally in the land development realm, have put forth the existence of TDRs to avoid finding a taking. For instance, in *Aptos Seascape Corporation v. County of Santa Cruz*, the Court found that the existence of TDRs precluded finding that an unconstitutional taking occurred.[32] The ordinance at issue prohibited all beachfront development, but the Court reasoned that its conclusion "rests on the premise that although development of the subject property is prohibited, the county's ordinance does permit the grant of compensating densities. . . ."[33]

ENDNOTES

[1] 123 U.S. 623 (1887).
[2] 369 U.S. 590 (1962).
[3] 480 U.S. 470 (1987).
[4] 112 S. Ct. 2886 (1992).
[5] *Keystone*, 480 U.S. at 473.
[6] 447 U.S. 255 (1980).
[7] *Id.*
[8] 112 S. Ct. 2886 (1992).
[9] *Id.*
[10] 483 U.S. 825 (1987).
[11] 114 S. Ct. 2309 (1994).
[12] *Id.*
[13] 12 Cal. 4th 854 (1996).
[14] 528 Pa. 12 (1991).
[15] *Id.*
[16] 535 Pa. 370 (1993).
[17] 482 U.S. 304 (1987).
[18] *See* discussion of temporary takings in Chapter 3.
[19] 42 U.S.C. § 4001(a).
[20] 114 S. Ct. 2309 (1994).
[21] *Id.*
[22] *Morris County Land Improvement Company v. Township of Parsippany Hills*, 193 A.2d. 232, 241-42 (N.J. 1963).
[23] 147 A. 294 (1929).
[24] *Dooley v. Town Planning and Zoning Commission of the Town of Fairfield*, 197 A.2d. 770, 774 (Conn. 1964).

[25] 376 U.S. 254 (1964).
[26] 114 S. Ct. 2309 (1994).
[27] 343 A.2d 408 (1975).
[28] *Id.*
[29] 827 P.2d 1270 (Mont. 1992).
[30] *Id.*
[31] *Penn Central Transportation Co. v. New York City.* 438 U.S. 104, 137 (1978).
[32] 188 Cal. Rptr. 191 (1983).
[33] *Id.* @ 200.

Chapter 8

DUE PROCESS, EQUAL PROTECTION AND GOVERNMENTAL SEIZURE OF PROPERTY

Immediately preceding the Just Compensation Clause of the Fifth Amendment, the Due Process Clause guarantees property and liberty interests against arbitrary government procedures. Implementing traditional notions of fairness and justice, the Due Process Clause requires regular government procedures that include fundamental protections such as notice of the proceedings, the opportunity to be heard, and a ruling by an impartial decision maker acting free of undue influences.

DUE PROCESS

When government deprives a person of a protected interest, it must do so using at least the minimum constitutionally required procedures. The specific procedural safeguards that must accompany substantive choices, however, are mandated by the specific context of the case.[1] Generally, the United States Supreme Court has held that some form of hearing is required before an individual may be deprived of a property interest.[2] At that hearing, an individual has a right to be heard.[3] That opportunity to be heard must take place at "a [reasonable] time and in a meaningful manner."[4] Rarely must the necessary hearing rise to the procedural level of an adjudicative function with extensive evidential analysis.[5]

Instead, the Court has developed an open-ended balancing test to decide what specific procedures are required. In *Mathews v. Eldridge*, the Court held that the constitutionally required administrative procedures are determined by an "analysis of the governmental and private interests that are affected."[6] Specifically, the Court noted three distinct factors:

> First, the private interest that will be affected by the official action; second, the risk of an erroneous deprivation of such interest through the procedures used, and the probable value, if any, of additional or substitute procedural safeguards; and finally, the Government's interest, including the function involved and the fiscal and administrative burdens that the additional or substitute procedural requirements would entail. While this utilitarian test has been criticized as requiring judges to make policy instead of legal decisions, subsequent cases have adopted this test.[7]

The Administrative Procedure Act: Statutory Due Process

In the Administrative Procedure Act (APA), Congress codified its notion of procedural due process for the majority of federal administrative agency proceedings. Before promulgating any rules, a federal agency must first publish notice of the proposed rule and provide opportunity for interested parties to comment upon the proposed rule. Indeed, the Supreme Court has held that the notice and comment procedures of Section 553 of the APA established the maximum procedural requirements which Congress was willing to have the courts impose upon agencies in conducting rulemaking procedures.[8] This decision put an end to "hybrid rulemaking," where courts imposed additional procedural requirements upon agencies beyond those required by the APA. However, the Court noted: "[t]his is not to say necessarily that there are no circumstances which would ever justify a court in overturning"[9] a rule. Therefore, generally, courts may not impose extra procedural hurdles for agency rulemaking when all APA requirements are met.

Courts, however, often aggressively enforce the APA's procedural requirements. For example, courts will strike down rules where agencies do not provide sufficient notice-and-comment to affected parties as required by due process and embodied in the APA by Section 553(b). While this section simply mandates notice by publication of proposed rules in the Federal Register, courts have required more than mere formality. In *Shell Oil Co. v. EPA*, the D.C. Court of Appeals overturned the "mixture and derived-from" rules promulgated under the Resource Conservation and Recovery Act (RCRA) on the grounds that the substantial difference between the proposed rule and the final rule deprived commentors of sufficient notice to allow them to constructively participate in formulation of the final rule.[10] In rejecting the EPA's argument that the final rule was the "logical outgrowth" of the proposed rule, the court commented that "[i]f the deviation [between] the proposal [of a rule and the final rule] is too sharp, the affected parties will not have had adequate notice and opportunity for comment."[11]

In *Corrosion Proof Fittings v. EPA*, the Fifth Circuit Court of Appeals overturned rules promulgated under the Toxic Substances Control Act because the EPA changed the methodology for calculating "analogous exposure" after closing the record.[12] The court held that "[f]ailure to seek public comment on such an important part of the EPA's analysis deprived its rule of the substantial evidence required to survive judicial scrutiny. . . ."[13] The agency's evidence that interested parties should have anticipated the change and thus had constructive notice was held insufficient.

As these cases show, courts will examine the basis for agency decisions as well as the procedures they undertake to make decisions. Such "hard look" review permits courts to engage in a rigorous examination of the substance of rulemaking by requiring an agency to build an adequate and fair record. Because environmental regulation is often complex and factually debatable, such record-making requirements impose significant limits to agency discretion even though the general rule is that courts give agencies wide latitude in formal rulemaking.

DUE PROCESS AS APPLIED TO PROPERTY RIGHTS

The Due Process Clause complements the Just Compensation Clause. Together, they ensure the protection of property rights against arbitrary deprivation, as well as just compensation when that deprivation occurs. When a state government takes private property, the right to just compensation is guaranteed by the Due Process Clause of the Fourteenth Amendment.

"Property" has been described by scholars in a variety of ways, reflecting concerns of pragmatism, justice, social function, and philosophy.[14] It is an uncontroversial, yet often unarticulated proposition that, in the absence of constitutional, statutory or common law rules, custom and usage may identify and create contract or property rights.[15,16]

The term "property" would appear to mean the same thing in both the Due Process and Just Compensation Clauses of the Fifth Amendment, although each area of the Amendment's jurisprudence developed separately. Recent cases recognized the relationship between the Due Process and Just Compensation Clauses. For example, in *Nixon v. United States*, the court defined former President Nixon's interest in his presidential papers for takings purposes.[17] The court drew upon the definitions of "property" in due process cases: "The essential character of property is that it is made up of mutually reinforcing understandings that are sufficiently well grounded to support a claim of entitlement."[18] These "mutually reinforcing understandings" can arise in a myriad of ways. For instance, state law may create entitlements through express or implied agreements, and property interests also may be created or reinforced through uniform custom and practice.

In the case of *Soldal v. Cook County, Ill.*, the Supreme Court confirmed the right of a mobile home owner to sue the county government for seizing his mobile home by removing it from the mobile home park without probable cause. The *Soldal* opinion affords an interesting, if untried, parallel to the "substantial advancement" test of *Nollan v. California Coastal Commission* for regulatory infringements on property rights under the Fifth Amendment. That is, what constitutes probable cause for the government to seize apples sprayed with Alar, a substance which subsequently proves to be benign? By what authority may the government seize shipments of grapes on the suspicion (erroneous, as it turns out) that they may be contaminated with cyanide? In order to seize imported computer chips manufactured with the use of ozone-depleting solvents, must the government demonstrate a nexus between environmental harm (*e.g.*, increased ultraviolet radiation at the earth's surface) and that manufacturing process?

The relationship between the Due Process and Just Compensation Clauses is also evident when government's restrictive orders affecting property owners pose constitutional problems regarding the boundaries of the restrictions. For example, Congress provided the Environmental Protection Agency (EPA) with the power to issue an order to stop the sale, use, or movement of a pesticide whenever there is reason to believe on the basis of inspections or tests that such pesticide or device is in violation of the Federal Insecticide, Fungicide, and Rodenticide Act (FIFRA). Since much of FIFRA is dedicated to procedural niceties, the "stop-sale" provision would appear to authorize the EPA to seize and destroy the entire stock of any product required to be registered under the statute, and to stop all future commerce in that product, on purely procedural grounds.

To add insult to injury, the EPA can require that the company store a pesticide for which a stop-sale order has been issued until the EPA is prepared to make arrangements for the disposal of the substance.[19] The Fourth Amendment's probable cause requirement, however, undoubtedly limits the reach of the stop-sale order, but the precise limitations imposed remain uncertain. Thus, in at least one case under FIFRA, a court invalidated as arbitrary and capricious an EPA decision to issue a stop-sale order.[20] Although the court did not base its decision on the theory of a Fourth Amendment violation, the lack of guidance FIFRA gives the EPA in issuing stop-sale orders resulted in the Court's finding. Similar constitutional problems can be posed by corrective action orders under RCRA, conditions placed upon Clear Air and Clear Water Act permits, and administrative cleanup orders issued under CERCLA.

DUE PROCESS AND UNREASONABLE DELAY

Perhaps the greatest threat to liberty and property interest in the environmental regulatory field is that of unreasonable delay. Failure to process a permit application, to approve a state implementation plan, to promulgate regulations, or to decide critical policy issues may destroy a constitutionally protected property or other liberty interest just as effectively as the denial of a pre-deprivation hearing. In its 1926 decision in *Smith v. Illinois Bell Telephone Co.*, the United States Supreme Court recognized that "long continued and unreasonable delay" by an agency may effectively deprive a party of his property in violation of the Constitution's Due Process guarantees.[21] Accordingly, courts have recognized the right of regulated persons to demand that government processes proceed with reasonable dispatch.

Whether unreasonable delay amounts to a violation of due process depends on the interests involved.[22] Under a test similar to that established by the United States Supreme Court in *Mathews v. Eldridge*, to analyze the government and private interests affected, courts must balance government interests such as administrative convenience against a complaining party's interest in a quick and efficient determination of his rights.[23] In *MCI Telecommunications Corp. v. FCC*, the Court compared the aggrieved party's interests in a rate-making by the Federal Communications Commission (FCC) to the policies that compel a "speedy" trial for criminal defendants or the implementation of civil decrees with "all deliberate speed."[24] The Court also noted that while "[t]hose situations generally involve protection of constitutional rights, . . . delay in the resolution of administrative proceedings can also deprive regulated entities, their competitors or the public of rights and economic opportunities without the due process the Constitution requires."[25] The court therefore remanded the case to the FCC to recom-mend a feasible schedule.

In delay cases, the plaintiff often argues that by unreasonably delaying a hearing, the agency has constructively denied the aggrieved party's right to a hearing.[26] Of course, one of the basic tenets of due process is that the deprivation of a protected interest requires a hearing in order to allow for sufficient fact-finding, reasoning, and fairness. Courts have long upheld the plaintiff's strong interests in a timely and meaningful hearing.[27] Moreover, in the administrative context, the APA will often specifically require a decision to be made in a "reasonable" time, creating a specific statutory right instead of the implicit constitutional right.

On the other hand, agencies may have important interests in managing their hearing schedules and otherwise allocating their resources. Thus, the issue becomes a determination of the "reasonableness" of the delay. The United States Supreme Court in *Smith v. Illinois Bell Telephone Co.* omitted any test of unreasonableness from its opinion, and the court in *MCI Telecommunications Corp. v. FCC* only marginally addressed the problem when it opined that a "rule of reason" governed the inquiry. Four years after *MCI*, however, the D.C. Circuit did fashion such a test in *Telecommunications Research and Action Center v. FCC [TRAC]*.[28] While the *TRAC* decision interpreted the word "reasonable" in the APA, such a test should apply in claims brought directly under the constitution as well.

The test in *TRAC* established a number of factors to aid in assessing whether an agency's delay was unreasonable. First, the time agencies take to make decisions must be governed by a "rule of reason," which is measured—where appropriate—by any timetable indicated by Congress in the enabling statute or otherwise. Second, courts must examine the consequences of an agency's delay. Economic harm is "clearly an important consideration and will, in some cases, justify court intervention."[29] Furthermore, delays that may be reasonable in the economic sphere are less tolerable when human health and welfare are at stake. Third, the court need not find any bad faith on the part of the agency, but only determine that the balance between an agency's need to delay decision making is outweighed by the nature and extent of interests prejudiced by the delay. Thus, while the complexity of the task, insufficient resources, and other agency explanations affect the reasonableness of the delay, such excuses are not always sufficient to justify lengthy delays. Each case of unreasonable delay is thus analyzed according to its own unique factors, and each case presents its own set of facts to consider.

Nevertheless, every intentional delay in the permitting process may not give rise to a constitutional claim [*PFZ v. Rodriguez*].[30] One court has even held that an agency's refusal to consider a building permit for over seven years was not a denial of due process, because the aggrieved party still had opportunities to seek redress through administrative and state judicial action. The facts of the case suggest the agency had and continued to deliberately delay processing the construction permit. The plaintiff in *PFZ* claimed that the delay of over seven years between submission of the original permit request and the filing of a complaint was a result of a deliberate decision by regulators to kill the project because of an increase in environmental concerns. Such cases suggest that courts will, at times, continue to avoid second-guessing agency procedures even where serious constitutional questions are raised.

SUBSTANTIVE DUE PROCESS AND PROPERTY RIGHTS

When the process afforded private property owners is unfair, or when local governments succumb to private biases or interests, then clearly the Due Process Clause is implicated. The Due Process Clause, quite simply, forbids all deprivations of property that are arbitrary, unreasonable, or violate fundamental principles of fairness.[31]

Moreover, the issue in a due process case is not whether the government has the power to "take" the property, but whether the deprivation of property has been accomplished in a manner violative of fundamental constitutional rights. In short, due process focuses upon the method by which land-use controls are imposed, while just compensation examines only the result of the process.

The United States Court of Appeals for the Ninth Circuit clearly set forth the basis for a due process cause of action in *Sinaloa Lake Owners Association v. City of Simi Valley*.[32]

> To establish a violation of substantive due process, [a plaintiff] must prove that the government's action was 'clearly arbitrary and unreasonable, having no substantial relation to the public health, safety, morals, or general welfare.' [33,34,35]

The court in *Sinaloa* recognized the overwhelming force represented by the government's police power, noting that such power is a double-edged sword; if wielded in an abusive, irrational or malicious fashion, it can cause grave harm. The *Sinaloa* court also stated that a decision that is simply wrong may not violate the Due Process Clause. Malicious, irrational, and plainly arbitrary actions are not within the legitimate purview of the state's power.

EQUAL PROTECTION AND PROPERTY RIGHTS

In various situations whereas an individual property owner is subject to arbitrary and unreasonable regulations that the public as a whole is exempt from, courts have enforced the property owner's right to equal protection so he does not alone bear the burden of the regulation.

In *Del Monte Dunes v. City of Monterey*[36], the court reversed the dismissal of plaintiff's equal protection claim, stating:

> The allegations, supported by affidavits, are adequate to state a claim if proved at trial. The allegations are that the City arbitrarily and unreasonably limited use and development of this property and set aside open space for public use, whereas owners of comparable property along

the Monterey Bay were not subjected to these conditions and restrictions.[37]

The *Del Monte Dunes* court went on to remind itself of the United States Supreme Court's holding in *Nollan v. California Coastal Commission*, that a property owner may not constitutionally be singled out to bear the burden of remedying a problem (such as lack of visual open space) to which he did not contribute disproportionately:

> If [particular property owners] were being singled out to bear the burden of California's attempt to remedy these problems, although they had not contributed to it more than other coastal landowners, the State's action, even if otherwise valid, might violate either the incorporated Takings Clause or the Equal Protection Clause.[38]

In *Fry v. City of Hayward*,[39] the plaintiff successfully stated a cause of action for denial of equal protection where her property, formerly a golf course, had been singled out by a city ordinance to remain as open space, while adjacent properties had been developed for residential and commercial purposes. Noting that "the record is devoid of any indication that Fry's property bears any unique characteristics that would warrant separate treatment,"[40] the *court* denied the City's Motion for Summary Judgment and granted Summary Judgment for the plaintiff. The court rejected the City's attempt to justify the open space requirement on environmental grounds: "Further, Fry obtained an environmental impact report indicating that development of the Golf Course would not have a detrimental effect on the region."[41]

Similarly in *Herrington v. County of Sonoma*,[42] the Ninth Circuit affirmed the jury's liability determination and award of injunctive relief for owners whose property had been down-sized to agricultural use, while similarly situated properties had been approved for residential development. Such disparate treatment of similarly situated properties constituted a denial of equal protection. The court stated "in regard to equal protection, the Herringtons showed that the county had approved sizable residential developments on three other agricultural properties shortly after it had rejected the Herrington proposal."[43]

FREEDOM FROM UNREASONABLE SEARCH AND SEIZURE

Before the American Revolution, many colonial subjects complained of the Crown's random ransacking of homes to search for any and all evidence of a crime. To protect against such practices in the newly formed United States, the framers of the Constitution drafted the Fourth Amendment, guaranteeing every citizen's right to privacy.[44] In *Frank v. Maryland*, the United States Supreme Court explained the rationale behind the Fourth Amendment, "because the necessary means of compelling self-accusation, falling upon the innocent as well as the guilty, would be both cruel and unjust; and it should seem, that search for evidence is disallowed upon the same principle. There too the innocent would be confounded with the guilty."[45]

In its Fourth Amendment jurisprudence, the Supreme Court has demarcated a broad range where individuals are guaranteed freedom from state action. In criminal cases, a person invokes the Amendment's protection by asserting that government evidence, obtained in violation of the right to be free from unreasonable searches or seizures, is inadmissible.[46] Criminal law applications, however, do not constitute the whole scope of Fourth Amendment protection; its strictures apply with equal force in the civil context.[47] The *Stanley v. Georgia* Court drew from Fourth Amendment jurisprudence to support its argument: "fundamental is the right to be free, except in very limited circumstances, from unwanted governmental intrusions into one's privacy."

In addition, the United States Supreme Court has unanimously affirmed that courts must interpret disjunctively the concepts of "search" and "seizure."[48] The Court emphasized that the concepts stand alone; that is, the Fourth Amendment protects against unreasonable seizures of property even where the government action does not implicate a privacy right. The Court believed that this reading mandated that "the [Fourth] Amendment protects property as well as privacy." The Court also made clear that, for Fourth Amendment purposes, a search occurs where the state infringes on a societally accepted privacy right, while a seizure takes place where the government "meaningful[ly] interferes with an individual's possessory interest in . . . property."[49]

Unreasonable Searches

In contrast to searches of homes, statutes which permit warrantless searches of commercial property for the purpose of "spot-checking" compliance with a regulatory scheme do not necessarily violate the Fourth Amendment.[50] The United States Supreme Court, however, has emphasized that the power of an administrative agency to conduct warrantless searches is not boundless. The restrictions are as follows: (1) Congress must have made rules governing the procedures that inspectors must follow, including the scope and frequency of inspections and which establishments to inspect, and (2) the subjected business must have a "long tradition of close governmental supervision" [*Dow Chemical Co. v. United States*]. As Justice Lewis Powell stated in *Dow Chemical*, the Court has never held that warrantless searches are generally acceptable under the Fourth Amendment. The agency need not have the same probable cause required in the criminal cases, but, where a regular scheme does not exist, a warrant is necessary in order to protect the owner from the "unbridled discretion [of] executive and administrative officers."[51] In the absence of this Fourth Amendment standard, the rule against arbitrary and capricious action would represent the only limitation on administrative searches.

Unreasonable Seizures

The Court has applied an even stricter standard to Fourth Amendment seizures. Although the Supreme Court decided that probable cause need not exist to conduct an administrative search, the Court has required more in the context of seizures.[52] A seizure occurs for purposes of the Fourth Amendment where "there is some meaningful interference with an individual's possessory interests in . . . property."[53] At the very least, in the absence of a warrant or consent, the government can justify seizures "only if they meet the probable cause standard . . . and if they are unaccompanied by unlawful trespass."[54] This standard applies even if the item seized is in plain view of the government agent.

Searches, Seizures, and Environmental Regulation

The protection of property rights guaranteed by the Fourth Amendment serves to shield against invasive searches and seizures that are sometimes authorized under environmental regulations. The Supreme Court traditionally has afforded substantial deference to congressionally adopted regulatory schemes that permit administrative searches and seizures as an integral part of the regulatory program. The assumption that the Court has made in these cases is two-fold: (1) that a highly regulated company, such as one subject to environmental regulation, has a diminished expectation of privacy, and (2) that the structure of a well-planned regulatory system will act as a surrogate for the protections guaranteed by the Fourth Amendment.[55] Even in such regulatory programs, however, the Constitution still stands between the regulatory body and its target.

ASSET FORFEITURE AND PROPERTY RIGHTS

Annually, the Department of Justice seizes approximately $1 billion worth of private property through its law enforcement actions. Of that, it retains $500 million.[56] Much of the money comes from asset forfeiture. Forfeiture is an important tool to fight crime, particularly organized crime and drug cartels. The theory behind asset forfeiture is that wrongdoers should not profit by their actions. The problem lies in the misuse of forfeiture by prosecutors.

Civil Forfeiture

The potential for abuse by the government is much greater in civil, as opposed to criminal, asset forfeiture cases. Operating under a civil asset forfeiture statute, the government may seize property without a hearing, operating merely on the belief that there is probable cause that the asset is contraband or a product of illegal behavior. The United States Supreme Court established the lower standard for civil asset forfeiture because the government is proceeding specifically against the property and not directly against the individual. A seeming unfairness arises when one observes that the owner must prove the noninvolvement of his property in the alleged enterprise using the preponderance of the evidence standard, and not the probable cause standard that applies to the government. Often deprived of assets of significant worth, owners are placed at a severe disadvantage in attempting to fully and fairly litigate their claims against the government.

Criminal Asset Forfeiture

Criminal asset forfeiture was not widely used until the passage of the Racketeer Influenced and Corrupt Act of 1970 (RICO). Under this and other criminal asset forfeiture statutes, the defendant receives the full benefit of criminal law protections. Additionally, the forfeiture is not performed without a hearing, but only done after a criminal trial results in a conviction. Therefore, asset forfeiture under criminal laws requires the government to first prove the guilt of the party beyond a reasonable doubt, and any subsequent forfeiture may be viewed as punishment for the crime.

Demonstrated by the United States Supreme Court's most recent criminal asset forfeiture case, seeming unfairness can occur when a third party is hurt by the forfeiture. In *Bennis v. Michigan*, a car that was jointly owned by a husband and wife was forfeited to the state when the husband was convicted for being involved with a prostitute in the automobile.[57] Ms. Bennis argued that she was denied due process because she was unaware of how her husband used the car.

Citing a "long and unbroken line of cases," the Supreme Court held that "property may be forfeited by reason of the use to which the property is put even though the owner did not know that it was to be put to such use."[58] Thus, the protections afforded a criminal defendant do not help a third party caught in an asset forfeiture case involving property used in criminal activity.

ENDNOTES

[1] *See Cafeteria Workers v. McElroy*, 367 U.S. 886, 895 (1961) ("Due process, unlike some legal rules, is not a technical conception with a fixed content unrelated to time, place, and circumstances.") (citations omitted).

[2] *Wolff v. McDonnell*, 418 U.S. 539, 557-58 (1974).

[3] *Joint Anti-Fascist Committee v. McGrath*, 341 U.S. 123, 168 (1951) (Frankfurter, J., concurring).

[4] *Armstrong v. Manzo*, 380 U.S. 545, 552 (1965).

[5] 397 U.S. 254, 266-71 (1970).

[6] 424 U.S. 319 (1976).

[7] *Id.*

[8] *Vermont Yankee Nuclear Power Corp. v. NRDC*, 435 U.S. 519, 524 (1977).

[9] *Id.*

[10] 950 F.2d 741 (D.C. Cir. 1991).

[11] *Id.*

[12] 947 F.2d 1201 (5th Cir. 1991).

[13] *Id.*

[14] *See generally* Frank I. Michelman, *Property, Utility, and Fairness: Comments on the Ethical Foundations of "Just Compensation" Law*, 80 HARV. L. REV. 1164 (1967).

[15] *See, e.g., First Victoria National Bank v. United States* ("law or custom may create property rights where none were earlier thought to exist"), 620 F.2d 1096, 1103 (1st Cir. 1980).

[16] *See also* Oliver W. Holmes, *The Path of the Law* (defining "property" as a thing used as such over an extended period of time; "[t]he law can ask no better justification"), 10 HARV. L. REV. 457, 477 (1897).

[17] 978 F.2d 1269 (D.C. Cir. 1992).
[18] *Id.*
[19] *Uniroyal v. Thomas*, 690 F. Supp. 593 (N.D. Ohio 1988).
[20] *Love v. Thomas*, 858 F.2d 1347 (9th Cir. 1988).
[21] 270 U.S. 587 (1926).
[22] *See, e.g., White v. Mathews*, 434 F. Supp. 1252, 1260-62 (D. Conn. 1976) *aff'd*, 559 F.2d 852, 858-60 (2d Cir. 1977) *cert. denied*, 435 U.S. 908 (1978) (stating that unreasonable, lengthy and persistent delays in disability appeals system contravened applicant's due process guarantees).
[23] *Air Line Pilots Association International v. Civil Aeronautics Board*, 750 F.2d 81 (D.C. Cir 1984).
[24] 627 F.2d 322 (1980).
[25] *Id.*
[26] *See, e.g., White v. Mathews* (lengthy and persistent delays in scheduling disability appeal hearings are unreasonable and deny due process rights to aggrieved party).
[27] *See Armstrong v. Manzo.*
[28] 750 F.2d 70 (D.C. Cir. 1984).
[29] *Cutler v. Hayes*, 818 F.2d 879, 898 (D.C. Cir. 1987).
[30] 729 F. Supp. 67 (D. Puerto Rico 1990).
[31] *DeBlasio v. Zoning Board of Adjustment*, 53 F.3d 592 (3d Cir. 1995).
[32] 882 F.2d 1398 (9th Cir. 1989).
[33] *Village of Euclid v. Ambler Realty Co.*, 272 U.S. 365, 395 (1926).
[34] *See Moore v. City of Cleveland*, 431 U.S. 494, 498 n.6 (1977).
[35] *Nectow v. City of Cambridge*, 277 U.S. 183 (1928).
[36] 920 F.2d 14967 (9th Cir. 1990).
[37] *Id.*
[38] *Id.*
[39] 701 F. Supp. 179 (N.D. Cal. 1988).
[40] *Id.*
[41] *Id.*
[42] 834 F.2d 1488 (9th Cir. 1987), *reh'g denied*, 857 F.2d 571 (9th Cir 1988).
[43] *Id.*
[44] *See Frank v. Maryland*, 359 U.S. 360, 363 (1959).
[45] *Id.* (citing *Entick v. Carrington*, 19 Howell's State Trials, col. 1029, 1073 (1765)).
[46] *See, e.g., Miranda v. Arizona*, 384 U.S. 436 (1966).

[47] *See, e.g., Stanley v. Georgia* (holding that the First Amendment protects the right of the individual to possess obscene materials in his or her home), 394 U.S. 557 (1969).
[48] *Soldal v. Cook County, Illinois*, 113 S. Ct. 538 (1992).
[49] *Soldal. (citing United States v. Jacobsen)*, 466 U.S. 109, 113 (1984).
[50] *Donovan v. Dewey*, 452 U.S. 594, 598 (1981).
[51] *Marshall v. Barlow's, Inc.*, 436 U.S. 307, 323 (1978).
[52] *Soldal v. Cook County, Ill.*
[53] *United States v. Jacobsen*, 466 U.S. 109, 113 (1984).
[54] *Soldal v. Cook County, Ill.*, 113 S. Ct. 538 (1992).
[55] *Dow Chemical Co. v. United States*, 476 U.S. 227 (1986).
[56] Linnet Meyers, *Ruling on Forfeitures is Bad News for the Guilty—and The Innocent*, CHICAGO TRIBUNE, March 12, 1996.
[57] 116 S. Ct. 994 (1996).
[58] *Id.*

Chapter 9

THE PRACTICAL DIFFICULTIES OF LITIGATING A TAKINGS CASE

The scales of justice are unfairly tipped in favor of the government when citizens are faced with the threat of losing their property due to regulatory burdens. Not only are the laws drafted to ease the litigation burden of the government, but the costs of takings litigation can range in the hundreds or thousands of dollars—too high for the average citizen to bear. Consequently, many citizens, when faced with a government takings claim, cannot pursue their rights under the Fifth Amendment. The government, on the other hand, does not face a similar shortage of resources (at least in comparison to the individual property owner) and can often pursue a vigorous defense of the case without constraint. Adding to the hardship, procedural hurdles often bar litigation on the merits of takings claims for anywhere from five to ten years.

The following are a few examples of reported cases that demonstrate how arduous and interminable the litigation of taking claims against the federal government can be:

On October 2, 1980, in the case of *Florida Rock Industries v. U.S.*, the company was denied a wetlands permit to mine limestone on its property in southern Florida. In 1982, the company filed suit against the federal government alleging an unconstitutional taking. Following a 1985 judgment in the company's favor, the government appealed and the case was reversed. In 1990, following another trial, the plaintiff won again, and the government appealed a second time. Again, the case was reversed in 1994. It is now pending yet a third trial. More than fourteen years after the original permit denial, the company is still waiting to be paid for the taking.

In 1983, the federal government placed groundwater monitoring wells on land owned by Mr. Hendler in southern California, and issued various orders forbidding certain uses of the property. In September of 1984, Mr. Hendler filed suit against the federal government alleging a taking and, after five years of bitter litigation, the case was dismissed in December 1989. Mr. Hendler appealed, and the case was reversed by the Court of Federal Appeals for the Federal Circuit in the summer of 1991. The matter is still in litigation, more than thirteen years after the government first physically invaded Hendler's property.

In January 1979, the Whitney Benefits Corporation was denied a permit to mine coal on its land in Wyoming. The company filed suit in the Claims Court in August 1983, and the case was dismissed the next year. In January 1985, the Court of Appeals reversed the dismissal and, following several years of litigation, the trial court entered judgment in favor of the plaintiff in October 1989. That judgment was affirmed in 1991, but has been followed by four more years of motions. Thus, more than sixteen years after the permit denial, Whitney Benefits has not yet received payment for the taking.

In May 1982, Loveladies Harbor, Inc. was denied a wetlands permit to develop property it owned in New Jersey and filed suit in the Claims Court in April 1983. After extensive litigation in both the Federal District Court and the Claims Court, the plaintiff was awarded judgment in 1990. The government appealed, then moved to dismiss the appeal. Finally, in 1994, the Court of Appeals for the Federal Circuit affirmed the judgment for the plaintiff—more than twelve years after the original permit denial.

CHOOSING THE RIGHT COURT:
STATE VERSUS FEDERAL

In *Williamson County Regional Planning Commission v. Hamilton Bank*,[1] the Supreme Court held that a claim was not ripe for federal court review if 1) the property owner had not obtained a "final decision" from the applicable administrative agency; and 2) the property owner had not first filed the claim in state court to challenge the government action. The Court stated that the second prong of its ripeness requirement was based on the Just Compensation Clause itself: "The nature of the constitutional right therefore requires that a property owner utilize procedures for obtaining compensation before bringing a Section 1983 action."[2]

Although requiring petitioners to start all over again plays right into the governmental defendant's litigation gamesmanship, many courts rigidly apply the second prong of *Williamson County* and dismiss cases as unripe. In *Reahard v. Lee County*,[3] the plaintiffs originally filed their lawsuit in the Twentieth Judicial Circuit Court of Florida in September of 1989. Subsequently, the governmental defendant voluntarily and intentionally removed the case from state to federal court, asserting that a federal question existed—*i.e.*, whether a Fifth Amendment taking requiring just compensation had occurred. It was not until after the case had been tried twice and appealed twice that the governmental defendant asserted that the case should have been tried first in state court. In holding that the case was not ripe, the *Reahard* court never explained why the initial filing of the lawsuit in state court did not satisfy the second prong of *Williamson County*. The result of this application of *Williamson County* is a ripeness standard that disregards the prudential concerns of the ripeness doctrine, and instead leads to gamesmanship and protracted litigation.

To avoid the technical trap of *Williamson County*'s second prong, some federal judges have allowed plaintiffs to plead their claims as something other than a takings claim. For example, a federal judge in Colorado recently refused to dismiss a lawsuit, concluding that the second prong of *Williamson County* did not bar property owners from going forward with their claim for money damages because the plaintiffs had alleged a "conspiracy" to take their property, not the actual "taking" of their property [*Oberndorf v. City of Denver*].[4] The judge noted that "if plaintiffs seek just compensation through inverse condemnation proceedings, then the objective, which defendants' conspiracy was designed to achieve, would be realized."[5] The *Oberndorf* court continued:

> This last point is key. If plaintiffs now execute their state court remedy, as defendants suggest, then they would be playing right into the scheme defendants [the government] have allegedly constructed. There are no further steps available to plaintiffs which might relieve them of the burdens created by the Urban Renewal Plan.[6]

Similarly, in *Simaloa Lake Owners Ass'n v. City of Simi Valley*,[7] the Ninth Circuit Court of Appeals avoided rewarding the government for failing to raise the ripeness issue in a timely fashion. Although the case was dismissed as unripe under *Williamson County* after six years of litigation because of the failure of the property owner to bring the case in state court, the court expressed dismay over the use of *Williamson County* as a delaying tactic. "Plaintiffs filed this lawsuit in December, 1983, yet it was not until May, 1986, one month before trial was to begin, that defendants first raised a ripeness challenge. It is clear they knew from the beginning that plaintiffs had not exhausted their state compensation remedies."[8] The solution arrived at by the court was to allow the plaintiffs to amend their federal complaint on remand to include a pendant state law takings claim. This would allow the district court judge to ascertain whether the state would afford the plaintiff just compensation as a pendant state claim.

If the plaintiff attempts to avoid a government ripeness challenge and first pursues a remedy for the takings claim in state court, the doctrine of *res judicata* would bar the plaintiff from raising the same claim in federal court. The doctrine of *res judicata* precludes parties from relitigating a claim that has received final judgment by a court of proper jurisdiction. Thus, potential takings claimants are presented with a Catch-22; either file their claim directly in federal court and risk the case's dismissal as unripe, or file the claim in state court and be barred from the federal court due to *res judicata*.[9]

A recent case in the Ninth Circuit Federal Court of Appeals offers takings litigants some hope of a judicial resolution of this dilemma. In *Dodd v. Hood River County*, the court held that the *Williamson County* state court remedy requirement had to be restricted to remedies available under state law.[10] In acknowledgment that *res judicata* would bar the federal review of constitutional issues already considered by a state court, the court stated, "The Fifth Amendment action is not more 'developed' or 'ripened' through presentation of the ultimate issue—the failure of a state to provide adequate compensation for a taking—to the state court. Indeed, such a requirement would not ripen the claim, rather it would extinguish the claim."[11] The court further resolved that in light of the difficulties encountered by litigants seeking to assert the Just Compensation Clause's guarantee, it was satisfied that the Supreme Court's ripeness requirements "may not be interpreted to command such a revolutionary concept and dacronian result."[12] The court concluded that it would be improper to interpret the Supreme Court's desire for ripe and final state decisions as a bar to federal court review of potential takings by a state.

It is arguable that the evolved state of takings jurisprudence in the ten years since the *Williamson County* decision brings the absolute nature of the strict, two-prong test into question. When *Williamson County* was decided in 1985, there were many unanswered questions in takings law. Chief among these were 1) whether a temporary taking was compensable under the Fifth Amendment; and 2) whether invalidation of the government action was the only remedy for a regulatory taking. Thus, the requirement that a plaintiff first litigate his case in state court before filing it in federal court reflected, in part, these uncertainties in the law. In 1987, however, the Court answered both of these questions, making clear that the plaintiff had a case for just compensation under the Fifth Amendment at the time the ordinance was passed in addition to the state court remedy for invalidation.[13] Therefore, a blanket requirement that a plaintiff bring a takings claim as a state action before a federal one fails to recognize the central concern of the ripeness bar: whether the case involves uncertain or contingent future events that may not occur as anticipated, or indeed may not occur at all.[14]

CHOOSING THE RIGHT FEDERAL COURT: DISTRICT COURT VERSUS COURT OF FEDERAL CLAIMS

The Just Compensation Clause of the Fifth Amendment contains the only express money damages remedy in the Constitution. Unlike most state judicial systems, the federal system divides the jurisdiction to decide Fifth Amendment claims between two separate courts. 28 U.S.C. Section 1331 provides that all questions under the Constitution and laws of the United States be decided in federal district court. In contrast, the Tucker Act removes all constitutional claims against the United States for money damages greater than $10,000 not founded on tort to the Court of Federal Claims.[15] The Tucker Act provides:

> The United States Claims Court shall have jurisdiction to render judgment upon any claim against the United States founded either upon the Constitution, or any Act of Congress or any regulation of an executive department, or upon any express or implied contract with the United States, or for liquidated or unliquidated damages in cases not sounding in tort.[16]

The result of this joint jurisdiction is that a property owner with a claim for just compensation must decide whether he will pursue his rights in one or more federal courts because no single court has broad enough jurisdiction to grant both monetary and equitable relief. To the extent that a property owner desires to invalidate the government's action—relief which is equitable in nature—his choice must be the federal district court. On the other hand, if the property owner desires to be compensated for the amount of money lost due to the regulation or other governmental acts, the claimant's remedy will only lie in the Court of Federal Claims. If, however, the owner wishes to seek injunctive relief against the government action and seek compensation for the value of his property already taken, at the same time he must bring separate suits in both courts.

CHOOSING A CLAIM: FACIAL VERSUS APPLIED CHALLENGES

Constitutional challenges to a government taking may be either "facial" or "as applied." A facial challenge argues that the government action by itself constitutes a taking. The less stringent "as applied" challenge must allege that the government action resulted in a specific injury to the plaintiff's property.

The United States Supreme Court declared in *Lucas v. South Carolina Coastal Council* that a taking claim that challenges the government's action as a violation of the Constitution "on its face" requires the plaintiff to prove that all economically viable use of the property was taken. *Lucas* also admonished potential litigants that, in the view of the Court, the occurrence of a complete deprivation was relatively uncommon. In *Keystone Bituminous Coal Association v. DeBenedictis*, the Court stated that takings litigants who bring a facial claim "face an uphill battle in making a facial attack" on the government action.[17] Further, a review of the takings cases brought before the Supreme Court illustrates the lack of success litigants have had in bringing Fifth Amendment facial challenges to a government action.[18] Faced with this judicial reception, common sense tells us that a facial challenge, proving that government action resulted in a total deprivation of *all* economically viable use of a parcel of property, will be an arduous, if not impossible, task.

In contrast, an "as applied" taking challenge does not require a similarly stringent level of proof to be successful. Reviewing an applied taking challenge requires a court to engage in an analysis that weighs the public and private interests to determine the constitutionality of the government action. In other words, the court will examine whether the government action results in a unconstitutional taking as applied to the specific piece of property of the litigant.[19] When both options are available, an applied challenge is to be preferred.

RIPENING THE CLAIM

In the landmark case of *Abbott Labs v. Gardner*, the Supreme Court explained that the purpose of the ripeness doctrine:

> is to prevent the courts, through avoidance of premature adjudication, from entangling themselves in abstract disagreements over administrative policies, and also to protect the agencies from judicial interference until an administrative decision has been formalized and its effects felt in concrete way by challenging parties.[20]

The *Abbott Labs* Court added, "the problem is best seen in a twofold aspect, requiring us to evaluate both the fitness of the issues for judicial decision and the hardship to the parties of withholding court consideration."[21] Thus, the ripeness doctrine has not generally been treated by the Court as a jurisdictional or strict procedural and mechanistic requirement mandating the trial and retrial of issues in multiple courts as a prelude to vindicating constitutionally protected rights. Professor Marla E. Mansfield states, quoting *Joint Anti-Fascist Refugee Committee v. McGrath*:[22]

> Justice Frankfurter's concurrence is telling. Despite his many opinions closing the courthouse door, he emphasized that '[f]inality is not . . . a principle inflexibly applied.' Crucial elements to consider include the probability that the plaintiff will be impacted and the burden created by procedures that exist for challenging the ultimate action.[23]

The praticality of the *Abbott Labs* ripeness doctrine is reflected in *Lucas v. South Carolina Coastal Council*.[24] In *Lucas*, the United States Supreme Court rejected the government's argument to apply the two-prong ripeness test of *Williamson County* requiring a final decision by an administrative agency and that such claims be filed first with state court. *Lucas* Court reexamined the requirements of *Williamson County* in light of recent amendments to the specific statute at issue. The amendments set up a variance process that, if applicable to the petitioner, would require the petitioner to apply for a variance and start all over again. In rejecting this course of action, the Court stated the case was ripe and "neither 'prudence' nor any other principle of judicial restraint requires that we remand. . . ."[25]

EXHAUSTING ADMINISTRATIVE REMEDIES

The necessity of exhausting all administrative options requires a litigant to have no remaining alternative but judicial review. In the takings context, the United States Supreme Court requires courts to examine whether the plaintiff exhausted his administrative remedies under the first prong of the *Williamson County* test. For example, a plaintiff may not immediately sue for a taking when his property is rezoned to prohibit the building of a structure the plaintiff desires. The plaintiff must first, if available, appeal the zoning restriction through the appropriate administrative channels before filing suit. The purpose of the exhaustion doctrine is to prevent the dockets of the judiciary from overflowing with takings claims due to a government action that an administrative appellate procedure might have overturned (or granted a variance if it was appealed).

STATUTE OF LIMITATIONS

There is no basis in the Fifth Amendment for holding that just compensation claims can be extinguished by a legislatively created time bar, particularly if the time limit is supplied by a brief administrative appeal period.[26] The Fifth Amendment of the United States Constitution contains no limitation or exception for its guarantee that when private property rights are taken for public use, just compensation must be paid to the owner: "[N]or shall private property be taken for public use, without just compensation."[27]

The obligation for just compensation attaches whenever government action works a taking of private property.[28] This constitutional obligation is so evident that the Supreme Court has held that an aggrieved property owner need not look to a statute or other legislative authorization in order to obtain the remedy of just compensation he is entitled.[29] As Justice William Brennan articulately explained in his dissenting opinion in *San Diego Gas & Electric Co. v. City of San Diego*, "This Court has consistently recognized that the just compensation requirement in the Fifth Amendment is not precatory: once there is a 'taking,' compensation *must* be awarded."[30] Justice Brennan concluded his opinion with the further observation that "the applicability of express constitutional guarantees is not a matter to be determined on the basis of policy judgments made by the legislative, executive or judicial branches."[31]

The most powerful analysis of the Fifth Amendment guarantee that individual rights are protected from confiscation by a statute passed by the sovereign is contained in *Jacobs v. United States*.[32] In *Jacobs*, the Court reviewed the constitutionality of a lower court's decision which held that interest was not recoverable on a property owner's claim for just compensation because the statute under which suit was brought did not authorize the payment of interest. The *Jacobs* Court rejected the lower court's conclusion that one's constitutional right to just compensation could be limited by statute:

> This ruling cannot be sustained. The suits were based on the right to recover just compensation for property taken by the United States for public use in the exercise of its power of eminent domain. That right was guaranteed by the Constitution. . . . The form of the remedy did not qualify the right. It rested upon the Fifth Amendment. Statutory recognition was not necessary. . . . The suits

> were . . . founded upon the Constitution of the United States. The amount recoverable was just compensation, not inadequate compensation. The concept of just compensation is comprehensive and includes all elements, 'and no specific command to include interest is necessary when interest or its equivalent is a part of such compensation.' The owner is not limited to the value of the property at the time of the taking; 'he is entitled to such addition as will produce the full equivalent of that value paid contemporaneously with the taking.'[33]

The *Jacobs* Court realized that to fulfill the constitutional promise of just compensation, that right cannot be taken away or qualified by statutory whim. The *Jacobs* decision gives credence to the constitutional guarantee considered essential "in a free government" wherein "almost all other rights would become worthless if the government possessed an uncontrollable power over the private fortune of every citizen."[34]

This Court has in other contexts similarly rejected attempts to limit the right of just compensation contained in the Fifth Amendment. In *First English Evangelical Lutheran Church of Glendale v. County of Los Angeles, California*, the Court flatly rejected the government's contention that the just compensation clause serves only as a limitation on the power of government and is not of itself a remedial provision:

> The cases cited in the text we think, refute the argument of the United States that 'the Constitution does not, of its own force, furnish a basis for a court to award money damages against the government. Though arising in various factual and jurisdictional settings, these cases make clear that it is the Constitution that dictates the remedy for interference with property rights amounting to a taking.'[35]

Given the explicit nature of the Just Compensation Clause and the long history of this Court's decisions which have maintained its vitality against attempts to legislatively limit it, it would seem anomalous to conclude that a cause of action can be extinguished on the basis of a statutory time limitation. This is not to say that statutes of limitation do not serve valid procedural interests in other contexts. Where the cause of action is created by statute or in instances involving a waiver of sovereign immunity, prudential concerns of screening out stale claims and putting a limit upon how long a defendant may be subject to a claim are legitimate. However, when a claim is based directly on an express provision of the Constitution, such limitations can only be viewed as substantive in effect because they extinguish both the right and the remedy for claims of just compensation.

ENDNOTES

[1] 473 U.S. 172 (1985).
[2] *Id.*
[3] 30 F.3d 1412 (11th Cir. 1994).
[4] 653 F. Supp. 304 (D. Colo. 1986).
[5] *Id.*
[6] *Id.*
[7] 882 F.2d 1398 (9th Cir. 1989).
[8] *Id.*
[9] 59 F.3d 852 (9th Cir. 1995).
[10] *See infra* Chapter 10.
[11] 59 F.3d 852, 860 (9th Cir., 1995).
[12] *Id.*
[13] *First English Evangelical Lutheran Church of Glendale v. County of Los Angeles*, 482 U.S. 304 (1987).
[14] 13A Charles A. Wright & Arthur R. Miller, Federal Practice and Procedure § 3532, at 126 (citing *Thomas v. Union Carbide Agr. Prods. Co.*, 473 U.S. 568, 580 (1985)).
[15] 28 U.S.C. § 1491(a)(1) (1988).
[16] *Id.*
[17] 480 U.S. 470 (1987).

[18] *See, e.g., Hodel v. Virginia Surface Mining & Reclamation Association*, 452 U.S. 264 (1981).
[19] *Penn Central v. City of New York.*
[20] 387 U.S. 136, 148-49 (1967).
[21] *Id.*
[22] 341 U.S. 123, 156 (1951) (Frankfurter, J., concurring).
[23] Marla E. Mansfield, *Standing and Ripeness Revisited: The Supreme Court's "Hypothetical" Barriers*, 68 N.D. L. REV. 1, 21-22 (1992).
[24] 112 S. Ct. 2886 (1992).
[25] *Id.*
[26] *Hensler v. City of Glendale*, 8 Cal.4th 1 (1994).
[27] U. S. CONST. AMEND. V.
[28] *Armstrong v. United States*, 364 U.S. 40, 49 (1960).
[29] *See, e.g., First English Evangelical Lutheran Church of Glendale v. County of Los Angeles.*
[30] 459 U.S. 621, 654 (1981).
[31] *Id.*
[32] 290 U.S. 13 (1933).
[33] *Id.*
[34] *Id.*
[35] 482 U.S. 304 (1987).

Chapter 10

DEVELOPING ISSUES REGARDING WHAT IS A TAKING

UNREASONABLE DELAY AS A TAKING

Unreasonable delay by an agency may, in and of itself, constitute a taking of private property. The notion encompasses two distinct claims. First, agency delay might deprive a party of a statutory "right to timely decision making."[1] The statutory duty under such a claim does not specify what course of action the agency must take, only that it must not unreasonably delay that action. Generally, agencies must exercise timely decision making due to the Administrative Procedure Act's broad prohibition against "unreasonable delay." Secondly, the agency's enabling statute may impose a duty of timeliness by either expressly imposing a deadline, exhorting timely behavior, or contemplating final action within a reasonable amount of time. The second group of "unreasonable delay" claims occurs when delay deprives a party of a right granted to it by Congress. For example, in analyzing the undue length of rate proceedings conducted by the Federal Communication Commission, one court found that an unreasonable delay in setting "just and reasonable" rates deprives ratepayers of their statutory right to such rates.[2]

In all instances, courts must examine the consequences of the agency's delay. Economic harm is "clearly an important consideration and will, in some cases, justify court intervention."[3] Furthermore, delays that might be reasonable in the sphere of economic regulation are less tolerable when human health and welfare are at stake.

Finally, courts need not find any "impropriety lurking behind agency lassitude in order to hold that agency action is 'unreasonably delayed.'"[4] Consequently, although the complexity of the task, insufficient resources, and other agency explanations affect the reasonableness of the delay, those excuses are not always sufficient to justify lengthy delays. Rather, justifications for delay must always be balanced against the nature and extent of the interests prejudiced by delay.[5] Moreover, while courts should consider the effect of expediting delayed action upon agency activities of a higher or competing priority, a lack of alternative means of eliminating or reducing a hazard adds to the finding that the delay is unreasonable.[6]

Each case of unreasonable delay must be analyzed according to its own unique circumstances; each case will present its own slightly different set of factors to consider.[7]

PARTIAL TAKINGS

"Partial takings" is a term that has grown up in the context of regulatory takings. Essentially, it refers to instances where the government takes less than the entire bundle of ownership rights. The property taken may be the property's value or a discrete component or unit of a larger parcel of land. Conceptually, there is no distinction between property taken by regulation and the government's condemnation of property through the exercise of the power of eminent domain. No matter how the basic entitlements contained within the bundle of ownership rights are divided and no matter how many times the division takes place, if property rights are taken, then the duty to compensate the owner is triggered.

Diminution in Value

One area of contention is whether a diminution of less than one hundred percent of the property's value due to regulatory action violates the Fifth Amendment. While the United States Supreme Court has yet to rule on this specific issue, a principled framework for analysis was provided by the United States Court of Appeals for the Federal Circuit. In *Florida Rock Industries, Inc. v. United States*, the Federal Circuit reviewed a case where a company purchased 1,560 acres of land west of suburban Miami in 1972 with the intent of mining the limestone found beneath it.[8] The United States Army Corps of Engineers, enforcing the Clean Water Act (passed after the purchase of the land), issued a cease-and-desist order against any mining operation. The company stopped mining, restored the wetlands, and applied for a permit to continue mining on 98 acres—the maximum area the Corps would consider for a permit. In 1980, the Corps denied the company's permit to resume operations, prompting Florida Rock to file suit against the government.

On appeal, the Federal Circuit ruled against the property owner on the issue of the property's value, holding that the property still retained some value contrary to the lower court's holding. However, the court set forth the proper takings analysis for property that retains partial value. Finding no logical distinction between the taking of the entire parcel—which is clearly compensable under *Lucas v. South Carolina Coastal Council*—and the taking of less than the full value of a parcel, the court stated:

> Logically, the amount of just compensation should be proportional to the value of the interest taken . . . whether the taking is by physical occupation for the public to use as a park, or by regulatory imposition to preserve the property as a wetland so that it maybe used by the public for ground water recharge and other ecological purposes.[9]

Relevant Parcel

Likewise, some question remains as to whether the taking of only a portion of a larger parcel of land is compensable. While the United States Supreme Court has yet to rule on this issue, the United States Court of Appeals for the Federal Circuit did so in *Loveladies Harbor,*

Inc. v. United States.[10] In *Loveladies Harbor*, investors bought 250 acres of undeveloped land in 1958 in Long Beach Township, New Jersey. The sole purpose of purchasing the land was to create a housing development. By 1982, 199 acres were developed. State and federal wetland regulations enacted in the 1970s barred the investors from developing the remaining fifty-one acres. After applying for and being denied a state permit to develop the remaining acreage, the investors reached a compromise with the state to develop 12.5 acres in exchange for creating the same amount of wetland elsewhere. The United States Army Corps of Engineers, however, rejected the plan. The investors filed suit, alleging that the refusal of the Army Corps to grant them a wetland permit violated the Fifth Amendment.

On appeal, the Federal Circuit held that the government had in fact violated the Fifth Amendment for failing to compensate the owners for the taking of the 12.5 acres. The court stated that although the 12.5 acres constituted only a part of the original property, it was the basis for determining whether the owner was deprived of "all economically beneficial use" of the property.

RES JUDICATA

In an effort to win takings litigation at the procedural stage, the government often argues that a claim is not ripe for review or that the plaintiff failed to exhaust all administrative remedies.[11] The contention that a case must be dismissed as unripe is often raised when a litigant has not pursued a remedy in state court before bringing an action in federal court.[12] However, due to the doctrine of *res judicata*, if a plaintiff pursued the takings claim in state court, the plaintiff would be barred from raising the same claim in federal court. Thus, potential takings claimants are presented with a Catch-22: either file their claim directly in federal court and risk the case's dismissal as unripe, or file the claim in state court and be barred from federal court due to *res judicata*.

A recent case in the Ninth Circuit Federal Court of Appeals offers takings litigants some hope of a judicial resolution to this dilemma.

In *Dodd v. Hood River County*, the court rejected the idea that the Supreme Court's ripeness requirement acts to deny a claimant a federal forum due to *res judicata*.[13] The court acknowledged that, with a few exceptions, case law prohibits federal courts from reviewing state court determinations of the same constitutional issues. However, while attempting to resolve the problem this creates for litigants seeking to assert the Just Compensation Clause's guarantee, the court stated that it was satisfied that the Supreme Court's ripeness requirements "may not be interpreted to command such a revolutionary concept and draconian result."[14] The court concluded that it would be improper to interpret the Supreme Court's desire for ripe and final state decisions as a bar to federal court review of potential takings by a state.

ENDNOTES

[1] *Sierra Club v. Thomas*, 828 F.2d 783, 794 (D.C. Cir. 1987).
[2] *Telecommunications Research and Action Center v. FCC* (*TRAC*), 750 F.2d 70, 80-81 (D.C. Cir. 1984). *See also Nader v. FCC*, 520 F.2d 182, 206 (D.C. Cir. 1975).
[3] *Cutler v. Hayes*, 818 F.2d 879, 898 (D.C. Cir. 1987).
[4] *Public Citizen Health Research Group v. FDA*, 740 F.2d 21, 34 (D.C. Cir. 1982).
[5] *Cutler*.
[6] *TRAC*; *Cutler*.
[7] *Air Line Pilots Association International v. Civil Aeronautics Board*, 750 F.2d 81, 86 (D.C. Cir. 1984).
[8] 91 F.2d 893 (Fed Cir. 1986), *cert. denied* 479 U.S. 1053 (1987).
[9] *Id*.
[10] 27 F.3d 1545 (Fed. Cir. 1994) (en banc).
[11] *See* Chapter 9.
[12] *See, e.g., Mission Oaks Mobile Home Park v. City of Hollister*, 989 F.2d 359, 361 (9th Cir. 1993).
[13] 59 F.3d 852 (9th Cir. 1995).
[14] *Id*.

Chapter 11

LEGISLATIVE SOLUTIONS TO THE PROPERTY RIGHTS PROBLEM

Is Property Rights Legislation Needed?

The Fifth Amendment provides that, when private property is taken for public use, the owner must be justly compensated, no matter how important the government objective. Yet, more and more, our federal, state, and local governments are regulating property and, in turn, destroying private property rights. As a result, countless individuals all across the country are being singled out to bear the cost of implementing policies that the government is unwilling or unable to pay for itself. As discussed earlier, the Constitution prohibits such government takings unless the property owner is justly compensated.

Through its ability to regulate, government "takes" these uses and benefits to property it needs, but because title to the property stays with the owner, the government often refuses to pay for it on the grounds that no taking has occurred. For example, through the wetlands regulatory regime, over 100 million acres of land in this country must remain in its natural condition. Indeed, Congress itself has never passed legislation defining what constitutes a wetland. Yet seventy-five percent of all wetland in this country is privately owned. The unlucky owner of wetland must leave his property untouched—or create new wetlands to mitigate against the use of the current wetlands—but will rarely receive any compensation from the government. Similarly, the protection of endangered species habitat locks up additional millions of acres of privately owned land across the country. Laws governing mining, manufacturing, home building, forestry, agriculture, coastlines, historic buildings, and a host of other social environmental issues may result in the transfer of private property rights to the public without compensation, in violation of the Fifth and Fourteenth Amendments.

Despite recent landmark rulings, the application of the Just Compensation Clause to claims of regulatory taking remains an uncertain, *ad hoc* enterprise whose outcome is heavily dependent upon the judge drawn and the facts of the particular case. As Justice William Brennan summed it up in an oft-quoted passage:

> While this Court has recognized that the "Fifth Amendment's guarantee . . . [is] designed to bar Government from forcing some people alone to bear public burdens which, in all fairness and justice, should be borne by the public as a whole," this Court, quite simply, has been unable to develop any "set formula" for determining when "justice and fairness" require that economic injuries caused by public action be compensated by the government, rather than remain disproportionately concentrated on a few persons. Indeed, we have frequently observed that whether a particular restriction will be rendered invalid by the government's failure to pay for any losses proximately caused by it depends largely "upon the particular circumstances [in that] case." *San Diego Gas & Electric Co. v. San Diego.* Moreover, it is still the exception rather than the rule that a property owner prevails in a regulatory takings case.[1]

The scales of justice are also unfairly tipped in favor of the government when citizens are faced with the threat of losing their property because of regulatory burdens. Not only are the laws drafted to ease the litigation burden of the government, but the cost of takings litigation can range from $50,000 to $500,000 or more—too great a burden for the average citizen to bear. The government, on the other hand, does not face a similar shortage of resources (at least in comparison to the individual property owner), and can often pursue the taking without constraint. Adding to the hardship, procedural hurdles bar litigation on the merits of takings claims for anywhere from five to ten years. Consequently, takings litigation today is a long and arduous process which only the most well-financed and dedicated property owner can endure. Thus, when presented with an opportunity to sue for compensation, many property owners will not or can not vindicate their rights under the Fifth Amendment.

To address this problem, legislation has been introduced in Congress to help more clearly define those government actions which will result in a compensable taking. Some states have gone even further. They have introduced bills which would ease the litigation burden facing both the state and the property owner by passing "compensation" legislation that specifically enumerates when compensable takings have occurred.

The federal government vigorously opposes such legislation, arguing that the present system is adequate to protect private property rights. The Associate Attorney General of the United States, John R. Schmidt, testified before Congress in 1995 that the government honors property rights.[2] "The right to own, use and enjoy private property is at the very core of our nation's heritage and our continued economic strength. Those rights must be protected from interference by both private individuals and protecting governments."[3] He went on to testify that current constitutional protections, as well as administrative ones, were adequate to protect private property rights.

Nevertheless, Chief Judge Loren Smith of the United States Court of Federal Claims—the court that is responsible for hearing all compensation cases brought against the United States government—has eloquently described the limitations of the court's ability to provide the detailed and definitive rules necessary to determine when compensation is due under each of the complex federal regulatory schemes.

> No set formula exists to determine whether compensation is constitutionally due for a government restriction on property. What emerges from the case law at a consti-

tutional minimum is that under the guise of regulation government cannot take from a property owner the core value of the property, leaving the owner with only a hollow deed. Nor can it force a discrete minority or single individual to bear the costs of public goods that should be borne by society as a whole.[4]

FEDERAL EXECUTIVE AND LEGISLATIVE ATTEMPTS TO PROTECT PROPERTY RIGHTS

Federal Executive Order—12630

During the 1987 term, the United States Supreme Court handed down a trilogy of decisions which redefined takings jurisprudence. One of the cases ruled for the first time that a regulatory taking required monetary compensation under the Constitution.[5] Theretofore, invalidation of the regulation causing the harm had been the only remedy available for a regulatory taking in at least most state courts. New requirements in Supreme Court cases such as *Nollan v. California Coastal Commission*, which stipulated that a regulation substantially relate to the asserted interest in health or safety and that the injury to the party pursuing compensation be proportional to the overall benefit that the regulation confers, helped refine the definition of what constitutes a taking. During the same term, the Court also decided *Hodel v. Irving*, holding that a statute depriving Indians of the right to inherit certain property constituted a taking of property without just compensation.[6] In light of these important developments in property rights law, the Executive Branch realized that changes in the administration of federal environmental regulations were necessary. Consequently, President Ronald Reagan issued Executive Order 12630 on March 15, 1988, imposing a new duty upon government agencies to protect property rights in the course of administering their regulatory programs.

Origins of the Executive Order

At the time of these landmark Supreme Court decisions, more than $1 billion in takings claims were pending against the federal government. For the most part, the plaintiffs in these actions did not challenge the right of the federal government to enact stringent environmental protections; rather, they asserted that the regulatory scheme in question had "taken" their property, thereby entitling them to just compensation under the Constitution. Through the Executive Order, the government hoped to be able to identify takings implications from the outset, and thus avoid regulatory takings. The Reagan administration's Order sought to formulate a policy to address the growing concern that the federal government must minimize governmental intrusion upon private property rights, and institute a budgetary planning process to pay just compensation when such intrusions occurred.

The coming of the Executive Order was foretold in President Reagan's State of the Union address of January 25, 1988. Embracing the Supreme Court's decisions, which, in large part, had adopted the position set forth in the government's *amicus* briefs in two previous cases, the President said:

> It was an axiom of our Founding Fathers and free Englishmen before them that the right to own and control property was the foundation of all other individual liberties. To protect these rights, the Administration has urged the courts to restore the constitutional right of a citizen to receive just compensation when government at any level takes private property through regulation or other means.
>
> Last spring, the Supreme Court adopted this view in *Nollan v. California Coastal Commission*. In a second case, the Court held that the Fifth Amendment requires government to compensate citizens for temporary losses that occur while they are challenging such a government regulatory "taking" in court.

In the wake of these decisions, this Administration is now implementing new procedures to ensure that federal regulations do not violate the Fifth Amendment prohibition on taking private property; or if they take a citizen's property for public use, to ensure that he receives constitutionally required just compensation.[7]

The Executive Order draws heavily upon the regulatory coordination function of the Office of Management and Budget. Threads of the environmental assessment process under the National Environmental Policy Act are woven into the fabric of this Order, as are aspects of the budgetary planning process. The Order reflected thoughtful consideration and vigorous debate throughout the affected government agencies, and established a practical and workable procedure for implementing the holdings in *Nollan* and *First English*.

Framework of the Executive Order

The legitimacy of the Executive Order is premised both upon the duty of the government to respect constitutional protections afforded by the Bill of Rights and upon the management principle that government should not undertake programs without knowing and planning for their potential costs:

> Responsible fiscal management and fundamental principles of good government require that government decision-makers evaluate carefully the effect of their administrative, regulatory, and legislative actions on constitutionally protected property rights. Executive departments and agencies should review their actions carefully to prevent unnecessary takings and should account in decision-making for those takings that are necessitated by statutory mandate.[8]

The Executive Order requires that "[i]n formulating or implementing policies that have takings implications, each Executive department and agency shall be guided"[9] by the principles established in *Nollan* and *First English*. These "general principles," set forth in Section 3 of the Executive Order, include the doctrines of nexus and proportionality established by *Nollan* and the self-actuating right to just compensation set forth in *First English*. Although some actions are exempted from coverage, most traditional government regulatory functions fall within the scope of the Order. The Order singles out permitting processes and the creation of restrictions upon private property use, requiring that all departments and agencies observe the doctrines of nexus and proportionality and that they minimize processing delays.

Perhaps the most challenging of the Order's requirements, however, is the "takings impact analysis" (TIA), which must be prepared "before undertaking any proposed action regulating private property use for the protection of public health or safety"[10] or for other purposes. When regulations focus on public health and safety purposes, the TIA must, "with as much specificity as possible": 1) identify the public health and safety risk created by the proposed private property use; 2) establish that the proposed governmental action "substantially advances the purpose of protecting public health and safety against the specifically identified risk;" 3) establish that the proposed restrictions are "not disproportionate" to the landowner's contribution to the overall risk; and 4) "estimate, to the extent possible, the potential cost to the government in the event that a court later determines that the action constituted a taking."[11] To encourage thoroughness and candor, the TIA will normally be considered an internal deliberative document not subject to production under the Freedom of Information Act, and, in any event, the Executive Order "is not intended to create any right or benefit, substantive or procedural, enforceable at law by a party against the United States, its agencies, its officers or any person."[12]

Finally, the Order requires that the Attorney General promulgate guidelines for the evaluation of risk and the avoidance of unanticipated takings "to which each Executive department or agency shall refer in making the evaluations required by this Order or in otherwise taking any action that is the subject of this Order."[13] To avoid obsolescence, particularly given the rapid changes of this emerging area of the

170 / Property Rights

law, expected subsequent revisions to the guidance will ensure consistency with developments in the law of takings.

The Executive Order was certainly a bold effort by the federal government to seize the initiative in a field where governmental intransigence or uncertainty can be very costly. Rather than entirely eliminating a government program due to its prohibitive costs or unconstitutionality, the Order seeks to prevent judicial disruptions to government regulatory programs in the field of health, safety, and the environment. Moreover, a takings impact analysis provides a clear and rational assessment of the costs and benefits of a proposed regulation *before* the government adopts it. Thus the Order is designed to produce a regulatory mechanism that is less intrusive upon the rights of the individual and more cost efficient.

Congressional Legislation

On December 21, 1995, the Senate Judiciary Committee favorably voted the Omnibus Property Rights Act (S. 605) out of committee with a bipartisan vote of ten to seven. In addition to the planning requirements for federal agencies set forth in President Reagan's Executive Order 12630, the S. 605 establishes a statutory right to judicial redress for citizens whose property may have been taken, and provides that compensation is triggered when the government takes thirty-three percent of an affected parcel's value under any federal statute. The act also establishes a special administrative appeals process for takings conflicts involving the Endangered Species Act and the wetlands provisions of the Clean Water Act. In an effort to promote additional care on the part of federal agencies, S. 605 would also require the agency that caused the taking to pay compensation out of its own appropriation.

The bill was later amended to narrow the definition of property, raise the trigger point for compensation to fifty percent, exempt civil rights laws, and remove a regulatory "look back" provision that would have made the takings impact analysis apply to all existing as well as new regulations. The new bill was designated S. 1954, and sponsored by Senator Orrin Hatch (R-UT).[14]

The House of Representatives passed The Private Property Protection Act of 1995 (H.R. 925) on March 3, 1995. This Act is not as broad as the Senate's Omnibus Private Rights Act. Although H.R. 925 compensates for the value of any affected portion of property that is reduced in value by twenty percent or more by government action, the Act limits the compensation trigger to the takings claims under the Endangered Species Act, the Federal Land Policy and Management Act, the Wetlands provisions of the Clean Water Act, and the Swampbuster provisions of the Food Security Act.

As of this writing, the federal government has not yet adopted property rights legislation. However, many in Congress have stated their intention to pursue the issue until property rights legislation is passed—either as a stand-alone bill or as part of the reauthorization of existing regulatory schemes. Thus, for example, bills to reauthorize the Endangered Species Act and the Wetlands Program contain provisions aimed at compensating property owners for regulatory takings.

STATE PROPERTY RIGHTS LEGISLATION

States have been very active in the pursuit of legislative solutions to the taking of property rights. There are generally two types of property rights bills being introduced in the states: (1) "planning" bills that are based directly on Executive Order 12630 and which require a takings impact analysis prior to the government's adopting new rules and regulations which could affect property rights; and (2) compensation bills that actually identify a numerical percentage of diminution in value which will trigger the requirement of just compensation.

Planning or "Look Before You Leap" Bills

Just as Executive Order 12630 does for the federal government, state planning bills require state governments to "look before they leap" regarding actions which might result in unconstitutional takings of private property.

In just three years, more than sixty planning bills, generally dubbed "Private Property Protection Acts," have been introduced at the state level. Twenty-five states have already signed property rights legislation into law, and almost every state in the country now has one or more property rights initiatives under consideration. *The National Law Journal* calls this mounting wave "The Property Rights' Revolt."

Planning bills first became state laws in 1991. After its governor vetoed a planning bill in 1990, the legislature for the State of Washington tacked a planning bill onto the Growth Management Act of 1991, which passed. Delaware enacted the first "stand alone" property rights law on January 21, 1992. It establishes procedures for assessing whether or not proposed state rules and regulations may result in a taking of private property.

Arizona almost followed suit on June 1, 1992, with a planning bill similar to the one in Delaware. But, in a campaign labeling the bill as "the worst anti-environmental law ever passed in the United States,"[15] the environmental lobby garnered 50,000 signatures on a petition and brought about a statewide referendum that repealed the law.

Meanwhile, Utah passed a law even stronger than the bill planning in Arizona. Indiana has also passed a law requiring the Attorney General to alert the Governor of any proposed rule that might entail a taking. Finally, a Virginia joint resolution has directed the creation of a joint subcommittee to study and if necessary change state procedures affecting property rights.

Compensation Bills

Planning bills do have a serious weakness, however. As Maryland Attorney General Ralph S. Tyler points out, "no meaningful analysis can be done" of the liability at stake in a taking when so much depends not just "upon the particular circumstances" of the case, but on the philosophy of the particular judge hearing the case. As Justice William Brennan admitted, the problem is the United States Supreme Court's failure "to develop any set formula" for determining when "justice and fairness require that economic injuries caused by public action be compensated by the government, rather than remain disproportionately concentrated on a few persons." The Court has refused to define "taking," "just compensation," "public use," and even "private property." When judges take this *ad hoc* approach to takings law, liability planning becomes a shot in the dark.

To address this problem, states are increasingly proposing legislation that will establish bright lines by specifying the exact diminution in value of property which will require compensation. This is the statutory "trigger point" at which a regulatory taking and inverse condemnation will be presumed to occur. Thus, this type of bill would entitle any property owner to automatic compensation if he could prove that his property lost, for example, twenty percent of its value as a result of government regulation.

It should be noted that compensation bills would not preclude property owners subject to regulatory takings which fall short of the specified trigger point from legally challenging regulatory action. In four states—California, Mississippi, New Hampshire, and Washington—a combination of planning and compensation bills were introduced. Although the Washington bill passed the legislature, it was defeated in a hard-fought referendum in November 1995.

In June 1995, the State of Texas enacted the most comprehensive property rights legislation to date. The statute contains planning provisions which require the preparation of a takings impact analysis where state actions are likely to unconstitutionally impact on private property rights. In early 1996, the Texas Attorney General promulgated for comment proposed guidelines to assist the State and local agencies in ascertaining the takings implications of their proposed activities.

The Texas bill also contains a compensation requirement where property value has been diminished by twenty percent as a result of actions taken by State and local governments (with a number of exceptions). Like other state compensation bills, the Texas statute provides an *additional* remedy beyond those already provided by the state's inverse condemnation statutes and the state and federal constitutions.

A number of states have looked to the Texas model for guidance in drafting their own combination of planning and compensation bills.

PROS AND CONS OF PROPERTY RIGHTS LEGISLATION

Planning Bills

Some regard private property protection laws, whether they be of the planning or the compensation variety, as a threat to environmental protection. The National Wildlife Federation worries that planning bills will "impose higher costs on state agencies," and the Wilderness Society asserts that they "will end up costing taxpayers millions of dollars." Their solution is to refuse to compensate individuals for takings, concentrating these same millions of dollars of costs upon the few whose property is actually physically taken.

"If the government is required in case after case to reward financially any party adversely affected by any environmental regulation, it [takings law] becomes the proverbial Damoclean sword hanging over environmental law," says Albert H. Myerhoff, an attorney with the Natural Resources Defense Council. "The reality is that the state simply cannot afford to pay off every landowner for every land-use decision," writes Terry J. Harris in *Chesapeake*, the newsletter of the Potomac, Maryland chapter of the Sierra Club. "So, should the legislative strategy [for passing Maryland's planning law] prevail, state and local governments are likely to throw out environmental protections as a too-expensive legal liability."

Of course, property rights bills do not require the payment of just compensation for takings—the Constitution does that. Planning bills merely require state agencies to assess the takings implications of their regulations before they are adopted. By requiring governments to "look before they leap," they reduce the likelihood that taxpayers will get stuck footing the bill for multi-million-dollar awards. Far from increasing costs, such legislation actually saves taxpayers money. In none of the states that have enacted property rights protection laws has the doomsday scenario of environmental neglect and cost explosion become a reality. Even compensation bills would not increase the net social cost of environmental regulation involving takings. By establishing an objective definition of takings, they would simply ensure that the cost be spread among the general public, rather than "forcing some people alone to bear public burdens which, in all fairness and justice, should be borne by the public as a whole."[16]

Compensation Bills

Environmental groups and others who support stricter regulatory schemes have consistently opposed compensation legislation in the field of property rights. In December 1995, the White House took the unusual step of informing the Senate Judiciary Committee, prior to the markup of its property rights bill, that President Bill Clinton intended to veto the legislation if it passed.

It should be noted that some property rights advocates also object to compensation bills. They are concerned that, by setting a threshold, compensation bills might disparage the rights of property owners who are the victims of takings that fail to meet the threshold. But, as discussed previously, compensation bills would not prevent property owners from obtaining compensation for takings that reduce property value by less than the established trigger. Such bills would simply require that once a taking crosses this threshold, the government must condemn and buy the property outright, or pay the property owner compensation for the loss in property value. While clarifying and mandating a compensation process for victims of takings that exceed the threshold, compensation bills would in no way impair the ability of property owners to obtain compensation for lesser takings.

Another final criticism of compensation bills is that they are arbitrary. Why set the trigger point at twenty, thirty-three, or fifty percent of property value? Why not higher? Or lower? Isn't that an arbitrary threshold?

176 / Property Rights

It is true that the specified percentage threshold is, to a degree, arbitrary. But the root problem in takings jurisprudence has been the inability of the courts to define a "taking" at all. To resolve this problem, it is necessary to establish a statutory definition. The only possible definitions that could not be called arbitrary would require condemnation proceedings for any diminution of value at all (even a fraction of a cent), or to permit the government to take everything without compensation. The first choice is entirely impractical, and the second means no limits on takings at all. Given the choice between an arbitrary limit and no limit, some would prefer a limit, however arbitrary.

Most property rights advocates argue that both planning and compensation bills make constitutional and budgetary sense. To them, government regulatory programs are bounded by constitutional protections of traditional notions of civil rights including property rights. They point out that the effect of property rights legislation would be that federal agencies would attempt to avoid paying compensation by modifying their decisions, processing permits more quickly, or otherwise changing their behavior.

Moreover, they contend, a price cannot be placed upon civil rights. Our constitutional system demands that government obey the restraints imposed upon its power by the Bill of Rights. The question: "How much does it cost to provide freedom of the press, freedom of religion, privacy in one's home or the right to jury trial?" is not—and should not—be asked.

ENDNOTES

[1] 438 U.S. 104, 124 (1978).

[2] Statement of John R. Schmidt, Associate Attorney General, Subcommittee on the Constitution, Committee on the Judiciary, United States House of Representatives. (Feb. 10, 1995).

[3] *Id.*

[4] *Bowles v. United States*, 31 Fed. Cl. 37, 44-45 (1994).

[5] *First English Evangelical Church v. County of Los Angeles*, 482 U.S. 304 (1987).
[6] 481 U.S. 704 (1987).
[7] State of the Union address, 1/25/88.
[8] Executive Order 12630.
[9] *Id.*
[10] *Id.*
[11] *Id.*
[12] *Id.*
[13] *Id.*
[14] Senate Majority Leader Trent Lott declined to bring the Omnibus Property Rights Act (S. 1954) to the Senate floor. This decision brought an end to property rights legislation in the 104th Congress.
[15] Marianne Lavelle, *The Property Rights "Revolt"*, Nat. L. J., May 10, 1993, at 34.
[16] *Armstrong v. United States*, 364 U.S. 40, 49 (1960).

Appendix A

The Bill of Rights and the 14th Amendment to the U.S. Constitution

Amendment I.*

Congress shall make no law respecting an establishment of religion, or prohibiting the free exercise thereof; or abridging the freedom of speech, or of the press, or the right of the people peaceably to assemble, and to petition the Government for a redress of grievances.

Amendment II.

A well regulated Militia, being necessary to the security of a free State, the right of the people to keep and bear Arms, shall not be infringed.

Amendment III.

No Soldier shall, in time of peace be quartered in any house, without the consent of the Owner, nor in time of war, but in a manner to be prescribed by law.

Amendment IV.

The right of the people to be secure in their persons, houses, papers, and effects, against unreasonable searches and seizures, shall not be violated, and no Warrants shall issue, but upon probable cause, supported by Oath or affirmation, and particularly describing the place to be searched, and the persons or things to be seized.

---

*The first ten Amendments (Bill of Rights) were ratified effective December 15, 1791.

Amendment V.

No person shall be held to answer for a capital, or otherwise infamous crime, unless on a presentment or indictment of a Grand Jury, except in cases arising in the land or naval forces, or in the Militia, when in actual service in time of War or public danger; nor shall any person be subject for the same offence to be twice put in jeopardy of life or limb, nor shall be compelled in any criminal case to be a witness against himself, nor be deprived of life, liberty, or property, without due process of law; nor shall private property be taken for public use without just compensation.

Amendment VI.

In all criminal prosecutions, the accused shall enjoy the right to a speedy and public trial, by an impartial jury of the State and district wherein the crime shall have been committed; which district shall have been previously ascertained by law, and to be informed of the nature and cause of the accusation; to be confronted with the witnesses against him; to have compulsory process for obtaining witnesses in his favor, and to have the assistance of counsel for his defence.

Amendment VII.

In Suits at common law, where the value in controversy shall exceed twenty dollars, the right of trial by jury shall be preserved, and no fact tried by a jury shall be otherwise re-examined in any Court of the United States, than according to the rules of the common law.

Amendment VIII.

Excessive bail shall not be required, nor excessive fines imposed, nor cruel and unusual punishments inflicted.

Amendment IX.

The enumeration in the Constitution of certain rights shall not be construed to deny or disparage others retained by the people.

Amendment X.

The powers not delegated to the United States by the Constitution, nor prohibited by it to the States, are reserved to the States respectively, or to the people.

Amendment XI.*

The Judicial power of the United States shall not be construed to extend to any suit in law or equity, commenced or prosecuted against one of the United States by Citizens of another State, or by Citizens or Subjects of any Foreign State.

[Note: Amendment XII is omitted due to lack of relevance.]

---

*The Eleventh Amendment was ratified February 7, 1795.

Amendment XIII.*

Section 1. Neither slavery nor involuntary servitude, except as a punishment for crime whereof the party shall have been duly convicted, shall exist within the United States, or any place subject to their jurisdiction.

Section 2. Congress shall have power to enforce this article by appropriate legislation.

Amendment XIV.**

Section 1. All persons born or naturalized in the United States and subject to the jurisdiction thereof, are citizens of the United States and of the State wherein they reside. No State shall make or enforce any law which shall abridge the privileges or immunities of citizens of the United States; nor shall any State deprive any person of life, liberty, or property, without due process of law; nor deny to any person within its jurisdiction the equal protection of the laws.

Section 2. Representatives shall be apportioned among the several States according to their respective numbers, counting the whole number of persons in each State, excluding Indians not

---

*The Thirteenth Amendment was ratified December 6, 1865.
**The Fourteenth Amendment was ratified July 9, 1868.

taxed. But when the right to vote at any election for the choice of electors for President and Vice President of the United States, Representatives in Congress, the Executive and Judicial officers of a State, or the members of the Legislature thereof, is denied to any of the male inhabitants of such State, being twenty-one years of age, and citizens of the United States, or in any way abridged, except for participation in rebellion, or other crime, the basis of representation therein shall be reduced in the proportion which the number of such male citizens shall bear to the whole number of male citizens twenty-one years of age in such State.

Section 3. No person shall be a Senator or Representative in Congress, or elector of President and Vice President, or hold any office, civil or military, under the United States, or under any State, who, having previously taken an oath, as a member of Congress, or as an officer of the United States, or as a member of any State legislature, or as an executive or judicial officer of any State, to support the Constitution of the United States, shall have engaged in insurrection or rebellion against the same, or given aid or comfort to the enemies thereof. But Congress may by a vote of two-thirds of each House, remove such disability.

Section 4. The validity of the public debt of the United States, authorized by law, including debts incurred for payment of pensions and bounties for services in suppressing insurrection or rebellion, shall not be questioned. But neither the United States nor any State shall assume or pay any debt or obligation incurred in aid of insurrection or rebellion against the United States, or any claim for the loss or emancipation of any slave; but all such debts, obligations and claims shall be held illegal and void.

Section 5. The Congress shall have power to enforce, by appropriate legislation, the provisions of this article.

Amendment XV.*

Section 1. The right of citizens of the United States to vote shall not be denied or abridged by the United States or by any State on account of race, color, or previous condition of servitude.

Section 2. The Congress shall have power to enforce this article by appropriate legislation.

Amendment XVI.**

The Congress shall have power to lay and collect taxes on incomes, from whatever source derived, without apportionment among the several States, and without regard to any census or enumeration.

[Note: Amendment XVII is omitted due to lack of relevance.]

---

*The Fifteenth Amendment was ratified February 3, 1870.
**The Sixteenth Amendment was ratified February 3, 1913.

Appendix B

Executive Order 12630

(President Reagan's
Executive Order
on Takings)

Appendix B: Executive Order 12630 / 189

Federal Register	**Presidential Documents**
Vol. 53, No. 53	
Friday, March 18, 1988	

Title 3—

The President

Executive Order 12630 of March 15, 1988

Governmental Actions and Interference With Constitutionally Protected Property Rights

By the authority vested in me as President by the Constitution and laws of the United States of America, and in order to ensure that government actions are undertaken on a well-reasoned basis with due regard for fiscal accountability, for the financial impact of the obligations imposed on the Federal government by the Just Compensation Clause of the Fifth Amendment, and for the Constitution, it is hereby ordered as follows:

Section 1. *Purpose.* (a) The Fifth Amendment of the United States Constitution provides that private property shall not be taken for public use without just compensation. Government historically has used the formal exercise of the power of eminent domain, which provides orderly processes for paying just compensation, to acquire private property for public use. Recent Supreme Court decisions, however, in reaffirming the fundamental protection of private property rights provided by the Fifth Amendment and in assessing the nature of governmental actions that have an impact on constitutionally protected property rights, have also reaffirmed that governmental actions that do not formally invoke the condemnation power, including regulations, may result in a taking for which just compensation is required.

(b) Responsible fiscal management and fundamental principles of good government require that government decision-makers evaluate carefully the effect of their administrative, regulatory, and legislative actions on constitutionally protected property rights. Executive departments and agencies should review their actions carefully to prevent unnecessary takings and should account in decision-making for those takings that are necessitated by statutory mandate.

(c) The purpose of this Order is to assist Federal departments and agencies in undertaking such reviews and in proposing, planning, and implementing actions with due regard for the constitutional protections provided by the Fifth Amendment and to reduce the risk of undue or inadvertent burdens on the public fisc resulting from lawful governmental action. In furtherance of the purpose of this Order, the Attorney General shall, consistent with the principles stated herein and in consultation with the Executive departments and agencies, promulgate Guidelines for the Evaluation of Risk and Avoidance of Unanticipated Takings to which each Executive department or agency shall refer in making the evaluations required by this Order or in otherwise taking any action that is the subject of this Order. The Guidelines shall be promulgated no later than May 1, 1988, and shall be disseminated to all units of each Executive department and agency no later than July 1, 1988. The Attorney General shall, as necessary, update these guidelines to reflect fundamental changes in takings law occurring as a result of Supreme Court decisions.

Sec. 2. *Definitions.* For the purpose of this Order: (a) "Policies that have takings implications" refers to Federal regulations, proposed Federal regulations, proposed Federal legislation, comments on proposed Federal legislation, or other Federal policy statements that, if implemented or enacted, could effect a taking, such as rules and regulations that propose or implement licensing, permitting, or other condition requirements or limitations on private property use, or that require dedications or exactions from owners of private property. "Policies that have takings implications" does not include:

(1) Actions abolishing regulations, discontinuing governmental programs, or modifying regulations in a manner that lessens interference with the use of private property;

(2) Actions taken with respect to properties held in trust by the United States or in preparation for or during treaty negotiations with foreign nations;

(3) Law enforcement actions involving seizure, for violations of law, of property for forfeiture or as evidence in criminal proceedings;

(4) Studies or similar efforts or planning activities;

(5) Communications between Federal agencies or departments and State or local land-use planning agencies regarding planned or proposed State or local actions regulating private property regardless of whether such communications are initiated by a Federal agency or department or are undertaken in response to an invitation by the State or local authority;

(6) The placement of military facilities or military activities involving the use of Federal property alone; or

(7) Any military or foreign affairs functions (including procurement functions thereunder) but not including the U.S. Army Corps of Engineers civil works program.

(b) Private property refers to all property protected by the Just Compensation Clause of the Fifth Amendment.

(c) "Actions" refers to proposed Federal regulations, proposed Federal legislation, comments on proposed Federal legislation, applications of Federal regulations to specific property, or Federal governmental actions physically invading or occupying private property, or other policy statements or actions related to Federal regulation or direct physical invasion or occupancy, but does not include:

(1) Actions in which the power of eminent domain is formally exercised;

(2) Actions taken with respect to properties held in trust by the United States or in preparation for or during treaty negotiations with foreign nations;

(3) Law enforcement actions involving seizure, for violations of law, of property for forfeiture or as evidence in criminal proceedings;

(4) Studies or similar efforts or planning activities;

(5) Communications between Federal agencies or departments and State or local land-use planning agencies regarding planned or proposed State or local actions regulating private property regardless of whether such communications are initiated by a Federal agency or department or are undertaken in response to an invitation by the State or local authority;

(6) The placement of military facilities or military activities involving the use of Federal property alone; or

(7) Any military or foreign affairs functions (including procurement functions thereunder), but not including the U.S. Army Corps of Engineers civil works program.

Sec. 3. *General Principles.* In formulating or implementing policies that have takings implications, each Executive department and agency shall be guided by the following general principles:

(a) Governmental officials should be sensitive to, anticipate, and account for, the obligations imposed by the Just Compensation Clause of the Fifth Amendment in planning and carrying out governmental actions so that they do not result in the imposition of unanticipated or undue additional burdens on the public fisc.

(b) Actions undertaken by governmental officials that result in a physical invasion or occupancy of private property, and regulations imposed on private property that substantially affect its value or use, may constitute a taking of property. Further, governmental action may amount to a taking even though the action results in less than a complete deprivation of all use or value, or of all separate and distinct interests in the same private property and even if the action constituting a taking is temporary in nature.

(c) Government officials whose actions are taken specifically for purposes of protecting public health and safety are ordinarily given broader latitude by courts before their actions are considered to be takings. However, the mere assertion of a public health and safety purpose is insufficient to avoid a taking. Actions to which this Order applies asserted to be for the protection of public health and safety, therefore, should be undertaken only in response to real and substantial threats to public health and safety, be designed to advance significantly the health and safety purpose, and be no greater than is necessary to achieve the health and safety purpose.

(d) While normal governmental processes do not ordinarily effect takings, undue delays in decision-making during which private property use if interfered with carry a risk of being held to be takings. Additionally, a delay in processing may increase significantly the size of compensation due if a taking is later found to have occurred.

(e) The Just Compensation Clause is self-actuating, requiring that compensation be paid whenever governmental action results in a taking of private property regardless of whether the underlying authority for the action contemplated a taking or authorized the payment of compensation. Accordingly, governmental actions that may have a significant impact on the use or value of private property should be scrutinized to avoid undue or unplanned burdens on the public fisc.

Sec. 4. *Department and Agency Action.* In addition to the fundamental principles set forth in Section 3, Executive departments and agencies shall adhere, to the extent permitted by law, to the following criteria when implementing policies that have takings implications:

(a) When an Executive department or agency requires a private party to obtain a permit in order to undertake a specific use of, or action with respect to, private property, any conditions imposed on the granting of a permit shall:

(1) Serve the same purpose that would have been served by a prohibition of the use or action; and

(2) Substantially advance that purpose.

(b) When a proposed action would place a restriction on a use of private property, the restriction imposed on the use shall not be disproportionate to the extent to which the use contributes to the overall problem that the restriction is imposed to redress.

(c) When a proposed action involves a permitting process or any other decision-making process that will interfere with, or otherwise prohibit, the use of private property pending the completion of the process, the duration of the process shall be kept to the minimum necessary.

(d) Before undertaking any proposed action regulating private property use for the protection of public health or safety, the Executive department or agency involved shall, in internal deliberative documents and any submissions to the Director of the Office of Management and Budget that are required:

(1) Identify clearly, with as much specificity as possible, the public health or safety risk created by the private property use that is the subject of the proposed action;

(2) Establish that such proposed action substantially advances the purpose of protecting public health and safety against the specifically identified risk;

(3) Establish to the extent possible that the restrictions imposed on the private property are not disproportionate to the extent to which the use contributes to the overall risk; and

(4) Estimate, to the extent possible, the potential cost to the government in the event that a court later determines that the action constituted a taking.

In instances in which there is an immediate threat to health and safety that constitutes an emergency requiring immediate response, this analysis may be done upon completion of the emergency action.

Sec. 5. *Executive Department and Agency Implementation.* (a) The head of each Executive department and agency shall designate an official to be responsible for ensuring compliance with this Order with respect to the actions of that department or agency.

(b) Executive departments and agencies shall, to the extent permitted by law, identify the takings implications of proposed regulatory actions and address the merits of those actions in light of the identified takings implications, if any, in all required submissions made to the Office of Management and Budget. Significant takings implications should also be identified and discussed in notices of proposed rule-making and messages transmitting legislative proposals to the Congress, stating the departments' and agencies' conclusions on the takings issues.

(c) Executive departments and agencies shall identify each existing Federal rule and regulation against which a takings award has been made or against which a takings claim is pending including the amount of each claim or award. A "takings" award has been made or a "takings" claim pending if the award was made, or the pending claim brought, pursuant to the Just Compensation Clause of the Fifth Amendment. An itemized compilation of all such awards made in Fiscal Years 1985, 1986, and 1987 and all such pending claims shall be submitted to the Director, Office of Management and Budget, on or before May 16, 1988.

(d) Each Executive department and agency shall submit annually to the Director, Office of Management and Budget, and to the Attorney General an itemized compilation of all awards of just compensation entered against the United States for takings, including awards of interest as well as monies paid pursuant to the provisions of the Uniform Relocation Assistance and Real Property Acquisition Policies Act of 1970, 42 U.S.C. 4601.

(e)(1) The Director, Office of Management and Budget, and the Attorney General shall each, to the extent permitted by law, take action to ensure that the policies of the Executive departments and agencies are consistent with the principles, criteria, and requirements stated in Sections 1 through 5 of this Order, and the Office of Management and Budget shall take action to ensure that all takings awards levied against agencies are properly accounted for in agency budget submissions.

(2) In addition to the guidelines required by Section 1 of this Order, the Attorney General shall, in consultation with each Executive department and agency to which this Order applies, promulgate such supplemental guidelines as may be appropriate to the specific obligations of that department or agency.

Sec. 6. *Judicial Review.* This Order is intended only to improve the internal management of the Executive branch and is not intended to create any right or benefit, substantive or procedural, enforceable at law by a party against the United States, its agencies, its officers, or any person.

Ronald Reagan

THE WHITE HOUSE,
March 15, 1988.

Appendix C

The U.S. Attorney General's Guidelines for Implementing Executive Order 12630

Guidelines 195

Index to Guidelines 222

Appendix to Guidelines 229

ATTORNEY GENERAL'S GUIDELINES
FOR THE EVALUATION OF RISK
AND AVOIDANCE OF UNANTICIPATED TAKINGS

Authority: Executive Order No. 12630
(53 Fed. Reg. 8859 (March 18, 1988))

Contents:
- Section I — Explanatory Note
- Section II — Scope of the Guidelines
- Section III — Agency Applicability
- Section IV — Definitions
- Section V — General Principles and Assessment Factors
- Section VI — Implementation, Management, and Special Reporting Requirements
- Section VII — Responsibilities of the Attorney General and the Director of the Office of Management and Budget
- Section VIII — Judicial Review and Enforcement

I. EXPLANATORY NOTE

A. Policy, Purpose, and Mandate

The Fifth Amendment to the United States Constitution provides that private property shall not be taken for public use without payment of just compensation. Over the course of our nation's history, this constitutional requirement has had important legal and fiscal consequences in the development and implementation of government policies and actions at the local, state, and national levels.

During the past year, the Supreme Court of the United States again examined the protection of private property under the Fifth Amendment. In *First English Evangelical Lutheran Church of Glendale v. County of Los Angeles*, 107 S. Ct. 2378 (1987) and *Nollan v. California Coastal Commission*, 107 S. Ct. 3141 (1987), the Supreme Court addressed the fundamental protections afforded by the Fifth Amendment whenever a government policy or action is determined to result in a taking of private property for public use.

The President issued Executive Order No. 12630, "Governmental Actions and Interference with Constitutionally Protected Property Rights," on March 15, 1988, pursuant to his authority as president and in service of his constitutional obligations to manage the executive branch and to ensure constitutionality of governmental actions. This Executive Order directs Executive Branch departments and agencies, as a part of their internal management process, to assess the takings implications of proposed policies and actions on private property interests protected by the Fifth Amendment. In this way, federal agency decisionmakers will be better informed about the potential effects of proposed agency activities and to the extent permitted by law, consistent with their statutory obligations, can minimize the impacts of such activities on constitutionally protected private property rights.

In Section 1(c) of Executive Order No. 12630, the President directed the Attorney General to promulgate, in consultation with the Executive Branch departments and agencies, Guidelines for the Evaluation of Risk and Avoidance of Unanticipated Takings. In accordance with the direction provided in the Executive Order, these Guidelines establish a basic, uniform framework for federal agencies to use in their internal evaluations of the takings implications of administrative, regulatory, and legislative policies and actions. Neither the Executive Order nor these Guidelines prevents an agency from making an independent decision about proceeding with a specific policy or action which the decisionmaker determines is statutorily required. Rather, their purpose is to assure that governmental decisionmakers are fully informed of any potential takings implications of proposed policies and actions, thereby enhancing the cost-efficient administration of agency programs. In those instances in which a range of alternatives are available, each of which would meet the statutorily required objective, prudent management requires selection of the least risk alternative. In instances in which alternatives are not available, the takings implications are noted.

As detailed in Section VIII of the Guidelines, the evaluations conducted under the Executive Order, the Guidelines, and the accompanying Appendix to the Guidelines for the Evaluation of Risk and Avoidance of Unanticipated Takings (incorporated by reference herein) are intended solely as internal and predecisional management aids for agency decisionmakers. Neither any part of the evaluation process nor any conclusions reached under that process are admissions of the existence -- possible, probable, or otherwise -- of takings or are otherwise subject to judicial review. Further, terms utilized in the process established in these Guidelines (for example, "takings implication" and "significant takings implications") are terms of art and their meanings are limited to the context of this evaluation process.

Appendix C: Guidelines for Implementing E.O. 12630 / 197

B.   Overview of the Guidelines

The Guidelines first present, in Sections II and III, information regarding the scope of policies and actions subject to evaluation under Executive Order No. 12630 and the agencies that must conduct these evaluations. Generally, an agency's administrative, regulatory, and legislative policies and actions that affect, or may affect, the use or value of private property must be evaluated. The policies and actions specifically excluded from review, for example, agency plans and studies, and policies and actions initiated prior to issuance of the Executive Order, are also set forth. Even as to excluded matters, however, agency decisionmakers must take steps to ensure that their constitutional obligations are recognized and fulfilled.

Section V of the Guidelines then explains the Fifth Amendment principles and specific assessment factors to be used in evaluating the takings implications of policies and actions. This evaluation, called the takings implication assessment (TIA), will enable the agency to determine whether, and to what extent, a proposed policy or action poses risks of a taking of private property and to estimate the potential financial exposure of the proposal. The basic elements of the TIA appear in Section VI of the Guidelines. Once completed, the TIA, which will usually be based on a specific factual setting, will serve as an evaluative tool for the agency decisionmaker. This predecisional assessment should be incorporated by the agency, in a form and manner chosen by the agency, into existing planning processes and procedures.

Section VI of the Guidelines explains specific executive branch management responsibilities with regard to the Executive Order and details special reporting requirements. For instance, Sections VI(B) and VI(C) address agency reporting requirements under Section 5(b) of the Executive Order to the Office of Management and Budget.

In addition, Section VI(D) of the Guidelines establishes a supplementation process enabling agencies to adapt these implementation procedures and management requirements to their specific program responsibilities. Through supplementation, an agency has flexibility, with the approval of the Attorney General, to exempt specific policies and actions from analysis under the Executive Order whenever such policies and actions, as a class, have no takings implications. For example, under current case law, no takings implication arises solely because an otherwise lawful permit system is established with respect to subsequent uses of property. In addition, through supplementation, an agency may make specific modifications, as necessary, to the management process. Supplementation may be initiated by an agency at any time, subject to review and approval by the Attorney General.

Section VII sets forth the general responsibilities of the Attorney General and the Director of the Office of Management and Budget in implementation of the Executive Order. The Attorney General is responsible for taking action, to the extent permitted by law, to ensure that the policies of the agencies are consistent with the principles, criteria, and administrative requirements established in the Executive Order and these Guidelines, and for revising and reissuing these Guidelines, as necessary, to reflect fundamental changes in takings law that occur as a result of United States Supreme Court decisions. Finally, in Section VIII of the Guidelines, the non-reviewability of actions taken under the Executive Order, the Guidelines, and the accompanying Appendix to the Guidelines is explained.

An Appendix to the Guidelines for the Evaluation of Risk and Avoidance of Unanticipated Takings has also been prepared and is incorporated by reference into these Guidelines. This Appendix provides further information for the use of departments and agencies regarding the case law surrounding considerations of whether a taking has occurred and the extent of any potential just compensation claim. As with the Guidelines themselves, this Appendix addresses only a general framework for the evaluation of takings implications of proposed agency policies and actions under the Executive Order and these Guidelines.

II. SCOPE OF THE GUIDELINES

    A. Policies and Actions Subject to Evaluation

        Except for the policies and actions specified in the exclusions in Subsections II(B) and (C) below, an agency must evaluate, for their takings implications, its administrative, regulatory, and legislative policies and actions that affect, or may affect, the use or value of private property in accordance with the framework established in these Guidelines. These will include, but are not limited to, the following.

        1. Administrative and Regulatory Policies and Actions

            An agency must evaluate its administrative and regulatory policies and actions that affect, or may affect, the use or value of private property. These policies and actions (as discussed in Sections 2(a) and 2(c) of Executive Order No. 12630) include, but are not limited to, federal regulations that propose or implement licensing or permitting requirements, conditions or restrictions otherwise imposed by an agency on private property use, and actions relating to or causing the physical occupancy or invasion of private property.

2. **Legislative Policies and Actions**

    An agency must evaluate its legislative policies and actions that affect, or may affect, the use or value of private property whenever such legislative policies and actions are subject to coordination and clearance by the Office of Management and Budget pursuant to Circular No. A-19, Revised, or succeeding management directives issued by the Office of Management and Budget for legislative coordination and clearance.

3. **Recommendations to Other Federal Agencies**

    Written agency comments or recommendations by other than the lead agency on policies or actions within the Executive Order are subject to evaluation under these Guidelines whenever such comments or recommendations are required by law. In that circumstance, the commenting agency shall prepare a limited takings implication assessment consisting only of an assessment of the likelihood that the proposed action or policy may effect a taking for which compensation is due pursuant to Section VI(A)(2)(c)(i), _infra_.

B. **Exclusions**

The following federal policies and actions are excluded from evaluation under these Guidelines. Although these specific policies and actions are excluded from evaluation, they should be conducted or undertaken by federal agencies with due regard for the Fifth Amendment. Accordingly, even as to excluded matters, federal agency decisionmakers must take steps to ensure that their constitutional obligations are recognized and fulfilled.

Those policies and actions explicitly excluded from coverage under Executive Order No. 12630 and these Guidelines are as follows:

1. **Programs or Regulations Reducing Federal Restrictions on Use of Private Property**

    Federal policies or actions involving amendments to regulations, deregulation, or discontinuance of federal programs in a manner that lessens interference with the use of private property are excluded from coverage under the Executive Order and these Guidelines.

2. **Trust Property and Treaty Negotiations**

   Those policies or actions involving the property of person(s) or identified groups (for example, a federally recognized Indian tribe) for which the United States is serving as trustee and those actions taken while the United States is preparing to enter into or undertaking treaty negotiations with a foreign nation are excluded from coverage under the Executive Order and these Guidelines. For purposes of this exclusion, properties held in trust do not include trust territories of the United States (such as the Trust Territories of the Pacific) or other properties over which the United States is acting as a government, rather than serving in the capacity of a statutory trustee.

3. **Seizures of Property**

   All policies or actions involving seizures of property, which will be used by federal civil or military law enforcement officers either as evidence in a criminal proceeding or for criminal or civil statutory forfeiture proceedings, are excluded from coverage under the Executive Order and these Guidelines. Property attached pursuant to law by court or administrative order in any proceeding initiated by the United States is also excluded.

4. **Agency Plans and Studies**

   Preliminary data gathering and evaluation activities, which occur prior to the agency's decision to implement a policy or action and which neither (1) physically occupy or invade private property nor (2) purport to regulate or otherwise restrict the use of private property, are excluded from coverage under the Executive Order and these Guidelines. Such activities are preliminary aids in the decisionmaking process and are excluded even though disclosure of their mere existence may, in certain instances, result in a drop in property values.

   Once a proposed policy or action has advanced beyond this preliminary stage, the agency's policy

Appendix C: Guidelines for Implementing E.O. 12630 / 201

or action is subject to evaluation under the Executive Order.

5. **Consultations Regarding Regulation of Private Property by State and Local Governments**

    Communications between federal agencies and state or local land-use planning agencies regarding planned or proposed state or local policies or actions regulating private property are excluded from coverage under the Executive Order and these Guidelines. This exclusion applies regardless of whether such communications are initiated by a federal agency or are undertaken by a federal agency in response to an invitation from the state or local authority. This exclusion does not apply to any policy or action for which a federal agency has decisionmaking authority, including authority to require or otherwise direct the state or local government to undertake or refrain from undertaking the activity in question.

6. **Military Property**

    Policies or actions involving placement of military facilities, in the exercise of the power of eminent domain, are excluded from coverage under the Executive Order and these Guidelines. Military activities that are undertaken solely on federal property, for example, artillery practice and military maneuvers and exercises, are also excluded.

7. **Exercise of the Power of Eminent Domain**

    The formal exercise of the power of eminent domain by federal agencies is excluded from coverage under the Executive Order and these Guidelines.

8. **Military and Foreign Affairs Activities**

    Policies and actions involving military and foreign affairs functions of the United States, such as foreign sanctions programs, military exercises, procurement activities, and regulation of personnel, are excluded from coverage under the Executive Order and these Guidelines. This exemption does not apply to regulation by the military of the use by citizens of private property, including the United States Army Corps of Engineers' civil works program. Thus, for purposes of this subsection, military functions do not include those activities in which the military component or personnel are substituting for, or performing as, a civilian regulatory body or agency.

9. <u>Pending or Imminent Litigation; Enforcement Actions Seeking Statutorily Authorized Penalties, Debt Collection, or the Like</u>

Policies and actions taken in furtherance of pending or imminent litigation, whether judicial or administrative, are excluded from coverage under these Guidelines. In addition, judicial and administrative adjudicatory actions brought pursuant to federal law seeking penalties, the collection of debts authorized by statute, or the like, are excluded from coverage under these Guidelines. Policies and actions of offices of the Inspector General under the Inspector General Act of 1978, as amended, are also excluded from coverage under these Guidelines.

C. <u>Special Exclusion for Agency Policies and Actions Initiated Prior to Issuance of Executive Order No. 12630</u>

Administrative, regulatory, or legislative policies and actions that were finally developed and implemented by an agency at the time of issuance of Executive Order No. 12630 are excluded from coverage under the Executive Order. Agency policies and actions proposed, but not initiated, prior to issuance of the Executive Order or these Guidelines are likewise excluded from coverage under the Executive Order. However, these categories of policies and actions should be evaluated in accordance with the Executive Order and these Guidelines to the maximum extent practicable in order to ensure that constitutional and managerial obligations are met.

III. **AGENCY APPLICABILITY**

Executive Order No. 12630 and these Guidelines apply, except as provided in Section 2 of the Executive Order and Section II(B) herein, to any executive department, agency, or military department of the United States Government, and to any United States Government corporation, United States Government controlled corporation, or other establishment in the Executive Branch of the United States Government other than those entities defined as "independent regulatory agencies" in 44 U.S.C. § 3502(10).

The term "agency," when used in these Guidelines, shall refer to any of the departments, corporations, or other establishments identified in this section.

IV. DEFINITIONS

A. "Private Property": "Private Property" includes all property protected by the Fifth Amendment to the United States Constitution, including, but not limited to, real and personal property and tangible and intangible property.

B. "Takings Implication": Any policy or action to which the Executive Order applies that, upon examination by the decisionmaker under Section V(D)(3), *infra*, appears to have an effect on private property sufficiently severe as to effectively deny economically viable use of any distinct legally protected property interest to its owner, or to have the effect of, or result in, a permanent or temporary physical occupation, invasion, or deprivation, shall be deemed to have a takings implication for purposes of the Executive Order and these Guidelines.

C. "Significant Takings Implications": For purposes of the Executive Order and these Guidelines, a "significant takings implication" exists when, on the basis of available information, the decisionmaker concludes as to any policy or action with a takings implication that:

   1. The proposed policy or action poses a substantial risk that a taking of private property may result, or

   2. Insufficient information as to facts or law exists to enable an accurate assessment of whether significant takings consequences may result from the proposed policy or action.

D. "Legislation": For purposes of an agency's evaluation and reporting responsibilities under the executive order and these guidelines, "legislation" is limited to those agency legislative policies and actions that are subject to coordination and clearance by the Office of Management and Budget pursuant to Circular No. A-19, Revised, or succeeding management directives issued by the Office of Management and Budget on legislative coordination and clearance. Examples of the types of legislative submissions subject to review include an agency's proposed legislation and agency comments or testimony concerning pending legislation.

E. "Lead Agency": This is the federal agency designated to supervise the preparation of the reviews and assessments directed by the Executive Order and these Guidelines.

1. Designation of a lead agency is necessary whenever more than one department or agency is involved in a group of policies or actions directly related to each other because of their functional interdependence or geographic proximity.

2. For purposes of all policies and actions subject to evaluation under the Executive Order and these Guidelines, the lead agency is the one which will have primary responsibility for implementing the proposed policy or action or whose program would otherwise be primarily affected by the proposed policy or action. Any other agency having interagency consultation and review responsibilities for the policy or action in question shall, to the maximum extent possible, work with the lead agency to identify any takings implications.

3. Potential lead agencies have the responsibility to coordinate and determine, in a timely manner, which agency will be lead agency and which will be cooperating agencies. If there is disagreement among the agencies, the following factors should be considered in resolving the lead agency question:

    a. Magnitude of the agency's involvement in the policy or action;

    b. The agency's approval/disapproval authority over the policy or action;

    c. Duration of the agency's involvement in the policy or action; and

    d. Sequence of the agencies' involvement in the policy or action.

4. When agencies are unable to resolve the choice of the lead agency, an official, to be

Appendix C: Guidelines for Implementing E.O. 12630 / 205

designated by the Office of the President, shall be responsible for selecting the lead agency.

V. GENERAL PRINCIPLES AND ASSESSMENT FACTORS

Section V of these Guidelines provides a discussion of the general principles and assessment factors which inform considerations of whether a takings implication (Section V(D)(3)) exists. Section V(A) surveys takings factors generally; Section V(B) addresses current takings law more specifically; and Section V(C) points to specific takings risks discussed in Executive Order No. 12630. The accompanying Attorney General's Appendix to these Guidelines further details case law considerations on the risk of a taking. Section V(D) describes the current legal criteria through which the factors identified in Section V are analyzed. And, Section V(D)(3) specifies the term of art risk assessment criteria -- "takings implication" -- used to assess risk. Section VI of the Guidelines, especially Section VI(A)(2), sets forth the general process for documentation of the agency's application of these factors and criteria.

A. Underlying Premises of the Fifth Amendment

1. The Fifth Amendment provides that "private property [shall not] be taken for public use, without just compensation." Ownership, use, and transfer of private property of all types are rights. They are not benefits or privileges bestowed by government. At the same time, government also has the obligation to lawfully govern. Thus, the rights of property owners are not absolute and government may, within limits, regulate the use of property. Where those regulations amount to a taking of private property, government must pay the owner just compensation for the property rights abridged. The fact that the government's actions are otherwise constitutionally authorized does not mean that those actions cannot effect a taking. On the other hand, government may not take property except for a public purpose within its constitutional authority, and only then, on the payment of just compensation.

2. Government has historically used the formal exercise of the power of eminent domain, which provides orderly processes for paying just compensation, to acquire private property for public use. However, government may become liable

- 11 -

for the payment of just compensation to private property owners whose property permanently or temporarily has been either physically occupied or invaded by government or others with the assistance or approval of government, or so affected by governmental regulation as to have been effectively taken despite the fact that the government has neither physically invaded, confiscated, or occupied the property nor taken legal title to the property.

3. So long as an action having consequences sufficiently severe as to constitute a taking is within the constitutional authority of the government, and the action taken is expressly or impliedly authorized by Congress or other constitutional source of authority (for example, an action directed by the President that the President may constitutionally authorize), the just compensation obligation will attach regardless of whether government contemplated or intended the taking to result. In contrast to the formal exercise of eminent domain, the private property owner can obtain compensation by filing what is called an "inverse condemnation" suit.

4. The Fifth Amendment's protection extends to all forms of property -- real and personal, tangible and intangible. Property is not defined by the Constitution, but by independent sources such as state, local, and federal law.

5. In planning and carrying out federal program policies and actions undertaken by statute and otherwise, government officials have the obligation to be fiscally responsible. In addition, they must respect the constitutional rights of individuals who are affected by those program policies and actions. Accordingly, officials must be aware of and avoid, to the extent possible and consistent with the obligations imposed by law, actions that may inadvertently result in takings. Where such taking risk cannot be wholly avoided, responsible government officials should, to the extent possible and consistent with the obligations imposed by law, minimize the potential financial impact of takings by appropriate planning and implementation. To do this, officials must make decisions informed by the general and specific principles of takings case law.

B. **The Nature of a Taking**

Takings may occur when permanent or temporary government actions result in the physical occupancy of property, the physical invasion of property, or the regulation of property.

1. **Physical Occupancies**

    Permanent or temporary physical occupancy is the most traditional type of taking and is therefore the most familiar and most easily recognized as a taking. As a general rule, where a physical occupancy exists no balancing of the economic impact on the owner and the public benefit will occur in the taking analysis. Examples of physical occupancy takings include not only formal condemnation exercises, such as the taking of land to build a highway, but also utility easements and access easements. [See Appendix to Guidelines, Section III(E)(1)]

2. **Physical Invasions**

    As a general rule, physical invasions of property, as distinguished from physical occupancies, may also give rise to a taking where the invasions are of a recurring and substantial nature. Examples of physical invasion takings include, among others, flooding and water related intrusions and overflight or aviation easement intrusions. [See Appendix to Guidelines, Section III(E)(2)]

3. **Regulatory Takings**

    a. Like physical occupations or invasions, regulation which affects the value, use, or transfer of property may constitute a taking if it goes too far. Pennsylvania Coal Company v. Mahon, 260 U.S. 393 (1922); Hodel v. Irving, 107 S. Ct. 2076 (1987); Nollan v. California Coastal Commission, 107 S. Ct. 3141 (1987). Regulation has gone too far and may result in takings liability if:

        i. The regulation in question does not substantially advance a legitimate governmental purpose; it is not enough that the regulation or action might rationally advance the purpose purported to be served; or

ii. In assessing the character of the government action, the economic impact of the action on the property interest involved, the extent to which the regulation interferes with the reasonable, investment-backed expectations of the owner of the property interest, and other relevant factors, justice and fairness require that the public, and not the private property owner, pay for the public use. Pennsylvania Coal v. Mahon, 260 U.S. 393 (1922); Penn Central Transportation Company v. New York City, 438 U.S. 104 (1978); Agins v. City of Tiburon, 447 U.S. 255 (1980); First English Evangelical Lutheran Church of Glendale v. Los Angeles County, 107 S. Ct. 2378, 2389, n.10 (1987).

b. Regulatory actions that closely resemble, or have the effect of, a physical invasion or occupation of property are more likely to be found to be takings. See, Nollan v. California Coastal Commission, 107 S. Ct. 2076 (1987). The greater the deprivation of use, the greater the likelihood that a taking will be found.

c. Regulation of an individual's property must not be disproportionate, within the limits of existing information or technology, to the degree to which the individual's property use is contributing to the overall problem. Thus, regulatory actions designed to compel public benefits, rather than prevent privately imposed harms, are also more likely to be takings.

[See Appendix to Guidelines, Section III(F)]

c. **Special Situations**

When implementing a regulatory policy or action and evaluating the takings implications of that policy or action, agencies should consider the following special factors:

- 14 -

Appendix C: Guidelines for Implementing E.O. 12630 / 209

1. Permitting Programs

    [Executive Order No. 12630, Section 4(a); Appendix to Guidelines, Section III(F)(2)]

    The programs of many agencies require private parties to obtain permits before making specific uses of, or acting with respect to, private property, without necessarily effecting a taking for which compensation is due. Those agencies may place conditions on the granting of such permits. However, a condition on the granting of a permit risks a takings implication unless:

    a. The condition serves the same purpose that would be served by a prohibition of the use or action; and

    b. The condition imposed substantially advances that purpose.

2. Public Health and Safety

    [Executive Order No. 12630, Section 4(d); Appendix to Guidelines, Section III(F)(5)]

    Policies or actions undertaken to protect public health and safety are ordinarily given greater latitude by courts before being held to give rise to takings. For purposes of that deference, however, the Supreme Court has ruled that "public health and safety" is not coextensive with the government's power to act. Public health and safety represents a component of that broader power. Again, that governmental power exists does not mean that its exercise is free of takings concerns. The deference discussed here extends only to public health and safety interests.

    a. Where public health and safety is the asserted regulatory purpose, then the health and safety risk posed by the property use to be regulated must be identified with as much specificity as possible and should be "real and substantial." That is, it must be more than speculative. It must present a genuine risk of harm to public health and safety and the claim of risk of harm must be supported by meaningful evidence, in light of available technology and information, that such harm may result from the use to be regulated.

b. Any action taken to regulate property use for public health and safety purposes must address the health and safety risk; that is, it must be designed to counter the identified risk and must substantially advance the public health and safety purpose. The action should also, within the limits of available technology and information, be no more restrictive than necessary to alleviate the health and safety risk created by the use to be regulated.

c. In assessing these issues, an agency should examine the following factors:

   i. The certainty that the property use to be regulated poses a health and safety risk in the absence of government action; and

   ii. The severity of the injury to public health and safety should the identified risk materialize, based on the best available information in the field involved.

   From the perspective of a takings implication analysis, the greater the certainty or the greater the severity, the more stringent measures are justified.

d. Although the ideal is that the response taken to counter the risk be "no greater than" the risk posed, reasonable proportionality presupposes available technology and information.

3. **Delay**

   [Executive Order No. 12630, Section 3(d); Appendix to Guidelines, Section IV]

   Undue delay in decisionmaking processes, whether intentional or unintentional, may give rise to takings liability, or increase the amount of compensation due if the decisionmaking process interferes with the use of property pending the decision. Hence, decision-making processes should be kept to the minimum time necessary to allow the agency to meet its obligations.

Appendix C: Guidelines for Implementing E.O. 12630 / 211

D. **Policy and Action Evaluation Criteria**

[Executive Order No. 12630, Section 4; Appendix to Guidelines, Sections II, III, and V]

When evaluating policies or actions for takings implications, the following criteria (informed by the guidance of Executive Order No. 12630, Sections V(A-C) of these Guidelines, the Appendix to these Guidelines, and applicable case law) will apply. These criteria will form the basis for the assessment of takings implications as outlined in Section VI(A)(2), infra.

1. **Takings Implication Considerations: Physical Intrusion**

    Physical intrusion takings analysis is appropriate where the action or policy involves physical presence by the government, or by others pursuant to government authorizations, on private property. Where that presence amounts to occupancy of the property, takings exposure is measured by the physical limits of the occupation. Where the intrusion is less than occupancy, takings exposure turns on both the character of the invasion (for example, overflight, flooding) and a physical presence that is the natural and probable consequence of authorized government action.

2. **Takings Implication Considerations: Regulatory Takings**

    As discussed in Section V(B)(3), regulation may result in a taking of property.

    a. **Character of the Government Action**

        In assessing the character of the government action, an agency should examine:

        i. The purpose intended to be served by the enabling statute, where the policy or action is taken pursuant to statute. Agencies should examine both the legislative history and the operative terms of the statute to determine that a legitimate purpose identified in the statute is being served.

        ii. Whether the policy or action will substantially advance a legitimate public purpose of the enabling statute, where the policy or action is in furtherance of obligations imposed or authorized by statute. The proposed policy or action both must have the purpose of furthering, and must substantially further, the purpose embodied in the statute. It is not enough that the policy or action or regulation might rationally advance the purpose purported to be served.

    iii. The degree to which the property-related activity or use that is the subject of the proposed policy or action contributes to a harm that the proposed policy or action is designed to address. The less direct, immediate, and demonstrable the contribution of the property-related activity to the harm to be addressed, the greater the risk that a taking will have occurred.

    iv. The extent to which the intended policy or action totally abrogates a property interest which has been historically viewed as an essential stick in the bundle of property rights.

b. <u>Economic Impact of the Proposed Policy or Action</u>

In assessing the economic impact of the proposed policy or action, an agency should examine:

    i. To the extent reasonably possible, what economic and property interests will be, or are likely to be, affected by the proposed policy or action. In that context, economic impact should be considered as to each property interest recognized by the applicable law.

    ii. The likely degree of economic impact on identified property and economic interests;

    iii. To the extent reasonably possible, among other relevant factors, the character and present use of the property, the anticipated duration of the proposed or intended action, and variations in state law;

    iv. Whether the proposed policy or action carries benefits to the private property owner that offset or otherwise mitigate the adverse economic impact of the proposed policy or action; and,

    v. Whether alternative actions are available that would achieve the underlying lawful governmental objective and would have a lesser economic impact.

  c. <u>Interference with Reasonable Investment-Backed Expectations</u>

To the extent reasonably possible, an agency should examine the degree to which the proposed policy or action will interfere with reasonable, investment-backed expectations of those private property owners affected by the proposed action, even if such expectations are not formally recognized as property interests under the generally applicable law.

3. <u>Determination of Policies or Actions Having Takings Implications or Significant Taking Implications</u>

  a. When an agency decisionmaker, in applying the Section V(D) criteria, determines that a policy or action appears to have an effect on private property sufficiently severe as to effectively deny economically viable use of any distinct legally protected property interest to its owner, or to have the effect of, or result in, a permanent or temporary physical occupation, invasion, or deprivation, that appearance shall be deemed to give rise to a takings implication for purposes of the Executive Order and these Guidelines. See Section IV(B), <u>supra</u> (definition of "takings implication").

  b. Similarly, a significant takings implication shall be deemed to exist for purposes of the Executive Order and these Guidelines when, on the basis of available information, the decisionmaker concludes as to any policy or action with a takings implication that:

i. The proposed policy or action poses a substantial risk that a taking of private property may result; or

ii. Insufficient information as to facts or law exists to enable an accurate assessment of whether significant takings consequences may result from the proposed policy or action.

See Section IV(B), *supra* (definition of "significant takings implication").

4. <u>Evaluation of Alternatives for Policies and Actions Having Takings Implications</u>

Agencies should strive to the extent permitted by law, consistent with their statutory obligations, to undertake policies or actions in a way which minimizes their takings implications. Where such implications cannot be wholly avoided, the agencies should take appropriate actions to minimize the potential financial impact of takings.

VI. <u>IMPLEMENTATION, MANAGEMENT, AND SPECIAL REPORTING REQUIREMENTS</u>

A. <u>Implementation and Management Requirements</u>

In order to apply the general principles contained in the Executive Order, Sections V(A)-(C) of these Guidelines, and the Appendix to these Guidelines, through the criteria detailed in Section V(D) of the Guidelines, Executive Order No. 12630 imposes the following obligations on agencies subject to its provisions.

1. <u>Federal Agency Contact</u>

The head of each agency required to review its policies and actions under Executive Order No. 12630 shall designate an agency official to be responsible for ensuring that agency's compliance with the Executive Order and these Guidelines. The designation of this official is solely within the discretion of the agency head. The designated federal agency contact shall serve as the agency's liaison on questions of compliance with the Executive Order and shall make information available to the Office of Management and Budget and/or the Attorney General, upon request, regarding the agency's compliance procedures and activities.

The identity of the designated official shall be communicated, by no later than July 15, 1988, to the Assistant Attorney General, Land and Natural Resources Division, Department of Justice, and the Director, Office of Management and Budget. Notification of any change in this designation shall also be forwarded within ten (10) working days of the effective date of the change.

2. **Takings Implication Assessment (TIA)**

Before undertaking any proposed action or implementing any policy or action subject to evaluation, each agency shall perform a Takings Implication Assessment (TIA). The TIA shall be made available to the agency decisionmaker responsible for determining whether and how to implement a policy or to undertake an action, in such form and in such manner as is calculated to ensure that the decisionmaker may make meaningful use of the TIA in formulating his or her decision.

   a. The TIA is to be integrated, in a form and manner in the agency's discretion, into normal agency decisionmaking processes.

   b. The TIA will serve as a tool for assessing the taking implications and related fiscal impact of policies and actions within the Executive Order. It is to provide candid, predecisional advice as a part of the continuing process of developing government policies and actions.

   c. For administrative and regulatory policies and actions subject to evaluation under the Executive Order and these Guidelines, a TIA must include:

       i. An assessment of the likelihood that the proposed action or policy may effect a taking for which compensation is due, in light of the principles referenced in the Executive Order and these Guidelines (see Section V, *supra*) and under applicable case law;

ii. Identification and consideration of alternatives, if any, to the proposed policy or action which also achieve the government's obligations under law but would reduce intrusions on the use or value of private property; and

iii. An estimate of the potential financial exposure to the government should a court find the proposed policy or action to be a taking. It is important to emphasize, in this respect, that this estimate is to be that -- an estimate. Agencies are encouraged to employ available data to the extent possible.

d. For legislative policies and actions subject to evaluation under the Executive Order and these Guidelines, a TIA must include:

i. An assessment of the likelihood that the proposed policy or action may effect a taking for which compensation is due, in light of the principles referenced in the Executive Order and these Guidelines (see Section V, supra) and under applicable case law;

ii. An assessment of whether there are alternatives to the proposed policy that could accomplish the legislative objective, but would present a lesser intrusion on the use or value of private property; and

iii. An estimate of the potential financial exposure to the government should a court find the proposed policy or action to be a taking. This estimate may be presented, in summary, in one of the following alternative forms, or in similar language in the agency's discretion:

a. If enacted as proposed, this legislation would pose a substantial risk of significant financial exposure for the United States.

b. If enacted as proposed, this legislation would pose a likelihood

- 22 -

of some degree of financial exposure for the United States.

c. If enacted as proposed, this legislation would pose a limited risk of financial exposure for the United States.

e. In instances in which there is an immediate threat to health and safety that constitutes an emergency requiring immediate response, the TIA may be done upon completion of the emergency action in a form and manner in the agency's discretion.

B. Special Reporting Requirements

1. Required Submissions to the Office of Management and Budget

For regulations submitted for Office of Management and Budget review under Executive Order No. 12291, each agency should include a discussion summarizing any identified takings implications, consistent with Section VI(A)(2)(c), and addressing the merits of the regulations in light of those implications, if the regulation is:

a. A "major" rule as defined or designated under Executive Order No. 12291;

b. Any rule that has "significant takings implications," regardless of whether it is properly classified as a "major rule"; or

c. Any rule otherwise designated by the Office of Management and Budget.

The agency should retain the Takings Implication Assessment and make it available, upon request, to the Office of Management and Budget.

2. Notices of Proposed Rulemaking

"Significant taking implications" shall be identified and discussed, in form and manner chosen by the agency, in notices of proposed rulemaking.

3. **Legislative Proposals**

   For legislative policies and actions subject to coordination and clearance by the Office of Management and Budget (OMB) under Circular No. A-19, Revised, or any successor directive or circular, each agency shall, consistent with Section VI(A)(2)(d), identify the takings implications of the legislation, if any, in such form and manner as the agency deems appropriate. When the agency then elects not to address an identified takings implication in the document submitted for legislative coordination and clearance, the agency shall notify OMB of the existence of such implication. Where an agency determines that a legislative policy or action has significant takings implications, it shall include an evaluation of such implications in its submission to OMB under Circular No. A-19, Revised.

   In every instance, agencies should retain the Takings Implication Assessment and make it available, upon request, to the Office of Management and Budget.

C. **Agency Budget Submissions**

   Separate guidance will be provided by the Office of Management and Budget regarding documentation requirements. (e.g., OMB Circular No. A-11)

D. **Agency Supplementation**

   1. **Purpose**

      Section 5(e)(2) of Executive Order No. 12630 directs that the Attorney General shall, in consultation with each agency, promulgate such supplemental guidelines as may be appropriate to the specific obligations of that agency. Supplemental guidelines may be issued for one specific agency or for a group of related agencies, as appropriate. The supplemental guidelines shall set forth implementing procedures that will aid an agency in administering its specific program responsibilities in accordance with the analytical and procedural framework presented in the Executive Order and these Guidelines. The supplemental guidelines should not be used to restate the terms of the Executive Order or these Guidelines.

Appendix C: Guidelines for Implementing E.O. 12630 / 219

2. **Initiation of Supplementation Process**

   The Guidelines supplementation process may be initiated either by an affected agency or by the Attorney General, as set forth below. However, in either event, the Attorney General is responsible for final approval and issuance of the supplemental guidelines.

   a. **Federal Agency Review**

   Each agency to which Executive Order No. 12630 applies is responsible, on a continuing basis, for reviewing its internal policies and procedures to ensure full compliance with the Executive Order. In conjunction with this review, each agency shall assess whether procedures to supplement these Guidelines (including, for example, exclusions supported by a Takings Implication Assessment, or special processes for certain categories of policies or actions) are necessary and appropriate in light of its specific statutory obligations. Whenever an agency determines that issuance of supplemental guidelines is warranted, the Secretary or head of the agency shall inform the Attorney General and submit proposed supplemental guidelines for review, approval, and issuance by the Attorney General.

   b. **Department of Justice Review**

   In conjunction with his responsibilities for oversight of agency implementation of Executive Order No. 12630, the Attorney General may initiate the preparation and issuance of supplemental guidelines for an individual agency or group of agencies. Initiation and development of such guidelines by the Attorney General may be appropriate, for example, to ensure that similar types of government program activities, conducted by several agencies, are evaluated in a comparable manner under the Executive Order. The Attorney General shall consult with the Secretary or head of the individual agency or agencies involved regarding the need for, and advisability of, issuance of such supplemental guidelines.

3. **Issuance of the Supplemental Guidelines**

   The Attorney General has the responsibility under section 5(e)(2) of the Executive Order to promulgate any such agency supplemental guidelines. Accordingly, the Attorney General shall review an agency's proposed supplemental guidelines, submitted in accordance with Section VI(D)(2)(a) above, for conformance with the Executive Order and these Guidelines. At the completion of this review, including consultation with the agency involved, the Attorney General may, in his discretion, issue agency supplemental guidelines. In the event the Attorney General has initiated preparation and development of agency supplemental guidelines, he shall consult with, and fully consider the recommendations of, the agency involved prior to issuance of Executive Order No. 12630 supplemental guidelines. Any policy or action for which a categorical exclusion has been created by supplemental guidelines will automatically lose that exclusion from the Executive Order No. 12630 process where such conduct is held by a court of competent jurisdiction to have the potential of a taking.

4. **National Security Exemption**

   Executive Order No. 12630 supplemental guidelines may include specific criteria for providing limited exceptions to the provisions of these guidelines for classified activities and actions. Such activities and actions are those specifically authorized under criteria established by an executive order or statute to be kept secret in the interest of national defense or foreign policy and are in fact properly classified pursuant to such executive order or statute.

VII. **RESPONSIBILITIES OF THE ATTORNEY GENERAL AND THE DIRECTOR OF THE OFFICE OF MANAGEMENT AND BUDGET**

   A. **Attorney General**

   In addition to the specific responsibilities for implementation of Executive Order No. 12630 set forth above, the Attorney General shall, to the extent permitted by law, take action to ensure that the policies of the agencies are consistent with the principles, criteria, and administrative requirements established in the Executive Order and these Guidelines. The Attorney General shall also revise and reissue these Guidelines, as necessary, to reflect fundamental changes in takings law that occur as a result of United States Supreme Court decisions.

B. <u>Director, Office of Management and Budget</u>

The Director, Office of Management and Budget, shall, to the extent permitted by law, take action to ensure that the policies of the agencies are consistent with the principles, criteria, and requirements stated in Executive Order No. 12630 and that all takings awards levied against agencies are properly accounted for in agency budget submissions.

VIII. <u>JUDICIAL REVIEW AND ENFORCEMENT</u>

Consistent with Section 6 of Executive Order No. 12630, these Guidelines and the Appendix to the Guidelines are intended only to improve the internal management of Executive Branch agencies and are therefore enforceable only by and within the Executive Branch. Accordingly, like the Executive Order itself, these Guidelines and the Appendix to the Guidelines shall not be deemed to create any right or benefit, substantive or procedural, enforceable by anyone in any court against the United States, its agencies, its officers, or any person. For these reasons, neither these Guidelines, the Appendix, nor the deliberative processes or products resulting from their implementation by agencies shall be treated as establishing criteria or standards that constitute any basis for judicial review of agency actions. Thus, the extent or quality of an agency's compliance with the Executive Order or these Guidelines shall not be justiciable in any proceeding for judicial review of agency action.

Issued in Washington, D.C. the _____ day of _____, 1988.

EDWIN MEESE III
Attorney General

INDEX

Term	Section	Page
Agency Plans and Studies	II(B)(4)	6
Alternatives		
Economic Impact	V(D)(2)(b)(v)	19
In General	V(A)(5)	12
Minimization	V(D)(4)	19
Special Reporting Requirements	VI(B)	23
Takings Implication Assessment	VI(A)(2)(c)(ii)	22
Attached Property	II(B)(3)	6
Attorney General		
Responsibilities	VII(A)	26
Available Technology and Information	V(B)(3)(c)	14
Budget	VI(C)	24
Character of Government Action	V(D)(2)(a)	17
Purpose to be Served	V(D)(2)(a)(i)	17
Policy or Action Significantly Advance Purpose	V(D)(2)(a)(ii)	17
Proportionality as Factor	V(D)(2)(a)(iii)	18
Consultation with State and Local Governments	II(B)(5)	7
Cost		
Estimate Only	VI(A)(2)(c)(iii)	22
Takings Implication Assessment	VI(A)(2)(c)(iii)	22
Data Gathering and Evaluation	II(B)(4)	6
Delay		
In General	V(C)(3)	16

INDEX

Term	Section	Page
Departments and Agencies		
Comments on Policies or Actions of Other Departments and Agencies	II(A)	4
Lead Agency	IV(E)	10
Within Executive Order 12630	III	8
Economic Impact		
In General	V(D)(2)(b)	18
Degree of Impact	V(D)(2)(b)(ii)	18
Number Affected	V(D)(2)(b)(i)	18
Reciprocal Benefits	V(D)(2)(b)(iv)	19
Relevant Factors	V(D)(2)(b)(iii)	18
Eminent Domain		
Power	II(B)(7)	7
Traditional use	V(A)(2)	11
Exemption		
Policies and Action Prior to Executive Order 12630	II(C)	8
Exclusions		
Agency Plans and Studies	II(B)(4)	6
Consultation with State and Local Governments	II(B)(5)	7
Eminent Domain Power	II(B)(7)	7
Military and Foreign Affairs Activities	II(B)(8)	7
Military Property	II(B)(6)	7
Reduction of Regulations	II(B)(1)	5
Seizures of Property	II(B)(3)	6
Trust Property and Treaty Negotiations	II(B)(2)	6

- 2 -

INDEX

Term	Section	Page
Executive Order		
History	I	1
Sections 2(a) and 2(c)	II(A)	4
Fifth Amendment		
Authority to Act	V(A)(3)	12
In General	I, II(B)	1, 5
Just Compensation		
Obligation	V(A)(1-3)	11, 12
General Principles and Assessment Factors	V	11
Guidelines		
Exclusions	II(B)	5
Overview	I	1
Policies and Actions Subject to Evaluation	II(A)	4
Purpose	I, V(B)(3)(c)	1, 14
Implementation, Management, and Special Reporting Requirements	VI(A)	20
Designation of Responsible Official	VI(A)(1)	20
Takings Implication Assessment	VI(A)(2)	21
Insufficient Information	IV(C)(2)	9
Inverse Condemnation		
Generally	V(A)(2)	11
Defined	V(A)(3)	12
Judicial Review	VIII	27
Land Use Planning Agencies	II(B)(4)	7

Appendix C: Guidelines for Implementing E.O. 12630 / 225

INDEX

Term	Section	Page
Legislation		
Pending	IV(D)	9
Proposed	IV(D)	9
Special Reporting		
Requirements	VI(B)(3)	24
Major Rule	VI(B)(1)	23
Military and Foreign		
Affairs Activities	II(B)(8)	7
Military Property	II(B)(6)	7
Minimization of Intrusion	V(A)(5), V(D)(4)	12, 20
Office of Management and Budget		
Responsibilities	VII(B)	27
Physical Intrusion		
Physical Invasion	II(B)(4), V(A)(2) V(D)(1)	6, 11, 17
Physical Occupancy	II(B)(4), V(A)(2) V(D)(1)	6, 11, 17
Police Power	V(C)(2)	15
Policies and Actions Prior to Executive Order 12630	II(C)	8
Policies and Actions Subject to Evaluation	II(A)	4
Private Property	IV(A)	9
Forms	V(A)(4)	12
Ownership and Use Not Privilege	V(A)(1)	11
Proportionality		
Character of Government Action	V(D)(2)(a)(iii)	18
In General	V(B)(3)(c)	14

- 4 -

INDEX

Term	Section	Page
Public Health and Safety	V(C)(2)(d)	16
Public Health and Safety		
Certainty and Severity Analysis	V(C)(2)(c)	16
Component of Broader Police Power	V(C)(2)	15
Deference	V(C)(2)	15
Health and Safety Risk	V(C)(2)(b)	16
Proportionality	V(C)(2)(d)	16
Purpose Analysis	V(C)(2)(a)	15
Substantially Advance Health and Safety Purpose	V(C)(2)(b)	16
Public Purpose		
In General	V(A)(1)	11
Reasonable Investment Backed Expectations	V(D)(2)(c)	19
Reciprocal Benefits		
Economic Impact	V(D)(2)(b)(iv)	18
Reduction of Regulations	II(B)(1)	5
Regulations		
Lawful Exercise Not Precluding Taking	V(A)(1)	11
Permitting	V(C)(1)	15
Public Health and Safety	V(C)(2)	15
Similarity to Physical Occupancy or Invasion	V(B)(3)(b)	14
Takings Implications	V(D)(2)	17
Responsible Official	VI(A)(1)	20

- 5 -

Term	INDEX Section	Page
Rulemaking	VI(B)(1)	23
Major Rule	VI(B)(1)(a)	23
Rule Otheriwse Designated	VI(B)(1)(c)	23
Rule with Significant Takings Implications	VI(B)(1)(b)	23
Significant Takings Implications		
Defined	IV(B)	9
Identify and Discuss	VI(B)(1)(b)	23
Special Reporting Requirements		
Budget	VI(B)(2)	23
In General	VI(B)	23
Legislative Proposals	VI(B)(3)	24
Rulemaking	VI(B)(1)	23
Special Situations	V(C)	
Permitting Programs	V(C)(1)	15
Public Health and Safety	V(C)(2)	15
Supplementation		
Department of Justice Review	VI(D)(1)(b)	25
Federal Agency Review	VI(D)(2)(a)	25
Initiation	VI(D)(2)	25
Issuance	VI(D)(3)	26
National Security Exemption	VI(D)(4)	26
Purpose	VI(D)(1)	24
Takings		
Nature of Takings	V(B)	13
Physical Invasions	V(B)(2)	13
Physical Occupancies	V(B)(1)	13
Regulatory	V(B)(3)	13

228 / Property Rights

```
                                INDEX
Term                            Section                 Page
```

Takings Implication Assessment

    Alternatives Assessment   VI(A)(2)(c)(ii)   22
    Budget Use   VI(C)   24
    Financial Exposure Estimate   VI(A)(2)(c)(iii)   22
    Evaluative Device   VI(A)(2)(b)   21
    Form and Manner, Agency Discretion   VI(A)(2)(a)   21
    In General   VI(A)(2)   21
    Likelihood of Taking   VI(A)(2)(c)(i)   21
    Predecisional Device   VI(A)(2)(b)   21
    Rulemaking Use   VI(B)(1)   23

Takings Implications

    Evaluation Criteria
        In General   V(D)   17
    Identify and Discuss Significant Takings Implications   VI(B)(1)(b)   23
    Identify Takings Implications of Regulatory Actions   VI(B)(1)   23
    Minimizing Risk   V(D)(4)   20
    Physical Intrusion   V(D)(1)   17
    Regulatory Takings
        In General   V(D)(2)   17
        Character of Government Action   V(D)(2)(a)   17
        Economic Impact   V(D)(2)(b)   18
        Reasonable Investment Backed Expectations   V(D)(2)(c)   19

    Test   V(D)(3)   19

Treaty Negotiations   II(B)(2)   6

Trust Property   II(B)(2)   6

APPENDIX
TO
GUIDELINES FOR THE EVALUATION OF RISK AND
AVOIDANCE OF UNANTICIPATED TAKINGS

I. **Introduction**

This Appendix is a part of, and incorporated by reference into, the Guidelines promulgated by the Attorney General pursuant to Executive Order No. 12630. It provides further detail for the case law parameters surrounding the consideration of the risk that a taking may have occurred. See Guidelines, Section V(A)(5). This discussion is not meant to be exhaustive. In that respect, the takings implication consideration and the evaluation of applicable case law will normally be one requiring close consultation between agency program personnel and agency counsel.

As with the Guidelines themselves, this Appendix speaks only to a general framework for the takings implication analysis under Executive Order No. 12630. Similarly, it is important to reiterate that Executive Order No. 12630 contemplates agency-specific supplemental guidelines. See Executive Order No. 12630, § 5(e)(2); Guidelines, § VI(D).

II. **General Considerations**

A. **The Framework**

Executive Order No. 12630, as further explained in the Guidelines, provides for: (a) completion of a Takings Implication Assessment (TIA) before undertaking any proposed action or implementing any policy as defined by Section 2(b) and 2(c) of the Executive Order (see Guidelines, § VI(A)(2)) and (b) certain Special Reporting Requirements, including the identification of takings implications of proposed regulatory actions in certain specific submissions to the Office of Management and Budget (OMB), and the identification and discussion of significant takings implications (as defined in the Guidelines) in notices of proposed rulemaking and, subject to the normal OMB legislative coordination and clearance process, messages transmitting legislative proposals to Congress. These obligations will be integrated, in ways to be determined by the agency in light of the particular program, into its normal decisionmaking processes.

The Guidelines contemplate that agency decisionmakers will continue to meet the obligations imposed upon them by statute. They do not, and should not be read to, preclude actions or policies which the decisionmaker determines necessary to meet those obligations. In those circumstances, the TIA process will identify the takings implications, if any, of the necessary governmental conduct while permitting that conduct to go forward.

B. The Takings Implication Assessment

The TIA serves as an evaluative tool for the takings implications of policies and actions within the Executive Order and provides candid advice on those implications. As a part of the continuing process of developing government policies and actions, the TIA focuses attention on the fiscal and policy concerns arising from takings risk. Intended as a predecisional document, the TIA will be available for meaningful use by the decisionmaker prior to the decision. See Guidelines, § VI(A)(2).

C. Significance of Factual Information to Takings Implication Analysis

Questions as to the existence of takings require the sifting of numerous facts for the isolation of significant and insignificant factors. This focus on facts also lies at the heart of the advice contemplated by the TIA. Thus, a separate TIA will normally be prepared for each policy or action within the Executive Order. Similarly, because the TIA's do evaluate specific factual settings, a TIA prepared for one policy or action will normally have no precedential value for another policy or action.

III. Takings Implications Analysis: General Principles and Framework

[See Executive Order No. 12630, §§ 1(b), 3(a); Guidelines, § V(D)]

A. Introduction

The Executive Order requires identification of takings implications. See Executive Order 12630, § 5(b). This Appendix now turns to a general discussion of the case law framework which provides the current background for assessing takings implications.

B. Fairness and Justice Under the Fifth Amendment

Ratified in 1791, the Fifth Amendment provides, for pertinent purposes:

> nor shall private property be taken for
> public use without just compensation.

Its terms do not prohibit the taking of private property for lawful purposes. Rather, they operate "to secure compensation in the event of otherwise proper interference amounting to a taking". First English Evangelical Lutheran Church of Glendale v. County of Los Angeles, 107 S. Ct. 2378, 2386 (1987). The constitutional guarantee of the Amendment precludes government "from forcing some people alone to bear public burdens which, in all fairness and justice, should be borne by the public as a whole." Armstrong v. United States, 364 U.S. 40, 49 (1959).

1. **Focus on Impact of Actions and Self-Executing Character**

The assessment of governmental interference under the Amendment turns ultimately not on what the government may say, or what it may intend, but on the impact of its actions. Hughes v. Washington, 389 U.S. 290, 298 (1967); Armstrong v. United States, 364 U.S. at 48-49. Moreover, where the interference effects a taking, that governmental action implicates a "constitutional obligation to pay just compensation." First English Evangelical Lutheran Church of Glendale v. County of Los Angeles, 107 S. Ct. at 2386. The Amendment has a "self-executing character . . . with respect to compensation." United States v. Clarke, 445 U.S. 253, 257 (1980)(citations omitted), quoted in First English Evangelical Lutheran Church of Glendale v. County of Los Angeles, id.

In the face of this self-executing obligation, it is not enough that an agency discontinue its intrusion when a court finds that a taking has occurred. First English Evangelical Lutheran Church of Glendale v. Country of Los Angeles, 107 S. Ct. at 2387-2389. In those circumstances, just compensation would still be due for the period between the point at which the government action created compensable interference (see Sections III(E-G), infra) and the termination of that intrusion. Id. at 2388-2389.

Nor is it necessary that just compensation be paid in advance of a taking, provided that a process is available for meeting the obligation. Williamson Co. Regional Planning v. Hamilton Bank, 105 S. Ct. 3108, 3121 (1985).

2. **Fact Sensitive Analysis**

The takings analysis proceeds in the particular factual circumstances of the governmental impact on property. This leads to what have been described as "ad hoc" analyses in the context of particular facts. See Hodel v. Irving, 107 S. Ct. 2076, 2082 (1987); Kaiser Aetna v. United States, 444 U.S.

164, 175 (1979); Penn Central Transportation Co. v. New York City, 438 U.S. 104, 124 (1978). See Section II(C), supra.

3. Public Use Requirement

The Amendment reaches the taking of private property for public use. In that respect, the "public use" requirement is "coterminous with the scope of the sovereign's police powers." Hawaii Housing Authority v. Midkiff, 104 S. Ct. 2321, 2329 (1984)(Hawaii Land Reform Act created condemnation process for transfer of title from lessors in land oligopoly to lessees in order to reduce concentration of land ownership). The Court will not "substitute its judgment for a legislature's judgment as to what constitutes a public use 'unless the use be palpably without reasonable foundation.'" Id. See also Berman v. Parker, 348 U.S. 26, 33 (1954)(comprehensive use of eminent domain power for slum redevelopment). Although analysis of the legislative public purpose may include the legislative statement of purpose and the legislative history, the operative terms and provisions of the statute will control any inconsistency between the former and the latter. See Keystone Bituminous Coal Association v. De Benedictis, 107 S. Ct. 1232, 1243 n.16 (1987)("examine the operative provisions of a statute, not just its stated purpose, in assessing its true nature"). That the Legislature has found a public use does not necessarily, however, answer the more critical question -- for Fifth Amendment purposes -- of whether the lawful exercise of governmental power effects a compensable taking. See Sections III(C-F), infra; Guidelines, § V.

C. Property Interests Within the Fifth Amendment

[See Executive Order No. 12630, § 2(b)]

"Property interests...are not created by the Constitution." Webb's Fabulous Pharmacies, Inc. v. Beckwith, 449 U.S. 155, 161 (1980). Instead, "they are created and their dimensions are defined by existing rules or understandings that stem from an independent source such as state law." Id. See also Ruckelshaus v. Monsanto Company, 467 U.S. 986, 1001 (1983) (trade secret property right). Federal statutes may, however, provide a basis for the perfection of property interests by individuals. For instance, subject to the federal law limitations for establishing that necessary predicates for the vesting of interests have occurred, federal mining claims are private property within the Fifth Amendment. Freese v. United States, 639 F.2d 754 (Ct. Cl. 1982). In a later opinion, Freese v. United States, 6 Cl. Ct. 1, aff'd, 770 F.2d 177 (Fed. Cir. 1984), the court found that plaintiffs had not perfected their claim. Cf. Cape Fox Corporation v. United States, 4 Cl. Ct. 223 (1983)(ANCSA "selections" contingent and speculative).

The Amendment reaches property interests of whatever specie -- realty, personalty, or intellectual. In the context of the Fifth Amendment, the word "property" is used in the sense of "the group of rights inhering in the citizen's relation to the physical thing, as the right to possess, to use and dispose of it." The provision addresses every sort of interest the citizen may possess. United States v. General Motors Corp., 323 U.S. 373, 378 (1945). See also United States v. Willow River Power Co., 324 U.S. 499, 502 (1945); but cf. Reichelderfer v. Quinn, 287 U.S. 315 (1932)(sovereign-created values may not be private property interests under the Fifth Amendment); Acton v. United States, 401 F.2d 896 (9th Cir. 1968), cert. denied, 395 U.S. 945 (1969)(no property rights accrued to licensee upon revocation which are compensable in condemnation). Nor are all economic interests property interests. United States v. Willow River Power Co., 324 U.S. 499, 502 (1945). Where a property interest exists, however, the authority of the government to limit the interest by legal redefinition is constrained by the Fifth Amendment. Ruckelshaus v. Monsanto Co., 467 U.S. 986, 1012 (1984).

And, even though the right to build on private property can be the subject of legitimate permitting regulation, that right "cannot remotely be described as a 'governmental benefit'." Nollan v. California Coastal Commission, 107 S.Ct. 3141, 3146 (1987).

Further, compensation due under the Amendment when a taking does occur accrues to the owner of the property interest at the time of the taking, not to the owner at an earlier or later date. United States v. Dow, 357 U.S. 17 (1958). For special statutory limitations with respect to the assignment of taking claims, see 31 U.S.C. § 3727 (1986).

D. Congressional Authorization to Act

[See Executive Order No. 12630, § 3(e)]

Congressional authorization to undertake the government action at issue is an essential element of a taking. See generally, Section 3(e), supra. The test is not whether Congress authorized or even contemplated a taking effect from action pursuant to its purpose. Rather, the test is whether the government conduct said to give rise to the taking was authorized. See Florida Rock Industries v. United States, 791 F.2d 893, 898 (Fed. Cir. 1986), citing Portsmouth Harbor Land and Hotel Company v. United States, 260 U.S. 327 (1922); NBH Land Company v. United States, 576 F.2d 317, 319 (Ct. Cl. 1978); Barnes v. United States, 538 F.2d 865, 871 (Ct. Cl. 1976). Where Congress has acted
so as to preclude implication of authority for takings purposes, however, a taking cannot lie. NBH Land Company v.

<u>United States</u>, 576 F.2d at 319; <u>Southern California Financial Corporation v. United States</u>, 634 F.2d 521, 524 (Ct. Cl. 1980).

E. **Physical Intrusion Takings: Physical Occupancy and Physical Invasion**

[<u>See</u> Executive Order No. 12630, § 3(b); Guidelines, § V(B)(1) & (2)]

1. <u>Physical Occupancy</u> [Guidelines, § V(B)(1)]

In general, governmental actions resulting in physical intrusions constitute property restrictions long viewed by the Supreme Court as having "an unusually serious character for purposes of the Takings Clause." <u>Loretto v. Teleprompter Manhattan CATV Corporation</u>, 458 U.S. 419, 426 (1982). Moreover, "when the physical intrusion reaches the extreme form of a permanent physical occupation, a taking has occurred." <u>Id</u>.

In the circumstances of a physical occupation, the taking reaches to "the extent of the occupation, without regard to whether the action achieves an important public benefit or has only minimal economic impact on the owner." <u>Id</u>., at 425-426. Thus, the presence of CATV cables and related boxes (occupying approximately 1 1/2 cubic feet) pursuant to New York law requiring landlords to permit the facilities on their rental property was a taking. <u>Id.</u> at 441.

2. <u>Physical Invasions</u> [Guidelines, § V(B)(2)]

The Supreme Court recognizes a distinction between instances of permanent physical occupation and those of physical invasions falling short of occupation. <u>Id.</u> at 430. Classic examples of the latter in federal law include, but are not limited to, aviation easement, or so-called overflight, and flooding taking cases.

Thus, where flights of government aircraft are so low and frequent over private property as to constitute a direct and immediate interference with the use and enjoyment of the subjacent land, compensable takings may arise. <u>United States v. Causby</u>, 328 U.S. 256 (1946). <u>See also</u> <u>Aaron v. United States</u>, 311 F.2d 798 (Ct. Cl. 1963)(finding overflight taking in navigable airspace); <u>Branning v. United States</u>, 654 F.2d 88 (Ct. Cl. 1981)(liability from flights over 500 feet AGL not precluded merely by that fact); <u>Stephens v. United States</u>, 11 Cl. Ct. 352 (1986)(vast majority of flights in navigable airspace and no peculiar circumstances warranting liability there). Where flights occurring below the navigable airspace are involved, those intruding flights must interfere "substantially with the use or enjoyment of the property" in order to risk taking liability. <u>Hero Lands Company v. United States</u>, 1 Cl. Ct. 102,

105 (flights in conjunction with operations of NAS-New Orleans), aff'd, 727 F.2d 1118 (Fed. Cir.), cert. denied, 466 U.S. 972 (1983).

Where flooding occurs as the natural and probable consequence of authorized government action and, although intermittent, is inevitably recurring, a taking also may be found. United States v. Cress, 243 U.S. 316, 330 (1917). See also Bartz v. United States, 633 F.2d 571 (Ct. Cl. 1980); Barnes v. United States, 538 F.2d 865 (Ct. Cl. 1976)(alteration of sedimentation patterns resulting in above high water flooding causing taking). The flooding must be productive of substantial interference in order to risk taking liability. Barnes v. United States, 538 F.2d at 870 (citing United States v. Cress, 243 U.S. at 328).

F. Regulatory Takings

[See Executive Order No. 12630, §§ 3(b), 3(c), 4(a), 4(d), 5(b); Guidelines, § V(B)(3)]

1. In General

Governmental regulatory conduct may go "too far", thus requiring just compensation. Pennsylvania Coal v. Mahon, 260 U.S. 393, 415 (1922)(statute prohibited the mining of anthracite coal in a manner causing surface subsidence and damage to overlying structures). Where the Mahon line is crossed and the vehicle for payment of just compensation provided by 28 U.S.C. § 1491 (1986) is unavailable, for instance, the Court has invalidated federal regulatory action. Specifically, in Hodel v. Irving, 107 S. Ct. 2076, 2084 (1987), the Supreme Court invalidated congressional legislation providing that certain property could not descend by intestacy or devise to successors in interest but, instead, would escheat to Indian tribes. Stressing the extraordinary character of the government regulation and the virtual "abrogation of the right to pass on a certain type of property," the Court concluded that the statute went "too far."

The Court has indicated, in land use regulation contexts, that the line will be crossed when a regulation does "not substantially advance legitimate state interests . . . or denies an owner economically viable use of his land." Agins v. Tiburon, 447 U.S. 255, 260 (1980)(zoning density restrictions neither prevented best use of proerty nor extinguished a "fundamental" attribute of ownership), cited in Nollan v. California Coastal Commission, 107 S. Ct. 3141, 3146 (1987) and United States v. Riverside Bayview Homes, Inc., 106 S. Ct. 455, 459 (1985). The existence of a permit system, for instance, and the requirement that an individual resort to the system before engaging in a property use does not effect a taking per se. Id.

"Only when a permit is denied and the effect of the denial is to prevent 'economically viable' use of the land in question can it be said that a taking has occurred." Id.

2. **Permitting Programs and Conditions Substantially Advancing Legitimate Government Purposes**

[See Executive Order No. 12630, § 4; Guidelines, § V(C)(1)]

a. **In General**

The programs of many agencies require private parties to obtain permits in order to undertake a specific use of, or action with respect to, private property. Takings precedent requires that permitting programs give special thought with respect to any conditions imposed on the granting of a permit. Specifically, in Nollan v. California Coastal Commission, 107 S. Ct. 3141, 3144 (1987), the Court addressed a situation where the California Coastal Commission granted property owners a permit to replace a small beachfront bungalow with a larger house on the condition that the owners provide, by easement, additional lateral access for the public to public beaches on the water side of the house.

Analyzing the case under the Takings Clause, the Court first reiterated the proposition that the right to exclude others from property was one of the most essential sticks in the property owners' bundle of rights. Id. at 3145. That the burden on this right resulted from a condition on a permit as contrasted to acquisition of an easement for access was insignificant. Id. Pointing to the permanent and continuous right given to individuals to traverse the lateral beachfront, the Court found a physical occupation. Id. Accord Loretto v. Teleprompter Manhattan CATV Corporation, 458 U.S. 419, 426 (1982).

Analyzing the question of whether exaction of this concession by permit condition effected a taking, Nollan cited Agins language and began with the proposition that "land use regulation would not effect a taking if it 'substantially advance[d] legitimate state interests' and [did] not 'den[y] an owner economically viable use of his land.'" Id. at 3146 (citing Agins v. City of Tiburon, 447 U.S. at 260). Significantly, the Court held that the regulatory requirement must "substantially advance" the legitimate interest and not merely be a requirement which might rationally achieve the governmental objective. Nollan v. California Coastal Commission, 107 S. Ct. at 3147, n.3.

Appendix C: Guidelines for Implementing E.O. 12630 / 237

The Court assumed, *arguendo*, the legitimacy of the government interest -- protecting the public's ability to see the beach -- in the first instance. Id. at 3147. Given that legitimacy, a "condition that would have protected the public's ability to see the beach notwithstanding construction of the new house," for example, would have been constitutional. Id. at 3148. Such a condition would have served the same governmental purpose as the building restriction in the first instance.

Where the condition imposed failed to advance the governmental interest which anchored the restriction in the first instance, but instead sought to achieve a different purpose without just compensation, "the building restriction [was] not a valid regulation of land use but 'an out and out plan of extortion'." Id. (citations omitted). In the Court's view, this nexus failure resulted, for Takings Clause purposes, in something beyond the "outer limits of 'legitimate state interests.'" Id.

b. **Executive Order and Guidelines Requirements**

Accordingly, in the interest of minimizing unanticipated takings, Section 4(a) of the Executive Order and Section V(C)(1) of the Guidelines provide that a permitting requirement imposing a condition on the granting of the permit should: (1) serve the same purpose that would have been served by a prohibition of the use or action; and, (2) substantially advance that purpose.

3. **Proportionality of Burden to Risk Created**

[See Executive Order No. 12630, § 4(b); Guidelines, § V(B)(3)(c)]

a. **In General**

It is also important to the justice and fairness analysis compelled by the Fifth Amendment to demonstrate, to the extent possible, that the restriction imposed is proportional to the contribution to that risk occasioned by the restricted use. Nollan v. California Coastal Commission, 107 S. Ct. 3141, 3143 n.4 (1987)("If . . . singled out to bear the burden . . . although they had not contributed to it more than other . . . landowners . . . [the action] might violate either the . . . Takings Clause or the Equal Protection Clause.").

b. **Executive Order and Guidelines Requirements**

Accordingly, Section 4(b) of Executive Order No. 12630 provides:

> When a proposed action would place a restriction
> on a use of private property, the restriction
> imposed on the use shall not be disproportionate
> to the extent to which the use contributes to
> the overall problem that the restriction is imposed
> to redress.

See also Guidelines, § V(B)(3)(c).

4. Three-Part Regulatory Taking Analysis

[Guidelines, § V(D)(2)]

a. In General

In addition to the specific requirements with respect to permitting conditions (Section III(F)(2), supra), the location of the Mahon "line" requires careful consideration of what has come to be viewed as a three-part regulatory taking test: (1) the character of the governmental action; (2) the economic impact of the action; and (3) the extent of interference with reasonable investment-backed expectations. Penn Central Transportation Company v. New York City, 438 U.S. 104, 124 (1978)(New York Landmark Law prohibited appellants from occupying airspace, i.e., developing, above Grand Central Station but permitted use of the remainder of the parcel as well as sanctioned the transfer of this precluded right to develop to other property; no taking found). This three-part test is applied in Section V(D) of the Guidelines when evaluating regulatory actions for their takings implications.

b. Examples of Application of Three-Part Analysis

The following are examples of the application of the three-tiered test: Hodel v. Irving, 107 S. Ct. at 2082 (act effected uncompensated taking; character of action, analogized significance of right to devise property to the right to exclude others; economic impact could be substantial and right to devise property "a valuable right"; taking found even though interference with investment backed expectations was not substantial; Connolly v. Pension Benefit Guaranty Corporation, 106 S. Ct. 1018, 1026 (1986)(withdrawal liability provisions of Multi-Employer Pension Plan Amendments of 1980 not takings; character of action, economic reallocation; economic impact, in proportion to experience with pension plan; interference with investment backed expectations, not substantial because of early notice to participants); Kaiser Aetna v. United States, 444 U.S. 164, 178 (1979)(action unlawful taking where petitioners, in presence of government consent and acquiesence, committed substantial investment of resources to link private body of water to navigable water; loss of right to exclude characterized as a

Appendix C: Guidelines for Implementing E.O. 12630 / 239

fundamental right of property; assertion of navigation servitude here would result in physical invasion; impact not insubstantial; expectancies evidenced by substantial investment of funds entitled to protection).

The ad hoc three-part test is not fully predictable, and therefore, proposed actions and policies should be sensitive to takings implications even if the case precedents finding a taking were decided on somewhat different facts. For example, even on the same subject matter, application of the tests can result in different takings conclusions. For instance, in Keystone Bituminous Coal Association v. De Benedictis, 107 S. Ct. 1232, 1242 (1987), the Court considered recent Pennsylvania legislation which -- like the Kohler Act analyzed in Mahon -- addressed concerns of subsidence damage associated with coal mining activities. The opinion finds the Mahon line unviolated for two reasons.

First, the 1966 Subsidence Act contained specific legislative findings that important public interests warranted the regulation, unlike the Kohler Act which involved "a balancing of the private economic interests of coal companies against the private interests of surface owners." 107 S. Ct. at 1242. Thus, the 1966 legislation brought to bear the "substantial" public interest in "preventing activities similar to public nuisances". 107 S. Ct. at 1246. See § III (F)(5)(a), infra. In determining the purposes, the Court emphasized that, although legislative declarations were important, the analysis required judicial consideration of the operative terms of the statute. 107 S. Ct. at 1243, n.16.

Second, Keystone petitioners demonstrated no material interference with reasonable investment backed expectations on the part of the coal industry. Specifically, the cases presented a facial challenge to the 1966 Act -- essentially, an allegation that the mere enactment of the legislation constituted a taking. 107 S. Ct. at 1242. Petitioners made no claim that the 1966 Act made continued mining of bituminous coal commercially impracticable. Nor did the Court have before it any evidence that the Act's requirement to leave certain coal in place had made mining unprofitable in those locations. These factors stood in contrast to Mahon's finding that the Kohler Act rendered mining commercially impracticable. Petitioners' "support estates" (which under Pennsylvania law included the right to remove coal underlying the surface or to leave those layers intact and which could be owned by either the surface or mineral estate owner), in the Court's view, had value only in that they protected or enhanced the mineral estates also owned by petitioners -- that is, the support estate was simply one strand in the bundle of rights owned by the coal owner. The Court stressed that petitioners "retain[ed] the right to mine virtually all of the coal in their mineral estates". Thus, the burden imposed on the surface estate did not constitute a taking.

    c. <u>Economic Impact Factors</u>

    [Guidelines, § V(D)(2)(b)]

Among the factors which may be relevant in assessing the economic impact of governmental action are the character of the property, the volatility of property values, variations in state property laws affecting the utility of the property, market, regional and demographic information, the existence of irretrievable economic opportunities, the anticipated duration of the proposed action, and the extent to which the property owner may have enhanced the existing use of the property. This list of factors is illustrative only and is neither exhaustive nor obligatory.

  5. <u>Regulation in the Service of Public Health and Safety</u>

    [<u>See</u> Executive Order No. 12630, § 4(d); Guidelines, § V(C)(2)]

    a. <u>In General: Deference in Matters of Public Health and Safety</u>

In evaluating government regulatory conduct under the Takings Clause, courts have evidenced a "hesitance" to find takings where the public purpose of the underlying legislation is to "restrain[] uses of property that are tantamount to public nuisances . . . " <u>Keystone Bituminous Coal Association v. De Benedictis</u>, 107 S. Ct. at 1245. Important to claiming the deference shown in such public nuisance regulation is recognition of the concept of "reciprocity of advantage" -- that, in demonstrable ways, each who is regulated benefits from the similar regulation of others. <u>Id. Cf. Mugler v. Kansas</u>, 123 U.S. 623 (1887)(prohibition of liquor sale in interest of health, safety, or morals of public); <u>Euclid v. Ambler</u>, 272 U.S. 365 (1926)(in a facial challenge, conclusion that noise and traffic might be very nearly a public nuisance in an area; thus, regulations bore substantial relationship to public welfare); <u>Miller v. Schoene</u>, 276 U.S. 272 (1928)(nuisance rationale sustains state's destruction of cedar rust trees); <u>Goldblatt v. Hempstead</u>, 369 U.S. 590, 595-596 (1961)(safety based regulation prohibiting further excavation of sand and gravel mine below water table not unreasonable; plaintiffs' failed to meet burden of showing that prohibition would further reduce value of property or that regulation unreasonable).

Appendix C: Guidelines for Implementing E.O. 12630 / 241

b. **Deference Not Coextensive with "Public Use"**

Although "public use" for purposes of the Fifth Amendment is coterminous with the governmental police power (Section III(B)(3), *supra*) the deferential "nuisance exception" discussed here is not coextensive with the police power. *Keystone Bituminous Coal Association v. De Benedictis*, 107 S. Ct. at 1245, n.20. In other words, even when governmental action is designed to protect health and safety, some consideration of that action's economic impact may nevertheless be appropriate. Thus, *Florida Rock v. United States*, 791 F.2d 893, 902 (Fed. Cir. 1986) has cautioned that a "regulation under the Clean Water Act can be a taking if its effect on a landowners's ability to put his property to productive use is sufficiently severe."

c. **Executive Order and Guidelines Requirements**

[*See* Executive Order 12630, § 5(d); Guidelines, § VI(A)]

With respect to public health and safety directed actions, then, management must, in any internal deliberative documents and any submissions to the Director, Office of Management and Budget, that are required:

i. Identify clearly, with as much specificity as possible, the public health or safety risk created by the private property use that is the subject of the proposed action;

ii. Establish that such proposed action substantially advances the purpose of protecting public health and safety against the specifically identified risk;

iii. Establish to the extent possible, that the restrictions imposed on the private property are not disproportionate to the extent to which the use contributes to the overall risk; and,

iv. Estimate, to the extent possible, the potential cost to the government in the event that a court later determines that the action constituted a taking. *See* § V, *infra*.

Under the Guidelines procedure, this reporting is accomplished by completion of the TIA process and consideration of the factors identified in Section V(C)(2) of the Guidelines for public health and safety actions. The "required submissions" are defined in Section VI(B) of the Guidelines.

6. **Examples of Regulatory Takings Litigation**

Although clearly not exhaustive, federal regulatory takings litigation include the following examples: Kirby Forest Industries v. United States, 467 U.S. 1, 4-6 (1984)(mere initiation of condemnation action does not result in taking even if accompanied by lis pendens); Yuba Goldfields v. United States, 723 F.2d 884 (Fed. Cir. 1983)(taking: government assertion of mineral rights title, was later found inaccurate by court ruling, and related "prohibition" of dredging activity); Deltona Corporation v. United States, 657 F.2d 1184 (Ct. Cl. 1981)(no taking: multi-stage development; permits as to early stages granted, but two permits under Section 10 of the Rivers and Harbors Act and Section 404 of the Clean Water Act denied as to latter stages; where many "economically viable uses" remain, denial of highest and best use not a taking); Jentgen v. United States, 657 F.2d 1210 (Ct. Cl. 1981)(no taking: Corps of Engineers denied section 404 permits, but offered modification; plaintiffs declined offer); Benenson v. United States, 548 F.2d 939 (Ct. Cl. 1977)(taking: statutory requirements for development of Pennsylvania Avenue property, in combination with congressionally imposed moratorium, in interest of preserving building facade deprived owner of any reasonable use); Hendler v. United States, 11 Cl. Ct. 91 (1986)(no taking: issuance of emergency access order under CERCLA alone not a taking; left open question of physical intrusion); Snowbank Enterprises v. United States, 6 Cl. Ct. 476 (1984)(no taking: regulatory constraints imposed by Boundary Waters Canoe Wilderness Act on access not so pervasive as to amount to a taking); Mesa Ranch Partnership v. United States, 2 Cl. Ct. 700 (1983)(no taking: threat of condemnation not a taking; interested party persuasion of local zoning body to down-zone property not a taking).

G. **Examples of Non-Categorical Takings Litigation**

Government action may not fall clearly into either a physical intrusion or regulatory burden category. In these instances, courts have proceeded to analyze the justice and fairness, in the context of Armstrong, supra, of the burden placed on the property owner. Examples include Eyherabide v. United States, 345 F.2d 565 (Ct. Cl. 1965)(taking: gunnery range around property; evidence of physical intrusion combined with other factors, such as signs indicating that area within ranch was a gunnery range); Drakes Bay Land Company v. United States, 424 F.2d 574 (Ct. Cl. 1970)(taking: government officials found to have ignored means, placed in their hands, to prevent economic harm from congressional taking; instead, found to have taken positive steps to prevent exploitation of land).

IV. Temporary Takings Resulting from Government Activity

[See Executive Order No. 12630, §§ 3(b), 3(d), 4(c) Guidelines, § V(C)(3)]

A. In General

"'[T]emporary' takings which ... deny a landowner all use of his property, are not different in kind from permanent takings, for which the Constitution clearly requires compensation." *First English Evangelical Lutheran Church of Glendale v. County of Los Angeles*, 107 S. Ct. at 2388 (finding that the Constitution's Takings Clause, as applicable to the states through the Fourteenth Amendment, compelled a cause of action for the government's payment for the value of the use of land during a temporary period). Where government action is found to occasion a temporary taking, "the government may elect to abandon its intrusion or discontinue regulations." *Id.* at 2387 (citations omitted). Time consumed by administrative processes in good faith which may be viewed as "normal delay" will likely raise no takings implication. *Id.* at 2389. However, government-imposed moratoria on use raise colorable takings considerations. *See, e.g., Benenson v. United States, supra.*

B. Executive Order and Guidelines Requirements

[See Executive Order No. 12630, § 3(d) & 4(c); Guidelines, § V(C)(3)]

Conversely, as the Executive Order highlights, "undue delays in decision-making during which private property use is interfered with carry a risk of being held to be takings." Executive Order No. 12630, § 3(d). In the interest of fiscal responsibility and minimizing the just compensation that might eventually be found due for any temporary taking, the Executive Order provides that:

> When a proposed action involves a permitting process or any other decision-making process that will interfere with, or otherwise prohibit, the use of private property pending the completion of the process, the duration of the process shall be kept to the minimum necessary.

Executive Order No. 12630, § 4(c). Types of delay requiring especially careful attention would include moratoria on the development or use or conduct which might be viewed as acquisitory in character.

V. Estimation of Potential Financial Exposure

[See Executive Order, § 4(d)(4); Guidelines, § VI(A)(2)(c)(3)]

A. In General

By way of overview, the United States may be held liable for the taking of a fee or lesser interest in property. See Benenson v. United States, 548 F.2d at 948 (fee interest); United States v. Causby, 328 U.S. at 267 (easement). Importantly, when the government takes, it acquires a property interest. With respect to the compensation due for the taking, the goal is to provide the monetary equivalent necessary to place the property owner in the same position he or she would have been had the taking not occurred. United States v. Reynolds, 397 U.S. 14, 15-16 (1970); Foster v. United States, 2 Cl. Ct. 426, 445 (1983). Where the taking is for less than a fee interest, the just compensation measure is frequently described as the difference between the value of the property before the taking and the value after the taking. Aaron v. United States, 311 F.2d at 802. Damages resulting from the loss or destruction of business incidental to the taking are not recoverable as part of the just compensation due. Mitchell v. United States, 267 U.S. 341, 346 (1925). But see Prudential Insurance Company of America v. United States, 801 F.2d 1295, 1300, n.13 (Fed. Cir. 1985).

The award of just compensation also entitles the successful plaintiff to interest from the date of the taking to the date of payment. See Jacobs v. United States, 290 U.S. 13, 16-17 (1933); Henry v. United States, 8 Cl. Ct. 389, 393-94 (1985); Foster v. United States, 3 Cl. Ct. 738, 745 (1983). Litigation expenses, including the reimbursement of reasonable attorney and appraisal fees, will also be available pursuant to the Uniform Relocation Assistance and Real Property Acquisition Policies Act, 42 U.S.C. § 4654(c)(1986).

B. Financial Exposure

The Guidelines require an estimation of potential financial exposure. First, it is critical to recognize that this is an estimation only. These estimates are not intended to be close approximations of ultimate takings liability, if any, in a given case. Second, the estimates will vary with the nature and scope of the government policy or action proposed. For instance, in the context of a proposed major rule under Executive Order No. 12291 for which a regulatory impact analysis has been prepared, that analysis may provide an appropriate vehicle for exposure estimation. See Sections 3(b) and (d), Executive Order No. 12291. In the context of other proposed rules, an economic assessment of the rule's impact on society will likely be prepared. See Sections 2(b)-(e), Executive Order No. 12291.

Appendix C: Guidelines for Implementing E.O. 12630 / 245

Treatment of the economic impact of the rule on the use or value of private property within that economic assessment may provide an appropriate vehicle for exposure estimation. In the context of legislation, economic assessments of the impact of such policies and action on the use or value of private property may provide an appropriate vehicle for exposure estimation. In the context of other policies and actions -- for example, permit applications -- applicants may be requested to supply the acquisition cost they paid for the property, adjusted for time to the date of the application.

Appendix D

The Dolan Decision*

*Source: West's CD ROM Libraries.

Material reprinted with permission.

114 S.Ct. 2309, Dolan v. City of Tigard, (U.S.Or. 1994)

*2309 114 S.Ct. 2309

38 ERC 1769, 129 L.Ed.2d 304, 62 USLW 4576, 24 Envtl. L. Rep. 21,083

**Florence DOLAN, Petitioner
v.
CITY OF TIGARD.**

No. 93-518.
Supreme Court of the United States
Argued March 23, 1994.
Decided June 24, 1994.

Landowner petitioned for judicial review of decision of Oregon Land Use Board of Appeals, affirming conditions placed by city on development of commercial property. The Court of Appeals, 113 Or.App. 162, 832 P.2d 853, affirmed, and landowner again appealed. The Oregon Supreme Court affirmed, 317 Or. 110, 854 P.2d 437, and certiorari was granted. The Supreme Court, Chief Justice Rehnquist, held that: (1) city's requirement that landowner dedicate portion of her property lying within flood plain for improvement of storm drainage system and property adjacent to flood plain as bicycle/pedestrian pathway, as condition for building permit allowing expansion of landowner's commercial property, had nexus with legitimate public purposes; (2) findings relied upon by city to require landowner to dedicate portion of her property in flood plain as public greenway, did not show required reasonable relationship necessary to satisfy requirements of Fifth Amendment; and (3) city failed to meet its burden of demonstrating that additional number of vehicle and bicycle trips generated by proposed commercial development reasonably related to city's requirement of dedication of pedestrian/bicycle pathway easement.

Reversed and remanded.

Justice Stevens filed dissenting opinion in which Justices Blackmun and Ginsburg joined.

Justice Souter filed dissenting opinion.

1.   EMINENT DOMAIN k1
     148 ----
     148I   Nature, Extent, and Delegation of Power
     148k1   Nature and source of power.

U.S.Or. 1994.

One of the principal purposes of the takings clause of the Fifth Amendment is to bar Government from forcing some people alone to bear public burdens which, in all fairness and justice, should be borne by public as a whole. U.S.C.A. Const.Amends. 5, 14.

2.   EMINENT DOMAIN k2(1.2)
     148 ----
     148I   Nature, Extent, and Delegation of Power
     148k2   What Constitutes a Taking; Police and Other Powers Distinguished
     148k2(1)   In General; Interference with Property Rights
     148k2(1.2)   Relating to zoning, planning, or land use.

[See headnote text below]

2.   ZONING AND PLANNING k40
     414 ----
     414II   Validity of Zoning Regulations
     414II(A)   In General
     414k40   Deprivation of property.

U.S.Or. 1994.
Land use regulation does not effect a taking if it substantially advances legitimate state interest and does not deny owner economically viable use of his or her land. U.S.C.A. Const.Amends. 5, 14.

3.   EMINENT DOMAIN k2(1.1)
     148 ----
     148I   Nature, Extent, and Delegation of Power
     148k2   What Constitutes a Taking; Police and Other Powers Distinguished
     148k2(1)   In General; Interference with Property Rights
     148k2(1.1)   Particular acts and regulations.

[See headnote text below]

3.   EMINENT DOMAIN k2(1.2)
     148 ----
     148I   Nature, Extent, and Delegation of Power
     148k2   What Constitutes a Taking; Police and Other Powers Distinguished
     148k2(1)   In General; Interference with Property Rights
     148k2(1.2)   Relating to zoning, planning, or land use.

Copyright (c) West Publishing Co. 1996 No claim to original U.S. Govt. works.

114 S.Ct. 2309, Dolan v. City of Tigard, (U.S.Or. 1994)

U.S.Or. 1994.
Under doctrine of "unconstitutional conditions," government may not require person to give up constitutional right in exchange for discretionary benefit conferred by government where property sought has little or no relationship to the benefit. U.S.C.A. Const.Amends. 5, 14.

See publication Words and Phrases for other judicial constructions and definitions.

4. EMINENT DOMAIN k2(1.2)
   148 ----
   148I   Nature, Extent, and Delegation of Power
   148k2   What Constitutes a Taking; Police and Other Powers Distinguished
   148k2(1)   In General; Interference with Property Rights
   148k2(1.2)   Relating to zoning, planning, or land use.

U.S.Or. 1994.
In evaluating landowner's claim that city's requirement that she dedicate a portion of her property as condition of further development was unconstitutional taking, Supreme Court was first required to determine whether "essential nexus" existed between legitimate state interest and permit condition exacted by city; if Court found that nexus existed, it was then required to decide required degree of connection between exactions and projected impact of proposed development. U.S.C.A. Const.Amends. 5, 14.

5. EMINENT DOMAIN k2(1.2)
   148 ----
   148I   Nature, Extent, and Delegation of Power
   148k2   What Constitutes a Taking; Police and Other Powers Distinguished
   148k2(1)   In General; Interference with Property Rights
   148k2(1.2)   Relating to zoning, planning, or land use.

[See headnote text below]

5. ZONING AND PLANNING k382.3
   414 ----
   414VIII Permits, Certificates and Approvals
   414VIII(A) In General
   414k382.1   Maps, Plats, or Plans, Conditions and Agreements
   414k382.3   Conveyance or dedication.

U.S.Or. 1994.
City's requirement that landowner dedicate portion of her property lying within flood plain for improvement of storm drainage system and property adjacent to flood plain as bicycle/pedestrian pathway, as condition for building permit allowing expansion of landowner's commercial property, had nexus with legitimate public purposes of preventing flooding along creek and reducing traffic congestion in city's central business district, for purposes of Fifth Amendment takings analysis. U.S.C.A. Const.Amends. 5, 14.

6. EMINENT DOMAIN k2(1.2)
   148 ----
   148I   Nature, Extent, and Delegation of Power
   148k2   What Constitutes a Taking; Police and Other Powers Distinguished
   148k2(1)   In General; Interference with Property Rights
   148k2(1.2)   Relating to zoning, planning, or land use.

[See headnote text below]

6. ZONING AND PLANNING k382.3
   414 ----
   414VIII Permits, Certificates and Approvals
   414VIII(A) In General
   414k382.1   Maps, Plats, or Plans, Conditions and Agreements
   414k382.3   Conveyance or dedication.

U.S.Or. 1994.
"Rough proportionality" test applied in determining whether degree of exactions required by city's building permit conditions bore required relationship to projected impact on proposed development to satisfy takings clause of Fifth Amendment; no precise mathematical calculation was required, but city was required to make some sort of individualized determination that required dedication was related both in nature and extent to impact of proposed development. U.S.C.A. Const.Amends. 5, 14.

See publication Words and Phrases for other judicial constructions and definitions.

7. CONSTITUTIONAL LAW k82(6.1)
   92 ----

Appendix D: The Dolan Decision / 251

114 S.Ct. 2309, Dolan v. City of Tigard, (U.S.Or. 1994)

> 92V   Personal, Civil and Political Rights
> 92k82   Constitutional Guaranties in General
> 92k82(6)   Particular Rights, Limitations, and Applications
> 92k82(6.1)   In general.

U.S.Or. 1994.

Simply denominating governmental interest as "business regulation" does not immunize it from constitutional challenge on grounds that it violates provision of the Bill of Rights. U.S.C.A. Const.Amends. 1-10.

8.   EMINENT DOMAIN k56
> 148 ----
> 148I   Nature, Extent, and Delegation of Power
> 148k54   Exercise of Delegated Power
> 148k56   Necessity for appropriation.

[See headnote text below]

8.   ZONING AND *2309 PLANNING k439
> 414 ----
> 414VIII Permits, Certificates and Approvals
> 414VIII(C) Proceedings to Procure
> 414k436   Hearing and Determination
> 414k439   Findings, conclusions, minutes, or records.

U.S.Or. 1994.

Findings relied upon by city to require landowner to dedicate portion of her property in flood plain as public greenway, as condition for constructing new commercial building, did not show required reasonable relationship between flood plain easement and landowner's proposed new building necessary to satisfy requirement of Fifth Amendment "takings" clause; although city found that paved parking lot that was included in proposed development would increase storm water flow from property, city never stated why public greenway, as opposed to private one, was required in interest of flood control. U.S.C.A. Const.Amends. 5, 14.

9.   ZONING AND PLANNING k382.3
> 414 ----
> 414VIII Permits, Certificates and Approvals
> 414VIII(A) In General
> 414k382.1   Maps, Plats, or Plans, Conditions and Agreements
> 414k382.3   Conveyance or dedication.

U.S.Or. 1994.

City failed to meet its burden of demonstrating that additional number of vehicle and bicycle trips generated by proposed commercial development were reasonably related to city's requirement of dedication of pedestrian/bicycle pathway easement as condition of granting building permit; city simply found that creation of pathway could offset some of the traffic demand and lessen increase in traffic congestion, but did not find that pathway was likely to offset traffic demand. U.S.C.A. Const.Amends. 5, 14.

10.   ZONING AND PLANNING k382.3
> 414 ----
> 414VIII Permits, Certificates and Approvals
> 414VIII(A) In General
> 414k382.1   Maps, Plats, or Plans, Conditions and Agreements
> 414k382.3   Conveyance or dedication.

U.S.Or. 1994.

Dedications for streets, sidewalks, and other public ways are generally reasonable exactions to avoid excessive congestion from proposed property use. U.S.C.A. Const.Amends. 5, 14.

2311 Syllabus (FN)

The City Planning Commission conditioned approval of petitioner Dolan's application to expand her store and pave her parking lot upon her compliance with dedication of land (1) for a public greenway along Fanno Creek to minimize flooding that would be exacerbated by the increases in impervious surfaces associated with her development and (2) for a pedestrian/bicycle pathway intended to relieve traffic congestion in the City's Central Business District. She appealed the Commission's denial of her request for variances from these standards to the Land Use Board of Appeals (LUBA), alleging that the land dedication requirements were not related to the proposed development and therefore constituted an uncompensated taking of her property under the Fifth Amendment. LUBA found a reasonable relationship between (1) the development and the requirement to dedicate land for a greenway, since the larger building and paved lot would increase the impervious surfaces and thus the runoff into the creek, and (2) alleviating the impact of increased traffic from the development and facilitating the provision of a pathway as an alternative means of transportation. Both the State Court of Appeals and the State

114 S.Ct. 2309, Dolan v. City of Tigard, (U.S.Or. 1994)

Supreme Court affirmed.

Held: The city's dedication requirements constitute an uncompensated taking of property. Pp. 2316-2321.

(a) Under the well-settled doctrine of "unconstitutional conditions," the government may not require a person to give up a constitutional right in exchange for a discretionary benefit conferred by the government where the property sought has little or no *2312 relationship to the benefit. In evaluating Dolan's claim, it must be determined whether an "essential nexus" exists between a legitimate state interest and the permit condition. *Nollan v. California Coastal Comm'n*, 483 U.S. 825, 837, 107 S.Ct. 3141, 3148, 97 L.Ed.2d 677. If one does, then it must be decided whether the degree of the exactions demanded by the permit conditions bears the required relationship to the projected impact of the proposed development. *Id.*, at 834, 107 S.Ct. at 3147. Pp. 2316-2317.

(b) Preventing flooding along Fanno Creek and reducing traffic congestion in the District are legitimate public purposes; and a nexus exists between the first purpose and limiting development within the creek's floodplain and between the second purpose and providing for alternative means of transportation. Pp. 2317-2318.

(c) In deciding the second question--whether the city's findings are constitutionally sufficient to justify the conditions imposed on Dolan's permit--the necessary connection required by the Fifth Amendment is "rough proportionality." No precise mathematical calculation is required, but the city must make some sort of individualized determination that the required dedication is related both in nature and extent to the proposed development's impact. This is essentially the "reasonable relationship" test adopted by the majority of the state courts. Pp. 2317-2318.

(d) The findings upon which the city relies do not show the required reasonable relationship between the floodplain easement and Dolan's proposed building. The Community Development Code already required that Dolan leave 15% of her property as open space, and the undeveloped floodplain would have nearly satisfied that requirement. However, the city has never said why a public, as opposed to a private, greenway is required in the interest of flood control. The difference to Dolan is the loss of her ability to exclude others from her property, yet the city has not attempted to make any individualized determination to support this part of its request. The city has also not met its burden of demonstrating that the additional number of vehicle and bicycle trips generated by Dolan's development reasonably relates to the city's requirement for a dedication of the pathway easement. The city must quantify its finding beyond a conclusory statement that the dedication could offset some of the traffic demand generated by the development. Pp. 2319-2321.

317 Ore. 110, 854 P.2d 437 (1993), reversed and remanded.

REHNQUIST, C.J., delivered the opinion of the Court, in which O'CONNOR, SCALIA, KENNEDY, and THOMAS, JJ., joined. STEVENS, J., filed a dissenting opinion, in which BLACKMUN and GINSBURG, JJ., joined. SOUTER, J., filed a dissenting opinion.

David B. Smith, Tigard, OR, for petitioner.

Timothy V. Ramis, Portland, OR, for respondent.

Edwin S. Kneedler, Washington, DC, for U.S., as amicus curiae by special leave of the Court.

For U.S. Supreme Court briefs, see:

1994 WL 249537 (Pet.Brief)

1994 WL 123754 (Resp.Brief)

1994 WL 82042 (Reply.Brief)

1994 WL 106731 (Resp.Supp.Brief)

For Transcript of Oral Argument See:

1994 WL 664939 (U.S.Oral.Arg.)

Chief Justice REHNQUIST delivered the opinion of the Court.

Petitioner challenges the decision of the Oregon Supreme Court which held that the city of Tigard could condition the approval of her building permit on the dedication of a portion of her property for flood control and traffic improvements. 317 Ore. 110, 854 P.2d 437 (1993). We granted certiorari to resolve a question left open by our decision in *Nollan*

114 S.Ct. 2309, Dolan v. City of Tigard, (U.S.Or. 1994)

v. *California Coastal Comm'n*, 483 U.S. 825, 107 S.Ct. 3141, 97 L.Ed.2d 677 (1987), of what is the required degree of connection between the exactions imposed by the city and the projected impacts of the proposed development.

*2313 I

The State of Oregon enacted a comprehensive land use management program in 1973. Ore.Rev.Stat. Secs. 197.005-197.860 (1991). The program required all Oregon cities and counties to adopt new comprehensive land use plans that were consistent with the statewide planning goals. Secs. 197.175(1), 197.250. The plans are implemented by land use regulations which are part of an integrated hierarchy of legally binding goals, plans, and regulations. Secs. 197.175, 197.175(2)(b). Pursuant to the State's requirements, the city of Tigard, a community of some 30,000 residents on the southwest edge of Portland, developed a comprehensive plan and codified it in its Community Development Code (CDC). The CDC requires property owners in the area zoned Central Business District to comply with a 15% open space and landscaping requirement, which limits total site coverage, including all structures and paved parking, to 85% of the parcel. CDC, ch. 18.66, App. to Pet. for Cert. G16-G17. After the completion of a transportation study that identified congestion in the Central Business District as a particular problem, the city adopted a plan for a pedestrian/bicycle pathway intended to encourage alternatives to automobile transportation for short trips. The CDC requires that new development facilitate this plan by dedicating land for pedestrian pathways where provided for in the pedestrian/bicycle pathway plan. (FN1)

The city also adopted a Master Drainage Plan (Drainage Plan). The Drainage Plan noted that flooding occurred in several areas along Fanno Creek, including areas near petitioner's property. Record, Doc. No. F, ch. 2, pp. 2-5 to 2-8; 4-2 to 4-6; Figure 4-1. The Drainage Plan also established that the increase in impervious surfaces associated with continued urbanization would exacerbate these flooding problems. To combat these risks, the Drainage Plan suggested a series of improvements to the Fanno Creek Basin, including channel excavation in the area next to petitioner's property. App. to Pet. for Cert. G13, G38. Other recommendations included ensuring that the floodplain remains free of structures and that it be preserved as greenways to minimize flood damage to structures. Record, Doc. No. F, ch. 5, pp. 5-16 to 5-21. The Drainage Plan concluded that the cost of these improvements should be shared based on both direct and indirect benefits, with property owners along the waterways paying more due to the direct benefit that they would receive. *Id.*, ch. 8, p. 8-11. CDC Chapters 18.84, 18.86 and CDC Sec. 18.164.100 and the Tigard Park Plan carry out these recommendations.

Petitioner Florence Dolan owns a plumbing and electric supply store located on Main Street in the Central Business District of the city. The store covers approximately 9,700 square feet on the eastern side of a 1.67-acre parcel, which includes a gravel parking lot. Fanno Creek flows through the southwestern corner of the lot and along its western boundary. The year-round flow of the creek renders the area within the creek's 100-year floodplain virtually unusable for commercial development. The city's comprehensive plan includes the Fanno Creek floodplain as part of the city's greenway system.

Petitioner applied to the city for a permit to redevelop the site. Her proposed plans called for nearly doubling the size of the store to 17,600 square feet, and paving a 39-space parking lot. The existing store, located on the opposite side of the parcel, would be razed in sections as construction progressed on the new building. In the second phase of the project, petitioner proposed to build an additional structure on the northeast side of *2314 the site for complementary businesses, and to provide more parking. The proposed expansion and intensified use are consistent with the city's zoning scheme in the Central Business District. CDC Sec. 18.66.030. App. to Brief for Petitioner C1-C2.

The City Planning Commission granted petitioner's permit application subject to conditions imposed by the city's CDC. The CDC establishes the following standard for site development review approval:

"Where landfill and/or development is allowed within and adjacent to the 100-year floodplain, the city shall require the dedication of sufficient open land area for greenway adjoining and within the floodplain. This area shall include portions at a suitable elevation for the construction of a pedestrian/bicycle pathway within the floodplain in accordance with the adopted pedestrian/ bicycle plan." CDC Sec. 18.120.180.A.8, App. to Brief for Respondent.

114 S.Ct. 2309, Dolan v. City of Tigard, (U.S.Or. 1994)

Thus, the Commission required that petitioner dedicate the portion of her property lying within the 100-year floodplain for improvement of a storm drainage system along Fanno Creek and that she dedicate an additional 15-foot strip of land adjacent to the floodplain as a pedestrian/bicycle pathway. (FN2) The dedication required by that condition encompasses approximately 7,000 square feet, or roughly 10% of the property. In accordance with city practice, petitioner could rely on the dedicated property to meet the 15% open space and landscaping requirement mandated by the city's zoning scheme. App. to Pet. for Cert. G28-G29. The city would bear the cost of maintaining a landscaped buffer between the dedicated area and the new store. *Id.*, at G44-G45.

Petitioner requested variances from the CDC standards. Variances are granted only where it can be shown that, owing to special circumstances related to a specific piece of the land, the literal interpretation of the applicable zoning provisions would cause "an undue or unnecessary hardship" unless the variance is granted. CDC Sec. 18.134.010. App. to Brief for Respondent B-47. (FN3) Rather than posing alternative mitigating measures to offset the expected impacts of her proposed development, as allowed under the CDC, petitioner simply argued that her proposed development would not conflict with the policies of the comprehensive plan. *Id.*, at E-4. The Commission denied the request.

The Commission made a series of findings concerning the relationship between the dedicated conditions and the projected impacts of petitioner's project. First, the Commission noted that "[i]t is reasonable to assume that customers and employees of the future uses of this site could utilize a pedestrian/bicycle pathway adjacent to this development for their transportation and recreational needs." ***2315** City of Tigard Planning Commission Final Order No. 91-09 PC, App. to Pet. for Cert. G24. The Commission noted that the site plan has provided for bicycle parking in a rack in front of the proposed building and "[i]t is reasonable to expect that some of the users of the bicycle parking provided for by the site plan will use the pathway adjacent to Fanno Creek if it is constructed." *Ibid.* In addition, the Commission found that creation of a convenient, safe pedestrian/bicycle pathway system as an alternative means of transportation "could offset some of the traffic demand on [nearby] streets and lessen the increase in traffic congestion." *Ibid.*

The Commission went on to note that the required floodplain dedication would be reasonably related to petitioner's request to intensify the use of the site given the increase in the impervious surface. The Commission stated that the "anticipated increased storm water flow from the subject property to an already strained creek and drainage basin can only add to the public need to manage the stream channel and floodplain for drainage purposes." *Id.*, at G37. Based on this anticipated increased storm water flow, the Commission concluded that "the requirement of dedication of the floodplain area on the site is related to the applicant's plan to intensify development on the site." *Ibid.* The Tigard City Council approved the Commission's final order, subject to one minor modification; the City Council reassigned the responsibility for surveying and marking the floodplain area from petitioner to the city's engineering department. *Id.*, at G-7.

Petitioner appealed to the Land Use Board of Appeals (LUBA) on the ground that the city's dedication requirements were not related to the proposed development, and, therefore, those requirements constituted an uncompensated taking of their property under the Fifth Amendment. In evaluating the federal taking claim, LUBA assumed that the city's findings about the impacts of the proposed development were supported by substantial evidence. *Dolan v. Tigard*, LUBA 91-161 (Jan. 7, 1992), reprinted at App. to Pet. for Cert. D-15, n. 9. Given the undisputed fact that the proposed larger building and paved parking area would increase the amount of impervious surfaces and the runoff into Fanno Creek, LUBA concluded that "there is a 'reasonable relationship' between the proposed development and the requirement to dedicate land along Fanno Creek for a greenway." *Id.*, at D-16. With respect to the pedestrian/bicycle pathway, LUBA noted the Commission's finding that a significantly larger retail sales building and parking lot would attract larger numbers of customers and employees and their vehicles. It again found a "reasonable relationship" between alleviating the impacts of increased traffic from the development and facilitating the provision of a pedestrian/bicycle pathway as an alternative means of transportation. *Ibid.*

The Oregon Court of Appeals affirmed, rejecting petitioner's contention that in *Nollan v. California Coastal Comm'n*, 483 U.S. 825, 107 S.Ct. 3141, 97 L.Ed.2d 677 (1987), we had abandoned the

114 S.Ct. 2309, Dolan v. City of Tigard, (U.S.Or. 1994)

"reasonable relationship" test in favor of a stricter "essential nexus" test. 113 Ore.App. 162, 832 P.2d 853 (1992). The Oregon Supreme Court affirmed. 317 Ore. 110, 854 P.2d 437 (1993). The court also disagreed with petitioner's contention that the *Nollan* Court abandoned the "reasonably related" test. *Id.*, at 118, 854 P.2d, at 442. Instead, the court read *Nollan* to mean that an "exaction is reasonably related to an impact if the exaction serves the same purpose that a denial of the permit would serve." *Id.*, at 120, 854 P.2d, at 443. The court decided that both the pedestrian/bicycle pathway condition and the storm drainage dedication had an essential nexus to the development of the proposed site. *Id.*, at 121, 854 P.2d, at 443. Therefore, the court found the conditions to be reasonably related to the impact of the expansion of petitioner's business. *Ibid.* (FN4) We *2316 granted certiorari, 510 U.S. ----, 114 S.Ct. 544, 126 L.Ed.2d 446 (1993), because of an alleged conflict between the Oregon Supreme Court's decision and our decision in *Nollan, supra.*

II

[1] The Takings Clause of the Fifth Amendment of the United States Constitution, made applicable to the States through the Fourteenth Amendment, *Chicago, B. & Q.R. Co. v. Chicago,* 166 U.S. 226, 239, 17 S.Ct. 581, 585, 41 L.Ed. 979 (1897), provides: "[N]or shall private property be taken for public use, without just compensation." (FN5) One of the principal purposes of the Takings Clause is "to bar Government from forcing some people alone to bear public burdens which, in all fairness and justice, should be borne by the public as a whole." *Armstrong v. United States,* 364 U.S. 40, 49, 80 S.Ct. 1563, 1569, 4 L.Ed.2d 1554 (1960). Without question, had the city simply required petitioner to dedicate a strip of land along Fanno Creek for public use, rather than conditioning the grant of her permit to redevelop her property on such a dedication, a taking would have occurred. *Nollan, supra,* 483 U.S., at 831, 107 S.Ct., at 3145. Such public access would deprive petitioner of the right to exclude others, "one of the most essential sticks in the bundle of rights that are commonly characterized as property." *Kaiser Aetna v. United States,* 444 U.S. 164, 176, 100 S.Ct. 383, 391, 62 L.Ed.2d 332 (1979).

[2] On the other side of the ledger, the authority of state and local governments to engage in land use planning has been sustained against constitutional challenge as long ago as our decision in *Euclid v. Ambler Realty Co.,* 272 U.S. 365, 47 S.Ct. 114, 71 L.Ed. 303 (1926). "Government hardly could go on if to some extent values incident to property could not be diminished without paying for every such change in the general law." *Pennsylvania Coal Co. v. Mahon,* 260 U.S. 393, 413, 43 S.Ct. 158, 159, 67 L.Ed. 322 (1922). A land use regulation does not effect a taking if it "substantially advance[s] legitimate state interests" and does not "den[y] an owner economically viable use of his land." *Agins v. Tiburon,* 447 U.S. 255, 260, 100 S.Ct. 2138, 2141, 65 L.Ed.2d 106 (1980). (FN6)

[3] The sort of land use regulations discussed in the cases just cited, however, differ in two relevant particulars from the present case. First, they involved essentially legislative determinations classifying entire areas of the city, whereas here the city made an adjudicative decision to condition petitioner's application for a building permit on an individual parcel. Second, the conditions imposed were not simply a limitation on the use petitioner might make of her own parcel, but a requirement that she deed portions of the property to the city. In *Nollan, supra,* we *2317 held that governmental authority to exact such a condition was circumscribed by the Fifth and Fourteenth Amendments. Under the well-settled doctrine of "unconstitutional conditions," the government may not require a person to give up a constitutional right--here the right to receive just compensation when property is taken for a public use--in exchange for a discretionary benefit conferred by the government where the property sought has little or no relationship to the benefit. See *Perry v. Sindermann,* 408 U.S. 593, 92 S.Ct. 2694, 33 L.Ed.2d 570 (1972); *Pickering v. Board of Ed. of Township High School Dist.,* 391 U.S. 563, 568, 88 S.Ct. 1731, 1734, 20 L.Ed.2d 811 (1968).

Petitioner contends that the city has forced her to choose between the building permit and her right under the Fifth Amendment to just compensation for the public easements. Petitioner does not quarrel with the city's authority to exact some forms of dedication as a condition for the grant of a building permit, but challenges the showing made by the city to justify these exactions. She argues that the city has identified "no special benefits" conferred on her, and has not identified any "special quantifiable burdens" created by her new store that would justify the particular dedications required from her which are not required from the public at large.

III

[4] In evaluating petitioner's claim, we must first determine whether the "essential nexus" exists between the "legitimate state interest" and the permit condition exacted by the city. Nollan, 483 U.S., at 837, 107 S.Ct., at 3148. If we find that a nexus exists, we must then decide the required degree of connection between the exactions and the projected impact of the proposed development. We were not required to reach this question in Nollan, because we concluded that the connection did not meet even the loosest standard. 483 U.S., at 838, 107 S.Ct., at 3149. Here, however, we must decide this question.

A

[5] We addressed the essential nexus question in Nollan. The California Coastal Commission demanded a lateral public easement across the Nollan's beachfront lot in exchange for a permit to demolish an existing bungalow and replace it with a three-bedroom house. 483 U.S., at 828, 107 S.Ct., at 3144. The public easement was designed to connect two public beaches that were separated by the Nollan's property. The Coastal Commission had asserted that the public easement condition was imposed to promote the legitimate state interest of diminishing the "blockage of the view of the ocean" caused by construction of the larger house.

We agreed that the Coastal Commission's concern with protecting visual access to the ocean constituted a legitimate public interest. Id., at 835, 107 S.Ct., at 3148. We also agreed that the permit condition would have been constitutional "even if it consisted of the requirement that the Nollans provide a viewing spot on their property for passersby with whose sighting of the ocean their new house would interfere." Id., at 836, 107 S.Ct., at 3148. We resolved, however, that the Coastal Commission's regulatory authority was set completely adrift from its constitutional moorings when it claimed that a nexus existed between visual access to the ocean and a permit condition requiring lateral public access along the Nollan's beachfront lot. Id., at 837, 107 S.Ct., at 3148. How enhancing the public's ability to "traverse to and along the shorefront" served the same governmental purpose of "visual access to the ocean" from the roadway was beyond our ability to countenance. The absence of a nexus left the Coastal Commission in the position of simply trying to obtain an easement through gimmickry, which converted a valid regulation of land use into "an out-and-out plan of extortion." Ibid., quoting J.E.D. Associates, Inc. v. Atkinson, 121 N.H. 581, 584, 432 A.2d 12, 14-15 (1981).

No such gimmicks are associated with the permit conditions imposed by the city in this case. Undoubtedly, the prevention of flooding *2318 along Fanno Creek and the reduction of traffic congestion in the Central Business District qualify as the type of legitimate public purposes we have upheld. Agins, supra, 447 U.S., at 260-262, 100 S.Ct., at 2141-2142. It seems equally obvious that a nexus exists between preventing flooding along Fanno Creek and limiting development within the creek's 100-year floodplain. Petitioner proposes to double the size of her retail store and to pave her now-gravel parking lot, thereby expanding the impervious surface on the property and increasing the amount of stormwater run-off into Fanno Creek.

The same may be said for the city's attempt to reduce traffic congestion by providing for alternative means of transportation. In theory, a pedestrian/bicycle pathway provides a useful alternative means of transportation for workers and shoppers: "Pedestrians and bicyclists occupying dedicated spaces for walking and/or bicycling ... remove potential vehicles from streets, resulting in an overall improvement in total transportation system flow." A. Nelson, Public Provision of Pedestrian and Bicycle Access Ways: Public Policy Rationale and the Nature of Private Benefits 11, Center for Planning Development, Georgia Institute of Technology, Working Paper Series (Jan. 1994). See also, Intermodal Surface Transportation Efficiency Act of 1991, Pub.L. 102-240, 105 Stat.1914; (recognizing pedestrian and bicycle facilities as necessary components of any strategy to reduce traffic congestion).

B

The second part of our analysis requires us to determine whether the degree of the exactions demanded by the city's permit conditions bear the required relationship to the projected impact of petitioner's proposed development. Nollan, supra, 483 U.S., at 834, 107 S.Ct., at 3147, quoting Penn Central, 438 U.S. 104, 127, 98 S.Ct. 2646, 2660, 57 L.Ed.2d 631 (1978) (" '[A] use restriction may constitute a taking if not reasonably necessary to the effectuation of a substantial government purpose' "). Here the Oregon Supreme Court deferred to what it termed the "city's unchallenged factual findings" supporting the dedication conditions and found them to be reasonably related to the impact of the

114 S.Ct. 2309, Dolan v. City of Tigard, (U.S.Or. 1994)

expansion of petitioner's business. 317 Ore., at 120-121, 854 P.2d, at 443.

The city required that petitioner dedicate "to the city as Greenway all portions of the site that fall within the existing 100-year floodplain [of Fanno Creek] ... and all property 15 feet above [the floodplain] boundary." In addition, the city demanded that the retail store be designed so as not to intrude into the greenway area. The city relies on the Commission's rather tentative findings that increased stormwater flow from petitioner's property "can only add to the public need to manage the [floodplain] for drainage purposes" to support its conclusion that the "requirement of dedication of the floodplain area on the site is related to the applicant's plan to intensify development on the site." City of Tigard Planning Commission Final Order No. 91-09 PC, App. to Pet. for Cert. G37.

The city made the following specific findings relevant to the pedestrian/bicycle pathway:

"In addition, the proposed expanded use of this site is anticipated to generate additional vehicular traffic thereby increasing congestion on nearby collector and arterial streets. Creation of a convenient, safe pedestrian/bicycle pathway system as an alternative means of transportation could offset some of the traffic demand on these nearby streets and lessen the increase in traffic congestion." *Id.*, at 24.

The question for us is whether these findings are constitutionally sufficient to justify the conditions imposed by the city on petitioner's building permit. Since state courts have been dealing with this question a good deal longer than we have, we turn to representative decisions made by them.

In some States, very generalized statements as to the necessary connection between the required dedication and the proposed development seem to suffice. See, *e.g.*, *Billings Properties, Inc. v. Yellowstone County*, 144 Mont. 25, 394 P.2d 182 (1964); **2319 Jenad, Inc. v. Scarsdale*, 18 N.Y.2d 78, 271 N.Y.S.2d 955, 218 N.E.2d 673 (1966). We think this standard is too lax to adequately protect petitioner's right to just compensation if her property is taken for a public purpose.

Other state courts require a very exacting correspondence, described as the "specifi[c] and uniquely attributable" test. The Supreme Court of Illinois first developed this test in *Pioneer Trust & Savings Bank v. Mount Prospect*, 22 Ill.2d 375, 380, 176 N.E.2d 799, 802 (1961). (FN7) Under this standard, if the local government cannot demonstrate that its exaction is directly proportional to the specifically created need, the exaction becomes "a veiled exercise of the power of eminent domain and a confiscation of private property behind the defense of police regulations." *Id.*, at 381, 176 N.E.2d, at 802. We do not think the Federal Constitution requires such exacting scrutiny, given the nature of the interests involved.

A number of state courts have taken an intermediate position, requiring the municipality to show a "reasonable relationship" between the required dedication and the impact of the proposed development. Typical is the Supreme Court of Nebraska's opinion in *Simpson v. North Platte*, 206 Neb. 240, 245, 292 N.W.2d 297, 301 (1980), where that court stated:

"The distinction, therefore, which must be made between an appropriate exercise of the police power and an improper exercise of eminent domain is whether the requirement has some reasonable relationship or nexus to the use to which the property is being made or is merely being used as an excuse for taking property simply because at that particular moment the landowner is asking the city for some license or permit."

Thus, the court held that a city may not require a property owner to dedicate private property for some future public use as a condition of obtaining a building permit when such future use is not "occasioned by the construction sought to be permitted." *Id.*, at 248, 292 N.W.2d, at 302.

Some form of the reasonable relationship test has been adopted in many other jurisdictions. See, *e.g.*, *Jordan v. Menomonee Falls*, 28 Wis.2d 608, 137 N.W.2d 442 (1965); *Collis v. Bloomington*, 310 Minn. 5, 246 N.W.2d 19 (1976) (requiring a showing of a reasonable relationship between the planned subdivision and the municipality's need for land); *College Station v. Turtle Rock Corp.*, 680 S.W.2d 802, 807 (Tex.1984); *Call v. West Jordan*, 606 P.2d 217, 220 (Utah 1979) (affirming use of the reasonable relation test). Despite any semantical differences, general agreement exists among the courts "that the dedication should have some reasonable relationship to the needs created by the

Copyright (c) West Publishing Co. 1996 No claim to original U.S. Govt. works.

[development]." *Ibid.* See generally, Morosoff, Take My Beach Please!: Nollan v. California Coastal Commission and a Rational--Nexus Constitutional Analysis of Development Exactions, 69 B.U.L.Rev. 823 (1989); see also *Parks v. Watson,* 716 F.2d 646, 651-653 (CA9 1983).

[6] We think the "reasonable relationship" test adopted by a majority of the state courts is closer to the federal constitutional norm than either of those previously discussed. But we do not adopt it as such, partly because the term "reasonable relationship" seems confusingly similar to the term "rational basis" which describes the minimal level of scrutiny under the Equal Protection Clause of the Fourteenth Amendment. We think a term such as "rough proportionality" best encapsulates what we hold to be the requirement of the Fifth Amendment. No precise mathematical calculation is required, but the city must make some sort of individualized determination that the required dedication *2320 is related both in nature and extent to the impact of the proposed development. (FN8)

[7] Justice STEVENS' dissent relies upon a law review article for the proposition that the city's conditional demands for part of petitioner's property are "a species of business regulation that heretofore warranted a strong presumption of constitutional validity." *Post,* at 2325. But simply denominating a governmental measure as a "business regulation" does not immunize it from constitutional challenge on the grounds that it violates a provision of the Bill of Rights. In *Marshall v. Barlow's, Inc.,* 436 U.S. 307, 98 S.Ct. 1816, 56 L.Ed.2d 305 (1978), we held that a statute authorizing a warrantless search of business premises in order to detect OSHA violations violated the Fourth Amendment. See also *Air Pollution Variance Board of Colo. v. Western Alfalfa Corp.,* 416 U.S. 861, 94 S.Ct. 2114, 40 L.Ed.2d 607 (1974); *New York v. Burger,* 482 U.S. 691, 107 S.Ct. 2636, 96 L.Ed.2d 601 (1982). And in *Central Hudson Gas & Electric Corp. v. Public Service Comm'n of N.Y.,* 447 U.S. 557, 100 S.Ct. 2343, 65 L.Ed.2d 341 (1980), we held that an order of the New York Public Service Commission, designed to cut down the use of electricity because of a fuel shortage, violated the First Amendment insofar as it prohibited advertising by a utility company to promote the use of electricity. We see no reason why the Takings Clause of the Fifth Amendment, as much a part of the Bill of Rights as the First Amendment or Fourth Amendment, should be relegated to the status of a poor relation in these comparable circumstances.

We turn now to analysis of whether the findings relied upon by the city here, first with respect to the floodplain easement, and second with respect to the pedestrian/bicycle path, satisfied these requirements.

[8] It is axiomatic that increasing the amount of impervious surface will increase the quantity and rate of storm-water flow from petitioner's property. Record, Doc. No. F, ch. 4, p. 4-29. Therefore, keeping the floodplain open and free from development would likely confine the pressures on Fanno Creek created by petitioner's development. In fact, because petitioner's property lies within the Central Business District, the Community Development Code already required that petitioner leave 15% of it as open space and the undeveloped floodplain would have nearly satisfied that requirement. App. to Pet. for Cert. G16-G17. But the city demanded more--it not only wanted petitioner not to build in the floodplain, but it also wanted petitioner's property along Fanno Creek for its Greenway system. The city has never said why a public greenway, as opposed to a private one, was required in the interest of flood control.

The difference to petitioner, of course, is the loss of her ability to exclude others. As we have noted, this right to exclude others is "one of the most essential sticks in the bundle of rights that are commonly characterized as property." *Kaiser Aetna,* 444 U.S., at 176, 100 S.Ct., at 391. It is difficult to see why recreational visitors trampling along petitioner's floodplain easement are sufficiently related to the city's legitimate interest in reducing flooding problems along Fanno Creek, and the city has not attempted to *2321 make any individualized determination to support this part of its request.

The city contends that recreational easement along the Greenway is only ancillary to the city's chief purpose in controlling flood hazards. It further asserts that unlike the residential property at issue in *Nollan,* petitioner's property is commercial in character and therefore, her right to exclude others is compromised. Brief for Respondent 41, quoting *United States v. Orito,* 413 U.S. 139, 142, 93 S.Ct. 2674, 2677, 37 L.Ed.2d 513 (1973) (" 'The Constitution extends special safeguards to the privacy of the home' "). The city maintains that "[t]here is nothing to suggest that preventing [petitioner] from prohibiting [the easements] will unreasonably impair the value of [her] property as a [retail store]." *PruneYard Shopping Center v. Robins,* 447 U.S. 74, 83, 100 S.Ct. 2035, 2042, 64 L.Ed.2d 741 (1980).

114 S.Ct. 2309, Dolan v. City of Tigard, (U.S.Or. 1994)

Admittedly, petitioner wants to build a bigger store to attract members of the public to her property. She also wants, however, to be able to control the time and manner in which they enter. The recreational easement on the Greenway is different in character from the exercise of state-protected rights of free expression and petition that we permitted in *PruneYard*. In *PruneYard*, we held that a major private shopping center that attracted more than 25,000 daily patrons had to provide access to persons exercising their state constitutional rights to distribute pamphlets and ask passersby to sign their petitions. *Id.*, at 85, 100 S.Ct., at 2042. We based our decision, in part, on the fact that the shopping center "may restrict expressive activity by adopting time, place, and manner regulations that will minimize any interference with its commercial functions." *Id.*, at 83, 100 S.Ct., at 2042. By contrast, the city wants to impose a permanent recreational easement upon petitioner's property that borders Fanno Creek. Petitioner would lose all rights to regulate the time in which the public entered onto the Greenway, regardless of any interference it might pose with her retail store. Her right to exclude would not be regulated, it would be eviscerated.

If petitioner's proposed development had somehow encroached on existing greenway space in the city, it would have been reasonable to require petitioner to provide some alternative greenway space for the public either on her property or elsewhere. See *Nollan*, 483 U.S., at 836, 107 S.Ct., at 3148 ("Although such a requirement, constituting a permanent grant of continuous access to the property, would have to be considered a taking if it were not attached to a development permit, the Commission's assumed power to forbid construction of the house in order to protect the public's view of the beach must surely include the power to condition construction upon some concession by the owner, even a concession of property rights, that serves the same end"). But that is not the case here. We conclude that the findings upon which the city relies do not show the required reasonable relationship between the floodplain easement and the petitioner's proposed new building.

[9][10] With respect to the pedestrian/bicycle pathway, we have no doubt that the city was correct in finding that the larger retail sales facility proposed by petitioner will increase traffic on the streets of the Central Business District. The city estimates that the proposed development would generate roughly 435 additional trips per day. (FN9) Dedications for streets, sidewalks, and other public ways are generally reasonable exactions to avoid excessive congestion from a proposed property use. But on the record before us, the city has not met its burden of demonstrating that the additional number of vehicle and bicycle trips generated by the petitioner's development reasonably relate to the city's requirement for a dedication of the pedestrian/bicycle pathway easement. The city simply found that the creation of the pathway "could offset some of the traffic *2322 demand ... and lessen the increase in traffic congestion." (FN10)

As Justice Peterson of the Supreme Court of Oregon explained in his dissenting opinion, however, "[t]he findings of fact that the bicycle pathway system '*could* offset some of the traffic demand' is a far cry from a finding that the bicycle pathway system *will*, or is *likely to*, offset some of the traffic demand." 317 Ore., at 127, 854 P.2d, at 447 (emphasis in original). No precise mathematical calculation is required, but the city must make some effort to quantify its findings in support of the dedication for the pedestrian/bicycle pathway beyond the conclusory statement that it could offset some of the traffic demand generated.

IV

Cities have long engaged in the commendable task of land use planning, made necessary by increasing urbanization particularly in metropolitan areas such as Portland. The city's goals of reducing flooding hazards and traffic congestion, and providing for public greenways, are laudable, but there are outer limits to how this may be done. "A strong public desire to improve the public condition [will not] warrant achieving the desire by a shorter cut than the constitutional way of paying for the change." *Pennsylvania Coal*, 260 U.S., at 416, 43 S.Ct., at 160.

The judgment of the Supreme Court of Oregon is reversed, and the case is remanded for further proceedings consistent with this opinion.

It is so ordered.

Justice STEVENS, with whom Justice BLACKMUN and Justice GINSBURG join, dissenting.

The record does not tell us the dollar value of petitioner Florence Dolan's interest in excluding the public from the greenway adjacent to her hardware

114 S.Ct. 2309, Dolan v. City of Tigard, (U.S.Or. 1994)

business. The mountain of briefs that the case has generated nevertheless makes it obvious that the pecuniary value of her victory is far less important than the rule of law that this case has been used to establish. It is unquestionably an important case.

Certain propositions are not in dispute. The enlargement of the Tigard unit in Dolan's chain of hardware stores will have an adverse impact on the city's legitimate and substantial interests in controlling drainage in Fanno Creek and minimizing traffic congestion in Tigard's business district. That impact is sufficient to justify an outright denial of her application for approval of the expansion. The city has nevertheless agreed to grant Dolan's application if she will comply with two conditions, each of which admittedly will mitigate the adverse effects of her proposed development. The disputed question is whether the city has violated the Fourteenth Amendment to the Federal Constitution by refusing to allow Dolan's planned construction to proceed unless those conditions are met.

The Court is correct in concluding that the city may not attach arbitrary conditions to a building permit or to a variance even when it can rightfully deny the application outright. I also agree that state court decisions dealing with ordinances that govern municipal development plans provide useful guidance in a case of this kind. Yet the Court's description of the doctrinal underpinnings of its decision, the phrasing of its fledgling test of "rough proportionality," and the application of that test to this case run contrary to the traditional treatment of these cases and break considerable and unpropitious new ground.

I

Candidly acknowledging the lack of federal precedent for its exercise in rulemaking, the Court purports to find guidance in 12 "representative" *2323 state court decisions. To do so is certainly appropriate. (FN1) The state cases the Court consults, however, either fail to support or decidedly undermine the Court's conclusions in key respects.

First, although discussion of the state cases permeates the Court's analysis of the appropriate test to apply in this case, the test on which the Court settles is not naturally derived from those courts' decisions. The Court recognizes as an initial matter that the city's conditions satisfy the "essential nexus" requirement announced in *Nollan v. California Coastal Comm'n*, 483 U.S. 825, 107 S.Ct. 3141, 97 L.Ed.2d 677 (1987), because they serve the legitimate interests in minimizing floods and traffic congestions. *Ante*, at 2317-2318. (FN2) The Court goes on, however, to erect a new constitutional hurdle in the path of these conditions. In addition to showing a rational nexus to a public purpose that would justify an outright denial of the permit, the city must also demonstrate "rough proportionality" between the harm caused by the new land use and the benefit obtained by the condition. *Ante*, at 2319. The Court also decides for the first time that the city has the burden of establishing the constitutionality of its conditions by making an "individualized determination" that the condition in question satisfies the proportionality requirement. See *ante*, at 2319.

Not one of the state cases cited by the Court announces anything akin to a "rough proportionality" requirement. For the most part, moreover, those cases that invalidated municipal ordinances did so on state law or unspecified grounds roughly equivalent to *Nollan* 's "essential nexus" requirement. See, *e.g., Simpson v. North Platte*, 206 Neb. 240, 245-248, 292 N.W.2d 297, 301-302 (1980) (ordinance lacking "reasonable relationship" or "rational nexus" to property's use violated Nebraska constitution); *J.E.D. Associates, Inc. v. Town of Atkinson*, 121 N.H. 581, 583-585, 432 A.2d 12, 14-15 (1981) (state constitutional grounds). One case purporting to apply the strict "specifically and uniquely attributable" test established by *Pioneer Trust & Savings Bank v. Mount Prospect*, 22 Ill.2d 375, 176 N.E.2d 799 (1961), nevertheless found that test was satisfied because the legislature had decided that the subdivision at issue created the need for a park or parks. *Billings Properties, Inc. v. Yellowstone County*, 144 Mont. 25, 33-36, 394 P.2d 182, 187-188 (1964). In only one of the seven cases upholding a land use regulation did the losing property owner petition this Court for certiorari. See *Jordan v. Village of Menomonee Falls*, 28 Wis.2d 608, 137 N.W.2d 442 (1965), appeal dism'd, 385 U.S. 4, 87 S.Ct. 36, 17 L.Ed.2d 3 (1966) (want of substantial federal question). Although 4 of the 12 opinions mention the Federal Constitution--two of those only in passing--it is quite obvious that neither the courts nor the litigants imagined they might be participating in the development of a new rule of federal law. Thus, although these state cases do lend support to the Court's reaffirmance of *Nollan* 's reasonable nexus requirement, the role the Court accords them in the announcement of its newly minted second phase of the constitutional inquiry is

114 S.Ct. 2309, Dolan v. City of Tigard, (U.S.Or. 1994)

remarkably inventive.

*2324 In addition, the Court ignores the state courts' willingness to consider what the property owner gains from the exchange in question. The Supreme Court of Wisconsin, for example, found it significant that the village's approval of a proposed subdivision plat "enables the subdivider to profit financially by selling the subdivision lots as homebuilding sites and thus realizing a greater price than could have been obtained if he had sold his property as unplatted lands." *Jordan v. Village of Menomonee Falls,* 28 Wis.2d 608, 619-620, 137 N.W.2d 442, 448 (1965). The required dedication as a condition of that approval was permissible "[i]n return for this benefit." *Ibid.* See also *Collis v. Bloomington,* 310 Minn. 5, 11-13, 246 N.W.2d 19, 23-24 (1976) (citing *Jordan*); *College Station v. Turtle Rock Corp.,* 680 S.W.2d 802, 806 (Tex.1984) (dedication requirement only triggered when developer *chooses* to develop land). In this case, moreover, Dolan's acceptance of the permit, with its attached conditions, would provide her with benefits that may well go beyond any advantage she gets from expanding her business. As the United States pointed out at oral argument, the improvement that the city's drainage plan contemplates would widen the channel and reinforce the slopes to increase the carrying capacity during serious floods, "confer[ring] considerable benefits on the property owners immediately adjacent to the creek." Tr. of Oral Arg. 41-42.

The state court decisions also are enlightening in the extent to which they required that the *entire parcel* be given controlling importance. All but one of the cases involve challenges to provisions in municipal ordinances requiring developers to dedicate either a percentage of the entire parcel (usually 7 or 10 percent of the platted subdivision) or an equivalent value in cash (usually a certain dollar amount per lot) to help finance the construction of roads, utilities, schools, parks and playgrounds. In assessing the legality of the conditions, the courts gave no indication that the transfer of an interest in realty was any more objectionable than a cash payment. See, *e.g., Jenad, Inc. v. Scarsdale,* 18 N.Y.2d 78, 271 N.Y.S.2d 955, 218 N.E.2d 673 (1966); *Jordan, supra; Collis, supra.* None of the decisions identified the surrender of the fee owner's "power to exclude" as having any special significance. Instead, the courts uniformly examined the character of the entire economic transaction.

II

It is not merely state cases, but our own cases as well, that require the analysis to focus on the impact of the city's action on the entire parcel of private property. In *Penn Central Transportation Co. v. New York City,* 438 U.S. 104, 98 S.Ct. 2646, 57 L.Ed.2d 631 (1978), we stated that takings jurisprudence "does not divide a single parcel into discrete segments and attempt to determine whether rights in a particular segment have been entirely abrogated." *Id.,* at 130-131, 98 S.Ct., at 2662. Instead, this Court focuses "both on the character of the action and on the nature and extent of the interference with rights in the parcel as a whole." *Ibid. Andrus v. Allard,* 444 U.S. 51, 100 S.Ct. 318, 62 L.Ed.2d 210 (1979), reaffirmed the nondivisibility principle outlined in *Penn Central,* stating that "[a]t least where an owner possesses a full 'bundle' of property rights, the destruction of one 'strand' of the bundle is not a taking, because the aggregate must be viewed in its entirety." *Id.,* at 65-66, 100 S.Ct., at 327. (FN3) As recently as last Term, we approved the principle again. See *Concrete Pipe & Products, Inc. v. Construction Laborers Pension Trust,* 508 U.S. ----, ----, 113 S.Ct. 2264, 2290, 124 L.Ed.2d 539 (1993) (explaining that "a claimant's parcel of property [cannot] first be divided into what was taken and what was left" to demonstrate a compensable taking). Although limitation of the right to exclude others undoubtedly constitutes a significant infringement upon property ***2325** ownership, *Kaiser Aetna v. United States,* 444 U.S. 164, 179-180, 100 S.Ct. 383, 393, 62 L.Ed.2d 332 (1979), restrictions on that right do not alone constitute a taking, and do not do so in any event unless they "unreasonably impair the value or use" of the property. *PruneYard Shopping Center v. Robins,* 447 U.S. 74, 82-84, 100 S.Ct. 2035, 2041-2042, 64 L.Ed.2d 741 (1980).

The Court's narrow focus on one strand in the property owner's bundle of rights is particularly misguided in a case involving the development of commercial property. As Professor Johnston has noted:

"The subdivider is a manufacturer, processor, and marketer of a product; land is but one of his raw materials. In subdivision control disputes, the developer is not defending hearth and home against the king's intrusion, but simply attempting to maximize his profits from the sale of a finished product. As applied to him,

114 S.Ct. 2309, Dolan v. City of Tigard, (U.S.Or. 1994)

subdivision control exactions are actually business regulations." Johnston, Constitutionality of Subdivision Control Exactions: The Quest for A Rationale, 52 Cornell L.Q. 871, 923 (1967). (FN4)

The exactions associated with the development of a retail business are likewise a species of business regulation that heretofore warranted a strong presumption of constitutional validity.

In Johnston's view, "if the municipality can demonstrate that its assessment of financial burdens against subdividers is rational, impartial, and conducive to fulfillment of authorized planning objectives, its action need be invalidated only in those extreme and presumably rare cases where the burden of compliance is sufficiently great to deter the owner from proceeding with his planned development." Id., at 917. The city of Tigard has demonstrated that its plan is rational and impartial and that the conditions at issue are "conducive to fulfillment of authorized planning objectives." Dolan, on the other hand, has offered no evidence that her burden of compliance has any impact at all on the value or profitability of her planned development. Following the teaching of the cases on which it purports to rely, the Court should not isolate the burden associated with the loss of the power to exclude from an evaluation of the benefit to be derived from the permit to enlarge the store and the parking lot.

The Court's assurances that its "rough proportionality" test leaves ample room for cities to pursue the "commendable task of land use planning," ante, at 2321--even twice avowing that "[n]o precise mathematical calculation is required," ante, at 2319, 2321--are wanting given the result that test compels here. Under the Court's approach, a city must not only "quantify its findings," ante, at 2319, and make "individualized determination[s]" with respect to the nature and the extent of the relationship between the conditions and the impact, ante, at 2319, 2320, but also demonstrate "proportionality." The correct inquiry should instead concentrate on whether the required nexus is present and venture beyond considerations of a condition's nature or germaneness only if the developer establishes that a concededly germane condition is so grossly disproportionate to the proposed development's adverse effects that it manifests motives other than land use regulation on the part of the city. (FN5) *2326 The heightened requirement the Court imposes on cities is even more unjustified when all the tools needed to resolve the questions presented by this case can be garnered from our existing case law.

III

Applying its new standard, the Court finds two defects in the city's case. First, while the record would adequately support a requirement that Dolan maintain the portion of the floodplain on her property as undeveloped open space, it does not support the additional requirement that the floodplain be dedicated to the city. Ante, at 2319-2321. Second, while the city adequately established the traffic increase that the proposed development would generate, it failed to quantify the offsetting decrease in automobile traffic that the bike path will produce. Ante, at 2320-2321. Even under the Court's new rule, both defects are, at most, nothing more than harmless error.

In her objections to the floodplain condition, Dolan made no effort to demonstrate that the dedication of that portion of her property would be any more onerous than a simple prohibition against any development on that portion of her property. Given the commercial character of both the existing and the proposed use of the property as a retail store, it seems likely that potential customers "trampling along petitioner's floodplain," ante, at 2320, are more valuable than a useless parcel of vacant land. Moreover, the duty to pay taxes and the responsibility for potential tort liability may well make ownership of the fee interest in useless land a liability rather than an asset. That may explain why Dolan never conceded that she could be prevented from building on the floodplain. The City Attorney also pointed out that absent a dedication, property owners would be required to "build on their own land" and "with their own money" a storage facility for the water runoff. Tr. of Oral Arg. 30-31. Dolan apparently "did have that option," but chose not to seek it. Id., at 31. If Dolan might have been entitled to a variance confining the city's condition in a manner this Court would accept, her failure to seek that narrower form of relief at any stage of the state administrative and judicial proceedings clearly should preclude that relief in this Court now.

The Court's rejection of the bike path condition amounts to nothing more than a play on words. Everyone agrees that the bike path "could" offset some of the increased traffic flow that the larger store will generate, but the findings do not unequivocally

114 S.Ct. 2309, Dolan v. City of Tigard, (U.S.Or. 1994)

state that it *will* do so, or tell us just how many cyclists will replace motorists. Predictions on such matters are inherently nothing more than estimates. Certainly the assumption that there will be an offsetting benefit here is entirely reasonable and should suffice whether it amounts to 100 percent, 35 percent, or only 5 percent of the increase in automobile traffic that would otherwise occur. If the Court proposes to have the federal judiciary micromanage state decisions of this kind, it is indeed extending its welcome mat to a significant new class of litigants. Although there is no reason to believe that state courts have failed to rise to the task, property owners have surely found a new friend today.

IV

The Court has made a serious error by abandoning the traditional presumption of constitutionality and imposing a novel burden of proof on a city implementing an admittedly valid comprehensive land use plan. Even more consequential than its incorrect disposition of this case, however, is the Court's resurrection of a species of substantive due process analysis that it firmly rejected decades ago. (FN6)

The Court begins its constitutional analysis by citing *Chicago, B. & Q.R. Co. v. Chicago,* 166 U.S. 226, 239, 17 S.Ct. 581, 585, 41 L.Ed. 979 (1897), for the proposition that the Takings Clause of the Fifth Amendment is "applicable to the States through the Fourteenth *2327 Amendment." *Ante,* at 2316. That opinion, however, contains no mention of either the Takings Clause or the Fifth Amendment; (FN7) it held that the protection afforded by the Due Process Clause of the Fourteenth Amendment extends to matters of substance as well as procedure, (FN8) and that the substance of "the due process of law enjoined by the Fourteenth Amendment requires compensation to be made or adequately secured to the owner of private property taken for public use under the authority of a State." *Chicago, B. & Q.R. Co.,* 166 U.S., at 235, 236-241, 17 S.Ct., at 584, 584-586. It applied the same kind of substantive due process analysis more frequently identified with a better known case that accorded similar substantive protection to a baker's liberty interest in working 60 hours a week and 10 hours a day. See *Lochner v. New York,* 198 U.S. 45, 25 S.Ct. 539, 49 L.Ed. 937 (1905). (FN9)

Later cases have interpreted the Fourteenth Amendment's substantive protection against uncompensated deprivations of private property by the States as though it incorporated the text of the Fifth Amendment's Takings Clause. See, *e.g., Keystone Bituminous Coal Assn. v. DeBenedictis,* 480 U.S. 470, 481, n. 10, 107 S.Ct. 1232, 1240, n. 10, 94 L.Ed.2d 472 (1987). There was nothing problematic about that interpretation in cases enforcing the Fourteenth Amendment against state action that involved the actual physical invasion of private property. See *Loretto v. Teleprompter Manhattan CATV Corp.,* 458 U.S. 419, 427-433, 102 S.Ct. 3164, 3172-3175, 73 L.Ed.2d 868 (1982); *Kaiser Aetna v. United States,* 444 U.S. 164, 178-180, 100 S.Ct. 383, 392-393, 62 L.Ed.2d 332 (1979). Justice Holmes charted a significant new course, however, when he opined that a state law making it "commercially impracticable to mine certain coal" had "very nearly the same effect for constitutional purposes as appropriating or destroying it." *Pennsylvania Coal Co. v. Mahon,* 260 U.S. 393, 414, 43 S.Ct. 158, 159, 67 L.Ed. 322 (1922). The so-called "regulatory takings" doctrine that the Holmes dictum (FN10) kindled has an obvious kinship with the line of substantive due process cases that *Lochner* exemplified. Besides having similar ancestry, both doctrines are potentially open-ended sources of judicial power to invalidate state economic regulations that Members of this Court view as unwise or unfair.

This case inaugurates an even more recent judicial innovation than the regulatory takings doctrine: the application of the "unconstitutional conditions" label to a mutually beneficial transaction between a property owner and a city. The Court tells us that the city's refusal to grant Dolan a discretionary benefit infringes her right to receive just compensation for the property interests that she has refused to dedicate to the city "where the property sought has little or no relationship to the benefit." (FN11) Although it is *2328 well settled that a government cannot deny a benefit on a basis that infringes constitutionally protected interests-- "especially [one's] interest in freedom of speech," *Perry v. Sindermann,* 408 U.S. 593, 597, 92 S.Ct. 2694, 2697, 33 L.Ed.2d 570 (1972)--the "unconstitutional conditions" doctrine provides an inadequate framework in which to analyze this case. (FN12)

Dolan has no right to be compensated for a taking unless the city acquires the property interests that she has refused to surrender. Since no taking has

114 S.Ct. 2309, Dolan v. City of Tigard, (U.S.Or. 1994)

yet occurred, there has not been any infringement of her constitutional right to compensation. See *Preseault v. ICC*, 494 U.S. 1, 11-17, 110 S.Ct. 921-925, 108 L.Ed.2d 1 (1990) (finding takings claim premature because property owner had not yet sought compensation under Tucker Act); *Hodel v. Virginia Surface Mining & Reclamation Assn., Inc.*, 452 U.S. 264, 294-295, 101 S.Ct. 2352, 2370, 69 L.Ed.2d 1 (1981) (no taking where no one "identified any property ... that has allegedly been taken").

Even if Dolan should accept the city's conditions in exchange for the benefit that she seeks, it would not necessarily follow that she had been denied "just compensation" since it would be appropriate to consider the receipt of that benefit in any calculation of "just compensation." See *Pennsylvania Coal Co. v. Mahon*, 260 U.S. 393, 415, 43 S.Ct. 158, 160, 67 L.Ed. 322 (1922) (noting that an "average reciprocity of advantage" was deemed to justify many laws); *Hodel v. Irving*, 481 U.S. 704, 715, 107 S.Ct. 2076, 2082, 95 L.Ed.2d 668 (1987) (such " 'reciprocity of advantage' " weighed in favor of a statute's constitutionality). Particularly in the absence of any evidence on the point, we should not presume that the discretionary benefit the city has offered is less valuable than the property interests that Dolan can retain or surrender at her option. But even if that discretionary benefit were so trifling that it could not be considered just compensation when it has "little or no relationship" to the property, the Court fails to explain why the same value would suffice when the required nexus is present. In this respect, the Court's reliance on the "unconstitutional conditions" doctrine is assuredly novel, and arguably incoherent. The city's conditions are by no means immune from constitutional scrutiny. The level of scrutiny, however, does not approximate the kind of review that would apply if the city had insisted on a surrender of Dolan's First Amendment rights in exchange *2329 for a building permit. One can only hope that the Court's reliance today on First Amendment cases, see *ante*, at 2317 (citing *Perry v. Sindermann, supra*, and *Pickering v. Board of Ed. of Township High School Dist.*, 391 U.S. 563, 568, 88 S.Ct. 1731, 1734, 20 L.Ed.2d 811 (1968)), and its candid disavowal of the term "rational basis" to describe its new standard of review, see *ante*, at 2319, do not signify a reassertion of the kind of superlegislative power the Court exercised during the *Lochner* era.

The Court has decided to apply its heightened scrutiny to a single strand--the power to exclude--in the bundle of rights that enables a commercial enterprise to flourish in an urban environment. That intangible interest is undoubtedly worthy of constitutional protection--much like the grandmother's interest in deciding which of her relatives may share her home in *Moore v. East Cleveland*, 431 U.S. 494, 97 S.Ct. 1932, 52 L.Ed.2d 531 (1977). Both interests are protected from arbitrary state action by the Due Process Clause of the Fourteenth Amendment. It is, however, a curious irony that Members of the majority in this case would impose an almost insurmountable burden of proof on the property owner in the *Moore* case while saddling the city with a heightened burden in this case. (FN13)

In its application of what is essentially the doctrine of substantive due process, the Court confuses the past with the present. On November 13, 1922, the village of Euclid, Ohio, adopted a zoning ordinance that effectively confiscated 75 percent of the value of property owned by the Ambler Realty Company. Despite its recognition that such an ordinance "would have been rejected as arbitrary and oppressive" at an earlier date, the Court (over the dissent of Justices Van Devanter, McReynolds and Butler) upheld the ordinance. Today's majority should heed the words of Justice Sutherland:

"Such regulations are sustained, under the complex conditions of our day, for reasons analogous to those which justify traffic regulations, which, before the advent of automobiles and rapid transit street railways, would have been condemned as fatally arbitrary and unreasonable. And in this there is no inconsistency, for while the meaning of constitutional guaranties never varies, the scope of their application must expand or contract to meet the new and different conditions which are constantly coming within the field of their operation. In a changing world, it is impossible that it should be otherwise." *Euclid v. Ambler Co.*, 272 U.S. 365, 387, 47 S.Ct. 114, 118, 71 L.Ed. 303 (1926).

In our changing world one thing is certain: uncertainty will characterize predictions about the impact of new urban developments on the risks of floods, earthquakes, traffic congestion, or environmental harms. When there is doubt concerning the magnitude of those impacts, the public interest in averting them must outweigh the private interest of the commercial entrepreneur. If the government can demonstrate that the conditions it

Copyright (c) West Publishing Co. 1996 No claim to original U.S. Govt. works.

114 S.Ct. 2309, Dolan v. City of Tigard, (U.S.Or. 1994)

has imposed in a land-use permit are rational, impartial and conducive to fulfilling the aims of a valid land-use plan, a strong presumption *2330 of validity should attach to those conditions. The burden of demonstrating that those conditions have unreasonably impaired the economic value of the proposed improvement belongs squarely on the shoulders of the party challenging the state action's constitutionality. That allocation of burdens has served us well in the past. The Court has stumbled badly today by reversing it.

I respectfully dissent.

Justice SOUTER, dissenting.

This case, like *Nollan v. California Coastal Comm'n*, 483 U.S. 825, 107 S.Ct. 3141, 97 L.Ed.2d 677 (1987), invites the Court to examine the relationship between conditions imposed by development permits, requiring landowners to dedicate portions of their land for use by the public, and governmental interests in mitigating the adverse effects of such development. *Nollan* declared the need for a nexus between the nature of an exaction of an interest in land (a beach easement) and the nature of governmental interests. The Court treats this case as raising a further question, not about the nature, but about the degree, of connection required between such an exaction and the adverse effects of development. The Court's opinion announces a test to address this question, but as I read the opinion, the Court does not apply that test to these facts, which do not raise the question the Court addresses.

First, as to the floodplain and Greenway, the Court acknowledges that an easement of this land for open space (and presumably including the five feet required for needed creek channel improvements) is reasonably related to flood control, see *ante*, at 2317-2318, 2320, but argues that the "permanent recreational easement" for the public on the Greenway is not so related, see *ante*, at 2317-2321. If that is so, it is not because of any lack of proportionality between permit condition and adverse effect, but because of a lack of any rational connection at all between exaction of a public recreational area and the governmental interest in providing for the effect of increased water runoff. That is merely an application of *Nollan* 's nexus analysis. As the Court notes, "[i]f petitioner's proposed development had somehow encroached on existing greenway space in the city, it would have been reasonable to require petitioner to provide some alternative greenway space for the public." *Ante*, at 2321. But that, of course, was not the fact, and the city of Tigard never sought to justify the public access portion of the dedication as related to flood control. It merely argued that whatever recreational uses were made of the bicycle path and the one foot edge on either side, were incidental to the permit condition requiring dedication of the 15-foot easement for an 8-foot-wide bicycle path and for flood control, including open space requirements and relocation of the bank of the river by some five feet. It seems to me such incidental recreational use can stand or fall with the bicycle path, which the city justified by reference to traffic congestion. As to the relationship the Court examines, between the recreational easement and a purpose never put forth as a justification by the city, the Court unsurprisingly finds a recreation area to be unrelated to flood control.

Second, as to the bicycle path, the Court again acknowledges the "theor[etically]" reasonable relationship between "the city's attempt to reduce traffic congestion by providing [a bicycle path] for alternative means of transportation," *ante*, at 2318, and the "correct" finding of the city that "the larger retail sales facility proposed by petitioner will increase traffic on the streets of the Central Business District." *Ante*, at 2321. The Court only faults the city for saying that the bicycle path "could" rather than "would" offset the increased traffic from the store, *ante*, at 2321-2322. That again, as far as I can tell, is an application of *Nollan*, for the Court holds that the stated connection ("could offset") between traffic congestion and bicycle paths is too tenuous; only if the bicycle path "would" offset the increased traffic by some amount, could the bicycle path be said to be related to the city's legitimate interest in reducing traffic congestion.

*2331. I cannot agree that the application of *Nollan* is a sound one here, since it appears that the Court has placed the burden of producing evidence of relationship on the city, despite the usual rule in cases involving the police power that the government is presumed to have acted constitutionally. (FN*) Having thus assigned the burden, the Court concludes that the City loses based on one word ("could" instead of "would"), and despite the fact that this record shows the connection the Court looks for. Dolan has put forward no evidence that the burden of granting a dedication for the bicycle path is unrelated in kind to the anticipated increase in traffic congestion, nor, if there exists a requirement that the

114 S.Ct. 2309, Dolan v. City of Tigard, (U.S.Or. 1994)

relationship be related in degree, has Dolan shown that the exaction fails any such test. The city, by contrast, calculated the increased traffic flow that would result from Dolan's proposed development to be 435 trips per day, and its Comprehensive Plan, applied here, relied on studies showing the link between alternative modes of transportation, including bicycle paths, and reduced street traffic congestion. See, e.g., Brief for Respondent A-5, quoting City of Tigard's Comprehensive Plan (" 'Bicycle and pedestrian pathway systems will result in some reduction of automobile trips within the community' "). *Nollan*, therefore, is satisfied, and on that assumption the city's conditions should not be held to fail a further rough proportionality test or any other that might be devised to give meaning to the constitutional limits. As Members of this Court have said before, "the common zoning regulations requiring subdividers to ... dedicate certain areas to public streets, are in accord with our constitutional traditions because the proposed property use would otherwise be the cause of excessive congestion." *Pennell v. San Jose*, 485 U.S. 1, 20, 108 S.Ct. 849, 862, 99 L.Ed.2d 1 (1988) (SCALIA, J., concurring in part and dissenting in part). The bicycle path permit condition is fundamentally no different from these.

In any event, on my reading, the Court's conclusions about the city's vulnerability carry the Court no further than *Nollan* has gone already, and I do not view this case as a suitable vehicle for taking the law beyond that point. The right case for the enunciation of takings doctrine seems hard to spot. See *Lucas v. South Carolina Coastal Council*, 505 U.S. ----, ----, 112 S.Ct. 2886, 2925, 120 L.Ed.2d 798 (1992) (statement of SOUTER, J.).

FN* The syllabus constitutes no part of the opinion of the Court but has been prepared by the Reporter of Decisions for the convenience of the reader. See *United States v. Detroit Lumber Co.*, 200 U.S. 321, 337, 26 S.Ct. 282, 287, 50 L.Ed. 499.

FN1. CDC Sec. 18.86.040.A.1.b provides: "The development shall facilitate pedestrian/bicycle circulation if the site is located on a street with designated bikepaths or adjacent to a designated greenway/open space/park. Specific items to be addressed [include]: (i) Provision of efficient, convenient and continuous pedestrian and bicycle transit circulation systems, linking developments by requiring dedication and construction of pedestrian and bikepaths identified in the comprehensive plan. If direct connections cannot be made, require that funds in the amount of the construction cost be deposited into an account for the purpose of constructing paths." (App. to Brief for Respondent B-33-34).

FN2. The city's decision includes the following relevant conditions: "1. The applicant shall dedicate to the City as Greenway all portions of the site that fall within the existing 100-year floodplain [of Fanno Creek] (*i.e.*, all portions of the property below elevation 150.0) and all property 15 feet above (to the east of) the 150.0 foot floodplain boundary. The building shall be designed so as not to intrude into the greenway area." App. to Pet. for Cert. G-43.

FN3. CDC Sec. 18.134.050 contains the following criteria whereby the decisionmaking authority can approve, approve with modifications, or deny a variance request:

"(1) The proposed variance will not be materially detrimental to the purposes of this title, be in conflict with the policies of the comprehensive plan, to any other applicable policies of the Community Development Code, to any other applicable policies and standards, and to other properties in the same zoning district or vicinity;

"(2) There are special circumstances that exist which are peculiar to the lot size or shape, topography or other circumstances over which the applicant has no control, and which are not applicable to other properties in the same zoning district;

"(3) The use proposed will be the same as permitted under this title and City standards will be maintained to the greatest extent possible, while permitting some economic use of the land;

"(4) Existing physical and natural systems, such as but not limited to traffic, drainage, dramatic land form or parks will not be adversely affected any more than would occur if the development were located as specified in the title; and

"(5) The hardship is not self-imposed and the variance requested is the minimum variance which would alleviate the hardship." App. to Brief for Respondent 49-50.

FN4. The Supreme Court of Oregon did not address the consequences of petitioner's failure to provide alternative mitigation measures in her variance

114 S.Ct. 2309, Dolan v. City of Tigard, (U.S.Or. 1994)

application and we take the case as it comes to us. Accordingly, we do not pass on the constitutionality of the city's variance provisions.

FN5. Justice STEVENS' dissent suggests that this case is actually grounded in "substantive" due process, rather than in the view that the Takings Clause of the Fifth Amendment was made applicable to the States by the Fourteenth Amendment. But there is no doubt that later cases have held that the Fourteenth Amendment does make the Takings Clause of the Fifth Amendment applicable to the States, see *Penn Central Transp. Co. v. New York City*, 438 U.S. 104, 122, 98 S.Ct. 2646, 2658, 57 L.Ed.2d 631 (1978); *Nollan v. California Coastal Comm'n*, 483 U.S. 825, 827, 107 S.Ct. 3141, 3143, 97 L.Ed.2d 677 (1987). Nor is there any doubt that these cases have relied upon *Chicago, B. & Q.R. Co. v. Chicago*, 166 U.S. 226, *2331. 17 S.Ct. 581, 41 L.Ed. 979 (1897), to reach that result. See, *e.g., Penn Central, supra*, 438 U.S., at 122, 98 S.Ct., at 2658 ("The issu[e] presented ... [is] whether the restrictions imposed by New York City's law upon appellants' exploitation of the Terminal site effect a 'taking' of appellants' property for a public use within the meaning of the Fifth Amendment, which of course is made applicable to the States through the Fourteenth Amendment, see *Chicago, B. & Q.R. Co. v. Chicago*, 166 U.S. 226, 239, 17 S.Ct. 581, 585, 41 L.Ed. 979 (1897)").

*2331_ FN6. There can be no argument that the permit conditions would deprive petitioner "economically beneficial us[e]" of her property as she currently operates a retail store on the lot. Petitioner assuredly is able to derive *some* economic use from her property. See, *e.g., Lucas v. South Carolina*, 505 U.S. ----, ----, 112 S.Ct. 2886, 2893, 120 L.Ed.2d 798 (1992); *Kaiser Aetna v. United States*, 444 U.S. 164, 175, 100 S.Ct. 383, 390, 62 L.Ed.2d 332 (1979); *Penn Central Transportation Co. v. New York City*, 438 U.S. 104, 124, 98 S.Ct. 2646, 2659, 57 L.Ed.2d 631 (1978).

FN7. The "specifically and uniquely attributable" test has now been adopted by a minority of other courts. See, *e.g., J.E.D. Associates., Inc. v. Atkinson*, 121 N.H. 581, 585, 432 A.2d 12, 15 (1981); *Divan Builders, Inc. v. Planning Bd. of Twp. of Wayne*, 66 N.J. 582, 600-601, 334 A.2d 30, 40 (1975); *McKain v. Toledo City Plan Comm'n*, 26 Ohio App.2d 171, 176, 270 N.E.2d 370, 374 (1971); *Frank Ansuini, Inc. v. Cranston*, 107 R.I. 63, 69, 264 A.2d 910, 913 (1970).

FN8. Justice STEVENS' dissent takes us to task for placing the burden on the city to justify the required dedication. He is correct in arguing that in evaluating most generally applicable zoning regulations, the burden properly rests on the party challenging the regulation to prove that it constitutes an arbitrary regulation of property rights. See, *e.g., Euclid v. Ambler Realty Co.*, 272 U.S. 365, 47 S.Ct. 114, 71 L.Ed. 303 (1926). Here, by contrast, the city made an adjudicative decision to condition petitioner's application for a building permit on an individual parcel. In this situation, the burden properly rests on the city. See *Nollan*, 483 U.S., at 836, 107 S.Ct., at 3148. This conclusion is not, as he suggests, undermined by our decision in *Moore v. East Cleveland*, 431 U.S. 494, 97 S.Ct. 1932, 52 L.Ed.2d 531 (1977), in which we struck down a housing ordinance that limited occupancy of a dwelling unit to members of a single family as violating the Due Process Clause of the Fourteenth Amendment. The ordinance at issue in *Moore* intruded on choices concerning family living arrangements, an area in which the usual deference to the legislature was found to be inappropriate. *Id.*, at 499, 97 S.Ct., at 1935.

FN9. The city uses a weekday average trip rate of 53.21 trips per 1000 square feet. Additional Trips Generated = 53.21 X (17,600-9720). App. to Pet. for Cert. G15.

FN10. In rejecting petitioner's request for a variance from the pathway dedication condition, the city stated that omitting the planned section of the pathway across petitioner's property would conflict with its adopted policy of providing a continuous pathway system. But the Takings Clause requires the city to implement its policy by condemnation unless the required relationship between the petitioner's development and added traffic is shown

FN1. Cf. *Moore v. East Cleveland*, 431 U.S. 494, 513-521, 97 S.Ct. 1932, 52 L.Ed.2d 531 (1977) (STEVENS, J., concurring in judgment).

FN2. In *Nollan* the Court recognized that a State agency may condition the grant of a land-use permit on the dedication of a property interest if the dedication serves a legitimate police-power purpose that would justify a refusal to issue the

114 S.Ct. 2309, Dolan v. City of Tigard, (U.S.Or. 1994)

permit. For the first time, however, it held that such a condition is unconstitutional if the condition "utterly fails" to further a goal that would justify the refusal. 483 U.S., at 837, 107 S.Ct., at 3148. In the *Nollan* Court's view, a condition would be constitutional even if it required the Nollans to provide a viewing spot for passersby whose view of the ocean was obstructed by their new house. *Id.*, at 836, 107 S.Ct., at 3148. "Although such a requirement, constituting a permanent grant of continuous access to the property, would have to be considered a taking if it were not attached to a development permit, the Commission's assumed power to forbid construction of the house in order to protect the public's view of the beach must surely include the power to condition construction upon some concession by the owner, even a concession of property rights, that serves the same end." *Ibid.*

*2331_ FN3. Similarly, in *Keystone Bituminous Coal Assn. v. DeBenedictis*, 480 U.S. 470, 498-499, 107 S.Ct. 1232, 1249, 94 L.Ed.2d 472 (1987), we concluded that "[t]he 27 million tons of coal do not constitute a separate segment of property for takings law purposes" and that "[t]here is no basis for treating the less than 2% of petitioners' coal as a separate parcel of property."

FN4. Johnston's article also sets forth a fair summary of the state cases from which the Court purports to derive its "rough proportionality" test. See 52 Cornell L.Q., at 917. Like the Court, Johnston observed that cases requiring a "rational nexus" between exactions and public needs created by the new subdivision--especially *Jordan v. Menomonee Falls*, 28 Wis.2d 608, 137 N.W.2d 442 (1965)-- "stee[r] a moderate course" between the "judicial obstructionism" of *Pioneer Trust & Savings Bank v. Mount Prospect*, 22 Ill.2d 375, 176 N.E.2d 799 (1961), and the "excessive deference" of *Billings Properties, Inc. v. Yellowstone County*, 144 Mont. 25, 394 P.2d 182 (1964). 52 Cornell L.Q., at 917.

FN5. Dolan's attorney overstated the danger when he suggested at oral argument that without some requirement for proportionality, "the City could have found that Mrs. Dolan's new store would have increased traffic by one additional vehicle trip per day [and] could have required her to dedicate 75, 95 percent of her land for a widening of Main Street." Tr. of Oral Arg. 52-53.

FN6. See, *e.g., Ferguson v. Skrupa*, 372 U.S. 726, 83 S.Ct. 1028, 10 L.Ed.2d 93 (1963).

FN7. An earlier case deemed it "well settled" that the Takings Clause "is a limitation on the power of the Federal government, and not on the States." *Pumpelly v. Green Bay Co.*, 13 Wall. 166, 177, 20 L.Ed. 557 (1872).

FN8. The Court held that a State "may not, by any of its agencies, disregard the prohibitions of the Fourteenth Amendment. Its judicial authorities may keep within the letter of the statute prescribing forms of procedure in the courts and give the parties interested the fullest opportunity to be heard, and yet it might be that its final action would be inconsistent with that amendment. In determining what is due process of law regard must be had to substance, not to form." *Chicago, B. & Q.R. Co. v. Chicago*, 166 U.S. 226, 234-235, 17 S.Ct. 581, 584, 41 L.Ed. 979 (1897).

FN9. The *Lochner* Court refused to presume that there was a reasonable connection between the regulation and the state interest in protecting the public health. 198 U.S., at 60-61, 25 S.Ct., at 544. A similar refusal to identify a sufficient nexus between an enlarged building with a newly paved parking lot and the state interests in minimizing the risks of flooding and traffic congestion proves fatal to the city's permit conditions in this case under the Court's novel approach.

FN10. See *Keystone Bituminous Coal Assn v. DeBenedictis*, 480 U.S. 470, 484, 107 S.Ct. 1232, 1241, 94 L.Ed.2d 472 (1987) (explaining why this portion of the opinion was merely "advisory").

FN11. *Ante*, at 2317. The Court's entire explanation reads: "Under the well-settled doctrine of 'unconstitutional conditions,' the government may not require a person to give up a constitutional right--here the right to receive just compensation when property is taken for a public use--in exchange for a discretionary benefit conferred by the government where the property sought has little or no relationship to the benefit." *Ibid.*

FN12. Although it has a long history, see *Home Ins. Co. v. Morse*, 20 Wall. 445, 451, 22 L.Ed. 365 (1874), the "unconstitutional conditions" doctrine has for just as long suffered from notoriously inconsistent application; it has never been an overarching principle of constitutional law that operates with equal force regardless of the nature

114 S.Ct. 2309, Dolan v. City of Tigard, (U.S.Or. 1994)

of the rights and powers in question. See, e.g., Sunstein, Why the Unconstitutional Conditions Doctrine is an Anachronism, 70 B.U.L.Rev. 593, 620 (1990) (doctrine is "too crude and too general to provide help in contested cases"); Sullivan, Unconstitutional Conditions, 102 Harv.L.Rev. 1415, 1416 (1989) (doctrine is "riven with inconsistencies"); Hale, Unconstitutional Conditions and Constitutional Rights, 35 Colum.L.Rev. 321, 322 (1935) ("The Supreme Court has sustained many such exertions of power even after announcing the broad doctrine that would invalidate them"). As the majority's case citations suggest, *ante*, at 2317, modern decisions invoking the doctrine have most frequently involved First Amendment liberties, see also, *e.g.*, *Connick v. Myers*, 461 U.S. 138, 143-144, 103 S.Ct. 1684, 1688, 75 L.Ed.2d 708 (1983); *Elrod v. Burns*, 427 U.S. 347, 361-363, 96 S.Ct. 2673, 2684, 49 L.Ed.2d 547 (1976) (plurality opinion); *Sherbert v. Verner*, 374 U.S. 398, 404, 83 S.Ct. 1790, 1794, 10 L.Ed.2d 965 (1963); *Speiser v. Randall*, 357 U.S. 513, 518-519, 78 S.Ct. 1332, 1338, 2 L.Ed.2d 1460 (1958). But see *Posadas de Puerto Rico Associates v. Tourism Co. of Puerto Rico*, 478 U.S. 328, 345-346, 106 S.Ct. 2968, 2979, 92 L.Ed.2d 266 (1986) ("the greater power to completely ban casino gambling necessarily includes the lesser power to ban advertising of casino gambling"). The necessary and traditional breadth of municipalities' power to regulate property development, together with the absence here of fragile and easily "chilled" constitutional rights such as that of free speech, make it quite clear that the Court is really writing on a clean slate rather than merely applying "well-settled" doctrine. See *ante*, at 2316.

*2331_ FN13. The author of today's opinion joined Justice Stewart's dissent in *Moore v. East Cleveland*, 431 U.S. 494, 97 S.Ct. 1932, 52 L.Ed.2d 531 (1977). There the dissenters found it sufficient, in response to my argument that the zoning ordinance was an arbitrary regulation of property rights, that "if the ordinance is a rational attempt to promote 'the city's interest in preserving the character of its neighborhoods,' *Young v. American Mini Theatres*, 427 U.S. 50, 71 [96 S.Ct. 2440, 2452, 49 L.Ed.2d 310 (1976)] (opinion of Stevens, J.), it is ... a permissible restriction on the use of private property under *Euclid v. Ambler Realty Co.*, 272 U.S. 365 [47 S.Ct. 114, 71 L.Ed. 303 (1926)], and *Nectow v. Cambridge*, 277 U.S. 183 [48 S.Ct. 447, 72 L.Ed. 842 (1928)]." *Id.*, 431 U.S., at 540, n. 10, 97 S.Ct., at 1956, n. 10. The dissent went on to state that my calling the city to task for failing to explain the need for enacting the ordinance *"place[d] the burden on the wrong party." Ibid.* (emphasis added). Recently, two other Members of today's majority severely criticized the holding in *Moore*. See *United States v. Carlton*, 512 U.S. ----, ---- 114 S.Ct. 2018, 2027, --- L.Ed.2d ---- (1994) (SCALIA, J., concurring in judgment); see also *id.*, at ----, 114 S.Ct. at 2020 (SCALIA, J., concurring in judgment) (calling the doctrine of substantive due process "an oxymoron").

FN* See, *e.g.*, *Goldblatt v. Hempstead*, 369 U.S. 590, 594-596, 82 S.Ct. 987, 990, 8 L.Ed.2d 130 (1962); *United States v. Sperry Corp.*, 493 U.S. 52, 60, 110 S.Ct. 387, 393-394, 107 L.Ed.2d 290 (1989). The majority characterizes this case as involving an "adjudicative decision" to impose permit conditions, *ante*, at ----, n. 8, but the permit conditions were imposed pursuant to Tigard's Community Development Code. See, *e.g.*, Sec. 18.84.040, App. to Brief for Respondent B-26. The adjudication here was of Dolan's requested variance from the permit conditions otherwise required to be imposed by the Code. This case raises no question about discriminatory, or "reverse spot" zoning, which "singles out a particular parcel for different, less favorable treatment than the neighboring ones." *Penn Central Transp. Co. v. New York City*, 438 U.S. 104, 132, 98 S.Ct. 2646, 2663, 57 L.Ed.2d 631 (1978).

Appendix E

The Lucas Decision*

*Source: West's CD ROM Libraries.

Material reprinted with permission.

112 S.Ct. 2886
120 L.Ed.2d 798, 60 USLW 4842, 34 ERC 1897, 22 Envtl. L. Rep. 21,104
(Cite as: 505 U.S. 1003, 112 S.Ct. 2886)

David H. LUCAS, Petitioner,
v.
SOUTH CAROLINA COASTAL COUNCIL.

No. 91-453.

Supreme Court of the United States

Argued March 2, 1992.

Decided June 29, 1992.

Owner of beachfront property brought action alleging that application of South Carolina Beachfront Management Act to his property constituted a taking without just compensation. The Common Pleas Court of Charleston County, Larry R. Patterson, Special Judge, awarded landowner damages and appeal was taken. The South Carolina Supreme Court, Toal, J., reversed, 304 S.C. 376, 404 S.E.2d 895. Certiorari was granted, 112 S.Ct. 436, and the Supreme Court, Justice Scalia held that: (1) property owner's claim was ripe for review, and (2) South Carolina Supreme Court erred in applying "harmful or noxious uses" principle to decide case.

Reversed and remanded.

Justice Kennedy, filed opinion concurring in the judgment.

Justices Blackmun and Stevens filed separate dissenting opinions.

Justice Souter filed separate statement.

[1] **FEDERAL COURTS** ⇐ 510
170Bk510
That South Carolina Beachfront Management Act, which landowner claimed deprived him of all economically viable use of property, was amended, after briefing and argument before South Carolina Supreme Court but prior to issuance of that court's opinion, to authorize issuance of special permits for construction or reconstruction of habitable structures in certain circumstances did not render unripe landowner's deprivation claim; South Carolina Supreme Court rested its judgment on merits of claim, rather than on ripeness grounds, thus precluding landowner from asserting any takings claim with respect to deprivation which had occurred prior to amendment, and landowner alleged injury-in-fact as to preamendment deprivation. S.C.Code 1976, §§ 48-39-250 et seq., 48-39-290(D)(1).

[2] **EMINENT DOMAIN** ⇐ 2(1)
148k2(1)
There are two discrete categories of regulatory deprivations that are compensable under Fifth Amendment without case-specific inquiry into public interest advanced in support of restraint; the first encompasses regulations that compel property owner to suffer physical invasion of his property, and the second concerns situation in which regulation denies all economically beneficial or productive use of land. U.S.C.A. Const.Amend. 5.

[3] **EMINENT DOMAIN** ⇐ 2(1)
148k2(1)
When owner of real property has been called upon to sacrifice all economically beneficial use of property in name of common good, that is, to leave his property economically idle, he has suffered a "taking" within meaning of Fifth Amendment. U.S.C.A. Const.Amend. 5.

See publication Words and Phrases for other judicial constructions and definitions.

[4] **EMINENT DOMAIN** ⇐ 2(1)
148k2(1)
There are a number of noneconomic interests in land, such as interest in excluding strangers from one's land, the impairment of which will invite exceedingly close scrutiny under takings clause. U.S.C.A. Const.Amend. 5.

[5] **FEDERAL COURTS** ⇐ 501
170Bk501
Where finding that was premise of petition for certiorari was not challenged in brief in opposition, court would not entertain argument in respondent's brief on the merits that such finding was erroneous.

Copr. © West 1996 No claim to orig. U.S. govt. works

112 S.Ct. 2886
(Cite as: 505 U.S. 1003, 112 S.Ct. 2886)

[6] EMINENT DOMAIN ⇐ 2(1.1)
148k2(1.1)
South Carolina Supreme Court erred in applying rule that harmful or noxious uses of property may be proscribed by government regulation without requirement of compensation to decide case in which property owner alleged that all economically viable use of his property was precluded by South Carolina Beachfront Management Act, which barred him from erecting any permanent habitable structures on his land; in order to avoid paying compensation, state had to identify background principles of nuisance and property law that prohibited use as landowner presently intended in circumstances in which property was presently found. U.S.C.A. Const.Amend. 5.

[7] EMINENT DOMAIN ⇐ 69
148k69
Where state seeks to sustain regulation that deprives land of all economically beneficial use, it may resist compensation only if logically antecedent inquiry into nature of owner's estate shows that proscribed use interests were not part of his title to begin with. U.S.C.A. Const.Amend. 5.

[8] EMINENT DOMAIN ⇐ 69
148k69
In order for state regulations prohibiting all economically beneficial use of land to be imposed without necessity of paying compensation to landowners, regulation must do no more than duplicate result that could have been achieved in the courts by adjacent landowners or other uniquely affected persons under state's law of private nuisance, or by state under its complimentary power to abate nuisances that affect public generally, or otherwise. U.S.C.A. Const.Amend. 5.

[9] EMINENT DOMAIN ⇐ 114.1
148k114.1
Formerly 148k114
Although state may elect to rescind regulation which prohibits all economically beneficial use of land, and thereby avoid having to pay compensation for permanent deprivation of land, where regulation has already worked a taking of all use of property, no subsequent action by government can relieve it of duty to provide compensation for period during which taking was effective. U.S.C.A. Const.Amend. 5.

**2887 Syllabus [FN*]

FN* The syllabus constitutes no part of the opinion of the Court but has been prepared by the Reporter of Decisions for the convenience of the reader. See United States v. Detroit Lumber Co., 200 U.S. 321, 337, 26 S.Ct. 282, 287, 50 L.Ed. 499.

*1003 In 1986, petitioner Lucas bought two residential lots on a South Carolina barrier island, intending to build single-family homes such as those on the immediately adjacent parcels. At that time, Lucas's lots were not subject to the State's coastal zone building permit requirements. In 1988, however, the state legislature enacted the Beachfront Management Act, which barred Lucas from erecting any permanent habitable structures on his parcels. He filed suit against respondent state agency, contending that, even though the Act may have been a lawful exercise of the State's police power, the ban on construction deprived him of all "economically viable use" of his property and therefore effected a "taking" under the Fifth and Fourteenth Amendments that required the payment of just compensation. See, e.g., Agins v. City of Tiburon, 447 U.S. 255, 261, 100 S.Ct. 2138, 2141, 65 L.Ed.2d 106. The state trial court agreed, finding that the ban rendered Lucas's parcels "valueless," and entered an award exceeding $1.2 million. In reversing, the State Supreme Court held itself bound, in light of Lucas's failure to attack the Act's validity, to accept the legislature's "uncontested ... findings" that new construction in the coastal zone threatened a valuable public resource. The court ruled that, under the Mugler v. Kansas, 123 U.S. 623, 8 S.Ct. 273, 31 L.Ed. 205, line of cases, when a regulation is designed to prevent "harmful or noxious uses" of property akin to public nuisances, no compensation is owing under the Takings Clause regardless of the regulation's effect on the property's value.

Held:

112 S.Ct. 2886
(Cite as: 505 U.S. 1003, *1003, 112 S.Ct. 2886, **2887)

1. Lucas's takings claim is not rendered unripe by the fact that he may yet be able to secure a special permit to build on his property under an amendment to the Act passed after briefing and argument before **2888 the State Supreme Court, but prior to issuance of that court's opinion. Because it declined to rest its judgment on ripeness grounds, preferring to dispose of the case on the merits, the latter court's decision precludes, both practically and legally, any takings claim with respect to Lucas's preamendment deprivation. Lucas has properly alleged injury in fact with respect to this preamendment deprivation, and it would not accord with sound process in these circumstances to insist that he pursue the late-created procedure before that component of his takings claim can be considered ripe. Pp. 2890-2892.

*1004 2. The State Supreme Court erred in applying the "harmful or noxious uses" principle to decide this case. Pp. 2892-2902.

(a) Regulations that deny the property owner all "economically viable use of his land" constitute one of the discrete categories of regulatory deprivations that require compensation without the usual case-specific inquiry into the public interest advanced in support of the restraint. Although the Court has never set forth the justification for this categorical rule, the practical--and economic--equivalence of physically appropriating and eliminating all beneficial use of land counsels its preservation. Pp. 2892-2895.

(b) A review of the relevant decisions demonstrates that the "harmful or noxious use" principle was merely this Court's early formulation of the police power justification necessary to sustain (without compensation) any regulatory diminution in value; that the distinction between regulation that "prevents harmful use" and that which "confers benefits" is difficult, if not impossible, to discern on an objective, value-free basis; and that, therefore, noxious-use logic cannot be the basis for departing from this Court's categorical rule that total regulatory takings must be compensated. Pp. 2896-2899.

(c) Rather, the question must turn, in accord with this Court's "takings" jurisprudence, on citizens' historic understandings regarding the content of, and the State's power over, the "bundle of rights" that they acquire when they take title to property. Because it is not consistent with the historical compact embodied in the Takings Clause that title to real estate is held subject to the State's subsequent decision to eliminate all economically beneficial use, a regulation having that effect cannot be newly decreed, and sustained, without compensation's being paid the owner. However, no compensation is owed--in this setting as with all takings claims--if the State's affirmative decree simply makes explicit what already inheres in the title itself, in the restrictions that background principles of the State's law of property and nuisance already place upon land ownership. Cf. Scranton v. Wheeler, 179 U.S. 141, 163, 21 S.Ct. 48, 57, 45 L.Ed. 126. Pp. 2899-2901.

(d) Although it seems unlikely that common-law principles would have prevented the erection of any habitable or productive improvements on Lucas's land, this state-law question must be dealt with on remand. To win its case, respondent cannot simply proffer the legislature's declaration that the uses Lucas desires are inconsistent with the public interest, or the conclusory assertion that they violate a common-law maxim such as sic utere tuo ut alienum non laedas, but must identify background principles of nuisance and property law that prohibit the uses Lucas now intends in the property's present circumstances. Pp. 2901-2902.

304 S.C. 376, 404 S.E.2d 895 (1991), reversed and remanded.

*1005 SCALIA, J., delivered the opinion of the Court, in which REHNQUIST, C.J., and WHITE, O'CONNOR, and THOMAS, JJ., joined. KENNEDY, J., filed an opinion concurring in the judgment, post, p. 2902. BLACKMUN, J., post, p. 2904, and STEVENS, J., post, p. 2917, filed dissenting opinions. SOUTER, J., filed a separate statement, post, p. 2925.

Copr. © West 1996 No claim to orig. U.S. govt. works

112 S.Ct. 2886
(Cite as: 505 U.S. 1003, *1005, 112 S.Ct. 2886, **2888)

A. Camden Lewis, Columbia, S.C., for petitioner.

**2889 C.C. Harness, III, Charleston, S.C., for respondent.

For U.S. Supreme Court Briefs See:

1991 WL 626699 (Pet.Brief)

1992 WL 672609 (Reply.Brief)

1992 WL 672613 (Resp.Brief)

For Transcript of Oral Argument See:

1992 WL 687838 (U.S.Oral.Arg.)

1992 WL 691954 (U.S.Oral.Arg.)

*1006 Justice SCALIA delivered the opinion of the Court.

In 1986, petitioner David H. Lucas paid $975,000 for two residential lots on the Isle of Palms in Charleston County, *1007 South Carolina, on which he intended to build single-family homes. In 1988, however, the South Carolina Legislature enacted the Beachfront Management Act, S.C.Code Ann. § 48-39-250 et seq. (Supp.1990), which had the direct effect of barring petitioner from erecting any permanent habitable structures on his two parcels. See § 48-39-290(A). A state trial court found that this prohibition rendered Lucas's parcels "valueless." App. to Pet. for Cert. 37. This case requires us to decide whether the Act's dramatic effect on the economic value of Lucas's lots accomplished a taking of private property under the Fifth and Fourteenth Amendments requiring the payment of "just compensation." U.S. Const., Amdt. 5.

I
A

South Carolina's expressed interest in intensively managing development activities in the so-called "coastal zone" dates from 1977 when, in the aftermath of Congress's passage of the federal Coastal Zone Management Act of 1972, 86 Stat. 1280, as amended, 16 U.S.C. § 1451 et seq., the legislature enacted a Coastal Zone Management Act of its own. See S.C.Code Ann. § 48-39-10 et seq. (1987). In its original form, the South Carolina Act required owners of coastal zone land that qualified as a "critical area" (defined in the legislation to include beaches and immediately adjacent sand dunes, *1008 § 48-39-10(J)) to obtain a permit from the newly created South Carolina Coastal Council (Council) (respondent here) prior to committing the land to a "use other than the use the critical area was devoted to on [September 28, 1977]." § 48-39-130(A).

In the late 1970's, Lucas and others began extensive residential development of the Isle of Palms, a barrier island situated eastward of the city of Charleston. Toward the close of the development cycle for one residential subdivision known as "Beachwood East," Lucas in 1986 purchased the two lots at issue in this litigation for his own account. No portion of the lots, which were located approximately 300 feet from the beach, qualified as a "critical area" under the 1977 Act; accordingly, at the time Lucas acquired these parcels, he was not legally obliged to obtain a permit from the Council in advance of any development activity. His intention with respect to the lots was to do what the owners of the immediately adjacent parcels had already done: erect single-family residences. He commissioned architectural drawings for this purpose.

The Beachfront Management Act brought Lucas's plans to an abrupt end. Under that 1988 legislation, the Council was directed to establish a "baseline" connecting the landward-most "point[s] of erosion ... during the past forty years" in the region of the Isle of Palms that includes Lucas's lots. S.C.Code Ann. § 48-39-280(A)(2) (Supp.1988). [FN1] In action not challenged here, the Council fixed this baseline landward of Lucas's parcels. That was significant, for under the Act *1009 construction of occupiable improvements [FN2] was flatly prohibited seaward of a line drawn **2890 20 feet landward of, and parallel to, the baseline. § 48-39-290(A). The Act provided no exceptions.

FN1. This specialized historical method of determining the baseline applied because the Beachwood East subdivision is located adjacent to a so-called "inlet erosion zone" (defined in the Act to mean "a segment of shoreline along or adjacent to tidal inlets which are directly influenced by the inlet and its associated shoals," S.C. Code Ann. § 48-39-270(7) (Supp.1988)) that is "not stabilized by jetties, terminal groins, or other structures," § 48-39-280(A)(2). For areas other than these unstabilized inlet erosion zones, the statute directs that the baseline be established along "the crest of an ideal primary oceanfront sand dune." § 48-39-280(A)(1).

FN2. The Act did allow the construction of certain nonhabitable improvements, e.g., "wooden walkways no larger in width than six feet," and "small wooden decks no larger than one hundred forty-four square feet." §§ 48-39-290(A)(1) and (2).

B

Lucas promptly filed suit in the South Carolina Court of Common Pleas, contending that the Beachfront Management Act's construction bar effected a taking of his property without just compensation. Lucas did not take issue with the validity of the Act as a lawful exercise of South Carolina's police power, but contended that the Act's complete extinguishment of his property's value entitled him to compensation regardless of whether the legislature had acted in furtherance of legitimate police power objectives. Following a bench trial, the court agreed. Among its factual determinations was the finding that "at the time Lucas purchased the two lots, both were zoned for single-family residential construction and ... there were no restrictions imposed upon such use of the property by either the State of South Carolina, the County of Charleston, or the Town of the Isle of Palms." App. to Pet. for Cert. 36. The trial court further found that the Beachfront Management Act decreed a permanent ban on construction insofar as Lucas's lots were concerned, and that this prohibition "deprive[d] Lucas of any reasonable economic use of the lots, ... eliminated the unrestricted right of use, and render[ed] them valueless." Id., at 37. The court thus concluded that Lucas's properties had been "taken" by operation of the Act, and it ordered respondent to pay "just compensation" in the amount of $1,232,387.50. Id., at 40.

The Supreme Court of South Carolina reversed. It found dispositive what it described as Lucas's concession "that the *1010 Beachfront Management Act [was] properly and validly designed to preserve ... South Carolina's beaches." 304 S.C. 376, 379, 404 S.E.2d 895, 896 (1991). Failing an attack on the validity of the statute as such, the court believed itself bound to accept the "uncontested ... findings" of the South Carolina Legislature that new construction in the coastal zone--such as petitioner intended--threatened this public resource. Id., at 383, 404 S.E.2d, at 898. The court ruled that when a regulation respecting the use of property is designed "to prevent serious public harm," id., at 383, 404 S.E.2d, at 899 (citing, inter alia, Mugler v. Kansas, 123 U.S. 623, 8 S.Ct. 273, 31 L.Ed. 205 (1887)), no compensation is owing under the Takings Clause regardless of the regulation's effect on the property's value.

Two justices dissented. They acknowledged that our Mugler line of cases recognizes governmental power to prohibit "noxious" uses of property--i.e., uses of property akin to "public nuisances"--without having to pay compensation. But they would not have characterized the Beachfront Management Act's "primary purpose [as] the prevention of a nuisance." 304 S.C., at 395, 404 S.E.2d, at 906 (Harwell, J., dissenting). To the dissenters, the chief purposes of the legislation, among them the promotion of tourism and the creation of a "habitat for indigenous flora and fauna," could not fairly be compared to nuisance abatement. Id., at 396, 404 S.E.2d, at 906. As a consequence, they would have affirmed the trial court's conclusion that the Act's obliteration of the value of petitioner's lots accomplished a taking.

We granted certiorari. 502 U.S. 966, 112 S.Ct. 436, 116 L.Ed.2d 455 (1991).

II

Copr. © West 1996 No claim to orig. U.S. govt. works

112 S.Ct. 2886
(Cite as: 505 U.S. 1003, *1010, 112 S.Ct. 2886, **2890)

[1] As a threshold matter, we must briefly address the Council's suggestion that this case is inappropriate for plenary review. After briefing and argument before the South Carolina Supreme Court, but prior to issuance of that court's opinion, the Beachfront Management Act was amended to *1011 authorize the Council, in certain circumstances, **2891 to issue "special permits" for the construction or reconstruction of habitable structures seaward of the baseline. See S.C.Code Ann. § 48-39-290(D)(1) (Supp.1991). According to the Council, this amendment renders Lucas's claim of a permanent deprivation unripe, as Lucas may yet be able to secure permission to build on his property. "[The Court's] cases," we are reminded, "uniformly reflect an insistence on knowing the nature and extent of permitted development before adjudicating the constitutionality of the regulations that purport to limit it." MacDonald, Sommer & Frates v. Yolo County, 477 U.S. 340, 351, 106 S.Ct. 2561, 2567, 91 L.Ed.2d 285 (1986). See also Agins v. City of Tiburon, 447 U.S. 255, 260, 100 S.Ct. 2138, 2141, 65 L.Ed.2d 106 (1980). Because petitioner "has not yet obtained a final decision regarding how [he] will be allowed to develop [his] property," Williamson County Regional Planning Comm'n v. Hamilton Bank of Johnson City, 473 U.S. 172, 190, 105 S.Ct. 3108, 3118, 87 L.Ed.2d 126 (1985), the Council argues that he is not yet entitled to definitive adjudication of his takings claim in this Court.

We think these considerations would preclude review had the South Carolina Supreme Court rested its judgment on ripeness grounds, as it was (essentially) invited to do by the Council. See Brief for Respondent 9, n. 3. The South Carolina Supreme Court shrugged off the possibility of further administrative and trial proceedings, however, preferring to dispose of Lucas's takings claim on the merits. Cf., e.g., San Diego Gas & Electric Co. v. San Diego, 450 U.S. 621, 631-632, 101 S.Ct. 1287, 1293-1294, 67 L.Ed.2d 551 (1981). This unusual disposition does not preclude Lucas from applying for a permit under the 1990 amendment for future construction, and challenging, on takings grounds, any denial. But it does preclude, both practically and legally, any takings claim with respect to Lucas's past deprivation, i.e., for his having been denied construction rights during the period before the 1990 amendment. See generally First English Evangelical Lutheran Church of Glendale v. County of Los Angeles, 482 U.S. 304, 107 S.Ct. 2378, 96 L.Ed.2d 250 (1987) (holding that *1012 temporary deprivations of use are compensable under the Takings Clause). Without even so much as commenting upon the consequences of the South Carolina Supreme Court's judgment in this respect, the Council insists that permitting Lucas to press his claim of a past deprivation on this appeal would be improper, since "the issues of whether and to what extent [Lucas] has incurred a temporary taking ... have simply never been addressed." Brief for Respondent 11. Yet Lucas had no reason to proceed on a "temporary taking" theory at trial, or even to seek remand for that purpose prior to submission of the case to the South Carolina Supreme Court, since as the Act then read, the taking was unconditional and permanent. Moreover, given the breadth of the South Carolina Supreme Court's holding and judgment, Lucas would plainly be unable (absent our intervention now) to obtain further state-court adjudication with respect to the 1988-1990 period.

In these circumstances, we think it would not accord with sound process to insist that Lucas pursue the late-created "special permit" procedure before his takings claim can be considered ripe. Lucas has properly alleged Article III injury in fact in this case, with respect to both the pre-1990 and post-1990 constraints placed on the use of his parcels by the Beachfront Management Act. [FN3] That there is a discretionary *1013 "special permit" **2892 procedure by which he may regain--for the future, at least--beneficial use of his land goes only to the prudential "ripeness" of Lucas's challenge, and for the reasons discussed we do not think it prudent to apply that prudential requirement here. See Esposito v. South Carolina Coastal Council, 939 F.2d 165, 168 (CA4 1991), cert. denied, 505 U.S. 1219, 112 S.Ct. 3027, 120 L.Ed.2d

898 (1992). [FN4] We leave for decision on remand, of course, the questions left unaddressed by the South *1014 Carolina Supreme Court as a consequence of its categorical disposition. [FN5]

FN3. Justice BLACKMUN insists that this aspect of Lucas's claim is "not justiciable," post, at 2907, because Lucas never fulfilled his obligation under Williamson County Regional Planning Comm'n v. Hamilton Bank of Johnson City, 473 U.S. 172, 105 S.Ct. 3108, 87 L.Ed.2d 126 (1985), to "submi[t] a plan for development of [his] property" to the proper state authorities, id., at 187, 105 S.Ct., at 3117. See post, at 2907. But such a submission would have been pointless, as the Council stipulated below that no building permit would have been issued under the 1988 Act, application or no application. Record 14 (stipulations). Nor does the peculiar posture of this case mean that we are without Article III jurisdiction, as Justice BLACKMUN apparently believes. See post, at 2907, and n. 5. Given the South Carolina Supreme Court's dismissive foreclosure of further pleading and adjudication with respect to the pre-1990 component of Lucas's takings claim, it is appropriate for us to address that component as if the case were here on the pleadings alone. Lucas properly alleged injury in fact in his complaint. See App. to Pet. for Cert. 154 (complaint); id., at 156 (asking "damages for the temporary taking of his property" from the date of the 1988 Act's passage to "such time as this matter is finally resolved"). No more can reasonably be demanded. Cf. First English Evangelical Lutheran Church of Glendale v. County of Los Angeles, 482 U.S. 304, 312-313, 107 S.Ct. 2378, 2384, 96 L.Ed.2d 250 (1987). Justice BLACKMUN finds it "baffling," post, at 2908, n. 5, that we grant standing here, whereas "just a few days ago, in Lujan v. Defenders of Wildlife, 504 U.S. 555, 112 S.Ct. 2130, 119 L.Ed.2d 351 (1992)," we denied standing. He sees in that strong evidence to support his repeated imputations that the Court "presses" to take this case, post, at 2904, is "eager to decide" it, post, at 2909, and is unwilling to "be denied," post, at 2907. He has a point: The decisions are indeed very close in time, yet one grants standing and the other denies it. The distinction, however, rests in law rather than chronology. Lujan, since it involved the establishment of injury in fact at the summary judgment stage, required specific facts to be adduced by sworn testimony; had the same challenge to a generalized allegation of injury in fact been made at the pleading stage, it would have been unsuccessful.

FN4. In that case, the Court of Appeals for the Fourth Circuit reached the merits of a takings challenge to the 1988 Beachfront Management Act identical to the one Lucas brings here even though the Act was amended, and the special permit procedure established, while the case was under submission. The court observed: "The enactment of the 1990 Act during the pendency of this appeal, with its provisions for special permits and other changes that may affect the plaintiffs, does not relieve us of the need to address the plaintiffs' claims under the provisions of the 1988 Act. Even if the amended Act cured all of the plaintiffs' concerns, the amendments would not foreclose the possibility that a taking had occurred during the years when the 1988 Act was in effect." Esposito v. South Carolina Coastal Council, 939 F.2d 165, 168 (1991).

FN5. Justice BLACKMUN states that our "intense interest in Lucas' plight ... would have been more prudently expressed by vacating the judgment below and remanding for further consideration in light of the 1990 amendments" to the Beachfront Management Act. Post, at 2909, n. 7. That is a strange suggestion, given that the South Carolina Supreme Court rendered its categorical disposition in this case after the Act had been amended, and after it had been invited to consider the effect of those amendments on Lucas's case. We have no reason to believe that the justices of the South Carolina Supreme Court are any more desirous of using a narrower ground now than they were then; and neither "prudence" nor any other principle of judicial restraint requires that we remand to find out whether they have changed their mind.

III
A

Prior to Justice Holmes's exposition in Pennsylvania Coal Co. v. Mahon, 260 U.S. 393, 43 S.Ct. 158, 67 L.Ed. 322 (1922), it was generally thought that the Takings Clause reached only a "direct appropriation" of property, Legal Tender Cases, 12 Wall. 457, 551, 20 L.Ed. 287 (1871), or the functional

112 S.Ct. 2886
(Cite as: 505 U.S. 1003, *1014, 112 S.Ct. 2886, **2892)

equivalent of a "practical ouster of [the owner's] possession," Transportation Co. v. Chicago, 99 U.S. 635, 642, 25 L.Ed. 336 (1879). See also Gibson v. United States, 166 U.S. 269, 275-276, 17 S.Ct. 578, 580, 41 L.Ed. 996 (1897). Justice Holmes recognized in Mahon, however, that if the protection against physical appropriations of private property was to be meaningfully enforced, the government's power to redefine the range of interests included in the ownership of property was necessarily constrained by constitutional limits. 260 U.S., at 414-415, 43 S.Ct., at 160. If, instead, the uses of private property were subject to unbridled, uncompensated qualification **2893 under the police power, "the natural tendency of human nature [would be] to extend the qualification more and more until at last private property disappear[ed]." Id., at 415, 43 S.Ct., at 160. These considerations gave birth in that case to the oft-cited maxim that, "while property may be regulated to a certain extent, if regulation goes too far it will be recognized as a taking." Ibid.

*1015 [2] Nevertheless, our decision in Mahon offered little insight into when, and under what circumstances, a given regulation would be seen as going "too far" for purposes of the Fifth Amendment. In 70-odd years of succeeding "regulatory takings" jurisprudence, we have generally eschewed any " 'set formula' " for determining how far is too far, preferring to "engag [e] in ... essentially ad hoc, factual inquiries." Penn Central Transportation Co. v. New York City, 438 U.S. 104, 124, 98 S.Ct. 2646, 2659, 57 L.Ed.2d 631 (1978) (quoting Goldblatt v. Hempstead, 369 U.S. 590, 594, 82 S.Ct. 987, 990, 8 L.Ed.2d 130 (1962)). See Epstein, Takings: Descent and Resurrection, 1987 S.Ct. Rev. 1, 4. We have, however, described at least two discrete categories of regulatory action as compensable without case-specific inquiry into the public interest advanced in support of the restraint. The first encompasses regulations that compel the property owner to suffer a physical "invasion" of his property. In general (at least with regard to permanent invasions), no matter how minute the intrusion, and no matter how weighty the public purpose behind it, we have required compensation. For example, in Loretto v. Teleprompter Manhattan CATV Corp., 458 U.S. 419, 102 S.Ct. 3164, 73 L.Ed.2d 868 (1982), we determined that New York's law requiring landlords to allow television cable companies to emplace cable facilities in their apartment buildings constituted a taking, id., at 435-440, 102 S.Ct., at 3175-3178, even though the facilities occupied at most only 1 1/2 cubic feet of the landlords' property, see id., at 438, n. 16, 102 S.Ct., at 3177. See also United States v. Causby, 328 U.S. 256, 265, and n. 10, 66 S.Ct. 1062, 1067, and n. 10, 90 L.Ed. 1206 (1946) (physical invasions of airspace); cf. Kaiser Aetna v. United States, 444 U.S. 164, 100 S.Ct. 383, 62 L.Ed.2d 332 (1979) (imposition of navigational servitude upon private marina).

The second situation in which we have found categorical treatment appropriate is where regulation denies all economically beneficial or productive use of land. See Agins, 447 U.S., at 260, 100 S.Ct., at 2141; see also Nollan v. California Coastal Comm'n, 483 U.S. 825, 834, 107 S.Ct. 3141, 3147, 97 L.Ed.2d 677 (1987); Keystone Bituminous Coal Assn. v. DeBenedictis, 480 U.S. 470, 495, 107 S.Ct. 1232, 1247, 94 L.Ed.2d 472 (1987); Hodel v. Virginia Surface Mining & Reclamation Assn., Inc., 452 *1016 U.S. 264, 295-296, 101 S.Ct. 2352, 2370, 69 L.Ed.2d 1 (1981). [FN6] As we have said on numerous occasions, **2894 the Fifth Amendment is violated when land-use regulation "does not substantially advance legitimate state interests or denies an owner economically viable use of his land." Agins, supra, 447 U.S., at 260, 100 S.Ct., at 2141 (citations omitted) (emphasis added). [FN7]

FN6. We will not attempt to respond to all of Justice BLACKMUN's mistaken citation of case precedent. Characteristic of its nature is his assertion that the cases we discuss here stand merely for the proposition "that proof that a regulation does not deny an owner economic use of his property is sufficient to defeat a facial takings challenge" and not for the point that "denial of such use is sufficient to establish a takings claim regardless of any other consideration." Post, at

Copr. © West 1996 No claim to orig. U.S. govt. works

112 S.Ct. 2886
(Cite as: 505 U.S. 1003, *1016, 112 S.Ct. 2886, **2894)

2911, n. 11. The cases say, repeatedly and unmistakably, that " '[t]he test to be applied in considering [a] facial [takings] challenge is fairly straightforward. A statute regulating the uses that can be made of property effects a taking if it "denies an owner economically viable use of his land." ' " Keystone, 480 U.S., at 495, 107 S.Ct., at 1247 (quoting Hodel, 452 U.S., at 295-296, 101 S.Ct., at 2370 (quoting Agins, 447 U.S., at 260, 100 S.Ct., at 2141)) (emphasis added). Justice BLACKMUN describes that rule (which we do not invent but merely apply today) as "alter[ing] the long-settled rules of review" by foisting on the State "the burden of showing [its] regulation is not a taking." Post, at 2909. This is of course wrong. Lucas had to do more than simply file a lawsuit to establish his constitutional entitlement; he had to show that the Beachfront Management Act denied him economically beneficial use of his land. Our analysis presumes the unconstitutionality of state land-use regulation only in the sense that any rule with exceptions presumes the invalidity of a law that violates it--for example, the rule generally prohibiting content-based restrictions on speech. See, e.g., Simon & Schuster, Inc. v. N.Y. Members of State Crime Victims Bd., 502 U.S. 105, 115, 112 S.Ct. 501, 508, 116 L.Ed.2d 476 (1991) ("A statute is presumptively inconsistent with the First Amendment if it imposes a financial burden on speakers because of the content of their speech"). Justice BLACKMUN's real quarrel is with the substantive standard of liability we apply in this case, a long-established standard we see no need to repudiate.

FN7. Regrettably, the rhetorical force of our "deprivation of all economically feasible use" rule is greater than its precision, since the rule does not make clear the "property interest" against which the loss of value is to be measured. When, for example, a regulation requires a developer to leave 90% of a rural tract in its natural state, it is unclear whether we would analyze the situation as one in which the owner has been deprived of all economically beneficial use of the burdened portion of the tract, or as one in which the owner has suffered a mere diminution in value of the tract as a whole. (For an extreme--and, we think, unsupportable--view of the relevant calculus, see Penn Central Transportation Co. v. New York City, 42 N.Y.2d 324, 333-334, 397 N.Y.S.2d 914, 920, 366 N.E.2d 1271, 1276-1277 (1977), aff'd, 438 U.S. 104, 98 S.Ct. 2646, 57 L.Ed.2d 631 (1978), where the state court examined the diminution in a particular parcel's value produced by a municipal ordinance in light of total value of the takings claimant's other holdings in the vicinity.) Unsurprisingly, this uncertainty regarding the composition of the denominator in our "deprivation" fraction has produced inconsistent pronouncements by the Court. Compare Pennsylvania Coal Co. v. Mahon, 260 U.S. 393, 414, 43 S.Ct. 158, 160, 67 L.Ed. 322 (1922) (law restricting subsurface extraction of coal held to effect a taking), with Keystone Bituminous Coal Assn. v. DeBenedictis, 480 U.S. 470, 497-502, 107 S.Ct. 1232, 1248-1251, 94 L.Ed.2d 472 (1987) (nearly identical law held not to effect a taking); see also id., at 515-520, 107 S.Ct., at 1257-1260 (REHNQUIST, C.J., dissenting); Rose, Mahon Reconstructed: Why the Takings Issue is Still a Muddle, 57 S.Cal.L.Rev. 561, 566-569 (1984). The answer to this difficult question may lie in how the owner's reasonable expectations have been shaped by the State's law of property--i.e., whether and to what degree the State's law has accorded legal recognition and protection to the particular interest in land with respect to which the takings claimant alleges a diminution in (or elimination of) value. In any event, we avoid this difficulty in the present case, since the "interest in land" that Lucas has pleaded (a fee simple interest) is an estate with a rich tradition of protection at common law, and since the South Carolina Court of Common Pleas found that the Beachfront Management Act left each of Lucas's beachfront lots without economic value.

*1017 We have never set forth the justification for this rule. Perhaps it is simply, as Justice Brennan suggested, that total deprivation of beneficial use is, from the landowner's point of view, the equivalent of a physical appropriation. See San Diego Gas & Electric Co. v. San Diego, 450 U.S., at 652, 101 S.Ct., at 1304 (dissenting opinion). "[F]or what is the land but the profits thereof[?]" 1 E. Coke, Institutes, ch. 1, § 1 (1st Am. ed. 1812). Surely, at least, in the extraordinary circumstance when no productive or economically beneficial use of land is permitted, it is less realistic to indulge our usual assumption that the legislature is simply "adjusting the benefits and burdens of economic life," Penn Central Transportation

Co., 438 *1018 U.S., at 124, 98 S.Ct., at 2659, in a manner that secures an "average reciprocity of advantage" to everyone concerned, Pennsylvania Coal Co. v. Mahon, 260 U.S., at 415, 43 S.Ct., at 160. And the functional basis for permitting the government, by regulation, to affect property values without compensation--that "Government hardly could go on if to some extent values incident to property could not be diminished without paying for every such change in the general law," id., at 413, 43 S.Ct., at 159--does not apply to the relatively rare situations where the government has deprived a landowner of all economically beneficial uses.

On the other side of the balance, affirmatively supporting a compensation requirement, is the fact that regulations that leave the owner of land without economically beneficial or productive options for its use-- typically, **2895 as here, by requiring land to be left substantially in its natural state--carry with them a heightened risk that private property is being pressed into some form of public service under the guise of mitigating serious public harm. See, e.g., Annicelli v. South Kingstown, 463 A.2d 133, 140-141 (R.I.1983) (prohibition on construction adjacent to beach justified on twin grounds of safety and "conservation of open space"); Morris County Land Improvement Co. v. Parsippany-Troy Hills Township, 40 N.J. 539, 552-553, 193 A.2d 232, 240 (1963) (prohibition on filling marshlands imposed in order to preserve region as water detention basin and create wildlife refuge). As Justice Brennan explained: "From the government's point of view, the benefits flowing to the public from preservation of open space through regulation may be equally great as from creating a wildlife refuge through formal condemnation or increasing electricity production through a dam project that floods private property." San Diego Gas & Elec. Co., supra, 450 U.S., at 652, 101 S.Ct., at 1304 (dissenting opinion). The many statutes on the books, both state and federal, that *1019 provide for the use of eminent domain to impose servitudes on private scenic lands preventing developmental uses, or to acquire such lands altogether, suggest the practical equivalence in this setting of negative regulation and appropriation. See, e.g., 16 U.S.C. § 410ff-1(a) (authorizing acquisition of "lands, waters, or interests [within Channel Islands National Park] (including but not limited to scenic easements)"); § 460aa-2(a) (authorizing acquisition of "any lands, or lesser interests therein, including mineral interests and scenic easements" within Sawtooth National Recreation Area); §§ 3921-3923 (authorizing acquisition of wetlands); N.C. Gen.Stat. § 113A-38 (1990) (authorizing acquisition of, inter alia, " 'scenic easements' " within the North Carolina natural and scenic rivers system); Tenn.Code Ann. §§ 11-15-101 to 11-15-108 (1987) (authorizing acquisition of "protective easements" and other rights in real property adjacent to State's historic, architectural, archaeological, or cultural resources).

[3][4] We think, in short, that there are good reasons for our frequently expressed belief that when the owner of real property has been called upon to sacrifice all economically beneficial uses in the name of the common good, that is, to leave his property economically idle, he has suffered a taking. [FN8]

FN8. Justice STEVENS criticizes the "deprivation of all economically beneficial use" rule as "wholly arbitrary," in that "[the] landowner whose property is diminished in value 95% recovers nothing," while the landowner who suffers a complete elimination of value "recovers the land's full value." Post, at 2919. This analysis errs in its assumption that the landowner whose deprivation is one step short of complete is not entitled to compensation. Such an owner might not be able to claim the benefit of our categorical formulation, but, as we have acknowledged time and again, "[t]he economic impact of the regulation on the claimant and ... the extent to which the regulation has interfered with distinct investment-backed expectations" are keenly relevant to takings analysis generally. Penn Central Transportation Co. v. New York City, 438 U.S. 104, 124, 98 S.Ct. 2646, 2659, 57 L.Ed.2d 631 (1978). It is true that in at least some cases the landowner with 95% loss will get nothing, while the landowner with total loss will recover in full. But that occasional result is no more strange than the gross disparity between the landowner whose premises are taken for a highway (who recovers in full) and the landowner whose property is reduced to 5% of its former value by the highway (who recovers nothing). Takings law is full of these "all-or-nothing" situations. Justice STEVENS similarly misinterprets our focus on "developmental" uses of property (the uses proscribed by the Beachfront Management Act) as betraying an "assumption that the only uses of property cognizable under the Constitution are developmental uses." Post, at 2919, n. 3. We make no such assumption. Though our prior takings cases evince an abiding concern for the productive use of, and economic investment in, land, there are plainly a number of noneconomic interests in land whose impairment will invite exceedingly close scrutiny under the Takings Clause. See, e.g., Loretto v. Teleprompter Manhattan CATV Corp., 458 U.S. 419, 436, 102 S.Ct. 3164, 3176, 73 L.Ed.2d 868 (1982) (interest in excluding strangers from one's land).

**2896 *1020 B

[5][6] The trial court found Lucas's two beachfront lots to have been rendered valueless by respondent's enforcement of the coastal-zone construction ban. [FN9] Under Lucas's theory of the case, which rested upon our "no economically viable use" statements, that finding entitled him to compensation. Lucas believed it unnecessary to take issue with either the purposes behind the Beachfront Management Act, or the means chosen by the South Carolina Legislature to effectuate those purposes. The South Carolina Supreme Court, however, thought otherwise. In its view, the Beachfront Management Act was no ordinary enactment, but involved an exercise of South Carolina's "police powers" to mitigate the harm to the public interest that petitioner's use of his *1021 land might occasion. 304 S.C., at 384, 404 S.E.2d, at 899. By neglecting to dispute the findings enumerated in the Act [FN10] or otherwise to challenge the legislature's purposes, *1022 petitioner "concede[d] that the beach/dune area of South Carolina's shores is an extremely valuable public resource; that the erection of new construction, inter alia, contributes to the erosion and destruction of this public resource; and that discouraging new construction in close proximity to the beach/dune area is necessary to prevent a great public harm." Id., at 382-383, 404 S.E.2d, at 898. In the court's view, these concessions brought petitioner's challenge within a long line of this Court's cases sustaining against **2897 Due Process and Takings Clause challenges the State's use of its "police powers" to enjoin a property owner from activities akin to public nuisances. See Mugler v. Kansas, 123 U.S. 623, 8 S.Ct. 273, 31 L.Ed. 205 (1887) (law prohibiting manufacture of alcoholic beverages); Hadacheck v. Sebastian, 239 U.S. 394, 36 S.Ct. 143, 60 L.Ed. 348 (1915) (law barring operation of brick mill in residential area); Miller v. Schoene, 276 U.S. 272, 48 S.Ct. 246, 72 L.Ed. 568 (1928) (order to destroy diseased cedar trees to prevent infection of nearby orchards); Goldblatt v. Hempstead, 369 U.S. 590, 82 S.Ct. 987, 8 L.Ed.2d 130 (1962) (law effectively preventing continued operation of quarry in residential area).

FN9. This finding was the premise of the petition for certiorari, and since it was not challenged in the brief in opposition we decline to entertain the argument in respondent's brief on the merits, see Brief for Respondent 45-50, that the finding was erroneous. Instead, we decide the question presented under the same factual assumptions as did the Supreme Court of South Carolina. See Oklahoma City v. Tuttle, 471 U.S. 808, 816, 105 S.Ct. 2427, 2432, 85 L.Ed.2d 791 (1985).

FN10. The legislature's express findings include the following: "The General Assembly finds that: "(1) The beach/dune system along the coast of South Carolina is extremely important to the people of this State and serves the following functions: "(a) protects life and property by serving as a storm barrier which dissipates wave energy and contributes to shoreline stability in an economical and effective manner; "(b) provides the basis for a tourism industry that generates approximately two-thirds of South Carolina's annual tourism industry revenue which constitutes a significant portion of the state's economy. The tourists who come to the South Carolina coast to enjoy the ocean and dry sand beach contribute significantly to state and local tax revenues; "(c) provides habitat for numerous species of plants and animals, several of which are threatened or endangered. Waters adjacent to the beach/dune system also provide habitat for many other marine species; "(d) provides a natural health environment for the citizens of South Carolina to spend leisure time which serves their physical and mental well-being. "(2) Beach/dune system vegetation is unique and extremely important to the vitality and preservation of the system. "(3) Many miles of South Carolina's beaches have been identified as critically eroding. "(4) ... [D]evelopment unwisely has been sited too close to the [beach/dune] system. This type of development has jeopardized the stability of the beach/dune system, accelerated erosion, and endangered adjacent property. It is in both the public and private interests to protect the system from this unwise development. "(5) The use of armoring in the form of hard erosion control devices such as seawalls, bulkheads, and rip-rap to protect erosion-threatened structures adjacent to the beach has not proven effective. These armoring devices have given a false sense of security to beachfront property owners. In reality, these hard structures, in many instances, have increased the vulnerability of beachfront property to damage from wind and waves while contributing to the deterioration and loss of the dry sand beach which is so important to the tourism industry. "(6) Erosion is a natural process which becomes a significant problem for man only when structures are erected in close proximity to the beach/dune system. It is in both the public and private interests to afford the beach/dune system space to accrete and erode in its natural cycle. This space can be provided only by discouraging new construction in close proximity to the beach/dune system and encouraging those who have erected structures too close to the system to retreat from it.

. . . . .

"(8) It is in the state's best interest to protect and to promote increased public access to South Carolina's beaches for out-of-state tourists and South Carolina residents alike." S.C. Code Ann. § 48-39-250 (Supp.1991).

It is correct that many of our prior opinions have suggested that "harmful or noxious uses" of property may be proscribed by government regulation without the requirement of compensation. For a number of reasons, however, we think the South Carolina Supreme Court was too quick to conclude that that principle decides the present case. The "harmful or noxious uses" principle was the Court's early attempt to describe in theoretical terms why government *1023 may, consistent with the Takings Clause, affect property values by regulation without incurring an obligation to compensate--a reality we nowadays acknowledge explicitly with respect to the full scope of the State's police power. See, e.g., Penn Central Transportation Co., 438 U.S., at 125, 98 S.Ct., at 2659 (where State "reasonably conclude[s] that 'the health, safety, morals, or general welfare' would be promoted by prohibiting particular contemplated uses of land," compensation need not accompany prohibition); see also Nollan v. California Coastal Comm'n, 483 U.S., at 834-835, 107 S.Ct., at 3147 ("Our cases have not elaborated on the standards for determining what constitutes a 'legitimate state interest[,]' [but] [t]hey have made clear ... that a broad range of governmental purposes and regulations satisfy these requirements"). We made this very point in Penn Central Transportation Co., where, in the course of sustaining New York City's landmarks preservation program against a takings challenge, we rejected the petitioner's suggestion that Mugler and the cases following it were premised on, and thus limited by, some objective conception of "noxiousness":

"[T]he uses in issue in Hadacheck, Miller, and Goldblatt were perfectly lawful in themselves. They involved no 'blameworthiness, ... moral wrongdoing or conscious act of dangerous risk-taking which induce[d society] to shift the cost to a pa[rt]icular individual.' Sax, Takings and the Police Power, 74 Yale L.J. 36, 50 (1964). These cases are better understood as resting not on any supposed 'noxious' quality of the prohibited uses but rather on the ground that the restrictions were reasonably related to the implementation of a policy--not unlike historic preservation--expected to produce a widespread public benefit and applicable to all similarly situated property." 438 U.S., at 133-134, n. 30, 98 S.Ct., at 2664, n. 30.

112 S.Ct. 2886
(Cite as: 505 U.S. 1003, *1023, 112 S.Ct. 2886, **2897)

"Harmful or noxious use" analysis was, in other words, simply the progenitor of our more contemporary statements that *1024 "land-use regulation does not effect a taking if it 'substantially advance[s] legitimate state interests'...." Nollan, supra, 483 U.S., at 834, 107 S.Ct., at 3147 (quoting Agins v. Tiburon, 447 U.S., at 260, 100 S.Ct., at 2141); see also Penn Central Transportation Co., supra, 438 U.S., at 127, 98 S.Ct., at 2660; Euclid v. Ambler Realty Co., 272 U.S. 365, 387-388, 47 S.Ct. 114, 118, 71 L.Ed. 303 (1926).

The transition from our early focus on control of "noxious" uses to our contemporary understanding of the broad realm within which government may regulate without compensation was an easy one, since the distinction between "harm-preventing" and "benefit-conferring" regulation is often in the eye of the beholder. It is quite possible, for **2898 example, to describe in either fashion the ecological, economic, and esthetic concerns that inspired the South Carolina Legislature in the present case. One could say that imposing a servitude on Lucas's land is necessary in order to prevent his use of it from "harming" South Carolina's ecological resources; or, instead, in order to achieve the "benefits" of an ecological preserve. [FN11] Compare, e.g., Claridge v. New Hampshire *1025 Wetlands Board, 125 N.H. 745, 752, 485 A.2d 287, 292 (1984) (owner may, without compensation, be barred from filling wetlands because landfilling would deprive adjacent coastal habitats and marine fisheries of ecological support), with, e.g., Bartlett v. Zoning Comm'n of Old Lyme, 161 Conn. 24, 30, 282 A.2d 907, 910 (1971) (owner barred from filling tidal marshland must be compensated, despite municipality's "laudable" goal of "preserv[ing] marshlands from encroachment or destruction"). Whether one or the other of the competing characterizations will come to one's lips in a particular case depends primarily upon one's evaluation of the worth of competing uses of real estate. See Restatement (Second) of Torts § 822, Comment g, p. 112 (1979) ("Practically all human activities unless carried on in a wilderness interfere to some extent with others or involve some risk of interference").

A given restraint will be seen as mitigating "harm" to the adjacent parcels or securing a "benefit" for them, depending upon the observer's evaluation of the relative importance of the use that the restraint favors. See Sax, Takings and the Police Power, 74 Yale L.J. 36, 49 (1964) ("[T]he problem [in this area] is not one of noxiousness or harm-creating activity at all; rather it is a problem of inconsistency between perfectly innocent and independently desirable uses"). Whether Lucas's construction of single-family residences on his parcels should be described as bringing "harm" to South Carolina's adjacent ecological resources thus depends principally upon whether the describer believes that the State's use interest in nurturing those resources is so important that any competing adjacent use must yield. [FN12]

FN11. In the present case, in fact, some of the "[South Carolina] legislature's 'findings' " to which the South Carolina Supreme Court purported to defer in characterizing the purpose of the Act as "harm-preventing," 304 S.C. 376, 385, 404 S.E.2d 895, 900 (1991), seem to us phrased in "benefit-conferring" language instead. For example, they describe the importance of a construction ban in enhancing "South Carolina's annual tourism industry revenue," S.C. Code Ann. § 48-39-250(1)(b) (Supp.1991), in "provid[ing] habitat for numerous species of plants and animals, several of which are threatened or endangered," § 48-39-250(1)(c), and in "provid[ing] a natural healthy environment for the citizens of South Carolina to spend leisure time which serves their physical and mental well-being," § 48-39-250(1)(d). It would be pointless to make the outcome of this case hang upon this terminology, since the same interests could readily be described in "harm-preventing" fashion. Justice BLACKMUN, however, apparently insists that we must make the outcome hinge (exclusively) upon the South Carolina Legislature's other, "harm-preventing" characterizations, focusing on the declaration that "prohibitions on building in front of the setback line are necessary to protect people and property from storms, high tides, and beach erosion." Post, at 2906. He says "[n]othing in the record undermines [this] assessment," ibid., apparently seeing no significance in the fact that the statute permits owners of existing structures to remain (and even to rebuild if their structures are not "destroyed beyond repair," S.C. Code Ann. § 48-39-290(B) (Supp.1988)), and in the fact that the 1990 amendment authorizes the Council to issue permits for new construction in violation of the uniform prohibition, see S.C. Code Ann. § 48-39-290(D)(1) (Supp.1991).

FN12. In Justice BLACKMUN's view, even with respect to regulations that deprive an owner of all developmental or economically beneficial land uses, the test for required compensation is whether the legislature has recited a harm-preventing justification for its action. See post, at 2906, 2910-2912. Since such a justification can be formulated in practically every case, this amounts to a test of whether the legislature has a stupid staff. We think the Takings Clause requires courts to do more than insist upon artful harm-preventing characterizations.

*1026 When it is understood that "prevention of harmful use" was merely our early formulation of the police power justification necessary to sustain (without compensation) any **2899 regulatory diminution in value; and that the distinction between regulation that "prevents harmful use" and that which "confers benefits" is difficult, if not impossible, to discern on an objective, value-free basis; it becomes self-evident that noxious-use logic cannot serve as a touchstone to distinguish regulatory "takings"--which require compensation--from regulatory deprivations that do not require compensation. A fortiori the legislature's recitation of a noxious-use justification cannot be the basis for departing from our categorical rule that total regulatory takings must be compensated. If it were, departure would virtually always be allowed. The South Carolina Supreme Court's approach would essentially nullify Mahon's affirmation of limits to the noncompensable exercise of the police power. Our cases provide no support for this: None of them that employed the logic of "harmful use" prevention to sustain a regulation involved an allegation that the regulation wholly eliminated the value of the claimant's land. See Keystone Bituminous Coal Assn., 480 U.S., at 513-514, 107 S.Ct., at 1257 (REHNQUIST, C.J., dissenting). [FN13]

FN13. E.g., Mugler v. Kansas, 123 U.S. 623, 8 S.Ct. 273, 31 L.Ed. 205 (1887) (prohibition upon use of a building as a brewery; other uses permitted); Plymouth Coal Co. v. Pennsylvania, 232 U.S. 531, 34 S.Ct. 359, 58 L.Ed. 713 (1914) (requirement that "pillar" of coal be left in ground to safeguard mine workers; mineral rights could otherwise be exploited); Reinman v. Little Rock, 237 U.S. 171, 35 S.Ct. 511, 59 L.Ed. 900 (1915) (declaration that livery stable constituted a public nuisance; other uses of the property permitted); Hadacheck v. Sebastian, 239 U.S. 394, 36 S.Ct. 143, 60 L.Ed. 348 (1915) (prohibition of brick manufacturing in residential area; other uses permitted); Goldblatt v. Hempstead, 369 U.S. 590, 82 S.Ct. 987, 8 L.Ed.2d 130 (1962) (prohibition on excavation; other uses permitted).

*1027 [7] Where the State seeks to sustain regulation that deprives land of all economically beneficial use, we think it may resist compensation only if the logically antecedent inquiry into the nature of the owner's estate shows that the proscribed use interests were not part of his title to begin with. [FN14] This accords, we think, with our "takings" jurisprudence, which has traditionally been guided by the understandings of our citizens regarding the content of, and the State's power over, the "bundle of rights" that they acquire when they obtain title to property. It seems to us that the property owner necessarily expects the uses of his property to be restricted, from time to time, by various measures newly enacted by the State in legitimate exercise of its police powers; "[a]s long recognized, some values are enjoyed under an implied limitation and must yield to the police power." Pennsylvania Coal Co. v. Mahon, 260 U.S., at 413, 43 S.Ct., at 159. And in the case of personal property, by reason of the State's traditionally high degree of control over commercial dealings, he ought to be aware of the possibility that new regulation might even render *1028 his property economically worthless (at least if the property's only economically productive use is sale or manufacture for sale). See Andrus v. Allard, 444 U.S. 51, 66-67, 100 S.Ct. 318, **2900 327, 62 L.Ed.2d 210 (1979) (prohibition on sale of eagle feathers). In the case of land, however, we think the notion pressed by the

112 S.Ct. 2886
(Cite as: 505 U.S. 1003, *1028, 112 S.Ct. 2886, **2900)

Council that title is somehow held subject to the "implied limitation" that the State may subsequently eliminate all economically valuable use is inconsistent with the historical compact recorded in the Takings Clause that has become part of our constitutional culture. [FN15]

> FN14. Drawing on our First Amendment jurisprudence, see, e.g., Employment Div., Dept. of Human Resources of Ore. v. Smith, 494 U.S. 872, 878-879, 110 S.Ct. 1595, 1600, 108 L.Ed.2d 876 (1990), Justice STEVENS would "loo[k] to the generality of a regulation of property" to determine whether compensation is owing. Post, at 2923. The Beachfront Management Act is general, in his view, because it "regulates the use of the coastline of the entire State." Post, at 2924. There may be some validity to the principle Justice STEVENS proposes, but it does not properly apply to the present case. The equivalent of a law of general application that inhibits the practice of religion without being aimed at religion, see Oregon v. Smith, supra, is a law that destroys the value of land without being aimed at land. Perhaps such a law--the generally applicable criminal prohibition on the manufacturing of alcoholic beverages challenged in Mugler comes to mind--cannot constitute a compensable taking. See 123 U.S., at 655-656, 8 S.Ct., at 293-294. But a regulation specifically directed to land use no more acquires immunity by plundering landowners generally than does a law specifically directed at religious practice acquire immunity by prohibiting all religions. Justice STEVENS's approach renders the Takings Clause little more than a particularized restatement of the Equal Protection Clause.

> FN15. After accusing us of "launch[ing] a missile to kill a mouse," post, at 2904, Justice BLACKMUN expends a good deal of throw-weight of his own upon a noncombatant, arguing that our description of the "understanding" of land ownership that informs the Takings Clause is not supported by early American experience. That is largely true, but entirely irrelevant. The practices of the States prior to incorporation of the Takings and Just Compensation Clauses, see Chicago, B. & Q.R. Co. v. Chicago, 166 U.S. 226, 17 S.Ct. 581, 41 L.Ed. 979 (1897)--which, as Justice BLACKMUN acknowledges, occasionally included outright physical appropriation of land without compensation, see post, at 2915 --were out of accord with any plausible interpretation of those provisions. Justice BLACKMUN is correct that early constitutional theorists did not believe the Takings Clause embraced regulations of property at all, see post, at 2915, and n. 23, but even he does not suggest (explicitly, at least) that we renounce the Court's contrary conclusion in Mahon. Since the text of the Clause can be read to encompass regulatory as well as physical deprivations (in contrast to the text originally proposed by Madison, see Speech Proposing Bill of Rights (June 8, 1789), in 12 J. Madison, The Papers of James Madison 201 (C. Hobson, R. Rutland, W. Rachal, & J. Sisson ed. 1979) ("No person shall be ... obliged to relinquish his property, where it may be necessary for public use, without a just compensation"), we decline to do so as well.

[8] Where "permanent physical occupation" of land is concerned, we have refused to allow the government to decree it anew (without compensation), no matter how weighty the asserted "public interests" involved, Loretto v. Teleprompter Manhattan CATV Corp., 458 U.S., at 426, 102 S.Ct., at 3171--though we assuredly would permit the government to assert a permanent easement that was a pre-existing limitation upon the landowner's *1029 title. Compare Scranton v. Wheeler, 179 U.S. 141, 163, 21 S.Ct. 48, 57, 45 L.Ed. 126 (1900) (interests of "riparian owner in the submerged lands ... bordering on a public navigable water" held subject to Government's navigational servitude), with Kaiser Aetna v. United States, 444 U.S., at 178-180, 100 S.Ct., at 392-393 (imposition of navigational servitude on marina created and rendered navigable at private expense held to constitute a taking). We believe similar treatment must be accorded confiscatory regulations, i.e., regulations that prohibit all economically beneficial use of land: Any limitation so severe cannot be newly legislated or decreed (without compensation), but must inhere in the title itself, in the restrictions that background principles of the State's law of property and nuisance already place upon land ownership. A law or decree with such an effect must, in other words, do no more than duplicate the result that could have been achieved in the courts--by adjacent

Copr. © West 1996 No claim to orig. U.S. govt. works

112 S.Ct. 2886
(Cite as: 505 U.S. 1003, *1029, 112 S.Ct. 2886, **2900)

landowners (or other uniquely affected persons) under the State's law of private nuisance, or by the State under its complementary power to abate nuisances that affect the public generally, or otherwise. [FN16]

> FN16. The principal "otherwise" that we have in mind is litigation absolving the State (or private parties) of liability for the destruction of "real and personal property, in cases of actual necessity, to prevent the spreading of a fire" or to forestall other grave threats to the lives and property of others. Bowditch v. Boston, 101 U.S. 16, 18-19, 25 L.Ed. 980 (1880); see United States v. Pacific R., Co., 120 U.S. 227, 238-239, 7 S.Ct. 490, 495-496, 30 L.Ed. 634 (1887).

[9] On this analysis, the owner of a lake-bed, for example, would not be entitled to compensation when he is denied the requisite permit to engage in a landfilling operation that would have the effect of flooding others' land. Nor the corporate owner of a nuclear generating plant, when it is directed to remove all improvements from its land upon discovery that the plant sits astride an earthquake fault. Such regulatory action may well have the effect of eliminating the land's only economically productive use, but it does **2901 not proscribe a productive use that was previously permissible *1030 under relevant property and nuisance principles. The use of these properties for what are now expressly prohibited purposes was always unlawful, and (subject to other constitutional limitations) it was open to the State at any point to make the implication of those background principles of nuisance and property law explicit. See Michelman, Property, Utility, and Fairness, Comments on the Ethical Foundations of "Just Compensation" Law, 80 Harv.L.Rev. 1165, 1239-1241 (1967). In light of our traditional resort to "existing rules or understandings that stem from an independent source such as state law" to define the range of interests that qualify for protection as "property" under the Fifth and Fourteenth Amendments, Board of Regents of State Colleges v. Roth, 408 U.S. 564, 577, 92 S.Ct. 2701, 2709, 33 L.Ed.2d 548 (1972); see, e.g., Ruckelshaus v. Monsanto Co., 467 U.S. 986, 1011-1012, 104 S.Ct. 2862, 2877, 81 L.Ed.2d 815 (1984); Hughes v. Washington, 389 U.S. 290, 295, 88 S.Ct. 438, 441, 19 L.Ed.2d 530 (1967) (Stewart, J., concurring), this recognition that the Takings Clause does not require compensation when an owner is barred from putting land to a use that is proscribed by those "existing rules or understandings" is surely unexceptional. When, however, a regulation that declares "off-limits" all economically productive or beneficial uses of land goes beyond what the relevant background principles would dictate, compensation must be paid to sustain it. [FN17]

> FN17. Of course, the State may elect to rescind its regulation and thereby avoid having to pay compensation for a permanent deprivation. See First English Evangelical Lutheran Church, 482 U.S., at 321, 107 S.Ct., at 2389. But "where the [regulation has] already worked a taking of all use of property, no subsequent action by the government can relieve it of the duty to provide compensation for the period during which the taking was effective." Ibid.

The "total taking" inquiry we require today will ordinarily entail (as the application of state nuisance law ordinarily entails) analysis of, among other things, the degree of harm to public lands and resources, or adjacent private property, *1031 posed by the claimant's proposed activities, see, e.g., Restatement (Second) of Torts §§ 826, 827, the social value of the claimant's activities and their suitability to the locality in question, see, e.g., id., §§ 828(a) and (b), 831, and the relative ease with which the alleged harm can be avoided through measures taken by the claimant and the government (or adjacent private landowners) alike, see, e.g., id., §§ 827(e), 828(c), 830. The fact that a particular use has long been engaged in by similarly situated owners ordinarily imports a lack of any common-law prohibition (though changed circumstances or new knowledge may make what was previously permissible no longer so, see id., § 827, Comment g. So also does the fact that other landowners, similarly situated, are permitted to continue the use denied to the claimant.

112 S.Ct. 2886
(Cite as: 505 U.S. 1003, *1031, 112 S.Ct. 2886, **2901)

It seems unlikely that common-law principles would have prevented the erection of any habitable or productive improvements on petitioner's land; they rarely support prohibition of the "essential use" of land, Curtin v. Benson, 222 U.S. 78, 86, 32 S.Ct. 31, 33, 56 L.Ed. 102 (1911). The question, however, is one of state law to be dealt with on remand. We emphasize that to win its case South Carolina must do more than proffer the legislature's declaration that the uses Lucas desires are inconsistent with the public interest, or the conclusory assertion that they violate a common-law maxim such as sic utere tuo ut alienum non laedas. As we have said, a "State, by ipse dixit, may not transform private property into public property without compensation...." Webb's Fabulous Pharmacies, Inc. v. Beckwith, 449 U.S. 155, 164, 101 S.Ct. 446, 452, 66 L.Ed.2d 358 (1980). Instead, as it would be required to do if it sought to restrain Lucas in a common-law action for public nuisance, South Carolina must identify background principles of nuisance and property law that prohibit the uses **2902 he now intends in the circumstances in which the property is presently found. Only on this showing can *1032 the State fairly claim that, in proscribing all such beneficial uses, the Beachfront Management Act is taking nothing. [FN18]

> FN18. Justice BLACKMUN decries our reliance on background nuisance principles at least in part because he believes those principles to be as manipulable as we find the "harm prevention"/ "benefit conferral" dichotomy, see post, at 2914. There is no doubt some leeway in a court's interpretation of what existing state law permits--but not remotely as much, we think, as in a legislative crafting of the reasons for its confiscatory regulation. We stress that an affirmative decree eliminating all economically beneficial uses may be defended only if an objectively reasonable application of relevant precedents would exclude those beneficial uses in the circumstances in which the land is presently found.

* * *

The judgment is reversed, and the case is remanded for proceedings not inconsistent with this opinion.

So ordered.

Justice KENNEDY, concurring in the judgment.

The case comes to the Court in an unusual posture, as all my colleagues observe. Ante, at 2890; post, at 2906 (BLACKMUN, J., dissenting); post, at 2917 (STEVENS, J., dissenting); post, at 2925 (statement of SOUTER, J.). After the suit was initiated but before it reached us, South Carolina amended its Beachfront Management Act to authorize the issuance of special permits at variance with the Act's general limitations. See S.C.Code Ann. § 48-39-290(D)(1) (Supp.1991). Petitioner has not applied for a special permit but may still do so. The availability of this alternative, if it can be invoked, may dispose of petitioner's claim of a permanent taking. As I read the Court's opinion, it does not decide the permanent taking claim, but neither does it foreclose the Supreme Court of South Carolina from considering the claim or requiring petitioner to pursue an administrative alternative not previously available.

The potential for future relief does not control our disposition, because whatever may occur in the future cannot undo *1033 what has occurred in the past. The Beachfront Management Act was enacted in 1988. S.C.Code Ann. § 48-39-250 et seq. (Supp.1990). It may have deprived petitioner of the use of his land in an interim period. § 48-39-290(A). If this deprivation amounts to a taking, its limited duration will not bar constitutional relief. It is well established that temporary takings are as protected by the Constitution as are permanent ones. First English Evangelical Lutheran Church of Glendale v. County of Los Angeles, 482 U.S. 304, 318, 107 S.Ct. 2378, 2387, 96 L.Ed.2d 250 (1987).

The issues presented in the case are ready for our decision. The Supreme Court of South Carolina decided the case on constitutional grounds, and its rulings are now before us.

112 S.Ct. 2886
(Cite as: 505 U.S. 1003, *1033, 112 S.Ct. 2886, **2902)

There exists no jurisdictional bar to our disposition, and prudential considerations ought not to militate against it. The State cannot complain of the manner in which the issues arose. Any uncertainty in this regard is attributable to the State, as a consequence of its amendment to the Beachfront Management Act. If the Takings Clause is to protect against temporary deprivations, as well as permanent ones, its enforcement must not be frustrated by a shifting background of state law.

Although we establish a framework for remand, moreover, we do not decide the ultimate question whether a temporary taking has occurred in this case. The facts necessary to the determination have not been developed in the record. Among the matters to be considered on remand must be whether petitioner had the intent and capacity to develop the property and failed to do so in the interim period because the State prevented him. Any failure by petitioner to comply **2903 with relevant administrative requirements will be part of that analysis.

The South Carolina Court of Common Pleas found that petitioner's real property has been rendered valueless by the State's regulation. App. to Pet. for Cert. 37. The finding appears to presume that the property has no significant market *1034 value or resale potential. This is a curious finding, and I share the reservations of some of my colleagues about a finding that a beach-front lot loses all value because of a development restriction. Post, at 2908 (BLACKMUN, J., dissenting); post, at 2919, n. 3 (STEVENS, J., dissenting); post, at 2925 (statement of SOUTER, J.). While the Supreme Court of South Carolina on remand need not consider the case subject to this constraint, we must accept the finding as entered below. See Oklahoma City v. Tuttle, 471 U.S. 808, 816, 105 S.Ct. 2427, 2432, 85 L.Ed.2d 791 (1985). Accepting the finding as entered, it follows that petitioner is entitled to invoke the line of cases discussing regulations that deprive real property of all economic value. See Agins v. City of Tiburon, 447 U.S. 255, 260, 100 S.Ct. 2138, 2141, 65 L.Ed.2d 106 (1980).

The finding of no value must be considered under the Takings Clause by reference to the owner's reasonable, investment-backed expectations. Kaiser Aetna v. United States, 444 U.S. 164, 175, 100 S.Ct. 383, 390, 62 L.Ed.2d 332 (1979); Penn Central Transportation Co. v. New York City, 438 U.S. 104, 124, 98 S.Ct. 2646, 2659, 57 L.Ed.2d 631 (1978); see also W.B. Worthen Co. v. Kavanaugh, 295 U.S. 56, 55 S.Ct. 555, 79 L.Ed. 1298 (1935). The Takings Clause, while conferring substantial protection on property owners, does not eliminate the police power of the State to enact limitations on the use of their property. Mugler v. Kansas, 123 U.S. 623, 669, 8 S.Ct. 273, 301, 31 L.Ed. 205 (1887). The rights conferred by the Takings Clause and the police power of the State may coexist without conflict. Property is bought and sold, investments are made, subject to the State's power to regulate. Where a taking is alleged from regulations which deprive the property of all value, the test must be whether the deprivation is contrary to reasonable, investment-backed expectations.

There is an inherent tendency towards circularity in this synthesis, of course; for if the owner's reasonable expectations are shaped by what courts allow as a proper exercise of governmental authority, property tends to become what courts say it is. Some circularity must be tolerated in these matters, however, as it is in other spheres. E.g., Katz v. *1035 United States, 389 U.S. 347, 88 S.Ct. 507, 19 L.Ed.2d 576 (1967) (Fourth Amendment protections defined by reasonable expectations of privacy). The definition, moreover, is not circular in its entirety. The expectations protected by the Constitution are based on objective rules and customs that can be understood as reasonable by all parties involved.

In my view, reasonable expectations must be understood in light of the whole of our legal tradition. The common law of nuisance is too narrow a confine for the exercise of regulatory power in a complex and interdependent society. Goldblatt v. Hempstead, 369 U.S. 590, 593, 82 S.Ct. 987, 989, 8 L.Ed.2d 130 (1962). The State should not be prevented

Appendix E: The Lucas Decision / 291

112 S.Ct. 2886
(Cite as: 505 U.S. 1003, *1035, 112 S.Ct. 2886, **2903)

from enacting new regulatory initiatives in response to changing conditions, and courts must consider all reasonable expectations whatever their source. The Takings Clause does not require a static body of state property law; it protects private expectations to ensure private investment. I agree with the Court that nuisance prevention accords with the most common expectations of property owners who face regulation, but I do not believe this can be the sole source of state authority to impose severe restrictions. Coastal property may present such unique concerns for a fragile land system that the State can go further in regulating its development and use than the common law of nuisance might otherwise permit.

The Supreme Court of South Carolina erred, in my view, by reciting the general purposes for which the state regulations **2904 were enacted without a determination that they were in accord with the owner's reasonable expectations and therefore sufficient to support a severe restriction on specific parcels of property. See 304 S.C. 376, 383, 404 S.E.2d 895, 899 (1991). The promotion of tourism, for instance, ought not to suffice to deprive specific property of all value without a corresponding duty to compensate. Furthermore, the means, as well as the ends, of regulation must accord with the owner's reasonable expectations. Here, the State did not act until after the property had been zoned for individual *1036 lot development and most other parcels had been improved, throwing the whole burden of the regulation on the remaining lots. This too must be measured in the balance. See Pennsylvania Coal Co. v. Mahon, 260 U.S. 393, 416, 43 S.Ct. 158, 160, 67 L.Ed. 322 (1922).

With these observations, I concur in the judgment of the Court.

Justice BLACKMUN, dissenting.

Today the Court launches a missile to kill a mouse.

The State of South Carolina prohibited petitioner Lucas from building a permanent structure on his property from 1988 to 1990. Relying on an unreviewed (and implausible) state trial court finding that this restriction left Lucas' property valueless, this Court granted review to determine whether compensation must be paid in cases where the State prohibits all economic use of real estate. According to the Court, such an occasion never has arisen in any of our prior cases, and the Court imagines that it will arise "relatively rarely" or only in "extraordinary circumstances." Almost certainly it did not happen in this case.

Nonetheless, the Court presses on to decide the issue, and as it does, it ignores its jurisdictional limits, remakes its traditional rules of review, and creates simultaneously a new categorical rule and an exception (neither of which is rooted in our prior case law, common law, or common sense). I protest not only the Court's decision, but each step taken to reach it. More fundamentally, I question the Court's wisdom in issuing sweeping new rules to decide such a narrow case. Surely, as Justice KENNEDY demonstrates, the Court could have reached the result it wanted without inflicting this damage upon our Takings Clause jurisprudence.

My fear is that the Court's new policies will spread beyond the narrow confines of the present case. For that reason, I, like the Court, will give far greater attention to this case than its narrow scope suggests--not because I can intercept *1037 the Court's missile, or save the targeted mouse, but because I hope perhaps to limit the collateral damage.

I
A

In 1972 Congress passed the Coastal Zone Management Act. 16 U.S.C. § 1451 et seq. The Act was designed to provide States with money and incentives to carry out Congress' goal of protecting the public from shoreline erosion and coastal hazards. In the 1980 amendments to the Act, Congress directed States to enhance their coastal programs by "[p]reventing or significantly reducing threats

Copr. © West 1996 No claim to orig. U.S. govt. works

to life and the destruction of property by eliminating development and redevelopment in high-hazard areas." [FN1] 16 U.S.C. § 1456b(a)(2) (1988 ed., Supp. II).

> FN1. The country has come to recognize that uncontrolled beachfront development can cause serious damage to life and property. See Brief for Sierra Club et al. as Amici Curiae 2-5. Hurricane Hugo's September 1989 attack upon South Carolina's coastline, for example, caused 29 deaths and approximately $6 billion in property damage, much of it the result of uncontrolled beachfront development. See Zalkin, Shifting Sands and Shifting Doctrines: The Supreme Court's Changing Takings Doctrine and South Carolina's Coastal Zone Statute, 79 Calif.L.Rev. 205, 212-213 (1991). The beachfront buildings are not only themselves destroyed in such a storm, "but they are often driven, like battering rams, into adjacent inland homes." Ibid. Moreover, the development often destroys the natural sand dune barriers that provide storm breaks. Ibid.

**2905 South Carolina began implementing the congressional directive by enacting the South Carolina Coastal Zone Management Act of 1977. Under the 1977 Act, any construction activity in what was designated the "critical area" required a permit from the South Carolina Coastal Council (Council), and the construction of any habitable structure was prohibited. The 1977 critical area was relatively narrow.

This effort did not stop the loss of shoreline. In October 1986, the Council appointed a "Blue Ribbon Committee on Beachfront Management" to investigate beach erosion and *1038 propose possible solutions. In March 1987, the Committee found that South Carolina's beaches were "critically eroding," and proposed land-use restrictions. Report of the South Carolina Blue Ribbon Committee on Beachfront Management i, 6-10 (Mar. 1987). In response, South Carolina enacted the Beachfront Management Act on July 1, 1988. S.C.Code Ann. § 48-39-250 et seq. (Supp.1990). The 1988 Act did not change the uses permitted within the designated critical areas. Rather, it enlarged those areas to encompass the distance from the mean high watermark to a setback line established on the basis of "the best scientific and historical data" available. [FN2] S.C.Code Ann. § 48-39-280 (Supp.1991).

> FN2. The setback line was determined by calculating the distance landward from the crest of an ideal oceanfront sand dune which is 40 times the annual erosion rate. S.C.Code Ann. § 48-39-280 (Supp.1991).

B

Petitioner Lucas is a contractor, manager, and part owner of the Wild Dune development on the Isle of Palms. He has lived there since 1978. In December 1986, he purchased two of the last four pieces of vacant property in the development. [FN3] The area is notoriously unstable. In roughly half of the last 40 years, all or part of petitioner's property was part of the beach or flooded twice daily by the ebb and flow of the tide. Tr. 84. Between 1957 and 1963, petitioner's property was under water. Id., at 79, 81-82. Between 1963 and 1973 the shoreline was 100 to 150 feet onto petitioner's property. Ibid. In 1973 the first line of stable vegetation was about halfway through the property. Id., at 80. Between 1981 and 1983, the Isle of Palms issued 12 emergency orders for *1039 sandbagging to protect property in the Wild Dune development. Id., at 99. Determining that local habitable structures were in imminent danger of collapse, the Council issued permits for two rock revetments to protect condominium developments near petitioner's property from erosion; one of the revetments extends more than halfway onto one of his lots. Id., at 102.

> FN3. The properties were sold frequently at rapidly escalating prices before Lucas purchased them. Lot 22 was first sold in 1979 for $96,660, sold in 1984 for $187,500, then in 1985 for $260,000, and, finally, to Lucas in 1986 for $475,000. He estimated its worth in 1991 at $650,000. Lot 24 had a similar past. The record does not indicate who purchased the properties prior to Lucas, or why none of the purchasers held on to the lots and built on them. Tr. 44-46.

C

112 S.Ct. 2886
(Cite as: 505 U.S. 1003, *1039, 112 S.Ct. 2886, **2905)

The South Carolina Supreme Court found that the Beachfront Management Act did not take petitioner's property without compensation. The decision rested on two premises that until today were unassailable-- that the State has the power to prevent any use of property it finds to be harmful to its citizens, and that a state statute is entitled to a presumption of constitutionality.

The Beachfront Management Act includes a finding by the South Carolina General Assembly that the beach/dune system serves the purpose of "protect[ing] life and property by serving as a storm barrier which dissipates wave energy and contributes to shoreline **2906 stability in an economical and effective manner." S.C.Code Ann. § 48-39-250(1)(a) (Supp.1990). The General Assembly also found that "development unwisely has been sited too close to the [beach/dune] system. This type of development has jeopardized the stability of the beach/dune system, accelerated erosion, and endangered adjacent property." § 48-39-250(4); see also § 48-39-250(6) (discussing the need to "afford the beach/dune system space to accrete and erode").

If the state legislature is correct that the prohibition on building in front of the setback line prevents serious harm, then, under this Court's prior cases, the Act is constitutional. "Long ago it was recognized that all property in this country is held under the implied obligation that the owner's use of it shall not be injurious to the community, and the Takings Clause did not transform that principle to one that requires compensation whenever the State asserts its power to enforce *1040 it." Keystone Bituminous Coal Assn. v. DeBenedictis, 480 U.S. 470, 491-492, 107 S.Ct. 1232, 1245, 94 L.Ed.2d 472 (1987) (internal quotation marks omitted); see also id., at 488-489, and n. 18, 107 S.Ct., at 1244, n. 18. The Court consistently has upheld regulations imposed to arrest a significant threat to the common welfare, whatever their economic effect on the owner. See, e.g., Goldblatt v. Hempstead, 369 U.S. 590, 592-593, 82 S.Ct. 987, 989, 8 L.Ed.2d 130 (1962); Euclid v. Ambler Realty Co., 272 U.S. 365, 47 S.Ct. 114, 71 L.Ed. 303 (1926); Gorieb v. Fox, 274 U.S. 603, 608, 47 S.Ct. 675, 677, 71 L.Ed. 1228 (1927); Mugler v. Kansas, 123 U.S. 623, 8 S.Ct. 273, 31 L.Ed. 205 (1887).

Petitioner never challenged the legislature's findings that a building ban was necessary to protect property and life. Nor did he contend that the threatened harm was not sufficiently serious to make building a house in a particular location a "harmful" use, that the legislature had not made sufficient findings, or that the legislature was motivated by anything other than a desire to minimize damage to coastal areas. Indeed, petitioner objected at trial that evidence as to the purposes of the setback requirement was irrelevant. Tr. 68. The South Carolina Supreme Court accordingly understood petitioner not to contest the State's position that "discouraging new construction in close proximity to the beach/dune area is necessary to prevent a great public harm," 304 S.C. 376, 383, 404 S.E.2d 895, 898 (1991), and "to prevent serious injury to the community." Id., at 387, 404 S.E.2d, at 901. The court considered itself "bound by these uncontested legislative findings ... [in the absence of] any attack whatsoever on the statutory scheme." Id., at 383, 404 S.E.2d, at 898.

Nothing in the record undermines the General Assembly's assessment that prohibitions on building in front of the setback line are necessary to protect people and property from storms, high tides, and beach erosion. Because that legislative determination cannot be disregarded in the absence of such evidence, see, e.g., Euclid, 272 U.S., at 388, 47 S.Ct., at 118; O'Gorman & Young, Inc. v. Hartford Fire Ins. Co., 282 U.S. 251, 257-258, 51 S.Ct. 130, 132, 75 L.Ed. 324 (1931) (Brandeis, J.), and because its determination *1041 of harm to life and property from building is sufficient to prohibit that use under this Court's cases, the South Carolina Supreme Court correctly found no taking.

II

My disagreement with the Court begins with its decision to review this case. This Court

112 S.Ct. 2886
(Cite as: 505 U.S. 1003, *1041, 112 S.Ct. 2886, **2906)

has held consistently that a land-use challenge is not ripe for review until there is a final decision about what uses of the property will be permitted. The ripeness requirement is not simply a gesture of good will to land-use planners. In the absence of "a final and authoritative determination of the type and intensity of development legally permitted on the subject property," MacDonald, Sommer & Frates v. Yolo County, 477 U.S. 340, 348, 106 S.Ct. 2561, 2566, 91 L.Ed.2d 285 (1986), and the utilization of **2907 state procedures for just compensation, there is no final judgment, and in the absence of a final judgment there is no jurisdiction, see San Diego Gas & Electric Co. v. San Diego, 450 U.S. 621, 633, 101 S.Ct. 1287, 1294, 67 L.Ed.2d 551 (1981); Agins v. City of Tiburon, 447 U.S. 255, 260, 100 S.Ct. 2138, 2141, 65 L.Ed.2d 106 (1980).

This rule is "compelled by the very nature of the inquiry required by the Just Compensation Clause," because the factors applied in deciding a takings claim "simply cannot be evaluated until the administrative agency has arrived at a final, definitive position regarding how it will apply the regulations at issue to the particular land in question." Williamson County Regional Planning Comm'n v. Hamilton Bank of Johnson City, 473 U.S. 172, 190, 191, 105 S.Ct. 3108, 3118, 3119, 87 L.Ed.2d 126 (1985). See also MacDonald, Sommer & Frates, 477 U.S., at 348, 106 S.Ct., at 2566 ("A court cannot determine whether a regulation has gone 'too far' unless it knows how far the regulation goes") (citation omitted).

The Court admits that the 1990 amendments to the Beachfront Management Act allowing special permits preclude Lucas from asserting that his property has been permanently taken. See ante, at 2890-2891. The Court agrees that such a claim would not be ripe because there has been no final decision by respondent on what uses will be permitted. *1042 The Court, however, will not be denied: It determines that petitioner's "temporary takings" claim for the period from July 1, 1988, to June 25, 1990, is ripe. But this claim also is not justiciable. [FN4]

FN4. The Court's reliance, ante, at 2892, on Esposito v. South Carolina Coastal Council, 939 F.2d 165, 168 (CA4 1991), cert. denied, 505 U.S. 1219, 112 S.Ct. 3027, 120 L.Ed.2d 898 (1992), in support of its decision to consider Lucas' temporary takings claim ripe is misplaced. In Esposito the plaintiffs brought a facial challenge to the mere enactment of the Act. Here, of course, Lucas has brought an as-applied challenge. See Brief for Petitioner 16. Facial challenges are ripe when the Act is passed; applied challenges require a final decision on the Act's application to the property in question.

From the very beginning of this litigation, respondent has argued that the courts
"lac[k] jurisdiction in this matter because the Plaintiff has sought no authorization from Council for use of his property, has not challenged the location of the baseline or setback line as alleged in the Complaint and because no final agency decision has been rendered concerning use of his property or location of said baseline or setback line." Tr. 10 (answer, as amended).
Although the Council's plea has been ignored by every court, it is undoubtedly correct.

Under the Beachfront Management Act, petitioner was entitled to challenge the setback line or the baseline or erosion rate applied to his property in formal administrative, followed by judicial, proceedings. S.C.Code Ann. § 48-39-280(E) (Supp.1991). Because Lucas failed to pursue this administrative remedy, the Council never finally decided whether Lucas' particular piece of property was correctly categorized as a critical area in which building would not be permitted. This is all the more crucial because Lucas argued strenuously in the trial court that his land was perfectly safe to build on, and that his company had studies to prove it. Tr. 20, 25, 36. If he was correct, the Council's *1043 final decision would have been to alter the setback line, eliminating the construction ban on Lucas' property.

That petitioner's property fell within the critical area as initially interpreted by the Council does not excuse petitioner's failure to challenge the Act's application to his property

112 S.Ct. 2886
(Cite as: 505 U.S. 1003, *1043, 112 S.Ct. 2886, **2907)

in the administrative process. The claim is not ripe until petitioner seeks a variance from that status. "[W]e have made it quite clear that the mere assertion of regulatory jurisdiction by a governmental body does not constitute a regulatory taking." United States v. Riverside Bayview Homes, Inc., 474 U.S. 121, 126, 106 S.Ct. 455, 459, 88 L.Ed.2d 419 (1985). See also Williamson County, **2908 473 U.S., at 188, 105 S.Ct., at 3117 (claim not ripe because respondent did not seek variances that would have allowed it to develop the property, notwithstanding the commission's finding that the plan did not comply with the zoning ordinance and subdivision regulations). [FN5]

> FN5. Even more baffling, given its decision, just a few days ago, in Lujan v. Defenders of Wildlife, 504 U.S. 555, 112 S.Ct. 2130, 119 L.Ed.2d 351 (1992), the Court decides petitioner has demonstrated injury in fact. In his complaint, petitioner made no allegations that he had any definite plans for using his property. App. to Pet. for Cert. 153-156. At trial, Lucas testified that he had house plans drawn up, but that he was "in no hurry" to build "because the lot was appreciating in value." Tr. 28-29. The trial court made no findings of fact that Lucas had any plans to use the property from 1988 to 1990. " '[S]ome day' intentions--without any description of concrete plans, or indeed even any specification of when the some day will be--do not support a finding of the 'actual or imminent' injury that our cases require." 504 U.S., at 564, 112 S.Ct., at 2138. The Court circumvents Defenders of Wildlife by deciding to resolve this case as if it arrived on the pleadings alone. But it did not. Lucas had a full trial on his claim for " 'damages for the temporary taking of his property' from the date of the 1988 Act's 'passage to such time as this matter is finally resolved,' " ante, at 2892, n. 3, quoting the complaint, and failed to demonstrate any immediate concrete plans to build or sell.

Even if I agreed with the Court that there were no jurisdictional barriers to deciding this case, I still would not try to decide it. The Court creates its new takings jurisprudence based on the trial court's finding that the property *1044 had lost all economic value. [FN6] This finding is almost certainly erroneous. Petitioner still can enjoy other attributes of ownership, such as the right to exclude others, "one of the most essential sticks in the bundle of rights that are commonly characterized as property." Kaiser Aetna v. United States, 444 U.S. 164, 176, 100 S.Ct. 383, 391, 62 L.Ed.2d 332 (1979). Petitioner can picnic, swim, camp in a tent, or live on the property in a movable trailer. State courts frequently have recognized that land has economic value where the only residual economic uses are recreation or camping. See, e.g., Turnpike Realty Co. v. Dedham, 362 Mass. 221, 284 N.E.2d 891 (1972) cert. denied, 409 U.S. 1108, 93 S.Ct. 908, 34 L.Ed.2d 689 (1973); Turner v. County of Del Norte, 24 Cal.App.3d 311, 101 Cal.Rptr. 93 (1972); Hall v. Board of Environmental Protection, 528 A.2d 453 (Me.1987). Petitioner also retains the right to alienate the land, which would have value for neighbors and for those prepared to enjoy proximity to the ocean without a house.

> FN6. Respondent contested the findings of fact of the trial court in the South Carolina Supreme Court, but that court did not resolve the issue. This Court's decision to assume for its purposes that petitioner had been denied all economic use of his land does not, of course, dispose of the issue on remand.

Yet the trial court, apparently believing that "less value" and "valueless" could be used interchangeably, found the property "valueless." The court accepted no evidence from the State on the property's value without a home, and petitioner's appraiser testified that he never had considered what the value would be absent a residence. Tr. 54-55. The appraiser's value was based on the fact that the "highest and best use of these lots ... [is] luxury single family detached dwellings." Id., at 48. The trial court appeared to believe that the property could be considered "valueless" if it was not available for its most profitable use. Absent that erroneous assumption, see Goldblatt, 369 U.S., at 592, 82 S.Ct., at 989, I find no evidence in the record supporting the trial court's conclusion that the damage to the lots by virtue of the restrictions *1045 was "total." Record 128 (findings of fact). I agree with the Court, ante, at 2896, n. 9, that it has the power to decide a case that turns on an erroneous finding, but I question the wisdom of deciding an issue based on a factual premise that does not exist in this case, and in the judgment of the Court will exist in the future only in "extraordinary circumstance[s]," ante, at 2894.

**2909 Clearly, the Court was eager to decide this case. [FN7] But eagerness, in the absence of proper jurisdiction, must--and in this case should have been--met with restraint.

FN7. The Court overlooks the lack of a ripe and justiciable claim apparently out of concern that in the absence of its intervention Lucas will be unable to obtain further adjudication of his temporary takings claim. The Court chastises respondent for arguing that Lucas' temporary takings claim is premature because it failed "so much as [to] commen[t]" upon the effect of the South Carolina Supreme Court's decision on petitioner's ability to obtain relief for the 2-year period, and it frets that Lucas would "be unable (absent our intervention now) to obtain further state-court adjudication with respect to the 1988-1990 period." Ante, at 2891. Whatever the explanation for the Court's intense interest in Lucas' plight when ordinarily we are more cautious in granting discretionary review, the concern would have been more prudently expressed by vacating the judgment below and remanding for further consideration in light of the 1990 amendments. At that point, petitioner could have brought a temporary takings claim in the state courts.

III

The Court's willingness to dispense with precedent in its haste to reach a result is not limited to its initial jurisdictional decision. The Court also alters the long-settled rules of review.

The South Carolina Supreme Court's decision to defer to legislative judgments in the absence of a challenge from petitioner comports with one of this Court's oldest maxims: "[T]he existence of facts supporting the legislative judgment is to be presumed." United States v. Carolene Products Co., 304 U.S. 144, 152, 58 S.Ct. 778, 783, 82 L.Ed. 1234 (1938). Indeed, we have said the legislature's judgment is "well-nigh conclusive." Berman v. Parker, *1046 348 U.S. 26, 32, 75 S.Ct. 98, 102, 99 L.Ed. 27 (1954). See also Sweet v. Rechel, 159 U.S. 380, 392, 16 S.Ct. 43, 45-46, 40 L.Ed. 188 (1895); Euclid, 272 U.S., at 388, 47 S.Ct., at 118 ("If the validity of the legislative classification for zoning purposes be fairly debatable, the legislative judgment must be allowed to control").

Accordingly, this Court always has required plaintiffs challenging the constitutionality of an ordinance to provide "some factual foundation of record" that contravenes the legislative findings. O'Gorman & Young, 282 U.S., at 258, 51 S.Ct., at 132. In the absence of such proof, "the presumption of constitutionality must prevail." Id., at 257, 51 S.Ct., at 132. We only recently have reaffirmed that claimants have the burden of showing a state law constitutes a taking. See Keystone Bituminous Coal, 480 U.S., at 485, 107 S.Ct., at 1242. See also Goldblatt, 369 U.S., at 594, 82 S.Ct., at 990 (citing "the usual presumption of constitutionality" that applies to statutes attacked as takings).

Rather than invoking these traditional rules, the Court decides the State has the burden to convince the courts that its legislative judgments are correct. Despite Lucas' complete failure to contest the legislature's findings of serious harm to life and property if a permanent structure is built, the Court decides that the legislative findings are not sufficient to justify the use prohibition. Instead, the Court "emphasize[s]" the State must do more than merely proffer its legislative judgments to avoid invalidating its law. Ante, at 2901. In this case, apparently, the State now has the burden of showing the regulation is not a taking. The Court offers no justification for its sudden hostility toward state legislators, and I doubt that it could.

IV

The Court does not reject the South Carolina Supreme Court's decision simply on the basis of its disbelief and distrust of the legislature's

112 S.Ct. 2886
(Cite as: 505 U.S. 1003, *1046, 112 S.Ct. 2886, **2909)

findings. It also takes the opportunity to create a new scheme for regulations that eliminate all economic value. From now on, there is a categorical rule finding these regulations to be a taking unless the use they *1047 prohibit is a background common-law nuisance or property principle. See ante, at 2899-2901.

**2910 A

I first question the Court's rationale in creating a category that obviates a "case-specific inquiry into the public interest advanced," ante, at 2893, if all economic value has been lost. If one fact about the Court's takings jurisprudence can be stated without contradiction, it is that "the particular circumstances of each case" determine whether a specific restriction will be rendered invalid by the government's failure to pay compensation. United States v. Central Eureka Mining Co., 357 U.S. 155, 168, 78 S.Ct. 1097, 1104, 2 L.Ed.2d 1228 (1958). This is so because although we have articulated certain factors to be considered, including the economic impact on the property owner, the ultimate conclusion "necessarily requires a weighing of private and public interests." Agins, 447 U.S., at 261, 100 S.Ct., at 2141. When the government regulation prevents the owner from any economically valuable use of his property, the private interest is unquestionably substantial, but we have never before held that no public interest can outweigh it. Instead the Court's prior decisions "uniformly reject the proposition that diminution in property value, standing alone, can establish a 'taking.'" Penn Central Transp. Co. v. New York City, 438 U.S. 104, 131, 98 S.Ct. 2646, 2663, 57 L.Ed.2d 631 (1978).

This Court repeatedly has recognized the ability of government, in certain circumstances, to regulate property without compensation no matter how adverse the financial effect on the owner may be. More than a century ago, the Court explicitly upheld the right of States to prohibit uses of property injurious to public health, safety, or welfare without paying compensation: "A prohibition simply upon the use of property for purposes that are declared, by valid legislation, to be injurious to the health, morals, or safety of the community, cannot, in any just sense, be deemed a taking or an appropriation of property." Mugler v. Kansas, 123 *1048 U.S., at 668-669, 8 S.Ct., at 301. On this basis, the Court upheld an ordinance effectively prohibiting operation of a previously lawful brewery, although the "establishments will become of no value as property." Id., at 664, 8 S.Ct., at 298; see also id., at 668, 8 S.Ct., at 300.

Mugler was only the beginning in a long line of cases. [FN8] In Powell v. Pennsylvania, 127 U.S. 678, 8 S.Ct. 992, 32 L.Ed. 253 (1888), the Court upheld legislation prohibiting the manufacture of oleomargarine, despite the owner's allegation that "if prevented from continuing it, the value of his property employed therein would be entirely lost and he be deprived of the means of livelihood." Id., at 682, 8 S.Ct., at 994. In Hadacheck v. Sebastian, 239 U.S. 394, 36 S.Ct. 143, 60 L.Ed. 348 (1915), the Court upheld an ordinance prohibiting a brickyard, although the owner had made excavations on the land that prevented it from being utilized for any purpose but a brickyard. Id., at 405, 36 S.Ct., at 143. In Miller v. Schoene, 276 U.S. 272, 48 S.Ct. 246, 72 L.Ed. 568 (1928), the Court held that the Fifth Amendment did not require Virginia to pay compensation to the owner of cedar trees ordered destroyed to prevent a disease from spreading to nearby apple orchards. The "preferment of [the public interest] over the property interest of the individual, to the extent even of its destruction, is one of the distinguishing characteristics of every exercise of the police power which affects property." Id., at 280, 48 S.Ct., at 247. Again, in Omnia Commercial Co. v. United States, 261 U.S. 502, 43 S.Ct. 437, 67 L.Ed. 773 (1923), the Court stated that "destruction of, or injury to, property is frequently accomplished without **2911 a 'taking' in the constitutional sense." Id., at 508, 43 S.Ct., at 437.

FN8. Prior to Mugler, the Court had held that owners whose real property is wholly destroyed to prevent the spread of a fire are not entitled to compensation. Bowditch v. Boston, 101 U.S. 16, 18-19, 25 L.Ed. 980 (1880). And the Court recognized in the License Cases, 5 How. 504, 589, 12 L.Ed. 256 (1847) (opinion of McLean, J.), that "[t]he acknowledged police power of a State extends often to the destruction of property."

More recently, in Goldblatt, the Court upheld a town regulation that barred continued operation of an existing sand and gravel operation in order to protect public safety. 369 *1049 U.S., at 596, 82 S.Ct., at 991. "Although a comparison of values before and after is relevant," the Court stated, "it is by no means conclusive." [FN9] Id., at 594, 82 S.Ct., at 990. In 1978, the Court declared that "in instances in which a state tribunal reasonably concluded that 'the health, safety, morals, or general welfare' would be promoted by prohibiting particular contemplated uses of land, this Court has upheld land-use regulation that destroyed ... recognized real property interests." Penn Central Transp. Co., 438 U.S., at 125, 98 S.Ct., at 2659. In First English Evangelical Lutheran Church of Glendale v. County of Los Angeles, 482 U.S. 304, 107 S.Ct. 2378, 96 L.Ed.2d 250 (1987), the owner alleged that a floodplain ordinance had deprived it of "all use" of the property. Id., at 312, 107 S.Ct., at 2384. The Court remanded the case for consideration whether, even if the ordinance denied the owner all use, it could be justified as a safety measure. [FN10] Id., at 313, 107 S.Ct., at 2385. And in Keystone Bituminous Coal, the Court summarized over 100 years of precedent: "[T]he Court has repeatedly upheld regulations that destroy or adversely affect real property interests." [FN11] 480 U.S., at 489, n. 18, 107 S.Ct., at 1244, n. 18.

FN9. That same year, an appeal came to the Court asking "[w]hether zoning ordinances which altogether destroy the worth of valuable land by prohibiting the only economic use of which it is capable effect a taking of real property without compensation." Juris. Statement, O.T.1962, No. 307, p. 5. The Court dismissed the appeal for lack of a substantial federal question. Consolidated Rock Products Co. v. Los Angeles, 57 Cal.2d 515, 20 Cal.Rptr. 638, 370 P.2d 342, appeal dism'd, 371 U.S. 36, 83 S.Ct. 145, 9 L.Ed.2d 112 (1962).

FN10. On remand, the California court found no taking in part because the zoning regulation "involves this highest of public interests--the prevention of death and injury." First Lutheran Church v. Los Angeles, 210 Cal.App.3d 1353, 1370, 258 Cal.Rptr. 893, 904 (1989), cert. denied, 493 U.S. 1056, 110 S.Ct. 866, 107 L.Ed.2d 950 (1990).

FN11. The Court's suggestion that Agins v. City of Tiburon, 447 U.S. 255, 100 S.Ct. 2138, 65 L.Ed.2d 106 (1980), a unanimous opinion, created a new per se rule, only now discovered, is unpersuasive. In Agins, the Court stated that "no precise rule determines when property has been taken" but instead that "the question necessarily requires a weighing of public and private interest." Id., at 260-262, 100 S.Ct., at 2141-2142. The other cases cited by the Court, ante, at 2893, repeat the Agins sentence, but in no way suggest that the public interest is irrelevant if total value has been taken. The Court has indicated that proof that a regulation does not deny an owner economic use of his property is sufficient to defeat a facial takings challenge. See Hodel v. Virginia Surface Mining & Reclamation Assn., Inc., 452 U.S. 264, 295-297, 101 S.Ct. 2352, 2370-2371, 69 L.Ed.2d 1 (1981). But the conclusion that a regulation is not on its face a taking because it allows the landowner some economic use of property is a far cry from the proposition that denial of such use is sufficient to establish a takings claim regardless of any other consideration. The Court never has accepted the latter proposition. The Court relies today on dicta in Agins, Hodel, Nollan v. California Coastal Comm'n, 483 U.S. 825, 107 S.Ct. 3141, 97 L.Ed.2d 677 (1987), and Keystone Bituminous Coal Assn. v. DeBenedictis, 480 U.S. 470, 107 S.Ct. 1232, 94 L.Ed.2d 472 (1987), for its new categorical rule. Ante, at 2893. I prefer to rely on the directly contrary holdings in cases such as Mugler v. Sebastian, 239 U.S. 394, 36 S.Ct. 143, 60 L.Ed. 348 (1915), and Hadacheck v. Kansas, 123 U.S. 623, 8 S.Ct. 273, 31 L.Ed. 205 (1887), not to mention contrary statements in the very cases on which the Court relies. See Agins, 447 U.S., at 260-262, 100 S.Ct., at 2141-2142; Keystone Bituminous Coal, 480 U.S., at 489, n. 18, 491-492, 107 S.Ct., at 1243-1244, n. 18, 1245-1246.

112 S.Ct. 2886
(Cite as: 505 U.S. 1003, *1050, 112 S.Ct. 2886, **2911)

*1050 The Court recognizes that "our prior opinions have suggested that 'harmful or noxious uses' of property may be proscribed by government regulation without the requirement of compensation," ante, at 2897, but seeks to reconcile them with its categorical rule by claiming that the Court never has upheld a regulation when the owner alleged the loss of all economic value. Even if the Court's factual premise were correct, its understanding of the Court's cases is distorted. In none of the cases did the Court suggest that the right of a State to prohibit certain activities without paying compensation **2912 turned on the availability of some residual valuable use. [FN12] Instead, the cases depended on whether the *1051 government interest was sufficient to prohibit the activity, given the significant private cost. [FN13]

FN12. Miller v. Schoene, 276 U.S. 272, 48 S.Ct. 246, 72 L.Ed. 568 (1928), is an example. In the course of demonstrating that apple trees are more valuable than red cedar trees, the Court noted that red cedar has "occasional use and value as lumber." Id., at 279, 48 S.Ct., at 247. But the Court did not discuss whether the timber owned by the petitioner in that case was commercially salable, and nothing in the opinion suggests that the State's right to require uncompensated felling of the trees depended on any such salvage value. To the contrary, it is clear from its unanimous opinion that the Schoene Court would have sustained a law requiring the burning of cedar trees if that had been necessary to protect apple trees in which there was a public interest: The Court spoke of preferment of the public interest over the property interest of the individual, "to the extent even of its destruction." Id., at 280, 48 S.Ct., at 247.

FN13. The Court seeks to disavow the holdings and reasoning of Mugler and subsequent cases by explaining that they were the Court's early efforts to define the scope of the police power. There is language in the earliest takings cases suggesting that the police power was considered to be the power simply to prevent harms. Subsequently, the Court expanded its understanding of what were government's legitimate interests. But it does not follow that the holding of those early cases--that harmful and noxious uses of property can be forbidden whatever the harm to the property owner and without the payment of compensation--was repudiated. To the contrary, as the Court consciously expanded the scope of the police power beyond preventing harm, it clarified that there was a core of public interests that overrode any private interest. See Keystone Bituminous Coal, 480 U.S., at 491, n. 20, 107 S.Ct., at 1245, n. 20.

These cases rest on the principle that the State has full power to prohibit an owner's use of property if it is harmful to the public. "[S]ince no individual has a right to use his property so as to create a nuisance or otherwise harm others, the State has not 'taken' anything when it asserts its power to enjoin the nuisance-like activity." Keystone Bituminous Coal, 480 U.S., at 491, n. 20, 107 S.Ct., at 1245, n. 20. It would make no sense under this theory to suggest that an owner has a constitutionally protected right to harm others, if only he makes the proper showing of economic loss. [FN14] See Pennsylvania Coal Co. v. Mahon, 260 U.S. 393, 418, 43 S.Ct. 158, 161, 67 L.Ed. 322 (1922) (Brandeis, J., dissenting) ("Restriction upon [harmful] use does not become inappropriate as a means, merely because it deprives the owner of the only use to which the property can then be profitably put").

FN14. "Indeed, it would be extraordinary to construe the Constitution to require a government to compensate private landowners because it denied them 'the right' to use property which cannot be used without risking injury and death." First Lutheran Church, 210 Cal.App.3d, at 1366, 258 Cal.Rptr., at 901-902.

*1052 B

Ultimately even the Court cannot embrace the full implications of its per se rule: It eventually agrees that there cannot be a categorical rule for a taking based on economic value that wholly disregards the public need asserted. Instead, the Court decides that it will permit a State to regulate all economic value only if the State prohibits uses that would not be permitted under "background principles of nuisance and property law." [FN15] Ante, at 2901.

FN15. Although it refers to state nuisance and property law, the Court apparently does not mean just any state nuisance and property law. Public nuisance was first a common-law creation, see Newark, The Boundaries of Nuisance, 65 L.Q.Rev. 480, 482 (1949) (attributing development of nuisance to 1535), but by the 1800's in both the United States and England, legislatures had the power to define what is a public nuisance, and particular uses often have been selectively targeted. See Prosser, Private Action for Public Nuisance, 52 Va.L.Rev. 997, 999-1000 (1966); J. Stephen, A General View of the Criminal Law of England 105-107 (2d ed. 1890). The Court's references to "common-law" background principles, however, indicate that legislative determinations do not constitute "state nuisance and property law" for the Court.

Until today, the Court explicitly had rejected the contention that the government's power to act without paying compensation **2913 turns on whether the prohibited activity is a common-law nuisance. [FN16] The brewery closed in Mugler itself was not a common-law nuisance, and the Court specifically stated that it was the role of the legislature to determine *1053 what measures would be appropriate for the protection of public health and safety. See 123 U.S., at 661, 8 S.Ct., at 297. In upholding the state action in Miller, the Court found it unnecessary to "weigh with nicety the question whether the infected cedars constitute a nuisance according to common law; or whether they may be so declared by statute." 276 U.S., at 280, 48 S.Ct., at 248. See also Goldblatt, 369 U.S., at 593, 82 S.Ct., at 989; Hadacheck, 239 U.S., at 411, 36 S.Ct., at 146. Instead the Court has relied in the past, as the South Carolina court has done here, on legislative judgments of what constitutes a harm. [FN17]

FN16. Also, until today the fact that the regulation prohibited uses that were lawful at the time the owner purchased did not determine the constitutional question. The brewery, the brickyard, the cedar trees, and the gravel pit were all perfectly legitimate uses prior to the passage of the regulation. See Mugler v. Kansas, 123 U.S., at 654, 8 S.Ct., at 293; Hadacheck v. Sebastian, 239 U.S. 394, 36 S.Ct. 143, 60 L.Ed. 348 (1915);

Miller, 276 U.S., at 272, 48 S.Ct., at 246; Goldblatt v. Hempstead, 369 U.S. 590, 82 S.Ct. 987, 8 L.Ed.2d 130 (1962). This Court explicitly acknowledged in Hadacheck that "[a] vested interest cannot be asserted against [the police power] because of conditions once obtaining. To so hold would preclude development and fix a city forever in its primitive conditions." 239 U.S., at 410, 36 S.Ct., at 145 (citation omitted).

FN17. The Court argues that finding no taking when the legislature prohibits a harmful use, such as the Court did in Mugler and the South Carolina Supreme Court did in the instant case, would nullify Pennsylvania Coal. See ante, at 2897. Justice Holmes, the author of Pennsylvania Coal, joined Miller v. Schoene, 276 U.S. 272, 48 S.Ct. 246, 72 L.Ed. 568 (1928), six years later. In Miller, the Court adopted the exact approach of the South Carolina court: It found the cedar trees harmful, and their destruction not a taking, whether or not they were a nuisance. Justice Holmes apparently believed that such an approach did not repudiate his earlier opinion. Moreover, this Court already has been over this ground five years ago, and at that point rejected the assertion that Pennsylvania Coal was inconsistent with Mugler, Hadacheck, Miller, or the others in the string of "noxious use" cases, recognizing instead that the nature of the State's action is critical in takings analysis. Keystone Bituminous Coal, 480 U.S., at 490, 107 S.Ct., at 1244.

The Court rejects the notion that the State always can prohibit uses it deems a harm to the public without granting compensation because "the distinction between 'harm-preventing' and 'benefit-conferring' regulation is often in the eye of the beholder." Ante, at 2897. Since the characterization will depend "primarily upon one's evaluation of the worth of competing uses of real estate," ante, at 2898, the Court decides a legislative judgment of this kind no longer can provide the desired "objective, value-free basis" for upholding a regulation, ante, at 2899. The Court, however, fails to explain how its proposed common-law alternative escapes the same trap.

*1054 The threshold inquiry for imposition of the Court's new rule, "deprivation of all

Appendix E: The Lucas Decision / 301

112 S.Ct. 2886
(Cite as: 505 U.S. 1003, *1054, 112 S.Ct. 2886, **2913)

economically valuable use," itself cannot be determined objectively. As the Court admits, whether the owner has been deprived of all economic value of his property will depend on how "property" is defined. The "composition of the denominator in our 'deprivation' fraction," ante, at 2894, n. 7, is the dispositive inquiry. Yet there is no "objective" way to define what that denominator should be. "We have long understood that any land-use regulation can be characterized as the 'total' deprivation of an aptly defined entitlement.... Alternatively, the same regulation can always be characterized as a mere 'partial' withdrawal from full, unencumbered ownership of the landholding affected by the regulation...." [FN18] Michelman, Takings, 1987, 88 Colum.L.Rev. 1600, 1614 (1988).

> FN18. See also Michelman, Property, Utility, and Fairness, Comments on the Ethical Foundations of "Just Compensation" Law, 80 Harv.L.Rev. 1165, 1192-1193 (1967); Sax, Takings and the Police Power, 74 Yale L.J. 36, 60 (1964).

The Court's decision in Keystone Bituminous Coal illustrates this principle perfectly. **2914 In Keystone, the Court determined that the "support estate" was "merely a part of the entire bundle of rights possessed by the owner." 480 U.S., at 501, 107 S.Ct., at 1250. Thus, the Court concluded that the support estate's destruction merely eliminated one segment of the total property. Ibid. The dissent, however, characterized the support estate as a distinct property interest that was wholly destroyed. Id., at 519, 107 S.Ct., at 1260. The Court could agree on no "value-free basis" to resolve this dispute.

Even more perplexing, however, is the Court's reliance on common-law principles of nuisance in its quest for a value-free takings jurisprudence. In determining what is a nuisance at common law, state courts make exactly the decision that the Court finds so troubling when made by the South Carolina General Assembly today: They determine whether the use is harmful. Common-law public and private nuisance *1055 law is simply a determination whether a particular use causes harm. See Prosser, Private Action for Public Nuisance, 52 Va.L.Rev. 997 (1966) ("Nuisance is a French word which means nothing more than harm"). There is nothing magical in the reasoning of judges long dead. They determined a harm in the same way as state judges and legislatures do today. If judges in the 18th and 19th centuries can distinguish a harm from a benefit, why not judges in the 20th century, and if judges can, why not legislators? There simply is no reason to believe that new interpretations of the hoary common-law nuisance doctrine will be particularly "objective" or "value free." [FN19] Once one abandons the level of generality of sic utere tuo ut alienum non laedas, ante, at 2901, one searches in vain, I think, for anything resembling a principle in the common law of nuisance.

> FN19. "There is perhaps no more impenetrable jungle in the entire law than that which surrounds the word 'nuisance.' It has meant all things to all people, and has been applied indiscriminately to everything from an alarming advertisement to a cockroach baked in a pie." W. Keeton, D. Dobbs, R. Keeton & D. Owen, Prosser and Keeton on The Law of Torts 616 (5th ed. 1984) (footnotes omitted). It is an area of law that "straddles the legal universe, virtually defies synthesis, and generates case law to suit every taste." W. Rodgers, Environmental Law § 2.4, p. 48 (1986) (footnotes omitted). The Court itself has noted that "nuisance concepts" are "often vague and indeterminate." Milwaukee v. Illinois, 451 U.S. 304, 317, 101 S.Ct. 1784, 1792, 68 L.Ed.2d 114 (1981).

C

Finally, the Court justifies its new rule that the legislature may not deprive a property owner of the only economically valuable use of his land, even if the legislature finds it to be a harmful use, because such action is not part of the " 'long recognized' " "understandings of our citizens." Ante, at 2899. These "understandings" permit such regulation only if the use is a nuisance under the common law. Any other course is "inconsistent with the historical compact recorded in the Takings Clause." Ante, at 2900. It is not clear from the Court's *1056 opinion where our

Copr. © West 1996 No claim to orig. U.S. govt. works

112 S.Ct. 2886
(Cite as: 505 U.S. 1003, *1056, 112 S.Ct. 2886, **2914)

"historical compact" or "citizens' understanding" comes from, but it does not appear to be history.

The principle that the State should compensate individuals for property taken for public use was not widely established in America at the time of the Revolution. "The colonists ... inherited ... a concept of property which permitted extensive regulation of the use of that property for the public benefit--regulation that could even go so far as to deny all productive use of the property to the owner if, as Coke himself stated, the regulation 'extends to the public benefit ... for this is for the public, and every one hath benefit by it.' " F. Bosselman, D. Callies, & J. Banta, The Taking Issue 80-81 (1973), quoting The Case of the King's Prerogative in Saltpetre, 12 Co.Rep. 12-13 (1606) (hereinafter **2915 Bosselman). See also Treanor, The Origins and Original Significance of the Just Compensation Clause of the Fifth Amendment, 94 Yale L.J. 694, 697, n. 9 (1985). [FN20]

> FN20. See generally Sax, 74 Yale L.J., at 56-59. "The evidence certainly seems to indicate that the mere fact that government activity destroyed existing economic advantages and power did not disturb [the English theorists who formulated the compensation notion] at all." Id., at 56. Professor Sax contends that even Blackstone, "remembered champion of the language of private property," did not believe that the Compensation Clause was meant to preserve economic value. Id., at 58-59.

Even into the 19th century, state governments often felt free to take property for roads and other public projects without paying compensation to the owners. [FN21] See M. Horwitz, The Transformation of American Law, 1780-1860, pp. 63-64 (1977) (hereinafter Horwitz); Treanor, 94 Yale L.J., at 695. As one court declared in 1802, citizens "were bound *1057 to contribute as much of [land], as by the laws of the country, were deemed necessary for the public convenience." M'Clenachan v. Curwin, 3 Yeates 362, 373 (Pa.1802). There was an obvious movement toward establishing the just compensation principle during the 19th century, but "there continued to be a strong current in American legal thought that regarded compensation simply as a 'bounty given ... by the State' out of 'kindness' and not out of justice." Horwitz 65, quoting Commonwealth v. Fisher, 1 Pen. & W. 462, 465 (Pa.1830). See also State v. Dawson, 3 Hill 100, 103 (S.C.1836)). [FN22]

> FN21. In 1796, the attorney general of South Carolina responded to property holders' demand for compensation when the State took their land to build a road by arguing that "there is not one instance on record, and certainly none within the memory of the oldest man now living, of any demand being made for compensation for the soil or freehold of the lands." Lindsay v. Commissioners, 2 S.C.L. 38, 49 (1796).

> FN22. Only the Constitutions of Vermont and Massachusetts required that compensation be paid when private property was taken for public use; and although eminent domain was mentioned in the Pennsylvania Constitution, its sole requirement was that property not be taken without the consent of the legislature. See Grant, The "Higher Law" Background of the Law of Eminent Domain, in 2 Selected Essays on Constitutional Law 912, 915-916 (1938). By 1868, five of the original States still had no just compensation clauses in their Constitutions. Ibid.

Although, prior to the adoption of the Bill of Rights, America was replete with land-use regulations describing which activities were considered noxious and forbidden, see Bender, The Takings Clause: Principles or Politics?, 34 Buffalo L.Rev. 735, 751 (1985); L. Friedman, A History of American Law 66-68 (1973), the Fifth Amendment's Takings Clause originally did not extend to regulations of property, whatever the effect. [FN23] See ante, at 2892. Most state courts agreed with this narrow interpretation of a taking. "Until the end of the nineteenth century ... jurists held that *1058 the constitution protected possession only, and not value." Siegel, Understanding the Nineteenth Century Contract Clause: The Role of the Property-Privilege Distinction and "Takings" Clause Jurisprudence, 60 S.Cal.L.Rev. 1, 76 (1986); Bosselman 106. Even indirect and consequential injuries to property resulting

112 S.Ct. 2886
(Cite as: 505 U.S. 1003, *1058, 112 S.Ct. 2886, **2915)

from regulations were excluded from the definition of a taking. See ibid.; Callender v. Marsh, 1 Pick. 418, 430 (Mass.1823).

> FN23. James Madison, author of the Takings Clause, apparently intended it to apply only to direct, physical takings of property by the Federal Government. See Treanor, The Origins and Original Significance of the Just Compensation Clause of the Fifth Amendment, 94 Yale L.J. 694, 711 (1985). Professor Sax argues that although "contemporary commentary upon the meaning of the compensation clause is in very short supply," 74 Yale L.J., at 58, the "few authorities that are available" indicate that the Clause was "designed to prevent arbitrary government action," not to protect economic value. Id., at 58-60.

Even when courts began to consider that regulation in some situations could constitute a taking, they continued to uphold bans on particular uses without paying compensation, notwithstanding the economic impact, under the rationale that no one can obtain a vested **2916 right to injure or endanger the public. [FN24] In the Coates cases, for example, the Supreme Court of New York found no taking in New York's ban on the interment of the dead within the city, although "no other use can be made of these lands." Coates v. City of New York, 7 Cow. 585, 592 (N.Y.1827). See also Brick Presbyterian Church v. City of New York, 5 Cow. 538 (N.Y.1826); Commonwealth v. Alger, 7 Cush. 53, 59, 104 (Mass.1851); St. Louis Gunning Advertisement Co. v. St. Louis, 235 Mo. 99, 146, 137 S.W. 929, 942 (1911), appeal dism'd, 231 U.S. 761, 34 S.Ct. 325, 58 L.Ed. 470 (1913). More recent cases reach the same result. See Consolidated Rock Products Co. v. Los Angeles, 57 Cal.2d 515, 20 Cal.Rptr. 638, 370 P.2d 342, appeal dism'd, 371 U.S. 36, 83 S.Ct. 145, 9 L.Ed.2d 112 (1962); Nassr v. *1059 Commonwealth, 394 Mass. 767, 477 N.E.2d 987 (1985); Eno v. Burlington, 125 Vt. 8, 209 A.2d 499 (1965); Turner v. County of Del Norte, 24 Cal.App.3d 311, 101 Cal.Rptr. 93 (1972).

> FN24. For this reason, the retroactive application of the regulation to formerly lawful uses was not a controlling distinction in the past. "Nor can it make any difference that the right is purchased previous to the passage of the by-law," for "[e]very right, from an absolute ownership in property, down to a mere easement, is purchased and holden subject to the restriction, that it shall be so exercised as not to injure others. Though, at the time, it be remote and inoffensive, the purchaser is bound to know, at his peril, that it may become otherwise." Coates v. City of New York, 7 Cow. 585, 605 (N.Y.1827). See also Brick Presbyterian Church v. City of New York, 5 Cow. 538, 542 (N.Y.1826); Commonwealth v. Tewksbury, 11 Metc. 55 (Mass.1846); State v. Paul, 5 R.I. 185 (1858).

In addition, state courts historically have been less likely to find that a government action constitutes a taking when the affected land is undeveloped. According to the South Carolina court, the power of the legislature to take unimproved land without providing compensation was sanctioned by "ancient rights and principles." Lindsay v. Commissioners, 2 S.C.L. 38, 57 (1796). "Except for Massachusetts, no colony appears to have paid compensation when it built a state-owned road across unimproved land. Legislatures provided compensation only for enclosed or improved land." Treanor, 94 Yale L.J., at 695 (footnotes omitted). This rule was followed by some States into the 1800's. See Horwitz 63-65.

With similar result, the common agrarian conception of property limited owners to "natural" uses of their land prior to and during much of the 18th century. See id., at 32. Thus, for example, the owner could build nothing on his land that would alter the natural flow of water. See id., at 44; see also, e.g., Merritt v. Parker, 1 Coxe 460, 463 (N.J.1795). Some more recent state courts still follow this reasoning. See, e.g., Just v. Marinette County, 56 Wis.2d 7, 201 N.W.2d 761, 768 (1972).

Nor does history indicate any common-law limit on the State's power to regulate harmful uses even to the point of destroying all economic value. Nothing in the discussions in Congress concerning the Takings Clause indicates that the Clause was limited by the common-law nuisance doctrine. Common-law courts themselves rejected an understanding. They regularly recognized that it is "for the legislature to interpose, and by positive enactment to prohibit a use of property which would be injurious to the public." *1060 Tewksbury, 11 Metc., at 57. [FN25] Chief Justice Shaw explained in upholding a regulation prohibiting construction of wharves, the existence of a taking did not depend on "whether a certain erection in tide water is a nuisance at common law or not." Alger, 7 Cush., at 104; see also State v. Paul, 5 R.I. 185, 193 (1858); Commonwealth v. Parks, 155 Mass. 531, 532, 30 N.E. 174 (1892) (Holmes, J.) ("[T]he legislature may change the common law as to nuisances, and may move the line either way, so as to make things nuisances **2917 which were not so, or to make things lawful which were nuisances").

> FN25. More recent state-court decisions agree. See, e.g., Lane v. Mt. Vernon, 38 N.Y.2d 344, 348-349, 379 N.Y.S.2d 798, 800, 342 N.E.2d 571, 573 (1976); Commonwealth v. Baker, 160 Pa.Super. 640, 641-642, 53 A.2d 829, 830 (1947).

In short, I find no clear and accepted "historical compact" or "understanding of our citizens" justifying the Court's new takings doctrine. Instead, the Court seems to treat history as a grab bag of principles, to be adopted where they support the Court's theory, and ignored where they do not. If the Court decided that the early common law provides the background principles for interpreting the Takings Clause, then regulation, as opposed to physical confiscation, would not be compensable. If the Court decided that the law of a later period provides the background principles, then regulation might be compensable, but the Court would have to confront the fact that legislatures regularly determined which uses were prohibited, independent of the common law, and independent of whether the uses were lawful when the owner purchased. What makes the Court's analysis unworkable is its attempt to package the law of two incompatible eras and peddle it as historical fact. [FN26]

> FN26. The Court asserts that all early American experience, prior to and after passage of the Bill of Rights, and any case law prior to 1897 are "entirely irrelevant" in determining what is "the historical compact recorded in the Takings Clause." Ante, at 2900 and n. 15. Nor apparently are we to find this compact in the early federal takings cases, which clearly permitted prohibition of harmful uses despite the alleged loss of all value, whether or not the prohibition was a common-law nuisance, and whether or not the prohibition occurred subsequent to the purchase. See supra, at 2910, 2912-2913, and n. 16. I cannot imagine where the Court finds its "historical compact," if not in history.

*1061 V

The Court makes sweeping and, in my view, misguided and unsupported changes in our takings doctrine. While it limits these changes to the most narrow subset of government regulation--those that eliminate all economic value from land--these changes go far beyond what is necessary to secure petitioner Lucas' private benefit. One hopes they do not go beyond the narrow confines the Court assigns them to today.

I dissent.

Justice STEVENS, dissenting.

Today the Court restricts one judge-made rule and expands another. In my opinion it errs on both counts. Proper application of the doctrine of judicial restraint would avoid the premature adjudication of an important constitutional question. Proper respect for our precedents would avoid an illogical expansion of the concept of "regulatory takings."

I

As the Court notes, ante, at 2890-2891, South Carolina's Beachfront Management Act has been amended to permit some construction of residences seaward of the line that frustrated petitioner's proposed use of his property. Until he exhausts his right to apply for a special permit under that amendment, petitioner is not entitled to an adjudication by this Court of the merits of his permanent takings claim. MacDonald, Sommer & Frates

112 S.Ct. 2886
(Cite as: 505 U.S. 1003, *1061, 112 S.Ct. 2886, **2917)

v. Yolo County, 477 U.S. 340, 351, 106 S.Ct. 2561, 2567, 91 L.Ed.2d 285 (1986).

It is also not clear that he has a viable "temporary takings" claim. If we assume that petitioner is now able to build on the lot, the only injury that he may have suffered is *1062 the delay caused by the temporary existence of the absolute statutory ban on construction. We cannot be sure, however, that that delay caused petitioner any harm because the record does not tell us whether his building plans were even temporarily frustrated by the enactment of the statute. [FN1] Thus, on the present record it is entirely possible that petitioner has suffered no injury **2918 in fact even if the state statute was unconstitutional when he filed this lawsuit.

> FN1. In this regard, it is noteworthy that petitioner acquired the lot about 18 months before the statute was passed; there is no evidence that he ever sought a building permit from the local authorities.

It is true, as the Court notes, that the argument against deciding the constitutional issue in this case rests on prudential considerations rather than a want of jurisdiction. I think it equally clear, however, that a Court less eager to decide the merits would follow the wise counsel of Justice Brandeis in his deservedly famous concurring opinion in Ashwander v. TVA, 297 U.S. 288, 341, 56 S.Ct. 466, 480, 80 L.Ed. 688 (1936). As he explained, the Court has developed "for its own governance in the cases confessedly within its jurisdiction, a series of rules under which it has avoided passing upon a large part of all the constitutional questions pressed upon it for decision." Id., at 346, 56 S.Ct., at 482. The second of those rules applies directly to this case.

"2. The Court will not 'anticipate a question of constitutional law in advance of the necessity of deciding it.' Liverpool, N.Y. & P.S.S. Co. v. Emigration Commissioners, 113 U.S. 33, 39 [5 S.Ct. 352, 355, 28 L.Ed. 899]; [citing five additional cases]. 'It is not the habit of the Court to decide questions of a constitutional nature unless absolutely necessary to a decision of the case.' Burton v. United States, 196 U.S. 283, 295 [25 S.Ct. 243, 245, 49 L.Ed. 482]." Id., at 346-347, 56 S.Ct., at 483.

Cavalierly dismissing the doctrine of judicial restraint, the Court today tersely announces that "we do not think it prudent to apply that prudential requirement here." Ante, at *1063 2892. I respectfully disagree and would save consideration of the merits for another day. Since, however, the Court has reached the merits, I shall do so as well.

II

In its analysis of the merits, the Court starts from the premise that this Court has adopted a "categorical rule that total regulatory takings must be compensated," ante, at 2899, and then sets itself to the task of identifying the exceptional cases in which a State may be relieved of this categorical obligation, ante, at 2899-2900. The test the Court announces is that the regulation must do no more than duplicate the result that could have been achieved under a State's nuisance law. Ante, at 2900. Under this test the categorical rule will apply unless the regulation merely makes explicit what was otherwise an implicit limitation on the owner's property rights.

In my opinion, the Court is doubly in error. The categorical rule the Court establishes is an unsound and unwise addition to the law and the Court's formulation of the exception to that rule is too rigid and too narrow.

The Categorical Rule

As the Court recognizes, ante, at 2892-2893, Pennsylvania Coal Co. v. Mahon, 260 U.S. 393, 43 S.Ct. 158, 67 L.Ed. 322 (1922), provides no support for its--or, indeed, any-- categorical rule. To the contrary, Justice Holmes recognized that such absolute rules ill fit the inquiry into "regulatory takings." Thus, in the paragraph that contains his famous observation that a regulation may go "too far" and thereby constitute a taking, the Justice wrote: "As we already have said, this is a question of degree--and therefore cannot be disposed of by general propositions." Id., at 416, 43 S.Ct., at 160. What he had "already ...

Copr. © West 1996 No claim to orig. U.S. govt. works

112 S.Ct. 2886
(Cite as: 505 U.S. 1003, *1063, 112 S.Ct. 2886, **2918)

said" made perfectly clear that Justice Holmes regarded economic injury to be merely one factor to be weighed: "One fact for consideration in determining such limits is the extent of the diminution *1064 [of value.] So the question depends upon the particular facts." Id., at 413, 43 S.Ct., at 159.

Nor does the Court's new categorical rule find support in decisions following Mahon. Although in dicta we have sometimes recited that a law "effects a taking if [it] ... denies an owner economically viable use of his land," Agins v. City of Tiburon, 447 U.S. 255, 260, 100 S.Ct. 2138, 2141, 65 L.Ed.2d 106 (1980), our rulings have rejected such an **2919 absolute position. We have frequently--and recently--held that, in some circumstances, a law that renders property valueless may nonetheless not constitute a taking. See, e.g., First English Evangelical Lutheran Church of Glendale v. County of Los Angeles, 482 U.S. 304, 313, 107 S.Ct. 2378, 2385, 96 L.Ed.2d 250 (1987); Goldblatt v. Hempstead, 369 U.S. 590, 596, 82 S.Ct. 987, 991, 8 L.Ed.2d 130 (1962); United States v. Caltex, 344 U.S. 149, 155, 73 S.Ct. 200, 203, 97 L.Ed. 157 (1952); Miller v. Schoene, 276 U.S. 272, 48 S.Ct. 246, 72 L.Ed. 568 (1928); Hadacheck v. Sebastian, 239 U.S. 394, 405, 36 S.Ct. 143, 143, 60 L.Ed. 348 (1915); Mugler v. Kansas, 123 U.S. 623, 657, 8 S.Ct. 273, 294, 31 L.Ed. 205 (1887); cf. Ruckelshaus v. Monsanto Co., 467 U.S. 986, 1011, 104 S.Ct. 2862, 2877, 81 L.Ed.2d 815 (1984); Connolly v. Pension Benefit Guaranty Corporation, 475 U.S. 211, 225, 106 S.Ct. 1018, 1026, 89 L.Ed.2d 166 (1986). In short, as we stated in Keystone Bituminous Coal Assn. v. DeBenedictis, 480 U.S. 470, 490, 107 S.Ct. 1232, 1244, 94 L.Ed.2d 472 (1987), " 'Although a comparison of values before and after' a regulatory action 'is relevant, ... it is by no means conclusive.' "

In addition to lacking support in past decisions, the Court's new rule is wholly arbitrary. A landowner whose property is diminished in value 95% recovers nothing, while an owner whose property is diminished 100% recovers the land's full value. The case at hand illustrates this arbitrariness well. The Beachfront Management Act not only prohibited the building of new dwellings in certain areas, it also prohibited the rebuilding of houses that were "destroyed beyond repair by natural causes or by fire." 1988 S.C. Acts 634, § 3; see also Esposito v. South Carolina Coastal Council, 939 F.2d 165, 167 (CA4 1991). [FN2] Thus, if the homes adjacent to Lucas' *1065 lot were destroyed by a hurricane one day after the Act took effect, the owners would not be able to rebuild, nor would they be assured recovery. Under the Court's categorical approach, Lucas (who has lost the opportunity to build) recovers, while his neighbors (who have lost both the opportunity to build and their homes) do not recover. The arbitrariness of such a rule is palpable.

FN2. This aspect of the Act was amended in 1990. See S.C. Code Ann. § 48-39-290(B) (Supp.1990).

Moreover, because of the elastic nature of property rights, the Court's new rule will also prove unsound in practice. In response to the rule, courts may define "property" broadly and only rarely find regulations to effect total takings. This is the approach the Court itself adopts in its revisionist reading of venerable precedents. We are told that--notwithstanding the Court's findings to the contrary in each case--the brewery in Mugler, the brickyard in Hadacheck, and the gravel pit in Goldblatt all could be put to "other uses" and that, therefore, those cases did not involve total regulatory takings. [FN3] Ante, at 2899, n. 13.

FN3. Of course, the same could easily be said in this case: Lucas may put his land to "other uses"-- fishing or camping, for example--or may sell his land to his neighbors as a buffer. In either event, his land is far from "valueless." This highlights a fundamental weakness in the Court's analysis: its failure to explain why only the impairment of "economically beneficial or productive use," ante, at 2893 (emphasis added), of property is relevant in takings analysis. I should think that a regulation arbitrarily prohibiting an owner from continuing to use her property for bird watching or sunbathing might constitute a taking under some circumstances; and, conversely, that such uses are of value to the owner. Yet the Court offers no basis for its assumption that the only uses of property

112 S.Ct. 2886
(Cite as: 505 U.S. 1003, *1065, 112 S.Ct. 2886, **2919)

cognizable under the Constitution are developmental uses.

On the other hand, developers and investors may market specialized estates to take advantage of the Court's new rule. The smaller the estate, the more likely that a regulatory change will effect a total taking. Thus, an investor may, for example, purchase the right to build a multifamily home on a specific lot, with the result that a zoning regulation that *1066 allows only single-**2920 family homes would render the investor's property interest "valueless." [FN4] In short, the categorical rule will likely have one of two effects: Either courts will alter the definition of the "denominator" in the takings "fraction," rendering the Court's categorical rule meaningless, or investors will manipulate the relevant property interests, giving the Court's rule sweeping effect. To my mind, neither of these results is desirable or appropriate, and both are distortions of our takings jurisprudence.

> FN4. This unfortunate possibility is created by the Court's subtle revision of the "total regulatory takings" dicta. In past decisions, we have stated that a regulation effects a taking if it "denies an owner economically viable use of his land," Agins v. City of Tiburon, 447 U.S. 255, 260, 100 S.Ct. 2138, 2141, 65 L.Ed.2d 106 (1980) (emphasis added), indicating that this "total takings" test did not apply to other estates. Today, however, the Court suggests that a regulation may effect a total taking of any real property interest. See ante, at 2894, n. 7.

Finally, the Court's justification for its new categorical rule is remarkably thin. The Court mentions in passing three arguments in support of its rule; none is convincing. First, the Court suggests that "total deprivation of feasible use is, from the landowner's point of view, the equivalent of a physical appropriation." Ante, at 2894. This argument proves too much. From the "landowner's point of view," a regulation that diminishes a lot's value by 50% is as well "the equivalent" of the condemnation of half of the lot. Yet, it is well established that a 50% diminution in value does not by itself constitute a taking. See Euclid v. Ambler Realty Co., 272 U.S. 365, 384, 47 S.Ct. 114, 117, 71 L.Ed. 303 (1926) (75% diminution in value). Thus, the landowner's perception of the regulation cannot justify the Court's new rule.

Second, the Court emphasizes that because total takings are "relatively rare" its new rule will not adversely affect the government's ability to "go on." Ante, at 2894. This argument proves too little. Certainly it is true that defining a small class of regulations that are per se takings will not *1067 greatly hinder important governmental functions--but this is true of any small class of regulations. The Court's suggestion only begs the question of why regulations of this particular class should always be found to effect takings.

Finally, the Court suggests that "regulations that leave the owner ... without economically beneficial ... use ... carry with them a heightened risk that private property is being pressed into some form of public service." Ibid. As discussed more fully below, see Part III, infra, I agree that the risks of such singling out are of central concern in takings law. However, such risks do not justify a per se rule for total regulatory takings. There is no necessary correlation between "singling out" and total takings: A regulation may single out a property owner without depriving him of all of his property, see, e.g., Nollan v. California Coastal Comm'n, 483 U.S. 825, 837, 107 S.Ct. 3141, 3149, 97 L.Ed.2d 677 (1987); J.E.D. Associates, Inc. v. Atkinson, 121 N.H. 581, 432 A.2d 12 (1981); and it may deprive him of all of his property without singling him out, see, e.g., Mugler v. Kansas, 123 U.S. 623, 8 S.Ct. 273, 31 L.Ed. 205 (1887); Hadacheck v. Sebastian, 239 U.S. 394, 36 S.Ct. 143, 60 L.Ed. 348 (1915). What matters in such cases is not the degree of diminution of value, but rather the specificity of the expropriating act. For this reason, the Court's third justification for its new rule also fails.

In short, the Court's new rule is unsupported by prior decisions, arbitrary and unsound in practice, and theoretically unjustified. In my opinion, a categorical rule as important as the one established by the Court today should be supported by more history or more reason than has yet been provided.

The Nuisance Exception

Like many bright-line rules, the categorical rule established in this case is only "categorical" for a page or two in the U.S. Reports. No sooner does the Court state that "total regulatory takings must be **2921 compensated," ante, at 2899, than it quickly establishes an exception to that rule.

*1068 The exception provides that a regulation that renders property valueless is not a taking if it prohibits uses of property that were not "previously permissible under relevant property and nuisance principles." Ante, at 2901. The Court thus rejects the basic holding in Mugler v. Kansas, 123 U.S. 623, 8 S.Ct. 273, 31 L.Ed. 205 (1887). There we held that a state-wide statute that prohibited the owner of a brewery from making alcoholic beverages did not effect a taking, even though the use of the property had been perfectly lawful and caused no public harm before the statute was enacted. We squarely rejected the rule the Court adopts today:

"It is true, that, when the defendants ... erected their breweries, the laws of the State did not forbid the manufacture of intoxicating liquors. But the State did not thereby give any assurance, or come under an obligation, that its legislation upon that subject would remain unchanged. [T]he supervision of the public health and the public morals is a governmental power, 'continuing in its nature,' and 'to be dealt with as the special exigencies of the moment may require;' ... 'for this purpose, the largest legislative discretion is allowed, and the discretion cannot be parted with any more than the power itself.' " Id., at 669, 8 S.Ct., at 301.

Under our reasoning in Mugler, a State's decision to prohibit or to regulate certain uses of property is not a compensable taking just because the particular uses were previously lawful. Under the Court's opinion today, however, if a State should decide to prohibit the manufacture of asbestos, cigarettes, or concealable firearms, for example, it must be prepared to pay for the adverse economic consequences of its decision. One must wonder if government will be able to "go on" effectively if it must risk compensation "for every such change in the general law." Mahon, 260 U.S., at 413, 43 S.Ct., at 159.

The Court's holding today effectively freezes the State's common law, denying the legislature much of its traditional *1069 power to revise the law governing the rights and uses of property. Until today, I had thought that we had long abandoned this approach to constitutional law. More than a century ago we recognized that "the great office of statutes is to remedy defects in the common law as they are developed, and to adapt it to the changes of time and circumstances." Munn v. Illinois, 94 U.S. 113, 134, 24 L.Ed. 77 (1877). As Justice Marshall observed about a position similar to that adopted by the Court today:

"If accepted, that claim would represent a return to the era of Lochner v. New York, 198 U.S. 45 [25 S.Ct. 539, 49 L.Ed. 937] (1905), when common-law rights were also found immune from revision by State or Federal Government. Such an approach would freeze the common law as it has been constructed by the courts, perhaps at its 19th-century state of development. It would allow no room for change in response to changes in circumstance. The Due Process Clause does not require such a result." PruneYard Shopping Center v. Robins, 447 U.S. 74, 93, 100 S.Ct. 2035, 2047, 64 L.Ed.2d 741 (1980) (concurring opinion).

Arresting the development of the common law is not only a departure from our prior decisions; it is also profoundly unwise. The human condition is one of constant learning and evolution--both moral and practical. Legislatures implement that new learning; in doing so they must often revise the definition of property and the rights of property owners. Thus, when the Nation came to understand that slavery was morally wrong and mandated the emancipation of all slaves, it, in effect,

112 S.Ct. 2886
(Cite as: 505 U.S. 1003, *1069, 112 S.Ct. 2886, **2921)

redefined "property." On a lesser scale, our ongoing self-education produces similar changes in the rights of property owners: New appreciation of the significance of endangered species, see, e.g., Andrus v. Allard, 444 U.S. 51, 100 S.Ct. 318, 62 L.Ed.2d 210 (1979); the importance of wetlands, see, e.g., 16 U.S.C. § 3801 et seq.; and **2922 the vulnerability of coastal *1070 lands, see, e.g., 16 U.S.C. § 1451 et seq., shapes our evolving understandings of property rights.

Of course, some legislative redefinitions of property will effect a taking and must be compensated--but it certainly cannot be the case that every movement away from common law does so. There is no reason, and less sense, in such an absolute rule. We live in a world in which changes in the economy and the environment occur with increasing frequency and importance. If it was wise a century ago to allow government " 'the largest legislative discretion' " to deal with " 'the special exigencies of the moment,' " Mugler, 123 U.S., at 669, 8 S.Ct. at 301, it is imperative to do so today. The rule that should govern a decision in a case of this kind should focus on the future, not the past. [FN5]

> FN5. Even measured in terms of efficiency, the Court's rule is unsound. The Court today effectively establishes a form of insurance against certain changes in land-use regulations. Like other forms of insurance, the Court's rule creates a "moral hazard" and inefficiencies: In the face of uncertainty about changes in the law, developers will overinvest, safe in the knowledge that if the law changes adversely, they will be entitled to compensation. See generally Farber, Economic Analysis and Just Compensation, 12 Int'l Rev. of Law & Econ. 125 (1992).

The Court's categorical approach rule will, I fear, greatly hamper the efforts of local officials and planners who must deal with increasingly complex problems in land-use and environmental regulation. As this case--in which the claims of an individual property owner exceed $1 million--well demonstrates, these officials face both substantial uncertainty because of the ad hoc nature of takings law and unacceptable penalties if they guess incorrectly about that law. [FN6]

> FN6. As the Court correctly notes, in regulatory takings, unlike physical takings, courts have a choice of remedies. See ante, at 2901, n. 17. They may "invalidat[e the] excessive regulation" or they may "allo[w] the regulation to stand and orde[r] the government to afford compensation for the permanent taking." First English Evangelical Lutheran Church of Glendale v. County of Los Angeles, 482 U.S. 304, 335, 107 S.Ct. 2378, 2396, 96 L.Ed.2d 250 (1987) (STEVENS, J., dissenting); see also id., at 319-321, 107 S.Ct., at 2388-2389. In either event, however, the costs to the government are likely to be substantial and are therefore likely to impede the development of sound land-use policy.

*1071 Viewed more broadly, the Court's new rule and exception conflict with the very character of our takings jurisprudence. We have frequently and consistently recognized that the definition of a taking cannot be reduced to a "set formula" and that determining whether a regulation is a taking is "essentially [an] ad hoc, factual inquir[y]." Penn Central Transportation Co. v. New York City, 438 U.S. 104, 124, 98 S.Ct. 2646, 2659, 57 L.Ed.2d 631 (1978) (quoting Goldblatt v. Hempstead, 369 U.S., at 594, 82 S.Ct., at 990. This is unavoidable, for the determination whether a law effects a taking is ultimately a matter of "fairness and justice," Armstrong v. United States, 364 U.S. 40, 49, 80 S.Ct. 1563, 1569, 4 L.Ed.2d 1554 (1960), and "necessarily requires a weighing of private and public interests," Agins, 447 U.S., at 261, 100 S.Ct., at 2141. The rigid rules fixed by the Court today clash with this enterprise: "fairness and justice" are often disserved by categorical rules.

III

It is well established that a takings case "entails inquiry into [several factors:] the character of the governmental action, its economic impact, and its interference with reasonable investment-backed expectations." PruneYard, 447 U.S., at 83, 100 S.Ct., at 2042. The Court's analysis today focuses on the last two of these three factors: The

112 S.Ct. 2886
(Cite as: 505 U.S. 1003, *1071, 112 S.Ct. 2886, **2922)

categorical rule addresses a regulation's "economic impact," while the nuisance exception recognizes that ownership brings with it only certain "expectations." Neglected by the Court today is the first and, in some ways, the most important factor in takings **2923 analysis: the character of the regulatory action.

The Just Compensation Clause "was designed to bar Government from forcing some people alone to bear public burdens which, in all fairness and justice, should be borne by the public as a whole." Armstrong, 364 U.S., at 49, 80 S.Ct., at 1569. Accordingly, one of the central concerns of our takings jurisprudence is "prevent[ing] the public from loading upon one individual more than his just share of the burdens of government." Monongahela Navigation Co. v. United *1072 States, 148 U.S. 312, 325, 13 S.Ct. 622, 626, 37 L.Ed. 463 (1893). We have, therefore, in our takings law frequently looked to the generality of a regulation of property. [FN7]

> FN7. This principle of generality is well rooted in our broader understandings of the Constitution as designed in part to control the "mischiefs of faction." See The Federalist No. 10, p. 43 (G. Wills ed. 1982) (J. Madison). An analogous concern arises in First Amendment law. There we have recognized that an individual's rights are not violated when his religious practices are prohibited under a neutral law of general applicability. For example, in Employment Div., Dept. of Human Resources of Oregon v. Smith, 494 U.S. 872, 879-880, 110 S.Ct. 1595, 1600, 108 L.Ed.2d 876 (1990), we observed: "[Our] decisions have consistently held that the right of free exercise does not relieve an individual of the obligation to comply with a 'valid and neutral law of general applicability on the ground that the law proscribes (or prescribes) conduct that his religion prescribes (or proscribes).' United States v. Lee, 455 U.S. 252, 263, n. 3, 102 S.Ct. 1051, 1054, n. 3, 71 L.Ed.2d 127 (1982) (STEVENS, J., concurring in judgment).... In Prince v. Massachusetts, 321 U.S. 158, 64 S.Ct. 438, 88 L.Ed. 645 (1944), we held that a mother could be prosecuted under the child labor laws for using her children to dispense literature in the streets, her religious motivation notwithstanding. We found no constitutional infirmity in 'excluding [these children] from doing there what no other children may do.' Id., at 171, 64 S.Ct., at 444. In Braunfeld v. Brown, 366 U.S. 599, 81 S.Ct. 1144, 6 L.Ed.2d 563 (1961) (plurality opinion), we upheld Sunday-closing laws against the claim that they burdened the religious practices of persons whose religions compelled them to refrain from work on other days. In Gillette v. United States, 401 U.S. 437, 461, 91 S.Ct. 828, 842, 28 L.Ed.2d 168 (1971), we sustained the military Selective Service System against the claim that it violated free exercise by conscripting persons who opposed a particular war on religious grounds." If such a neutral law of general applicability may severely burden constitutionally protected interests in liberty, a comparable burden on property owners should not be considered unreasonably onerous.

For example, in the case of so-called "developmental exactions," we have paid special attention to the risk that particular landowners might "b[e] singled out to bear the burden" of a broader problem not of his own making. Nollan, 483 U.S., at 835, n. 4, 107 S.Ct., at 3148, n. 4; see also Pennell v. San Jose, 485 U.S. 1, 23, 108 S.Ct. 849, 863, 99 L.Ed.2d 1 (1988). Similarly, in distinguishing between the Kohler Act (at issue in Mahon) and the Subsidence Act (at issue in Keystone), we found significant that the regulatory function of the latter was substantially broader. Unlike the Kohler *1073 Act, which simply transferred back to the surface owners certain rights that they had earlier sold to the coal companies, the Subsidence Act affected all surface owners--including the coal companies--equally. See Keystone, 480 U.S., at 486, 107 S.Ct., at 1242. Perhaps the most familiar application of this principle of generality arises in zoning cases. A diminution in value caused by a zoning regulation is far less likely to constitute a taking if it is part of a general and comprehensive land-use plan, see Euclid v. Ambler Realty Co., 272 U.S. 365, 47 S.Ct. 114, 71 L.Ed. 303 (1926); conversely, "spot zoning" is far more likely to constitute a taking, see Penn Central, 438 U.S., at 132, and n. 28, 98 S.Ct., at 2663, and n. 28.

The presumption that a permanent physical occupation, no matter how slight, effects a taking is wholly consistent with this principle. A physical taking entails a certain amount of "singling out." [FN8] Consistent with this principle, physical occupations by third parties are more likely to effect takings than other physical occupations. Thus, a regulation **2924 requiring the installation of a junction box owned by a third party, Loretto v. Teleprompter Manhattan CATV Corp., 458 U.S. 419, 102 S.Ct. 3164, 73 L.Ed.2d 868 (1982), is more troubling than a regulation requiring the installation of sprinklers or smoke detectors; just as an order granting third parties access to a marina, Kaiser Aetna v. United States, 444 U.S. 164, 100 S.Ct. 383, 62 L.Ed.2d 332 (1979), is more troubling than an order requiring the placement of safety buoys in the marina.

FN8. See Levmore, Takings, Torts, and Special Interests, 77 Va.L.Rev. 1333, 1352-1354 (1991).

In analyzing takings claims, courts have long recognized the difference between a regulation that targets one or two parcels of land and a regulation that enforces a statewide policy. See, e.g., A.A. Profiles, Inc. v. Ft. Lauderdale, 850 F.2d 1483, 1488 (CA11 1988); Wheeler v. Pleasant Grove, 664 F.2d 99, 100 (CA5 1981); Trustees Under Will of Pomeroy v. Westlake, 357 So.2d 1299, 1304 (La.App.1978); see also Burrows v. Keene, 121 N.H. 590, 596, 432 A.2d 15, 21 (1981); Herman Glick Realty Co. v. St. Louis County, 545 S.W.2d 320, 324-325 (Mo.App.1976); Huttig v. Richmond Heights, *1074 372 S.W.2d 833, 842-843 (Mo.1963). As one early court stated with regard to a waterfront regulation, "If such restraint were in fact imposed upon the estate of one proprietor only, out of several estates on the same line of shore, the objection would be much more formidable." Commonwealth v. Alger, 61 Mass. 53, 102 (1851).

In considering Lucas' claim, the generality of the Beachfront Management Act is significant. The Act does not target particular landowners, but rather regulates the use of the coastline of the entire State. See S.C. Code Ann. § 48-39-10 (Supp.1990). Indeed, South Carolina's Act is best understood as part of a national effort to protect the coastline, one initiated by the federal Coastal Zone Management Act of 1972. Pub.L. 92-583, 86 Stat. 1280, codified as amended at 16 U.S.C. § 1451 et seq. Pursuant to the federal Act, every coastal State has implemented coastline regulations. [FN9] Moreover, the Act did not single out owners of undeveloped land. The Act also prohibited owners of developed land from rebuilding if their structures were destroyed, see 1988 S.C. Acts 634, § 3, [FN10] and what is equally significant, from repairing erosion control devices, such as seawalls, see S.C. Code Ann. § 48-39-290(B)(2) (Supp.1990). In addition, in some situations, owners of developed land were required to "renouris[h] the beach ... on a yearly basis with an amount ... of sand ... not ... less than one and one-half times the yearly volume of sand lost due to erosion." 1988 S.C. Acts 634, § 3, p. 5140. [FN11] In short, the South Carolina Act imposed substantial burdens on owners of developed and undeveloped *1075 land alike. [FN12] This generality indicates that the Act is not an effort to expropriate owners of undeveloped land.

FN9. See Zalkin, Shifting Sands and Shifting Doctrines: The Supreme Court's Changing Takings Doctrine and South Carolina's Coastal Zone Statute, 79 Calif.L.Rev. 205, 216-217, nn. 46-47 (1991) (collecting statutes).

FN10. This provision was amended in 1990. See S.C. Code Ann. § 48-39-290(B) (Supp.1990).

FN11. This provision was amended in 1990; authority for renourishment was shifted to local governments. See S.C. Code Ann. § 48-39-350(A) (Supp.1990).

FN12. In this regard, the Act more closely resembles the Subsidence Act in Keystone than the Kohler Act in Pennsylvania Coal Co. v. Mahon, 260 U.S. 393, 43 S.Ct. 158, 67 L.Ed. 322 (1922), and more closely resembles the general zoning scheme in Euclid v. Ambler Realty Co., 272 U.S. 365, 47 S.Ct. 114, 71 L.Ed. 303 (1926), than the specific landmark designation in Penn Central Transportation Co. v. New York City, 438 U.S. 104, 98 S.Ct. 2646, 57 L.Ed.2d 631 (1978).

112 S.Ct. 2886
(Cite as: 505 U.S. 1003, *1075, 112 S.Ct. 2886, **2924)

Admittedly, the economic impact of this regulation is dramatic and petitioner's investment-backed expectations are substantial. Yet, if anything, the costs to and expectations of the owners of developed land are even greater: I doubt, however, that the cost to owners of developed land of renourishing the beach and allowing their seawalls to deteriorate effects a taking. The costs imposed on **2925 the owners of undeveloped land, such as petitioner, differ from these costs only in degree, not in kind.

The impact of the ban on developmental uses must also be viewed in light of the purposes of the Act. The legislature stated the purposes of the Act as "protect[ing], preserv[ing], restor[ing] and enhanc[ing] the beach/dune system" of the State not only for recreational and ecological purposes, but also to "protec[t] life and property." S.C. Code Ann. § 48-39-260(1)(a) (Supp.1990). The State, with much science on its side, believes that the "beach/dune system [acts] as a buffer from high tides, storm surge, [and] hurricanes." Ibid. This is a traditional and important exercise of the State's police power, as demonstrated by Hurricane Hugo, which in 1989, caused 29 deaths and more than $6 billion in property damage in South Carolina alone. [FN13]

FN13. Zalkin, 79 Calif.L.Rev., at 212-213.

In view of all of these factors, even assuming that petitioner's property was rendered valueless, the risk inherent in investments of the sort made by petitioner, the generality of the Act, and the compelling purpose motivating the South *1076 Carolina Legislature persuade me that the Act did not effect a taking of petitioner's property.

Accordingly, I respectfully dissent.

Statement of Justice SOUTER.
I would dismiss the writ of certiorari in this case as having been granted improvidently. After briefing and argument it is abundantly clear that an unreviewable assumption on which this case comes to us is both questionable as a conclusion of Fifth Amendment law and sufficient to frustrate the Court's ability to render certain the legal premises on which its holding rests.

The petition for review was granted on the assumption that the State by regulation had deprived the owner of his entire economic interest in the subject property. Such was the state trial court's conclusion, which the State Supreme Court did not review. It is apparent now that in light of our prior cases, see, e.g., Keystone Bituminous Coal Assn. v. DeBenedictis, 480 U.S. 470, 493-502, 107 S.Ct. 1232, 1246-1251, 94 L.Ed.2d 472 (1987); Andrus v. Allard, 444 U.S. 51, 65-66, 100 S.Ct. 318, 326-327, 62 L.Ed.2d 210 (1979); Penn Central Transportation Corp. v. New York City, 438 U.S. 104, 130-131, 98 S.Ct. 2646, 2662, 57 L.Ed.2d 631 (1978), the trial court's conclusion is highly questionable. While the respondent now wishes to contest the point, see Brief for Respondent 45-50, the Court is certainly right to refuse to take up the issue, which is not fairly included within the question presented, and has received only the most superficial and one-sided treatment before us.

Because the questionable conclusion of total deprivation cannot be reviewed, the Court is precluded from attempting to clarify the concept of total (and, in the Court's view, categorically compensable) taking on which it rests, a concept which the Court describes, see ante, at 2893, n. 6, as so uncertain under existing law as to have fostered inconsistent pronouncements by the Court itself. Because that concept is left uncertain, so is the significance of the exceptions to the compensation requirement that the Court proceeds to recognize. *1077 This alone is enough to show that there is little utility in attempting to deal with this case on the merits.

The imprudence of proceeding to the merits in spite of these unpromising circumstances is underscored by the fact that, in doing so, the Court cannot help but assume something about the scope of the uncertain concept of total deprivation, even when it is barred from explicating total deprivation directly. Thus,

Copr. © West 1996 No claim to orig. U.S. govt. works

112 S.Ct. 2886
(Cite as: 505 U.S. 1003, *1077, 112 S.Ct. 2886, **2925)

when the Court concludes that the application of nuisance law provides an exception to the general rule that complete denial of economically beneficial use of property amounts to a compensable taking, the Court will be understood to suggest (if it does not assume) that there are in fact circumstances **2926 in which state-law nuisance abatement may amount to a denial of all beneficial land use as that concept is to be employed in our takings jurisprudence under the Fifth and Fourteenth Amendments. The nature of nuisance law, however, indicates that application of a regulation defensible on grounds of nuisance prevention or abatement will quite probably not amount to a complete deprivation in fact. The nuisance enquiry focuses on conduct, not on the character of the property on which that conduct is performed, see 4 Restatement (Second) of Torts § 821B (1979) (public nuisance); id., § 822 (private nuisance), and the remedies for such conduct usually leave the property owner with other reasonable uses of his property, see W. Keeton, D. Dobbs, R. Keeton, & D. Owen, Prosser and Keeton on Law of Torts § 90 (5th ed. 1984) (public nuisances usually remedied by criminal prosecution or abatement), id., § 89 (private nuisances usually remedied by damages, injunction, or abatement); see also, e.g., Mugler v. Kansas, 123 U.S. 623, 668-669, 8 S.Ct. 273, 301, 31 L.Ed. 205 (1887) (prohibition on use of property to manufacture intoxicating beverages "does not disturb the owner in the control or use of his property for lawful purposes, nor restrict his right to dispose of it, but is only a declaration by the State that its use ... for certain forbidden purposes, is prejudicial to the public interests"); Hadacheck v. Sebastian, *1078 239 U.S. 394, 412, 36 S.Ct. 143, 146, 60 L.Ed. 348 (1915) (prohibition on operation of brickyard did not prohibit extraction of clay from which bricks were produced). Indeed, it is difficult to imagine property that can be used only to create a nuisance, such that its sole economic value must presuppose the right to occupy it for such seriously noxious activity.

The upshot is that the issue of what constitutes a total deprivation is being addressed by indirection, and with uncertain results, in the Court's treatment of defenses to compensation claims. While the issue of what constitutes total deprivation deserves the Court's attention, as does the relationship between nuisance abatement and such total deprivation, the Court should confront these matters directly. Because it can neither do so in this case, nor skip over those preliminary issues and deal independently with defenses to the Court's categorical compensation rule, the Court should dismiss the instant writ and await an opportunity to face the total deprivation question squarely. Under these circumstances, I believe it proper for me to vote to dismiss the writ, despite the Court's contrary preference. See, e.g., Welsh v. Wisconsin, 466 U.S. 740, 755, 104 S.Ct. 2091, 2100, 80 L.Ed.2d 732 (1984) (Burger, C.J.); United States v. Shannon, 342 U.S. 288, 294, 72 S.Ct. 281, 285, 96 L.Ed. 321 (1952) (Frankfurter, J.).

Index

A

Administrative Procedure Act (APA), 126-128, 157
American Farm Bureau Federation, 52-53
Anderson & Middleton Logging Co., 88
APA, 126-128, 157
Asset forfeiture, 137-139
  civil, 138
  criminal, 138-139

B

Baucus, Max, 49
Bill of Rights, 1-2, 168, 176
  property rights and, 2
Billboards, 18-19
Birds
  Florida scrub jay, 81-83
  golden-cheeked warbler, 83-84
Blackmun, Harry, 15
Brennan, William, 23, 26, 28, 33, 152, 164, 172
Britton, Ray, 67
Bunton Lucius, 86-87

C

CERCLA, 94-99, 105
Chinook salmon, 87
Civil asset forfeiture, 138
Clean Air Act, 103-104, 107

Clean Water Act, 43, 44, 48, 50, 55, 63, 104, 159, 170
  Section 309, 53-54
  Section 404, 46, 49-50, 51, 56, 58
  Section 505, 54
Clinton, Bill, 175
Coastal Zone Management Act of 1972 (CZMA), 106
Comal Springs salamander, 86
Commerce Clause, 47
Communism, 3
Communist Manifesto, 3
Comprehensive Environmental Response, Compensation, and Liability Act of 1980 (CERCLA), 94, 95, 96, 105
  court cases, 96-99
  property rights and, 94-99
  regulatory scheme, 94-95
  Section 104, 95
  Section 107, 95
Condemnation blight, 120-122
Conservation Reserve Program, 55
Constitution
  Contracts Clause, 2
  Fifth Amendment, 2, 12, 60-61, 114, 121, 147, 152, 160, 163, 168
  Due Process Clause, 2, 125-133
  Just Compensation Clause, 4, 13, 14, 24, 37, 55, 121, 128, 147, 148, 153
  potential violations of, 24-28, 24

315

316 / Property Rights

Constitution (*continued*)
  First Amendment, 57
  founding fathers of, 1
  Fourteenth Amendment, 2, 57
    Due Process Clause, 128
  Fourth Amendment, 2, 57, 129, 135-136
  property rights, 1-9
  Tenth Amendment, 88-89
Contracts, 14 (*see also* Property)
Court cases (*see also* Litigation)
  Abbott Labs v. Gardner, 150-151
  Agins v. City of Tiburon, 24, 40, 113-114
  Allied-General Nuclear Services v. United States, 17-18
  Aptos Seascape Corporation v. County of Santa Cruz, 122-123
  Armstrong v. United States, 34
  Babbitt v. Sweet Home Chapter of Communities for a Great Oregon, 79-80, 89
  Bennis v. Michigan, 138
  Bowles v. Willingham, 38
  Cafeteria Workers v. McElroy, 139
  Ciampetti v. United States, 69
  Cohen v. California, 68
  Concrete Pipe of Calif. v. Laborers Pension Trust, 15
  Connolly v. PBGC Corp., 15
  Corrosion Proof Fittings v. EPA, 127
  Cox v. Louisiana, 67
  Dames & Moore v. Regan, 16
  Del Monte Dunes v. City of Monterey, 133-134
  Dodd v. Hood River County, 147, 161
  Dolan v. City of Tigard, 116, 117, 119, 121
  Dow v. United States, 6
  Dow Chemical Co. v. United States, 136
  Ehrlich v. City of Culver City et. al., 116-117
  First English Evangelical Lutheran Church v. County of Los Angeles, California, 37, 118, 153, 168, 169
  First Victoria National Bank v. United States, 139
  Florida Rock Industries Inc. v. United States, 36, 58-59, 60, 143, 159
  Frank v. Maryland, 135
  Fry v. City of Hayward, 134
  General Offshore Corp. v. Farrelly, 14
  Goldblatt v. Hempstead, 111-112
  Gwaltney of Smithfield Ltd. v. Chesapeake Bay Foundation Inc., 54
  Heart of Atlanta Motel Inc. v. United States, 68
  Henderson v. United States, 68
  Hendler v. United States, 96-98, 144
  Herrington v. County of Sonoma, 134
  Hodel v. Irving, 24, 32, 33, 166
  Hoffman Homes Inc. v. EPA, 46, 47
  Jacobs v. United States, 152-153
  Joint Anti-Fascist Refugee Committee v. McGrath, 150
  Juda v. United States, 16
  Keystone Bituminous Coal Association v. DeBenedictis, 102, 112, 149

Court cases (*continued*)
 Knight v. City of Missoula, 122
 Loretto v. TelePrompter Manhattan CATV Corp., 6-7
 Loveladies Harbor, Inc. v. United States, 29, 40, 60-61, 69, 144, 159-160
 Lucas v. South Carolina Coastal Council, 13, 24, 27, 37, 114, 149, 151, 159
 Mathews v. Eldridge, 126, 130
 MCI Telecommunications Corp. v. FCC, 130, 131
 Miller v. Schoene, 40
 Mugler v. Kansas, 37, 111, 112
 Natural Resources Defense Council Inc. v. Callaway, 66
 New York Times Co. v. Sullivan, 120-121
 Nixon v. United States, 128
 Nollan v. California Coastal Commission, 24, 25, 26, 28, 115, 117, 129, 134, 166, 167, 168, 169
 Oberndorf v. City of Denver, 146
 Penn Central Transp. Co. v. New York City, 24, 28, 29, 30, 32, 33-34, 122
 Pennsylvania Coal Co. v. Mahon, 23, 28, 30, 102
 Pension Benefit Guaranty Corp. v. R.A. Gray, 16
 PFZ v. Rodriguez, 132
 Reahard v. Lee County, 145
 Richardson v. City and County of Honolulu, 26
 Ruckelshaus v. Monsanto Co., 11, 13, 30, 39
 San Diego Gas & Electric Co. v. City of San Diego, 23, 152
 Seawall Associates v. City of New York, 26
 Shell Oil Co. v. EPA, 127
 Simaloa Lake Owners Association v. City of Simi Valley, 133, 146
 Smith v. Illinois Bell Telephone Co., 130, 131
 Soldal v. Cook County, Illinois, 128-129
 Stanley v. Georgia, 135, 140
 State v. Hillman, 120
 Tabb Lakes Ltd. v. United States, 66
 Triumph, Idaho property taking, 98-99
 TVA v. Hill, 72, 80
 United Artists Theater Circuit Inc. v. City of Philadelphia, 117
 United Nuclear Corp. v. United States, 31, 33
 United States v. Billie, 77
 United States v. James J. Wilson, 65
 United States v. Ocie Mills and Carey C. Mills, 63-64
 United States v. Paul Tudor Jones, II and William B. Ellen, 61-63
 United States v. Riverside Bayview Homes Inc., 66
 United States v. St. Onge, 77
 Washington Market Enterprises v. City of Trenton, 121
 Webb's Fabulous Pharmacies Inc. v. Beckwith, 14
 White v. Mathews, 140
 Whitney Benefits Inc. v. United States, 29-30, 102, 144

318 / Property Rights

Court cases (*continued*)
  Williamson County Regional Planning Commission v. Hamilton Bank, 145-146, 147, 151
  Yancey v. United States, 17, 33-34
  Yuba Natural Resources Inc. v. United States, 37-38
Criminal asset forfeiture, 138-139
Critical habitat, definition, 90-91
CZMA, 106

D

Delta smelt, 87
Department of Environmental Resources, 51, 52
Department of Housing and Urban Development (HUD), 65
Downzoning, 112-113
Due process, 125-133
  as applied to property rights, 128-130
  property rights and substantive, 132-133
  statutory, 126-128
  unreasonable delay and, 130-132

E

Earth Day, 102
Edwards Aquifer, 86-87
Endangered species
  Chinook salmon, 87
  Comal Springs salamander, 86
  definition, 90
  delta smelt, 87
  Florida scrub jay, 81-83
  golden-cheeked warbler, 83-84
  ranching and farming and, 84-85
  San Marcos fountain darter, 86
  San Marcos salamander, 86
  timber harvesting and, 88
  Tipton kangaroo rat, 84
Endangered Species Act of 1973 (ESA), 71-91, 106, 170, 171
  civil and criminal enforcement provisions, 76-77
  conservation plan, 74, 75-76
  court cases, 79-81
  criminal prosecution statistics, 78
  definition of "harm", 73, 81
  incidental take permits, 75-76
  jeopardy opinions, 76
  overview, 71
  prohibitions on Federal agencies, 73-74
  regulatory scheme, 72-76
  Section 4(d), 90
  Section 4(f), 74
  Section 5, 74
  Section 7, 75, 82
  Section 7(a)(1), 74
  Section 7(a)(2), 73, 76
  Section 9, 72, 88
  Section 9(a)(1), 71
  Section 9(a)(1)(B), 71, 75
  Section 10(a), 82
  Section 10(a)(2)(A), 75
  Section 11, 77
  state land use regulation and development, 88-90
  "take" prohibition, 72-73
  timber harvesting and, 88
  water rights and, 85-87
Endangered species habitat
  case studies on habitat modification, 81-84
  "critical habitat" definition, 90-91
  property rights and, 78-88

Environmental Protection Agency (EPA), 30, 47, 48, 53, 96, 98, 129
Environmental regulations, 93-108
  costs to Americans, 93
  legislation (*see* Legislation)
  mining, 99-102
  overview, 93
  search and seizure and, 137
  statutes
    Federal, 102-106
    State, 106-108
  Superfund and property rights, 94-99
EPA, 30, 47, 48, 53, 96, 98, 129
Equal protection, property rights and, 133-135
ESA (*see* Endangered Species Act of 1973)
Exactions, 115-117
Executive Order (*see* Federal Executive Order 12630)

F

FCC, 130
Federal Communications Commission (FCC), 130
Federal Executive Order 12630, 166-170, 171
  framework of, 168-170
  origin, 167-168
Federal Insecticide, Fungicide, and Rodenticide Act (FIFRA), 30-31, 106, 129
Federal Land Policy and Management Act, 171
Federal Water Pollution Control Act of 1972, 43

FIFRA, 30-31, 106, 129
Fish
  Chinook salmon, 87
  definition, 90
  delta smelt, 87
Flood plain zoning, 118-120
  property rights and, 119-120
  regulatory scheme, 118-119
Florida scrub jay, 81-83
Food Security Act, 48, 171

G

Golden-cheeked warbler, 83-84
Government, property rights and (*see* Property rights)
Growth Management Act of 1991, 172

H

Harris, Terry J., 174
Hatch, Orrin, 170
Hazardous Substances Response Trust Fund (*see* Superfund)
Historic preservation zoning, 117-118
Holmes, Oliver Wendell, 7, 23, 139
HUD, 65

I

Indian Land Consolidation Act, 32
Industries, heavily regulated, 17-18
Intellectual property, trade secrets and, 13-14 (*see also* Property)
Interstate General Company (IGC), 65

J

Jay, Florida scrub, 81-83
Jefferson, Thomas, 1
Justinian Code, 1

L

Land (*see also* Property)
Lazarus, Richard, 13
Legislation
   Administrative Procedure Act (APA), 126-128, 157
   Clean Air Act, 103-104, 107
   Clean Water Act, 43, 44, 48, 50, 55, 63, 104, 159, 170
     Section 309, 53-54
     Section 404, 46, 49-50, 51, 56, 58
     Section 505, 54
   Coastal Zone Management Act of 1972 (CZMA), 106
   Comprehensive Environmental Response, Compensation, and Liability Act (CERCLA), 94, 105
     court cases, 96-99
     property rights and, 94-99
     regulatory scheme, 94-95
     Section 104, 95
     Section 107, 95
   congressional, 170-171
   Endangered Species Act of 1973 (ESA), 71-91, 106, 170, 171
     civil and criminal enforcement provisions, 76-77
     conservation plan, 74, 75-76
     court cases, 79-81
     criminal prosecution statistics, 78
     definition of "harm", 73, 81
     incidental take permits, 75-76
     jeopardy opinions, 76
     overview, 71
     prohibitions on Federal agencies, 73-74
     regulatory scheme, 72-76
     Section 4(d), 90
     Section 4(f), 74
     Section 5, 74
     Section 7, 75, 82
     Section 7(a)(1), 74
     Section 7(a)(2), 73, 76
     Section 9, 72, 88
     Section 9(a)(1), 71
     Section 9(a)(1)(B), 71, 75
     Section 10(a), 82
     Section 10(a)(2)(A), 75
     Section 11, 77
     state land use regulation and development, 88-90
     "take" prohibition, 72-73
     timber harvesting and, 88
     water rights and, 85-87
   Federal Insecticide, Fungicide, and Rodenticide Act (FIFRA), 30-31, 106, 129
   Federal Land Policy and Management Act, 171
   Federal Water Pollution Control Act of 1972, 43
   Food Security Act, 48, 171
   Growth Management Act of 1991, 172
   Indian Land Consolidation Act, 32

Legislation *(continued)*
  Marine Protection Resources and Sanctuaries Act (MPRSA), 106
  Multiemployer Pension Plan Amendments Act of 1980 (MPPAA), 15
  National Environmental Policy Act (NEPA), 103
  Oil Pollution Act of 1990, 105
  Omnibus Property Rights Act, 170, 177
  Private Property Protection Act of 1995, 171
  property rights, 163-177
    advantages/disadvantages, 174-176
    compensation bills, 175-176
    planning bills, 174-175
    State, 171-174
  Racketeer Influenced and Corrupt Act of 1970 (RICO), 138
  Resource Conservation and Recovery Act (RCRA), 104-105, 127
  Rivers and Harbors Act of 1899, 54
  Safe Drinking Water Act (SDWA), 106
  South Carolina Beachfront Management Act, 114
  Superfund Amendment and Reauthorization Act (SARA), 105
  Surface Mining Control and Reclamation Act of 1977 (SMCRA), 29, 99-102, 105-106
    Section 501, 99-100
    Section 501(a), 100
    Section 501(b), 101
    Section 502(c), 100
    Section 503, 101
  Toxic Substances Control Act (TSCA), 106, 127
  Tucker Act, 39, 148
  Virgin Islands Wrongful Discharge Act, 14
Litigation, 143-155 *(see also* Court cases)
  choosing a claim, 149-150
  choosing the right court, 145-148
  choosing the right Federal court, 148-149
  District Court vs. Court of Federal Claims, 148-149
  exhausting administrative remedies, 151
  res judicata doctrine, 160-161
  ripening the claim, 150-151
  State courts vs. Federal courts, 145-148
  statute of limitations, 151-154
Long Beach Equities Inc., 113
Lott, Trent, 177

M

Madison, James, 1, 11
Magna Carta, 1
Mansfield, Marla E., 150
Marine Protection Resources and Sanctuaries Act (MPRSA), 106
Marx, Karl, 3
Mining, 99-102
Money, 14-15 *(see also* Property)
MPPAA, 15
MPRSA, 106
Muir, John, 102

Multiemployer Pension Plan Amendments Act of 1980 (MPPAA), 15
Myerhoff, Albert H., 174

N

National Academy of Sciences, 49
National Environmental Policy Act (NEPA), 103
National Flood Insurance Program (NFIP), 118
National Historic Trust, 117
National Marine Fisheries Service, 47
National Pollution Discharge Elimination System (NPDES), 104
National Wildlife Federation (NWF), 174
Natural Resources Defense Council, 174
NEPA, 103
NFIP, 118
Nixon, Richard, 12, 128
NPDES, 104
Nuisance exception, 34-37
NWF, 174

O

Oil Pollution Act of 1990, 105
Omnibus Property Rights Act, 170, 177
Open space zoning, 113-114

P

Pension plans, 15-16 (*see also* Property)

Pinchot, Gifford, 102
Pollutants, permits for discharging, 55
Pollution (*see also* Clean Air Act; Clean Water Act)
water, 43, 55-56
Powell, Lewis, 136
Private Property Protection Act of 1995, 171
Property, 11-21
billboards, 18-19
business interests in, 17
contracts, 14
definition, 2, 12
definition by James Madison, 11
endangered species on (*see* Endangered Species Act of 1973)
environmental regulations, 93-108
governmental causes of action against, 16-17
governmental takings of, 23-41 (*see also* Takings)
character of the government's action, 32-33
definition, 23
deprivation of beneficial/productive use of property, 27
destruction of power to exclude others, 27-28
economic impact considerations, 28-30
fact-based inquiries, 28-34
interference with investment-backed expectations, 30-32
litigating, 143-155
no substantial advancement of a state in, 25-26
nuisance exception, 34-37
potential violations, 24-28

Property (*continued*)
   temporary takings, 37-38
   wetlands, 58-61
   heavily regulated industries and, 17-18
   intellectual, trade secrets and, 13-14
   land, 13
   land use restrictions, 111-123
   mining, 99-102
   money, 14-15
   new forms of, 19
   pension plans, 15-16
   physical invasions or occupations of, 6-7
   public usage of, 4
   regulatory takings, 7-8
   search and seizure of, 135-137
   taking (*see* Takings)
   temporary occupancy of, 6
   value determination, 5
   water rights, 18
   wetlands (*see* Wetlands)
   zoning regulations, 111-123
Property rights
   asset forfeiture and, 137-139
   condemnation blight, 120-122
   developing issues regarding what is a taking, 157-161
   due process and, 128-130
   eminent domain, 3-5
   endangered species habitat and, 78-88
   equal protection and, 133-135
   exactions, 115-117
   Federal Executive Order 12630 to protect, 166-170
   flood plain zoning and, 119-120
   freedom from unreasonable search and seizure, 135-137
   legislation benefits, 163-177
   origins of Constitutionally protected, 1-9
   physical infringements on, 7
   private, 2
   government involvement in, 3-5
   substantive due process and, 132-133
   Superfund and, 94-99
   Transferable Development Rights (TDRs), 122-123
   wetlands and, 54-65

R

Racketeer Influenced and Corrupt Act of 1970 (RICO), 138
Rat, Tipton kangaroo, 84
RCRA, 104, 127
Reagan, Ronald, 166, 167
Res judicata doctrine, 160-161
Resource Conservation and Recovery Act (RCRA), 104-105, 127
RICO, 138
Rivers and Harbors Act of 1899, 54
Roosevelt, Theodore, 102

S

Safe Drinking Water Act (SDWA), 106
Salamanders
   Comal Springs, 86
   San Marcos, 86
Salmon, Chinook, 87
San Marcos fountain darter, 86
San Marcos salamander, 86
SARA, 105
Scalia, Antonin, 25, 112

Schmidt, John R., 165
SDWA, 106
Search and seizure, 135-137
   environmental regulations and, 137
   freedom from unreasonable, 135-137
   unreasonable searches, 136
   unreasonable seizures, 136-137
Secretary of the Interior, 71
SMCRA, 29, 99-102
Smith, Loren, 165
Soil Conservation Service, 47
South Carolina Beachfront Management Act, 114
St. Charles Associates, 65
Statute of limitations, 151-154
Stevens, John Paul, 112
Substantive due process, 132-133
Superfund
   court cases, 96-99
   property rights and, 94-99
   regulatory scheme, 94-95
Superfund Amendment and Reauthorization Act (SARA), 105
Surface Mining Control and Reclamation Act of 1977 (SMCRA), 29, 99-102, 105-106
   Section 501, 99-100
   Section 501(a), 100
   Section 501(b), 101
   Section 502(c), 100
   Section 503, 101

T

Takings
   developing issues regarding what is a taking, 157-161
   governmental, 23-41
      character of the government's action, 32
      definition, 23
      deprivation of beneficial/productive use, 27
      destruction of power to exclude others, 27
      economic impact considerations, 28-30
      fact-based inquiries, 28-34
      interference with investment-backed experience, 30
      litigating, 143-155
      no substantial advancement of a state in, 25
      nuisance exception, 34-37
      potential violations, 24-28
      temporary takings, 37-38
      wetlands, 58-61
   partial, 158-160
      diminution in value, 158-159
      relevant parcel, 159-160
   prohibition, 72-73
   regulatory, 7-8
   res judicata doctrine, 160-161
   temporary, 37-38
   unreasonable delay as a taking, 157-158
Takings Impact Analysis (TIA), 169
TIA, 169
Timber harvesting, endangered species and, 88
Tipton kangaroo rat, 84
Toxic Substances Control Act (TSCA), 106, 127
Trade secrets, intellectual property and, 13-14
Transferable Development Rights (TDRs), 122-123

TSCA, 106, 127
Tuang, Ming-Lin, 84
Tucker Act, 39, 148
Two Treatises of John Locke, 1
Tyler, Ralph S., 172

U

United States Constitution (*see* Constitution)
United States Fish and Wildlife Service, 47, 48, 50-51, 72, 73-74, 78, 82, 83

V

Virgin Islands Wrongful Discharge Act, 14

W

Warbler, golden-cheeked, 83-84
Water pollution, 43 (*see also* Clean Water Act)
   regulating, 55-56
Water rights, 18, 85-87
   Edwards Aquifer and, 86-87
   Kern County California, 87
Waters regulations governing, 45
Webster, Noah, 3
Wetlands, 29, 43-69
   case study—wetland definition and agency contradiction, 50-53
   criminal prosecutions, 61-65
   definition, 47-48
   enforcement provisions, 53-54
   importance of, 43
   isolated, 46-47
   manuals, 49-50
   property rights and, 54-65
   property rights defense of, 56-57
   protection of, 43
   regulatory scheme, 44-53
   takings of, 58-61
Wetlands Reserve Program, 55
Wilderness Society, 174
Wildlife, definition, 90

Z

Zoning regulations, 111-123
   alcoholic beverage production, 111
   downzoning, 112-113
   early, 111
   exactions, 115-117
   flood plain, 118-120
   historic preservation, 117-118
   open space zoning, 113-114
   when do they go too far?, 112-114

More Environmental Books from Government Institutes

Wetland Mitigation: Mitigation Banking and Other Strategies for Development and Compliance

Regulations require that development projects in wetland areas restore or replace lost wetland functions and values. This new book provides the most comprehensive, in-depth treatment of wetland mitigation options available! A practical reference, this book outlines the various regulations involved in wetland development, mitigation requirements, and the permitting process.
Hardcover, Index, 272 pages, Jan '97, ISBN: 0-86587-534-0 **$75**

Environmental Law Handbook, 14th Edition

The authoritative reference on environmental law has been completely updated in this new edition. Written by 14 highly-regarded environmental attorneys, this book enjoys a reputation as one of the most basic and useful texts in the environmental field. With a copy in your reference collection, you'll have easy access to a wealth of information on every major environmental topic—all written in clearly understandable, everyday English.
Hardcover, Index, 550 pages, Mar '97, ISBN: 0-86587-560-X **$79**

State Wildlife Laws Handbook

The first comprehensive analysis of wildlife management and protection laws for all fifty states. The book is organized into three parts: **Part I** provides an overview of wildlife law and issues of concern, with an entire chapter devoted to wildlife poaching in the U.S.; **Part II** contains summaries of each of the fish and wildlife codes for all fifty states in a standard format; **Part III** discusses the states' provisions and compares topics from state to state. Appendices include a glossary of important wildlife terms for each state, a suggested reading list, and addresses for state fish and wildlife agencies.
Harcover, 854 pages, 1993, ISBN: 0-86587-357-7 **$94**

To obtain a catalog of our books, write or call:

Government Institutes
4 Research Place
Rockville, MD 20850
(301) 921-2355